APUS ePress
World Literature Anthology:
Through the Renaissance

Volume I

Linda Silva: Volume Editor

Contributing Editors: Linda Silva
William Overton
Program Director: Kimberly Jacobs
Production Editor: Judith Novak
Editor-in-Chief: Fred Stielow

APUS *e*Press
Production

APUS™

2011

Production Editor Judith Novak
Contributing Editors: Linda Silva
William Overton
Editor:Fred Stielow
Text Design: Judith Novak
Jessica Radlich
Artwork: Victor Montoya

Printed in the United States of America

This text was compiled in Charles Town WV by APUS ePress

Printed by Lightning Source Inc.
La Vergne, TN

Cover Illustration: Victor Montoya,
American Public University System Visual Arts

Series contents include excepts of classical literature from around the world through the Renaissance

ISBN 978-1-937381-00-4, 978-1-937381-01-1, 978-1-937381-02-8
Collection ISBN 978-1-937381-03-5

ISBN 978-1-937381-00-4

American Public University Electronic Press
111 West Congress Street
Charles Town, WV 25414

www.apus.edu

Literature 201
Volume I

Volume III

Introduction
Volume I

The aim of this text is to give you a taste of the writings from nearly every continent - to expand your knowledge about people and places by reading works from many different regions. Our goal is to offer some of the greatest pieces of literature in the world in one three volume textbook.

In Volume I, you will have the opportunity to:

- Read works from Ancient Greece and Rome
- Meet heroes like Odysseus, Achilles, and Aeneas
- Follow the Hero Quest

In Volume II, you will read the stories of people in far off lands:

- Read the thoughts of Confucius in Ancient China
- Follow the adventures of mythical heroes of India
- Explore the folk tales of Africa

In Volume III, more adventure tales await you:

- Travel through Hell with Dante and his guide
- Meet the Knights of King Arthur's Court
- Meet Medieval Princes, both wise and not so wise

To study literature is to open oneself to years and years of wisdom from some of the greatest minds to ever walk the planet. Theirs are not mere stories; theirs are histories that, when completely opened, enable each of us to grow as students, as writers, and as people. When students engage in the study of literature, close reading is inter-related with writing about what one has read. Having a deeper understanding of the meaning allows us to take a glimpse into the world of our past - to see what was important to a culture or society, to grasp what urged them forward or held them back. It is, in essence, a privileged peek into the underpinnings of a culture from the authors' points of view.

Literary works are best read in their social, historical, and literary contexts. They do not exist in a vacuum and ought not to be read as though they did. Every piece tells its own story. Every work is colored by the time in which it was written - by the author's opinions, thoughts, and feelings and by the hundreds of critical analyses written over the years.

While most students know how to read literature, writing about it can be frustrating. The key isn't to find the right answer. It is to have an opinion based on what you have read and understood and then using the literature to support your response. Let the works be your guide, your friend, your support. Show that you read and understood the work by using it as evidence to back up your ideas. With proper support, your papers can be just as correct as those critics who spend their days dissecting a work to death, but with a greater meaning to you. To find this meaning you may have to read a piece two or three times - but it is worth the effort.

Let the work speak to you - to tell you about the author who wrote it and the audience for whom it was written. Enjoy the stories, the moral struggles, the ethical battles, the heroic moments, and the abysmal failures. Read these as you would watch a movie, immersed as the drama unfolds. But most of all, be willing to have an opinion, to support that opinion, and to use the text as your expert witness.

Especially in Volume I, you will follow heroes on their quests for adventure, revenge, to gain the spoils of war, and to establish kingdoms and nations.

The Odyssey

By Homer

WRITTEN 800 B.C.E | TRANSLATED BY SAMUEL BUTLER

Book I

Tell me, O muse, of that ingenious hero who travelled far and wide after he had sacked the famous town of Troy. Many cities did he visit, and many were the nations with whose manners and customs he was acquainted; moreover he suffered much by sea while trying to save his own life and bring his men safely home; but do what he might he could not save his men, for they perished through their own sheer folly in eating the cattle of the Sun-god Hyperion; so the god prevented them from ever reaching home. Tell me, too, about all these things, O daughter of Jove, from whatsoever source you may know them.

So now all who escaped death in battle or by shipwreck had got safely home except Ulysses, and he, though he was longing to return to his wife and country, was detained by the goddess Calypso, who had got him into a large cave and wanted to marry him. But as years went by, there came a time when the gods settled that he should go back to Ithaca; even then, however, when he was among his own people, his troubles were not yet over; nevertheless all the gods had now begun to pity him except Neptune, who still persecuted him without ceasing and would not let him get home.

Now Neptune had gone off to the Ethiopians, who are at the world's end, and lie in two halves, the one looking West and the other East. He had gone there to accept a hecatomb of sheep and oxen, and was enjoying himself at his festival; but the other gods met in the house of Olympian Jove, and the sire of gods and men spoke first. At that moment he was thinking of Aegisthus, who had been killed by Agamemnon's son Orestes; so he said to the other gods:

"See now, how men lay blame upon us gods for what is after all nothing but their own folly. Look at Aegisthus; he must needs make love to Agamemnon's wife unrighteously and then kill Agamemnon, though he knew it would be the death of him; for I sent Mercury to warn him not to do either of these things, inasmuch as Orestes would be sure to take his revenge when he grew up and wanted to return home. Mercury told him this in all good will but he would not listen, and now he has paid for everything in full."

Then Minerva said, "Father, son of Saturn, King of kings, it served Aegisthus right, and so it would any one else who does as he did; but Aegisthus is neither here nor there; it is for Ulysses that my heart bleeds, when I think of his sufferings in that lonely sea-girt island, far away, poor man, from all his friends. It is an island covered with forest, in the very middle of the sea, and a goddess lives there, daughter of the magician Atlas, who looks after the bottom of the ocean, and carries the great columns that keep heaven and earth asunder. This daughter of Atlas has got hold of poor unhappy Ulysses, and keeps trying by every kind of blandishment to make him forget his home, so that he is tired of life, and thinks of nothing but how he may once more see the smoke of his own chimneys. You, sir, take no heed of this, and yet when Ulysses was before Troy did he not propitiate you with many a burnt sacrifice? Why then should you keep on being so angry with him?"

And Jove said, "My child, what are you talking about? How can I forget Ulysses than whom there is no more capable man on earth, nor more liberal in his offerings to the immortal gods that live in heaven? Bear in mind, however, that Neptune is still furious with Ulysses for having blinded an eye of Polyphemus king of the Cyclopes. Polyphemus is son to Neptune by the nymph Thoosa, daughter to the sea-king Phorcys; therefore though he will not kill Ulysses outright, he torments him by preventing him from getting home. Still, let us lay our heads together and see how we can help him to return; Neptune will then be pacified, for if we are all of a mind he can hardly stand out against us."

And Minerva said, "Father, son of Saturn, King of kings, if, then, the gods now mean that Ulysses should get home, we should first send Mercury to the Ogygian island to tell Calypso that we have made up our minds and that he is to return. In the meantime I will go to Ithaca, to put heart into Ulysses' son Telemachus; I will embolden him to call the Achaeans in assembly, and speak out to the suitors of his mother Penelope, who persist in eating up any number of his sheep and oxen; I will also conduct him to Sparta and to Pylos, to see if he can hear anything about the return of his dear father- for this will make people speak well of him."

So saying she bound on her glittering golden sandals, imperishable, with which she can fly like the wind over land or sea; she grasped the redoubtable bronze-shod spear, so stout and sturdy and strong, wherewith she quells the ranks of heroes who have displeased her, and down she darted from the topmost summits of Olympus, whereon forthwith she was in Ithaca, at the gateway of Ulysses' house, disguised as a visitor, Mentes, chief of the Taphians, and she held a bronze spear in her hand. There she found the lordly suitors seated on hides of the oxen which they had killed and eaten, and playing draughts in front of the house. Men-servants and pages were bustling about to wait upon them, some mixing wine with water in the mixing-bowls, some cleaning down the tables with wet sponges and laying them out again, and some cutting up great quantities of meat.

Telemachus saw her long before any one else did. He was sitting moodily among the suitors thinking about his brave father, and how he would send them flying out of the house, if he were to come to his own again and be honoured as in days gone by. Thus brooding as he sat among them, he caught sight of Minerva and went straight to the gate, for he was vexed that a stranger should be kept waiting for admittance. He took her right hand in his own, and bade her give him her spear. "Welcome," said he, "to our house, and when you have partaken of food you shall tell us what you have come for."

He led the way as he spoke, and Minerva followed him. When they were within he took her spear and set it in the spear- stand against a strong bearing-post along with the many other spears of his unhappy father, and he conducted her to a richly decorated seat under which he threw a cloth of damask. There was a footstool also for her feet, and he set another seat near her for himself, away from the suitors, that she might not be annoyed while eating by their noise and insolence, and that he might ask her more freely about his father.

A maid servant then brought them water in a beautiful golden ewer and poured it into a silver basin for them to wash their hands, and she drew a clean table beside them. An upper servant brought them bread, and offered them many good things of what there was in the house, the carver fetched them plates of all manner of meats and set cups of gold by their side, and a man-servant brought them wine and poured it out for them.

Then the suitors came in and took their places on the benches and seats. Forthwith men servants poured water over their hands, maids went round with the bread-baskets, pages filled the mixing-bowls with wine and water, and they laid their hands upon the good things that were before them. As soon as they had had enough to eat and drink they wanted music and dancing, which are the crowning embellishments of a banquet, so a servant brought a lyre to Phemius, whom they compelled perforce to sing to them. As soon as he touched his lyre and began to sing Telemachus spoke low to Minerva, with his head close to hers that no man might hear.

"I hope, sir," said he, "that you will not be offended with what I am going to say. Singing comes cheap to those who do not pay for it, and all this is done at the cost of one whose bones lie rotting in some wilderness or grinding to powder in the surf. If these men were to see my father come back to Ithaca they would pray for longer legs rather than a longer purse, for money would not serve them; but he, alas, has fallen on an ill fate, and even when people do sometimes say that he is coming, we no longer heed them; we shall never see him again. And now, sir, tell me and tell me true, who you are and where you come from. Tell me of your town and parents, what manner of ship you came in, how your crew brought you to Ithaca, and of what nation they declared themselves to be- for you cannot have come by land. Tell me also truly, for I want to know, are you a stranger to this house, or have you been here in my father's time? In the old days we had many visitors for my father went about much himself."

And Minerva answered, "I will tell you truly and particularly all about it. I am Mentes, son of Anchialus, and I am King of the Taphians. I have come here with my ship and crew, on a voyage to men of a foreign tongue being bound for Temesa with a cargo of iron, and I shall bring back copper. As for my ship, it lies over yonder off the open country away from the town, in the harbour Rheithron under the wooded mountain Neritum. Our fathers were friends before us, as old Laertes will tell you, if you will go and ask him. They say, however, that he never comes to town now, and lives by himself in the country, faring hardly, with an old woman to look after him and get his dinner for him, when he comes in tired from pottering about his vineyard. They told me your father was at home again, and that was why I came, but it seems the gods are still keeping him back, for he is not dead yet not on the mainland. It is more likely he is on some sea-girt island in mid ocean, or a prisoner among savages who are detaining him against his will I am no prophet, and know very little about omens, but I speak as it is borne in upon me from heaven, and assure you that he will not be away much longer; for he is a man of such resource that even though he were in chains of iron he would find some means of getting home again. But tell me, and tell me true, can Ulysses really have such a fine looking fellow for a son? You are indeed wonderfully like him about the head and eyes, for we were close friends before he set sail for Troy where the flower of all the Argives went also. Since that time we have never either of us seen the other."

"My mother," answered Telemachus, tells me I am son to Ulysses, but it is a wise child that knows his own father. Would that I were son to one who had grown old upon his own estates, for, since you ask me, there is no more ill-starred man under heaven than he who they tell me is my father."

And Minerva said, "There is no fear of your race dying out yet, while Penelope has such a fine son as you are. But tell me, and tell me true, what is the meaning of all this feasting, and who are these people? What is it all about? Have you some banquet, or is there a wedding in the family- for no one seems to be bringing any provisions of his own? And the guests- how atrociously they are behaving; what riot they make over the whole house; it is enough to disgust any respectable person who comes near them."

"Sir," said Telemachus, "as regards your question, so long as my father was here it was well with us and with the house, but the gods in their displeasure have willed it otherwise, and have hidden him away more closely than mortal man was ever yet hidden. I could have borne it better even though he were dead, if he had fallen with his men before Troy, or had died with friends around him when the days of his fighting were done; for then the Achaeans would have built a mound over his ashes, and I should myself have been heir to his renown; but now the storm-winds have spirited him away we know not wither; he is gone without leaving so much as a trace behind him, and I inherit nothing but dismay. Nor does the matter end simply with grief for the loss of my father; heaven has laid sorrows upon me of yet another kind; for the chiefs from all our islands, Dulichium, Same, and the woodland island of Zacynthus, as also all the principal men of Ithaca itself, are eating up my house under the pretext of paying their court to my mother, who will neither point blank say that she will not marry, nor yet bring matters to an end; so they are making havoc of my estate, and before long will do so also with myself."

"Is that so?" exclaimed Minerva, "then you do indeed want Ulysses home again. Give him his helmet, shield, and a couple lances, and if he is the man he was when I first knew him in our house, drinking and making merry, he would soon lay his hands about these rascally suitors, were he to stand once more upon his own threshold. He was then coming from Ephyra, where he had been to beg poison for his arrows from Ilus, son of Mermerus. Ilus feared the ever-living gods and would not give him any, but my father let him have some, for he was very fond of him. If Ulysses is the man he then was these suitors will have a short shrift and a sorry wedding.

"But there! It rests with heaven to determine whether he is to return, and take his revenge in his own house or no; I would, however, urge you to set about trying to get rid of these suitors at once. Take my advice, call the Achaean heroes in assembly to-morrow -lay your case before them, and call heaven to bear you witness. Bid the suitors take themselves off, each to his own place, and if your mother's mind is set on marrying again, let her go back to her father, who will find her a husband and provide her with all the marriage gifts that so dear a daughter may expect. As for yourself, let me prevail upon you to take the best ship you can get, with a crew of twenty men, and go in quest of your father who has so long been missing. Some one may tell you something, or (and people often hear things in this way) some heaven-sent message may direct you. First go to Pylos and ask Nestor; thence go on to Sparta and visit Menelaus, for he got home last of all the Achaeans; if you hear that your father is alive and on his way home, you can put up with the waste these suitors will make for yet another twelve months. If on the other hand you hear of his death, come home at once, celebrate his funeral rites with all due pomp, build a barrow to his memory, and make your mother marry again. Then, having done all this, think it well over in your mind how, by fair means or foul, you may kill these suitors in your own house. You are too old to plead infancy any longer; have you not heard how people are singing Orestes' praises for having killed his father's murderer Aegisthus? You are a fine, smart looking fellow; show your mettle, then, and make yourself a name in story. Now, however, I must go back to my ship and to my crew, who will be impatient if I keep them waiting longer; think the matter over for yourself, and remember what I have said to you."

"Sir," answered Telemachus, "it has been very kind of you to talk to me in this way, as though I were your own son, and I will do all you tell me; I know you want to be getting on with your voyage, but stay a little longer till you have taken a bath and refreshed yourself. I will then give you a present, and you shall go on your way rejoicing; I will give you one of great beauty and value- a keepsake such as only dear friends give to one another."

Minerva answered, "Do not try to keep me, for I would be on my way at once. As for any present you may be disposed to make me, keep it till I come again, and I will take it home with me. You shall give me a very good one, and I will give you one of no less value in return."

With these words she flew away like a bird into the air, but she had given Telemachus courage, and had made him think more than ever about his father. He felt the change, wondered at it, and knew that the stranger had been a god, so he went straight to where the suitors were sitting.

Phemius was still singing, and his hearers sat rapt in silence as he told the sad tale of the return from Troy, and the ills Minerva had laid upon the Achaeans. Penelope, daughter of Icarius, heard his song from her room upstairs, and came down by the great staircase, not alone, but attended by two of her handmaids. When she reached the suitors she stood by one of the bearing posts that supported the roof of the cloisters with a staid maiden on either side of her. She held a veil, moreover, before her face, and was weeping bitterly.

"Phemius," she cried, "you know many another feat of gods and heroes, such as poets love to celebrate. Sing the suitors some one of these, and let them drink their wine in silence, but cease this sad tale, for it breaks my sorrowful heart, and reminds me of my lost husband whom I mourn ever without ceasing, and whose name was great over all Hellas and middle Argos."

"Mother," answered Telemachus, "let the bard sing what he has a mind to; bards do not make the ills they sing of; it is Jove, not they, who makes them, and who sends weal or woe upon mankind according to his own good pleasure. This fellow means no harm by singing the ill-fated return of the Danaans, for people always applaud the latest songs most warmly. Make up your mind to it and bear it; Ulysses is not the only man who never came back from Troy, but many another went down as well as he. Go, then, within the house and busy yourself with your daily duties, your loom, your distaff, and the ordering of your servants; for speech is man's matter, and mine above all others- for it is I who am master here."

She went wondering back into the house, and laid her son's saying in her heart. Then, going upstairs with her handmaids into her room, she mourned her dear husband till Minerva shed sweet sleep over her eyes. But the suitors were clamorous throughout the covered cloisters, and prayed each one that he might be her bed fellow.

Then Telemachus spoke, "Shameless," he cried, "and insolent suitors, let us feast at our pleasure now, and let there be no brawling, for it is a rare thing to hear a man with such a divine voice as Phemius has; but in the morning meet me in full assembly that I may give you formal notice to depart, and feast at one another's houses, turn and turn about, at your own cost. If on the other hand you choose to persist in spunging upon one man, heaven help me, but Jove shall reckon with you in full, and when you fall in my father's house there shall be no man to avenge you."

The suitors bit their lips as they heard him, and marvelled at the boldness of his speech. Then, Antinous, son of Eupeithes, said, "The gods seem to have given you lessons in bluster and tall talking; may Jove never grant you to be chief in Ithaca as your father was before you."

Telemachus answered, "Antinous, do not chide with me, but, god willing,

I will be chief too if I can. Is this the worst fate you can think of for me? It is no bad thing to be a chief, for it brings both riches and honour. Still, now that Ulysses is dead there are many great men in Ithaca both old and young, and some other may take the lead among them; nevertheless I will be chief in my own house, and will rule those whom Ulysses has won for me."

Then Eurymachus, son of Polybus, answered, "It rests with heaven to decide who shall be chief among us, but you shall be master in your own house and over your own possessions; no one while there is a man in Ithaca shall do you violence nor rob you. And now, my good fellow, I want to know about this stranger. What country does he come from? Of what family is he, and where is his estate? Has he brought you news about the return of your father, or was he on business of his own? He seemed a well-to-do man, but he hurried off so suddenly that he was gone in a moment before we could get to know him."

"My father is dead and gone," answered Telemachus, "and even if some rumour reaches me I put no more faith in it now. My mother does indeed sometimes send for a soothsayer and question him, but I give his prophecyings no heed. As for the stranger, he was Mentes, son of Anchialus, chief of the Taphians, an old friend of my father's." But in his heart he knew that it had been the goddess.

The suitors then returned to their singing and dancing until the evening; but when night fell upon their pleasuring they went home to bed each in his own abode. Telemachus's room was high up in a tower that looked on to the outer court; hither, then, he hied, brooding and full of thought. A good old woman, Euryclea, daughter of Ops, the son of Pisenor, went before him with a couple of blazing torches. Laertes had bought her with his own money when she was quite young; he gave the worth of twenty oxen for her, and shewed as much respect to her in his household as he did to his own wedded wife, but he did not take her to his bed for he feared his wife's resentment. She it was who now lighted Telemachus to his room, and she loved him better than any of the other women in the house did, for she had nursed him when he was a baby. He opened the door of his bed room and sat down upon the bed; as he took off his shirt he gave it to the good old woman, who folded it tidily up, and hung it for him over a peg by his bed side, after which she went out, pulled the door to by a silver catch, and drew the bolt home by means of the strap. But Telemachus as he lay covered with a woollen fleece kept thinking all night through of his intended voyage of the counsel that Minerva had given him.

Book II

Now when the child of morning, rosy-fingered Dawn, appeared, Telemachus rose and dressed himself. He bound his sandals on to his comely feet, girded his sword about his shoulder, and left his room looking like an immortal god. He at once sent the criers round to call the people in assembly, so they called them and the people gathered thereon; then, when they were got together, he went to the place of assembly spear in hand- not alone, for his two hounds went with him. Minerva endowed him with a presence of such divine comeliness that all marvelled at him as he went by, and when he took his place' in his father's seat even the oldest councillors made way for him.

Aegyptius, a man bent double with age, and of infinite experience, the first to speak His son Antiphus had gone with Ulysses to Ilius, land of noble steeds, but the savage Cyclops had killed him when they were all shut up in the cave, and had cooked his last dinner for him, He had three sons left, of whom two still worked on their father's land, while the third, Eurynomus, was one of the suitors; nevertheless their father could not get over the loss of Antiphus, and was still weeping for him when he began his speech.

"Men of Ithaca," he said, "hear my words. From the day Ulysses left us there has been no meeting of our councillors until now; who then can it be, whether old or young, that finds it so necessary to convene us? Has he got wind of some host approaching, and does he wish to warn us, or would he speak upon some other matter of public moment? I am sure he is an excellent person, and I hope Jove will grant him his heart's desire."

Telemachus took this speech as of good omen and rose at once, for he was bursting with what he had to say. He stood in the middle of the assembly and the good herald Pisenor brought him his staff. Then, turning to Aegyptius, "Sir," said he, "it is I, as you will shortly learn, who have convened you, for it is I who am the most aggrieved. I have not got wind of any host approaching about which I would warn you, nor is there any matter of public moment on which I would speak. My grieveance is purely personal, and turns on two great misfortunes which have fallen upon my house. The first of these is the loss of my excellent father, who was chief among all you here present, and was like a father to every one of you; the second is much more serious, and ere long will be the utter ruin of my estate. The sons of all the chief men among you are pestering my mother to marry them against her will. They are afraid to go to her father Icarius, asking him to choose the one he likes best, and to provide marriage gifts for his daughter, but day by day they keep hanging about my father's house, sacrificing our oxen, sheep, and fat goats for their banquets, and never giving so much as a thought to the quantity of wine they drink. No estate can stand such recklessness; we have now no Ulysses to ward off harm from our doors, and I cannot hold my own against them. I shall never all my days be as good a man as he was, still I would indeed defend myself if I had power to do so, for I cannot stand such treatment any longer; my house is being disgraced and ruined. Have respect, therefore, to your own consciences and to public opinion. Fear, too, the wrath of heaven, lest the gods should be displeased and turn upon you. I pray you by Jove and Themis, who is the beginning and the end of councils, [do not] hold back, my friends, and leave me singlehanded- unless it be that my brave father Ulysses did some wrong to the Achaeans which you would now avenge on me, by aiding and abetting these suitors. Moreover, if I am to be eaten out of house and home at all, I had rather you did the eating yourselves, for I could then take action against you to some purpose, and serve you with notices from house to house till I got paid in full, whereas now I have no remedy."

With this Telemachus dashed his staff to the ground and burst into tears. Every one was very sorry for him, but they all sat still and no one ventured to make him an angry answer, save only Antinous, who spoke thus:

"Telemachus, insolent braggart that you are, how dare you try to throw the blame upon us suitors? It is your mother's fault not ours, for she is a very artful woman. This three years past, and close on four, she has been driving us out of our minds, by encouraging each one of us, and sending him messages without meaning one word of what she says. And then there was that other trick she played us. She set up a great tambour frame in her room, and began to work on an enormous piece of fine needlework. 'Sweet hearts,' said she, 'Ulysses is indeed dead, still do not press me to marry again immediately, wait- for I would not have skill in needlework perish unrecorded- till I have completed a pall for the hero Laertes, to be in readiness against the time when death shall take him. He is very rich, and the women of the place will talk if he is laid out without a pall.'

"This was what she said, and we assented; whereon we could see her working on her great web all day long, but at night she would unpick the stitches again by torchlight. She fooled us in this way for three years and we never found her out, but as time wore on and she was now in her fourth year, one of her maids who knew what she was doing told us, and we caught her in the act of undoing her work, so she had to finish it whether she would or no. The suitors, therefore, make you this answer, that both you and the Achaeans may understand-'Send your mother away, and bid her marry the man of her own and of her father's choice'; for I do not know what will happen if she goes on plaguing us much longer with the airs she gives herself on the score of the accomplishments Minerva has taught her, and because she is so clever. We never yet heard of such a woman; we know all about Tyro, Alcmena, Mycene, and the famous women of old, but they were nothing to your mother, any one of them. It was not fair of her to treat us in that way, and as long as she continues in the mind with which heaven has now endowed her, so long shall we go on eating up your estate; and I do not see why she should change, for she gets all the honour and glory, and it is you who pay for it, not she. Understand, then, that we will not go back to our lands, neither here nor elsewhere, till she has made her choice and married some one or other of us."

Telemachus answered, "Antinous, how can I drive the mother who bore me from my father's house? My father is abroad and we do not know whether he is alive or dead. It will be hard on me if I have to pay Icarius the large sum which I must give him if I insist on sending his daughter back to him. Not only will he deal rigorously with me, but heaven will also punish me; for my mother when she leaves the house will calf on the Erinyes to avenge her; besides, it would not be a creditable thing to do, and I will have nothing to say to it. If you choose to take offence at this, leave the house and feast elsewhere at one another's houses at your own cost turn and turn about. If, on the other hand, you elect to persist in spunging upon one man, heaven help me, but Jove shall reckon with you in full, and when you fall in my father's house there shall be no man to avenge you."

As he spoke Jove sent two eagles from the top of the mountain, and they flew on and on with the wind, sailing side by side in their own lordly flight. When they were right over the middle of the assembly they wheeled and circled about, beating the air with their wings and glaring death into the eyes of them that were below; then, fighting fiercely and tearing at one another, they flew off towards the right over the town. The people wondered as they saw them, and asked each other what an this might be; whereon Halitherses, who was the best prophet and reader of omens among them, spoke to them plainly and in all honesty, saying:

"Hear me, men of Ithaca, and I speak more particularly to the suitors, for I see mischief brewing for them. Ulysses is not going to be away much longer; indeed he is close at hand to deal out death and destruction, not on them alone, but on many another of us who live in Ithaca. Let us then be wise in time, and put a stop to this wickedness before he comes. Let the suitors do so of their own accord; it will be better for them, for I am not prophesying without due knowledge; everything has happened to Ulysses as I foretold when the Argives set out for Troy, and he with them. I said that after going through much hardship and losing all his men he should come home again in the twentieth year and that no one would know him; and now all this is coming true."

Eurymachus son of Polybus then said, "Go home, old man, and prophesy to your own children, or it may be worse for them. I can read these omens myself much better than you can; birds are always flying about in the sunshine somewhere or other, but they seldom mean anything. Ulysses has died in a far country, and it is a pity you are not dead along with him, instead of prating here about omens and adding fuel to the anger of Telemachus which is fierce enough as it is. I suppose you think he will give you something for your family, but I tell you- and it shall surely be- when an old man like you, who should know better, talks a young one over till he becomes troublesome, in the first place his young friend will only fare so much the worse- he will take nothing by it, for the suitors will prevent this- and in the next, we will lay a heavier fine, sir, upon yourself than you will at all like paying, for it will bear hardly upon you. As for Telemachus, I warn him in the presence of you all to send his mother back to her father, who will find her a husband and provide her with all the marriage gifts so dear a daughter may expect. Till we shall go on harassing him with our suit; for we fear no man, and care neither for him, with all his fine speeches, nor for any fortune-telling of yours. You may preach as much as you please, but we shall only hate you the more. We shall go back and continue to eat up Telemachus's estate without paying him, till such time as his mother leaves off tormenting us by keeping us day after day on the tiptoe of expectation, each vying with the other in his suit for a prize of such rare perfection. Besides we cannot go after the other women whom we should marry in due course, but for the way in which she treats us."

Then Telemachus said, "Eurymachus, and you other suitors, I shall say no more, and entreat you no further, for the gods and the people of Ithaca now know my story. Give me, then, a ship and a crew of twenty men to take me hither and thither, and I will go to Sparta and to Pylos in quest of my father who has so long been missing. Some one may tell me something, or (and people often hear things in this way) some heaven-sent message may direct me. If I can hear of him as alive and on his way home I will put up with the waste you suitors will make for yet another twelve months. If on the other hand I hear of his death, I will return at once, celebrate his funeral rites with all due pomp, build a barrow to his memory, and make my mother marry again."

With these words he sat down, and Mentor who had been a friend of Ulysses, and had been left in charge of everything with full authority over the servants, rose to speak. He, then, plainly and in all honesty addressed them thus:

"Hear me, men of Ithaca, I hope that you may never have a kind and well-disposed ruler any more, nor one who will govern you equitably; I hope that all your chiefs henceforward may be cruel and unjust, for there is not one of you but has forgotten Ulysses, who ruled you as though he were your father. I am not half so angry with the suitors, for if they choose to do violence in the naughtiness of their hearts, and wager their heads that Ulysses will not return, they can take the high hand and eat up his estate, but as for you others I am shocked at the way in which you all sit still without even trying to stop such scandalous goings on-which you could do if you chose, for you are many and they are few."

Leiocritus, son of Evenor, answered him saying, "Mentor, what folly is all this, that you should set the people to stay us? It is a hard thing for one man to fight with many about his victuals. Even though Ulysses himself were to set upon us while we are feasting in his house, and do his best to oust us, his wife, who wants him back so very badly, would have small cause for rejoicing, and his blood would be upon his own head if he fought against such great odds. There is no sense in what you have been saying. Now, therefore, do you people go about your business, and let his father's old friends, Mentor and Halitherses, speed this boy on his journey, if he goes at all- which I do not think he will, for he is more likely to stay where he is till some one comes and tells him something."

On this he broke up the assembly, and every man went back to his own abode, while the suitors returned to the house of Ulysses.

Then Telemachus went all alone by the sea side, washed his hands in the grey waves, and prayed to Minerva.

"Hear me," he cried, "you god who visited me yesterday, and bade me sail the seas in search of my father who has so long been missing. I would obey you, but the Achaeans, and more particularly the wicked suitors, are hindering me that I cannot do so."

As he thus prayed, Minerva came close up to him in the likeness and with the voice of Mentor. "Telemachus," said she, "if you are made of the same stuff as your father you will be neither fool nor coward henceforward, for Ulysses never broke his word nor left his work half done. If, then, you take after him, your voyage will not be fruitless, but unless you have the blood of Ulysses and of Penelope in your veins I see no likelihood of your succeeding. Sons are seldom as good men as their fathers; they are generally worse, not better; still, as you are not going to be either fool or coward henceforward, and are not entirely without some share of your father's wise discernment, I look with hope upon your undertaking. But mind you never make common cause with any of those foolish suitors, for they have neither sense nor virtue, and give no thought to death and to the doom that will shortly fall on one and all of them, so that they shall perish on the same day. As for your voyage, it shall not be long delayed; your father was such an old friend of mine that I will find you a ship, and will come with you myself. Now, however, return home, and go about among the suitors; begin getting provisions ready for your voyage; see everything well stowed, the wine in jars, and the barley meal, which is the staff of life, in leathern bags, while I go round the town and beat up volunteers at once. There are many ships in Ithaca both old and new; I will run my eye over them for you and will choose the best; we will get her ready and will put out to sea without delay."

Thus spoke Minerva daughter of Jove, and Telemachus lost no time in doing as the goddess told him. He went moodily and found the suitors flaying goats and singeing pigs in the outer court. Antinous came up to him at once and laughed as he took his hand in his own, saying, "Telemachus, my fine fire-eater, bear no more ill blood neither in word nor deed, but eat and drink with us as you used to do. The Achaeans will find you in everything- a ship and a picked crew to boot- so that you can set sail for Pylos at once and get news of your noble father."

"Antinous," answered Telemachus, "I cannot eat in peace, nor take pleasure of any kind with such men as you are. Was it not enough that you should waste so much good property of mine while I was yet a boy? Now that I am older and know more about it, I am also stronger, and whether here among this people, or by going to Pylos, I will do you all the harm I can. I shall go, and my going will not be in vain though, thanks to you suitors, I have neither ship nor crew of my own, and must be passenger not captain."

As he spoke he snatched his hand from that of Antinous. Meanwhile the others went on getting dinner ready about the buildings, jeering at him tauntingly as they did so.

"Telemachus," said one youngster, "means to be the death of us; I suppose he thinks he can bring friends to help him from Pylos, or again from Sparta, where he seems bent on going. Or will he go to Ephyra as well, for poison to put in our wine and kill us?"

Another said, "Perhaps if Telemachus goes on board ship, he will be like his father and perish far from his friends. In this case we should have plenty to do, for we could then divide up his property amongst us: as for the house we can let his mother and the man who marries her have that."

This was how they talked. But Telemachus went down into the lofty and spacious store-room where his father's treasure of gold and bronze lay heaped up upon the floor, and where the linen and spare clothes were kept in open chests. Here, too, there was a store of fragrant olive oil, while casks of old, well-ripened wine, unblended and fit for a god to drink, were ranged against the wall in case Ulysses should come home again after all. The room was closed with well-made doors opening in the middle; moreover the faithful old house-keeper Euryclea, daughter of Ops the son of Pisenor, was in charge of everything both night and day. Telemachus called her to the store-room and said:

"Nurse, draw me off some of the best wine you have, after what you are keeping for my father's own drinking, in case, poor man, he should escape death, and find his way home again after all. Let me have twelve jars, and see that they all have lids; also fill me some well-sewn leathern bags with barley meal- about twenty measures in all. Get these things put together at once, and say nothing about it. I will take everything away this evening as soon as my mother has gone upstairs for the night. I am going to Sparta and to Pylos to see if I can hear anything about the return of my dear father.

When Euryclea heard this she began to cry, and spoke fondly to him, saying, "My dear child, what ever can have put such notion as that into your head? Where in the world do you want to go to- you, who are the one hope of the house? Your poor father is dead and gone in some foreign country nobody knows where, and as soon as your back is turned these wicked ones here will be scheming to get you put out of the way, and will share all your possessions among themselves; stay where you are among your own people, and do not go wandering and worrying your life out on the barren ocean."

"Fear not, nurse," answered Telemachus, "my scheme is not without heaven's sanction; but swear that you will say nothing about all this to my mother, till I have been away some ten or twelve days, unless she hears of my having gone, and asks you; for I do not want her to spoil her beauty by crying."

The old woman swore most solemnly that she would not, and when she had completed her oath, she began drawing off the wine into jars, and getting the barley meal into the bags, while Telemachus went back to the suitors.

Then Minerva bethought her of another matter. She took his shape, and went round the town to each one of the crew, telling them to meet at the ship by sundown. She went also to Noemon son of Phronius, and asked him to let her have a ship- which he was very ready to do. When the sun had set and darkness was over all the land, she got the ship into the water, put all the tackle on board her that ships generally carry, and stationed her at the end of the harbour. Presently the crew came up, and the goddess spoke encouragingly to each of them.

Furthermore she went to the house of Ulysses, and threw the suitors into a deep slumber. She caused their drink to fuddle them, and made them drop their cups from their hands, so that instead of sitting over their wine, they went back into the town to sleep, with their eyes heavy and full of drowsiness. Then she took the form and voice of Mentor, and called Telemachus to come outside.

"Telemachus," said she, "the men are on board and at their oars, waiting for you to give your orders, so make haste and let us be off."

On this she led the way, while Telemachus followed in her steps. When they got to the ship they found the crew waiting by the water side, and Telemachus said, "Now my men, help me to get the stores on board; they are all put together in the cloister, and my mother does not know anything about it, nor any of the maid servants except one."

With these words he led the way and the others followed after. When they had brought the things as he told them, Telemachus went on board, Minerva going before him and taking her seat in the stern of the vessel, while Telemachus sat beside her. Then the men loosed the hawsers and took their places on the benches. Minerva sent them a fair wind from the West, that whistled over the deep blue waves whereon Telemachus told them to catch hold of the ropes and hoist sail, and they did as he told them. They set the mast in its socket in the cross plank, raised it, and made it fast with the forestays; then they hoisted their white sails aloft with ropes of twisted ox hide. As the sail bellied out with the wind, the ship flew through the deep blue water, and the foam hissed against her bows as she sped onward. Then they made all fast throughout the ship, filled the mixing-bowls to the brim, and made drink offerings to the immortal gods that are from everlasting, but more particularly to the grey-eyed daughter of Jove.

Thus, then, the ship sped on her way through the watches of the night from dark till dawn.

Book III

But as the sun was rising from the fair sea into the firmament of heaven to shed light on mortals and immortals, they reached Pylos the city of Neleus. Now the people of Pylos were gathered on the sea shore to offer sacrifice of black bulls to Neptune lord of the Earthquake. There were nine guilds with five hundred men in each, and there were nine bulls to each guild. As they were eating the inward meats and burning the thigh bones [on the embers] in the name of Neptune, Telemachus and his crew arrived, furled their sails, brought their ship to anchor, and went ashore.

Minerva led the way and Telemachus followed her. Presently she said, "Telemachus, you must not be in the least shy or nervous; you have taken this voyage to try and find out where your father is buried and how he came by his end; so go straight up to Nestor that we may see what he has got to tell us. Beg of him to speak the truth, and he will tell no lies, for he is an excellent person."

"But how, Mentor," replied Telemachus, "dare I go up to Nestor, and how am I to address him? I have never yet been used to holding long conversations with people, and am ashamed to begin questioning one who is so much older than myself."

"Some things, Telemachus," answered Minerva, "will be suggested to you by your own instinct, and heaven will prompt you further; for I am assured that the gods have been with you from the time of your birth until now."

She then went quickly on, and Telemachus followed in her steps till they reached the place where the guilds of the Pylian people were assembled. There they found Nestor sitting with his sons, while his company round him were busy getting dinner ready, and putting pieces of meat on to the spits while other pieces were cooking. When they saw the strangers they crowded round them, took them by the hand and bade them take their places. Nestor's son Pisistratus at once offered his hand to each of them, and seated them on some soft sheepskins that were lying on the sands near his father and his brother Thrasymedes. Then he gave them their portions of the inward meats and poured wine for them into a golden cup, handing it to Minerva first, and saluting her at the same time.

"Offer a prayer, sir," said he, "to King Neptune, for it is his feast that you are joining; when you have duly prayed and made your drink-offering, pass the cup to your friend that he may do so also. I doubt not that he too lifts his hands in prayer, for man cannot live without God in the world. Still he is younger than you are, and is much of an age with myself, so I he handed I will give you the precedence."

As he spoke he handed her the cup. Minerva thought it very right and proper of him to have given it to herself first; she accordingly began praying heartily to Neptune. "O thou," she cried, "that encirclest the earth, vouchsafe to grant the prayers of thy servants that call upon thee. More especially we pray thee send down thy grace on Nestor and on his sons; thereafter also make the rest of the Pylian people some handsome return for the goodly hecatomb they are offering you. Lastly, grant Telemachus and myself a happy issue, in respect of the matter that has brought us in our to Pylos."

When she had thus made an end of praying, she handed the cup to Telemachus and he prayed likewise. By and by, when the outer meats were roasted and had been taken off the spits, the carvers gave every man his portion and they all made an excellent dinner. As soon as they had had enough to eat and drink, Nestor, knight of Gerene, began to speak.

"Now," said he, "that our guests have done their dinner, it will be best to ask them who they are. Who, then, sir strangers, are you, and from what port have you sailed? Are you traders? or do you sail the seas as rovers with your hand against every man, and every man's hand against you?"

Telemachus answered boldly, for Minerva had given him courage to ask about his father and get himself a good name.

"Nestor," said he, "son of Neleus, honour to the Achaean name, you ask whence we come, and I will tell you. We come from Ithaca under Neritum, and the matter about which I would speak is of private not public import. I seek news of my unhappy father Ulysses, who is said to have sacked the town of Troy in company with yourself. We know what fate befell each one of the other heroes who fought at Troy, but as regards Ulysses heaven has hidden from us the knowledge even that he is dead at all, for no one can certify us in what place he perished, nor say whether he fell in battle on the mainland, or was lost at sea amid the waves of Amphitrite. Therefore I am suppliant at your knees, if haply you may be pleased to tell me of his melancholy end, whether you saw it with your own eyes, or heard it from some other traveller, for he was a man born to trouble. Do not soften things out of any pity for me, but tell me in all plainness exactly what you saw. If my brave father Ulysses ever did you loyal service, either by word or deed, when you Achaeans were harassed among the Trojans, bear it in mind now as in my favour and tell me truly all."

"My friend," answered Nestor, "you recall a time of much sorrow to my mind, for the brave Achaeans suffered much both at sea, while privateering under Achilles, and when fighting before the great city of king Priam. Our best men all of them fell there- Ajax, Achilles, Patroclus peer of gods in counsel, and my own dear son Antilochus, a man singularly fleet of foot and in fight valiant. But we suffered much more than this; what mortal tongue indeed could tell the whole story? Though you were to stay here and question me for five years, or even six, I could not tell you all that the Achaeans suffered, and you would turn homeward weary of my tale before it ended. Nine long years did we try every kind of stratagem, but the hand of heaven was against us; during all this time there was no one who could compare with your father in subtlety- if indeed you are his son- I can hardly believe my eyes- and you talk just like him too- no one would say that people of such different ages could speak so much alike. He and I never had any kind of difference from first to last neither in camp nor council, but in singleness of heart and purpose we advised the Argives how all might be ordered for the best.

"When however, we had sacked the city of Priam, and were setting sail in our ships as heaven had dispersed us, then Jove saw fit to vex the Argives on their homeward voyage; for they had Not all been either wise or understanding, and hence many came to a bad end through the displeasure of Jove's daughter Minerva, who brought about a quarrel between the two sons of Atreus.

"The sons of Atreus called a meeting which was not as it should be, for it was sunset and the Achaeans were heavy with wine. When they explained why they had called- the people together, it seemed that Menelaus was for sailing homeward at once, and this displeased Agamemnon, who thought that we should wait till we had offered hecatombs to appease the anger of Minerva. Fool that he was, he might have known that he would not prevail with her, for when the gods have made up their minds they do not change them lightly. So the two stood bandying hard words, whereon the Achaeans sprang to their feet with a cry that rent the air, and were of two minds as to what they should do.

"That night we rested and nursed our anger, for Jove was hatching mischief against us. But in the morning some of us drew our ships into the water and put our goods with our women on board, while the rest, about half in number, stayed behind with Agamemnon. We- the other half- embarked and sailed; and the ships went well, for heaven had smoothed the sea. When we reached Tenedos we offered sacrifices to the gods, for we were longing to get home; cruel Jove, however, did not yet mean that we should do so, and raised a second quarrel in the course of which some among us turned their ships back again, and sailed away under Ulysses to make their peace with Agamemnon; but I, and all the ships that were with me pressed forward, for I saw that mischief was brewing. The son of Tydeus went on also with me, and his crews with him. Later on Menelaus joined us at Lesbos, and found us making up our minds about our course- for we did not know whether to go outside Chios by the island of Psyra, keeping this to our left, or inside Chios, over against the stormy headland of Mimas. So we asked heaven for a sign, and were shown one to the effect that we should be soonest out of danger if we headed our ships across the open sea to Euboea. This we therefore did, and a fair wind sprang up which gave us a quick passage during the night to Geraestus, where we offered many sacrifices to Neptune for having helped us so far on our way. Four days later Diomed and his men stationed their ships in Argos, but I held on for Pylos, and the wind never fell light from the day when heaven first made it fair for me.

"Therefore, my dear young friend, I returned without hearing anything about the others. I know neither who got home safely nor who were lost but, as in duty bound, I will give you without reserve the reports that have reached me since I have been here in my own house. They say the Myrmidons returned home safely under Achilles' son Neoptolemus; so also did the valiant son of Poias, Philoctetes. Idomeneus, again, lost no men at sea, and all his followers who escaped death in the field got safe home with him to Crete. No matter how far out of the world you live, you will have heard of Agamemnon and the bad end he came to at the hands of Aegisthus- and a fearful reckoning did Aegisthus presently pay. See what a good thing it is for a man to leave a son behind him to do as Orestes did, who killed false Aegisthus the murderer of his noble father. You too, then- for you are a tall, smart-looking fellow- show your mettle and make yourself a name in story."

"Nestor son of Neleus," answered Telemachus, "honour to the Achaean name, the Achaeans applaud Orestes and his name will live through all time for he has avenged his father nobly. Would that heaven might grant me to do like vengeance on the insolence of the wicked suitors, who are ill treating me and plotting my ruin; but the gods have no such happiness in store for me and for my father, so we must bear it as best we may."

"My friend," said Nestor, "now that you remind me, I remember to have heard that your mother has many suitors, who are ill disposed towards you and are making havoc of your estate. Do you submit to this tamely, or are public feeling and the voice of heaven against you? Who knows but what Ulysses may come back after all, and pay these scoundrels in full, either single-handed or with a force of Achaeans behind him? If Minerva were to take as great a liking to you as she did to Ulysses when we were fighting before Troy (for I never yet saw the gods so openly fond of any one as Minerva then was of your father), if she would take as good care of you as she did of him, these wooers would soon some of them him, forget their wooing."

Telemachus answered, "I can expect nothing of the kind; it would be far too much to hope for. I dare not let myself think of it. Even though the gods themselves willed it no such good fortune could befall me."

On this Minerva said, "Telemachus, what are you talking about? Heaven has a long arm if it is minded to save a man; and if it were me, I should not care how much I suffered before getting home, provided I could be safe when I was once there. I would rather this, than get home quickly, and then be killed in my own house as Agamemnon was by the treachery of Aegisthus and his wife. Still, death is certain, and when a man's hour is come, not even the gods can save him, no matter how fond they are of him."

"Mentor," answered Telemachus, "do not let us talk about it any more. There is no chance of my father's ever coming back; the gods have long since counselled his destruction. There is something else, however, about which I should like to ask Nestor, for he knows much more than any one else does. They say he has reigned for three generations so that it is like talking to an immortal. Tell me, therefore, Nestor, and tell me true; how did Agamemnon come to die in that way? What was Menelaus doing? And how came false Aegisthus to kill so far better a man than himself? Was Menelaus away from Achaean Argos, voyaging elsewhither among mankind, that Aegisthus took heart and killed Agamemnon?"

"I will tell you truly," answered Nestor, "and indeed you have yourself divined how it all happened. If Menelaus when he got back from Troy had found Aegisthus still alive in his house, there would have been no barrow heaped up for him, not even when he was dead, but he would have been thrown outside the city to dogs and vultures, and not a woman would have mourned him, for he had done a deed of great wickedness; but we were over there, fighting hard at Troy, and Aegisthus who was taking his ease quietly in the heart of Argos, cajoled Agamemnon's wife Clytemnestra with incessant flattery.

"At first she would have nothing to do with his wicked scheme, for she was of a good natural disposition; moreover there was a bard with her, to whom Agamemnon had given strict orders on setting out for Troy, that he was to keep guard over his wife; but when heaven had counselled her destruction, Aegisthus thus this bard off to a desert island and left him there for crows and seagulls to batten upon- after which she went willingly enough to the house of Aegisthus. Then he offered many burnt sacrifices to the gods, and decorated many temples with tapestries and gilding, for he had succeeded far beyond his expectations.

"Meanwhile Menelaus and I were on our way home from Troy, on good terms with one another. When we got to Sunium, which is the point of Athens, Apollo with his painless shafts killed Phrontis the steersman of Menelaus' ship (and never man knew better how to handle a vessel in rough weather) so that he died then and there with the helm in his hand, and Menelaus, though very anxious to press forward, had to wait in order to bury his comrade and give him his due funeral rites. Presently, when he too could put to sea again, and had sailed on as far as the Malean heads, Jove counselled evil against him and made it it blow hard till the waves ran mountains high. Here he divided his fleet and took the one half towards Crete where the Cydonians dwell round about the waters of the river Iardanus. There is a high headland hereabouts stretching out into the sea from a place called Gortyn, and all along this part of the coast as far as Phaestus the sea runs high when there is a south wind blowing, but arter Phaestus the coast is more protected, for a small headland can make a great shelter. Here this part of the fleet was driven on to the rocks and wrecked; but the crews just managed to save themselves. As for the other five ships, they were taken by winds and seas to Egypt, where Menelaus gathered much gold and substance among people of an alien speech. Meanwhile Aegisthus here at home plotted his evil deed. For seven years after he had killed Agamemnon he ruled in Mycene, and the people were obedient under him, but in the eighth year Orestes came back from Athens to be his bane, and killed the murderer of his father. Then he celebrated the funeral rites of his mother and of false Aegisthus by a banquet to the people of Argos, and on that very day Menelaus came home, with as much treasure as his ships could carry.

"Take my advice then, and do not go travelling about for long so far from home, nor leave your property with such dangerous people in your house; they will eat up everything you have among them, and you will have been on a fool's errand. Still, I should advise you by all means to go and visit Menelaus, who has lately come off a voyage among such distant peoples as no man could ever hope to get back from, when the winds had once carried him so far out of his reckoning; even birds cannot fly the distance in a twelvemonth, so vast and terrible are the seas that they must cross. Go to him, therefore, by sea, and take your own men with you; or if you would rather travel by land you can have a chariot, you can have horses, and here are my sons who can escort you to Lacedaemon where Menelaus lives. Beg of him to speak the truth, and he will tell you no lies, for he is an excellent person."

As he spoke the sun set and it came on dark, whereon Minerva said, "Sir, all that you have said is well; now, however, order the tongues of the victims to be cut, and mix wine that we may make drink-offerings to Neptune, and the other immortals, and then go to bed, for it is bed time. People should go away early and not keep late hours at a religious festival."

Thus spoke the daughter of Jove, and they obeyed her saying. Men servants poured water over the hands of the guests, while pages filled the mixing-bowls with wine and water, and handed it round after giving every man his drink-offering; then they threw the tongues of the victims into the fire, and stood up to make their drink-offerings. When they had made their offerings and had drunk each as much as he was minded, Minerva and Telemachus were forgoing on board their ship, but Nestor caught them up at once and stayed them.

"Heaven and the immortal gods," he exclaimed, "forbid that you should leave my house to go on board of a ship. Do you think I am so poor and short of clothes, or that I have so few cloaks and as to be unable to find comfortable beds both for myself and for my guests? Let me tell you I have store both of rugs and cloaks, and shall not permit the son of my old friend Ulysses to camp down on the deck of a ship- not while I live- nor yet will my sons after me, but they will keep open house as have done."

Then Minerva answered, "Sir, you have spoken well, and it will be much better that Telemachus should do as you have said; he, therefore, shall return with you and sleep at your house, but I must go back to give orders to my crew, and keep them in good heart. I am the only older person among them; the rest are all young men of Telemachus' own age, who have taken this voyage out of friendship; so I must return to the ship and sleep there. Moreover to-morrow I must go to the Cauconians where I have a large sum of money long owing to me. As for Telemachus, now that he is your guest, send him to Lacedaemon in a chariot, and let one of your sons go with him. Be pleased also to provide him with your best and fleetest horses."

When she had thus spoken, she flew away in the form of an eagle, and all marvelled as they beheld it. Nestor was astonished, and took Telemachus by the hand. "My friend," said he, "I see that you are going to be a great hero some day, since the gods wait upon you thus while you are still so young. This can have been none other of those who dwell in heaven than Jove's redoubtable daughter, the Trito-born, who showed such favour towards your brave father among the Argives." "Holy queen," he continued, "vouchsafe to send down thy grace upon myself, my good wife, and my children. In return, I will offer you in sacrifice a broad-browed heifer of a year old, unbroken, and never yet brought by man under the yoke. I will gild her horns, and will offer her up to you in sacrifice."

Thus did he pray, and Minerva heard his prayer. He then led the way to his own house, followed by his sons and sons-in-law. When they had got there and had taken their places on the benches and seats, he mixed them a bowl of sweet wine that was eleven years old when the housekeeper took the lid off the jar that held it. As he mixed the wine, he prayed much and made drink-offerings to Minerva, daughter of Aegis-bearing Jove. Then, when they had made their drink-offerings and had drunk each as much as he was minded, the others went home to bed each in his own abode; but Nestor put Telemachus to sleep in the room that was over the gateway along with Pisistratus, who was the only unmarried son now left him. As for himself, he slept in an inner room of the house, with the queen his wife by his side.

Now when the child of morning, rosy-fingered Dawn, appeared, Nestor left his couch and took his seat on the benches of white and polished marble that stood in front of his house. Here aforetime sat Neleus, peer of gods in counsel, but he was now dead, and had gone to the house of Hades; so Nestor sat in his seat, sceptre in hand, as guardian of the public weal. His sons as they left their rooms gathered round him, Echephron, Stratius, Perseus, Aretus, and

Thrasymedes; the sixth son was Pisistratus, and when Telemachus joined them they made him sit with them. Nestor then addressed them.

"My sons," said he, "make haste to do as I shall bid you. I wish first and foremost to propitiate the great goddess Minerva, who manifested herself visibly to me during yesterday's festivities. Go, then, one or other of you to the plain, tell the stockman to look me out a heifer, and come on here with it at once. Another must go to Telemachus's ship, and invite all the crew, leaving two men only in charge of the vessel. Some one else will run and fetch Laerceus the goldsmith to gild the horns of the heifer. The rest, stay all of you where you are; tell the maids in the house to prepare an excellent dinner, and to fetch seats, and logs of wood for a burnt offering. Tell them also- to bring me some clear spring water."

On this they hurried off on their several errands. The heifer was brought in from the plain, and Telemachus's crew came from the ship; the goldsmith brought the anvil, hammer, and tongs, with which he worked his gold, and Minerva herself came to the sacrifice. Nestor gave out the gold, and the smith gilded the horns of the heifer that the goddess might have pleasure in their beauty. Then Stratius and Echephron brought her in by the horns; Aretus fetched water from the house in a ewer that had a flower pattern on it, and in his other hand he held a basket of barley meal; sturdy Thrasymedes stood by with a sharp axe, ready to strike the heifer, while Perseus held a bucket. Then Nestor began with washing his hands and sprinkling the barley meal, and he offered many a prayer to Minerva as he threw a lock from the heifer's head upon the fire.

When they had done praying and sprinkling the barley meal Thrasymedes dealt his blow, and brought the heifer down with a stroke that cut through the tendons at the base of her neck, whereon the daughters and daughters-in-law of Nestor, and his venerable wife Eurydice (she was eldest daughter to Clymenus) screamed with delight. Then they lifted the heifer's head from off the ground, and Pisistratus cut her throat. When she had done bleeding and was quite dead, they cut her up. They cut out the thigh bones all in due course, wrapped them round in two layers of fat, and set some pieces of raw meat on the top of them; then Nestor laid them upon the wood fire and poured wine over them, while the young men stood near him with five-pronged spits in their hands. When the thighs were burned and they had tasted the inward meats, they cut the rest of the meat up small, put the pieces on the spits and toasted them over the fire.

Meanwhile lovely Polycaste, Nestor's youngest daughter, washed Telemachus. When she had washed him and anointed him with oil, she brought him a fair mantle and shirt, and he looked like a god as he came from the bath and took his seat by the side of Nestor. When the outer meats were done they drew them off the spits and sat down to dinner where they were waited upon by some worthy henchmen, who kept pouring them out their wine in cups of gold. As soon as they had had had enough to eat and drink Nestor said, "Sons, put Telemachus's horses to the chariot that he may start at once."

Thus did he speak, and they did even as he had said, and yoked the fleet horses to the chariot. The housekeeper packed them up a provision of bread, wine, and sweetmeats fit for the sons of princes. Then Telemachus got into the chariot, while Pisistratus gathered up the reins and took his seat beside him. He lashed the horses on and they flew forward nothing loth into the open country, leaving the high citadel of Pylos behind them. All that day did they travel, swaying the yoke upon their necks till the sun went down and darkness was over all the land. Then they reached Pherae where Diocles lived, who was son to Ortilochus and grandson to Alpheus. Here they passed the night and Diocles entertained them hospitably. When the child of morning, rosy-fingered Dawn; appeared, they again yoked their horses and drove out through the gateway under the echoing gatehouse. Pisistratus lashed the horses on and they flew forward nothing loth; presently they came to the corn lands Of the open country, and in the course of time completed their journey, so well did their steeds take them.

Now when the sun had set and darkness was over the land,

Book IV

They reached the low lying city of Lacedaemon them where they drove straight to the of abode Menelaus [and found him in his own house, feasting with his many clansmen in honour of the wedding of his son, and also of his daughter, whom he was marrying to the son of that valiant warrior Achilles. He had given his consent and promised her to him while he was still at Troy, and now the gods were bringing the marriage about; so he was sending her with chariots and horses to the city of the Myrmidons over whom Achilles' son was reigning. For his only son he had found a bride from Sparta, daughter of Alector. This son, Megapenthes, was born to him of a bondwoman, for heaven vouchsafed Helen no more children after she had borne Hermione, who was fair as golden Venus herself.

So the neighbours and kinsmen of Menelaus were feasting and making merry in his house. There was a bard also to sing to them and play his lyre, while two tumblers went about performing in the midst of them when the man struck up with his tune.

Telemachus and the son of Nestor stayed their horses at the gate, whereon Eteoneus servant to Menelaus came out, and as soon as he saw them ran hurrying back into the house to tell his Master. He went close up to him and said, "Menelaus, there are some strangers come here, two men, who look like sons of Jove. What are we to do? Shall we take their horses out, or tell them to find friends elsewhere as they best can?"

Menelaus was very angry and said, "Eteoneus, son of Boethous, you never used to be a fool, but now you talk like a simpleton. Take their horses out, of course, and show the strangers in that they may have supper; you and I have stayed often enough at other people's houses before we got back here, where heaven grant that we may rest in peace henceforward."

So Eteoneus bustled back and bade other servants come with him. They took their sweating hands from under the yoke, made them fast to the mangers, and gave them a feed of oats and barley mixed. Then they leaned the chariot against the end wall of the courtyard, and led the way into the house. Telemachus and Pisistratus were astonished when they saw it, for its splendour was as that of the sun and moon; then, when they had admired everything to their heart's content, they went into the bath room and washed themselves.

When the servants had washed them and anointed them with oil, they brought them woollen cloaks and shirts, and the two took their seats by the side of Menelaus. A maidservant brought them water in a beautiful golden ewer, and poured it into a silver basin for them to wash their hands; and she drew a clean table beside them. An upper servant brought them bread, and offered them many good things of what there was in the house, while the carver fetched them plates of all manner of meats and set cups of gold by their side.

Menelaus then greeted them saying, "Fall to, and welcome; when you have done supper I shall ask who you are, for the lineage of such men as you cannot have been lost. You must be descended from a line of sceptre-bearing kings, for poor people do not have such sons as you are."

On this he handed them a piece of fat roast loin, which had been set near him as being a prime part, and they laid their hands on the good things that were before them; as soon as they had had enough to eat and drink, Telemachus said to the son of Nestor, with his head so close that no one might hear, "Look, Pisistratus, man after my own heart, see the gleam of bronze and gold- of amber, ivory, and silver. Everything is so splendid that it is like seeing the palace of Olympian Jove. I am lost in admiration."

Menelaus overheard him and said, "No one, my sons, can hold his own with Jove, for his house and everything about him is immortal; but among mortal men- well, there may be another who has as much wealth as I have, or there may not; but at all events I have travelled much and have undergone much hardship, for it was nearly eight years before I could get home with my fleet. I went to Cyprus, Phoenicia and the Egyptians; I went also to the Ethiopians, the Sidonians, and the Erembians, and to Libya where the lambs have horns as soon as they are born, and the sheep lamb down three times a year. Every one in that country, whether master or man, has plenty of cheese, meat, and good milk, for the ewes yield all the year round. But while I was travelling and getting great riches among these people, my brother was secretly and shockingly murdered through the perfidy of his wicked wife, so that I have no pleasure in being lord of all this wealth. Whoever your parents may be they must have told you about all this, and of my heavy loss in the ruin of a stately mansion fully and magnificently furnished. Would that I had only a third of what I now have so that I had stayed at home, and all those were living who perished on the plain of Troy, far from Argos. I of grieve, as I sit here in my house, for one and all of them. At times I cry aloud for sorrow, but presently I leave off again, for crying is cold comfort and one soon tires of it. Yet grieve for these as I may, I do so for one man more than for them all. I cannot even think of him without loathing both food and sleep, so miserable does he make me, for no one of all the Achaeans worked so hard or risked so much as he did. He took nothing by it, and has left a legacy of sorrow to myself, for he has been gone a long time, and we know not whether he is alive or dead. His old father, his long-suffering wife Penelope, and his son Telemachus, whom he left behind him an infant in arms, are plunged in grief on his account."

Thus spoke Menelaus, and the heart of Telemachus yearned as he bethought him of his father. Tears fell from his eyes as he heard him thus mentioned, so that he held his cloak before his face with both hands. When Menelaus saw this he doubted whether to let him choose his own time for speaking, or to ask him at once and find what it was all about.

While he was thus in two minds Helen came down from her high vaulted and perfumed room, looking as lovely as Diana herself. Adraste brought her a seat, Alcippe a soft woollen rug while Phylo fetched her the silver work-box which Alcandra wife of Polybus had given her. Polybus lived in Egyptian Thebes, which is the richest city in the whole world; he gave Menelaus two baths, both of pure silver, two tripods, and ten talents of gold; besides all this, his wife gave Helen some beautiful presents, to wit, a golden distaff, and a silver work-box that ran on wheels, with a gold band round the top of it. Phylo now placed this by her side, full of fine spun yarn, and a distaff charged with violet coloured wool was laid upon the top of it. Then Helen took her seat, put her feet upon the footstool, and began to question her husband.

"Do we know, Menelaus," said she, "the names of these strangers who have come to visit us? Shall I guess right or wrong?-but I cannot help saying what I think. Never yet have I seen either man or woman so like somebody else (indeed when I look at him I hardly know what to think) as this young man is like Telemachus, whom Ulysses left as a baby behind him, when you Achaeans went to Troy with battle in your hearts, on account of my most shameless self."

"My dear wife," replied Menelaus, "I see the likeness just as you do. His hands and feet are just like Ulysses'; so is his hair, with the shape of his head and the expression of his eyes. Moreover, when I was talking about Ulysses, and saying how much he had suffered on my account, tears fell from his eyes, and he hid his face in his mantle."

Then Pisistratus said, "Menelaus, son of Atreus, you are right in thinking that this young man is Telemachus, but he is very modest, and is ashamed to come here and begin opening up discourse with one whose conversation is so divinely interesting as your own. My father, Nestor, sent me to escort him hither, for he wanted to know whether you could give him any counsel or suggestion. A son has always trouble at home when his father has gone away leaving him without supporters; and this is how Telemachus is now placed, for his father is absent, and there is no one among his own people to stand by him."

"Bless my heart," replied Menelaus, "then I am receiving a visit from the son of a very dear friend, who suffered much hardship for my sake. I had always hoped to entertain him with most marked distinction when heaven had granted us a safe return from beyond the seas. I should have founded a city for him in Argos, and built him a house. I should have made him leave Ithaca with his goods, his son, and all his people, and should have sacked for them some one of the neighbouring cities that are subject to me. We should thus have seen one another continually, and nothing but death could have interrupted so close and happy an intercourse. I suppose, however, that heaven grudged us such great good fortune, for it has prevented the poor fellow from ever getting home at all."

Thus did he speak, and his words set them all a weeping. Helen wept, Telemachus wept, and so did Menelaus, nor could Pisistratus keep his eyes from filling, when he remembered his dear brother Antilochus whom the son of bright Dawn had killed. Thereon he said to Menelaus,

"Sir, my father Nestor, when we used to talk about you at home, told me you were a person of rare and excellent understanding. If, then, it be possible, do as I would urge you. I am not fond of crying while I am getting my supper. Morning will come in due course, and in the forenoon I care not how much I cry for those that are dead and gone. This is all we can do for the poor things. We can only shave our heads for them and wring the tears from our cheeks. I had a brother who died at Troy; he was by no means the worst man there; you are sure to have known him- his name was Antilochus; I never set eyes upon him myself, but they say that he was singularly fleet of foot and in fight valiant."

"Your discretion, my friend," answered Menelaus, "is beyond your years. It is plain you take after your father. One can soon see when a man is son to one whom heaven has blessed both as regards wife and offspring- and it has blessed Nestor from first to last all his days, giving him a green old age in his own house, with sons about him who are both we disposed and valiant. We will put an end therefore to all this weeping, and attend to our supper again. Let water be poured over our hands. Telemachus and I can talk with one another fully in the morning."

On this Asphalion, one of the servants, poured water over their hands and they laid their hands on the good things that were before them.

Then Jove's daughter Helen bethought her of another matter. She drugged the wine with an herb that banishes all care, sorrow, and ill humour. Whoever drinks wine thus drugged cannot shed a single tear all the rest of the day, not even though his father and mother both of them drop down dead, or he sees a brother or a son hewn in pieces before his very eyes. This drug, of such sovereign power and virtue, had been given to Helen by Polydamna wife of Thon, a woman of Egypt, where there grow all sorts of herbs, some good to put into the mixing-bowl and others poisonous. Moreover, every one in the whole country is a skilled physician, for they are of the race of Paeeon. When Helen had put this drug in the bowl, and had told the servants to serve the wine round, she said:

"Menelaus, son of Atreus, and you my good friends, sons of honourable men (which is as Jove wills, for he is the giver both of good and evil, and can do what he chooses), feast here as you will, and listen while I tell you a tale in season. I cannot indeed name every single one of the exploits of Ulysses, but I can say what he did when he was before Troy, and you Achaeans were in all sorts of difficulties. He covered himself with wounds and bruises, dressed himself all in rags, and entered the enemy's city looking like a menial or a beggar. and quite different from what he did when he was among his own people. In this disguise he entered the city of Troy, and no one said anything to him. I alone recognized him and began to question him, but he was too cunning for me. When, however, I had washed and anointed him and had given him clothes, and after I had sworn a solemn oath not to betray him to the Trojans till he had got safely back to his own camp and to the ships, he told me all that the Achaeans meant to do. He killed many Trojans and got much information before he reached the Argive camp, for all which things the Trojan women made lamentation, but for my own part I was glad, for my heart was beginning to oam after my home, and I was unhappy about wrong that Venus had done me in taking me over there, away from my country, my girl, and my lawful wedded husband, who is indeed by no means deficient either in person or understanding."

Then Menelaus said, "All that you have been saying, my dear wife, is true. I have travelled much, and have had much to do with heroes, but I have never seen such another man as Ulysses. What endurance too, and what courage he displayed within the wooden horse, wherein all the bravest of the Argives were lying in wait to bring death and destruction upon the Trojans. At that moment you came up to us; some god who wished well to the Trojans must have set you on to it and you had Deiphobus with you. Three times did you go all round our hiding place and pat it; you called our chiefs each by his own name, and mimicked all our wives -Diomed, Ulysses, and I from our seats inside heard what a noise you made. Diomed and I could not make up our minds whether to spring out then and there, or to answer you from inside, but Ulysses held us all in check, so we sat quite still, all except Anticlus, who was beginning to answer you, when Ulysses clapped his two brawny hands over his mouth, and kept them there. It was this that saved us all, for he muzzled Anticlus till Minerva took you away again."

"How sad," exclaimed Telemachus, "that all this was of no avail to save him, nor yet his own iron courage. But now, sir, be pleased to send us all to bed, that we may lie down and enjoy the blessed boon of sleep."

On this Helen told the maid servants to set beds in the room that was in the gatehouse, and to make them with good red rugs, and spread coverlets on the top of them with woollen cloaks for the guests to wear. So the maids went out, carrying a torch, and made the beds, to which a man-servant presently conducted the strangers. Thus, then, did Telemachus and Pisistratus sleep there in the forecourt, while the son of Atreus lay in an inner room with lovely Helen by his side.

When the child of morning, rosy-fingered Dawn, appeared, Menelaus rose and dressed himself. He bound his sandals on to his comely feet, girded his sword about his shoulders, and left his room looking like an immortal god. Then, taking a seat near Telemachus he said:

"And what, Telemachus, has led you to take this long sea voyage to Lacedaemon? Are you on public or private business? Tell me all about it."

"I have come, sir replied Telemachus, "to see if you can tell me anything about my father. I am being eaten out of house and home; my fair estate is being wasted, and my house is full of miscreants who keep killing great numbers of my sheep and oxen, on the pretence of paying their addresses to my mother. Therefore, I am suppliant at your knees if haply you may tell me about my father's melancholy end, whether you saw it with your own eyes, or heard it from some other traveller; for he was a man born to trouble. Do not soften things out of any pity for myself, but tell me in all plainness exactly what you saw. If my brave father Ulysses ever did you loyal service either by word or deed, when you Achaeans were harassed by the Trojans, bear it in mind now as in my favour and tell me truly all."

Menelaus on hearing this was very much shocked. "So," he exclaimed, "these cowards would usurp a brave man's bed? A hind might as well lay her new born young in the lair of a lion, and then go off to feed in the forest or in some grassy dell: the lion when he comes back to his lair will make short work with the pair of them- and so will Ulysses with these suitors. By father Jove, Minerva, and Apollo, if Ulysses is still the man that he was when he wrestled with Philomeleides in Lesbos, and threw him so heavily that all the Achaeans cheered him- if he is still such and were to come near these suitors, they would have a short shrift and a sorry wedding. As regards your questions, however, I will not prevaricate nor deceive you, but will tell you without concealment all that the old man of the sea told me.

"I was trying to come on here, but the gods detained me in Egypt, for my hecatombs had not given them full satisfaction, and the gods are very strict about having their dues. Now off Egypt, about as far as a ship can sail in a day with a good stiff breeze behind her, there is an island called Pharos- it has a good harbour from which vessels can get out into open sea when they have taken in water- and the gods becalmed me twenty days without so much as a breath of fair wind to help me forward. We should have run clean out of provisions and my men would have starved, if a goddess had not taken pity upon me and saved me in the person of Idothea, daughter to Proteus, the old man of the sea, for she had taken a great fancy to me.

"She came to me one day when I was by myself, as I often was, for the men used to go with their barbed hooks, all over the island in the hope of catching a fish or two to save them from the pangs of hunger. 'Stranger,' said she, 'it seems to me that you like starving in this way- at any rate it does not greatly trouble you, for you stick here day after day, without even trying to get away though your men are dying by inches.'

"'Let me tell you,' said I, 'whichever of the goddesses you may happen to be, that I am not staying here of my own accord, but must have offended the gods that live in heaven. Tell me, therefore, for the gods know everything. which of the immortals it is that is hindering me in this way, and tell me also how I may sail the sea so as to reach my home.'

"'Stranger,' replied she, 'I will make it all quite clear to you. There is an old immortal who lives under the sea hereabouts and whose name is Proteus. He is an Egyptian, and people say he is my father; he is Neptune's head man and knows every inch of ground all over the bottom of the sea. If you can snare him and hold him tight, he will tell you about your voyage, what courses you are to take, and how you are to sail the sea so as to reach your home. He will also tell you, if you so will, all that has been going on at your house both good and bad, while you have been away on your long and dangerous journey.'

"'Can you show me,' said I, 'some stratagem by means of which I may catch this old god without his suspecting it and finding me out? For a god is not easily caught- not by a mortal man.'

"'Stranger,' said she, 'I will make it all quite clear to you. About the time when the sun shall have reached mid heaven, the old man of the sea comes up from under the waves, heralded by the West wind that furs the water over his head. As soon as he has come up he lies down, and goes to sleep in a great sea cave, where the seals- Halosydne's chickens as they call them- come up also from the grey sea, and go to sleep in shoals all round him; and a very strong and fish-like smell do they bring with them. Early to-morrow morning I will take you to this place and will lay you in ambush. Pick out, therefore, the three best men you have in your fleet, and I will tell you all the tricks that the old man will play you.

"'First he will look over all his seals, and count them; then, when he has seen them and tallied them on his five fingers, he will go to sleep among them, as a shepherd among his sheep. The moment you see that he is asleep seize him; put forth all your strength and hold him fast, for he will do his very utmost to get away from you. He will turn himself into every kind of creature that goes upon the earth, and will become also both fire and water; but you must hold him fast and grip him tighter and tighter, till he begins to talk to you and comes back to what he was when you saw him go to sleep; then you may slacken your hold and let him go; and you can ask him which of the gods it is that is angry with you, and what you must do to reach your home over the seas.'

"Having so said she dived under the waves, whereon I turned back to the place where my ships were ranged upon the shore; and my heart was clouded with care as I went along. When I reached my ship we got supper ready, for night was falling, and camped down upon the beach.

"When the child of morning, rosy-fingered Dawn, appeared, I took the three men on whose prowess of all kinds I could most rely, and went along by the sea-side, praying heartily to heaven. Meanwhile the goddess fetched me up four seal skins from the bottom of the sea, all of them just skinned, for she meant playing a trick upon her father. Then she dug four pits for us to lie in, and sat down to wait till we should come up. When we were close to her, she made us lie down in the pits one after the other, and threw a seal skin over each of us. Our ambuscade would have been intolerable, for the stench of the fishy seals was most distressing- who would go to bed with a sea monster if he could help it?-but here, too, the goddess helped us, and thought of something that gave us great relief, for she put some ambrosia under each man's nostrils, which was so fragrant that it killed the smell of the seals.

"We waited the whole morning and made the best of it, watching the seals come up in hundreds to bask upon the sea shore, till at noon the old man of the sea came up too, and when he had found his fat seals he went over them and counted them. We were among the first he counted, and he never suspected any guile, but laid himself down to sleep as soon as he had done counting. Then we rushed upon him with a shout and seized him; on which he began at once with his old tricks, and changed himself first into a lion with a great mane; then all of a sudden he became a dragon, a leopard, a wild boar; the next moment he was running water, and then again directly he was a tree, but we stuck to him and never lost hold, till at last the cunning old creature became distressed, and said, Which of the gods was it, Son of Atreus, that hatched this plot with you for snaring me and seizing me against my will? What do you want?'

"'You know that yourself, old man,' I answered, 'you will gain nothing by trying to put me off. It is because I have been kept so long in this island, and see no sign of my being able to get away. I am losing all heart; tell me, then, for you gods know everything, which of the immortals it is that is hindering me, and tell me also how I may sail the sea so as to reach my home?'

"Then,' he said, 'if you would finish your voyage and get home quickly, you must offer sacrifices to Jove and to the rest of the gods before embarking; for it is decreed that you shall not get back to your friends, and to your own house, till you have returned to the heaven fed stream of Egypt, and offered holy hecatombs to the immortal gods that reign in heaven. When you have done this they will let you finish your voyage.'

"I was broken hearted when I heard that I must go back all that long and terrible voyage to Egypt; nevertheless, I answered, 'I will do all, old man, that you have laid upon me; but now tell me, and tell me true, whether all the Achaeans whom Nestor and I left behind us when we set sail from Troy have got home safely, or whether any one of them came to a bad end either on board his own ship or among his friends when the days of his fighting were done.'

"'Son of Atreus,' he answered, 'why ask me? You had better not know what I can tell you, for your eyes will surely fill when you have heard my story. Many of those about whom you ask are dead and gone, but many still remain, and only two of the chief men among the Achaeans perished during their return home. As for what happened on the field of battle- you were there yourself. A third Achaean leader is still at sea, alive, but hindered from returning. Ajax was wrecked, for Neptune drove him on to the great rocks of Gyrae; nevertheless, he let him get safe out of the water, and in spite of all Minerva's hatred he would have escaped death, if he had not ruined himself by boasting. He said the gods could not drown him even though they had tried to do so, and when Neptune heard this large talk, he seized his trident in his two brawny hands, and split the rock of Gyrae in two pieces. The base remained where it was, but the part on which Ajax was sitting fell headlong into the sea and carried Ajax with it; so he drank salt water and was drowned.

"'Your brother and his ships escaped, for Juno protected him, but when he was just about to reach the high promontory of Malea, he was caught by a heavy gale which carried him out to sea again sorely against his will, and drove him to the foreland where Thyestes used to dwell, but where Aegisthus was then living. By and by, however, it seemed as though he was to return safely after all, for the gods backed the wind into its old quarter and they reached home; whereon Agamemnon kissed his native soil, and shed tears of joy at finding himself in his own country.

"'Now there was a watchman whom Aegisthus kept always on the watch, and to whom he had promised two talents of gold. This man had been looking out for a whole year to make sure that Agamemnon did not give him the slip and prepare war; when, therefore, this man saw Agamemnon go by, he went and told Aegisthus who at once began to lay a plot for him. He picked twenty of his bravest warriors and placed them in ambuscade on one side the cloister, while on the opposite side he prepared a banquet. Then he sent his chariots and horsemen to Agamemnon, and invited him to the feast, but he meant foul play. He got him there, all unsuspicious of the doom that was awaiting him, and killed him when the banquet was over as though he were butchering an ox in the shambles; not one of Agamemnon's followers was left alive, nor yet one of Aegisthus', but they were all killed there in the cloisters.'

"Thus spoke Proteus, and I was broken hearted as I heard him. I sat down upon the sands and wept; I felt as though I could no longer bear to live nor look upon the light of the sun. Presently, when I had had my fill of weeping and writhing upon the ground, the old man of the sea said, 'Son of Atreus, do not waste any more time in crying so bitterly; it can do no manner of good; find your way home as fast as ever you can, for Aegisthus be still alive, and even though Orestes has beforehand with you in kilting him, you may yet come in for his funeral.'

"On this I took comfort in spite of all my sorrow, and said, 'I know, then, about these two; tell me, therefore, about the third man of whom you spoke; is he still alive, but at sea, and unable to get home? or is he dead? Tell me, no matter how much it may grieve me.'

"'The third man,' he answered, 'is Ulysses who dwells in Ithaca. I can see him in an island sorrowing bitterly in the house of the nymph Calypso, who is keeping him prisoner, and he cannot reach his home for he has no ships nor sailors to take him over the sea. As for your own end, Menelaus, you shall not die in Argos, but the gods will take you to the Elysian plain, which is at the ends of the world. There fair-haired Rhadamanthus reigns, and men lead an easier life than any where else in the world, for in Elysium there falls not rain, nor hail, nor snow, but Oceanus breathes ever with a West wind that sings softly from the sea, and gives fresh life to all men. This will happen to you because you have married Helen, and are Jove's son-in-law.'

"As he spoke he dived under the waves, whereon I turned back to the ships with my companions, and my heart was clouded with care as I went along. When we reached the ships we got supper ready, for night was falling, and camped down upon the beach. When the child of morning, rosy-fingered Dawn appeared, we drew our ships into the water, and put our masts and sails within them; then we went on board ourselves, took our seats on the benches, and smote the grey sea with our oars. I again stationed my ships in the heaven-fed stream of Egypt, and offered hecatombs that were full and sufficient. When I had thus appeased heaven's anger, I raised a barrow to the memory of Agamemnon that his name might live for ever, after which I had a quick passage home, for the gods sent me a fair wind.

"And now for yourself- stay here some ten or twelve days longer, and I will then speed you on your way. I will make you a noble present of a chariot and three horses. I will also give you a beautiful chalice that so long as you live you may think of me whenever you make a drink-offering to the immortal gods."

"Son of Atreus," replied Telemachus, "do not press me to stay longer; I should be contented to remain with you for another twelve months; I find your conversation so delightful that I should never once wish myself at home with my parents; but my crew whom I have left at Pylos are already impatient, and you are detaining me from them. As for any present you may be disposed to make me, I had rather that it should he a piece of plate. I will take no horses back with me to Ithaca, but will leave them to adorn your own stables, for you have much flat ground in your kingdom where lotus thrives, as also meadowsweet and wheat and barley, and oats with their white and spreading ears; whereas in Ithaca we have neither open fields nor racecourses, and the country is more fit for goats than horses, and I like it the better for that. None of our islands have much level ground, suitable for horses, and Ithaca least of all."

Menelaus smiled and took Telemachus's hand within his own. "What you say," said he, "shows that you come of good family. I both can, and will, make this exchange for you, by giving you the finest and most precious piece of plate in all my house. It is a mixing-bowl by Vulcan's own hand, of pure silver, except the rim, which is inlaid with gold. Phaedimus, king of the Sidonians, gave it me in the course of a visit which I paid him when I returned thither on my homeward journey. I will make you a present of it."

Thus did they converse [and guests kept coming to the king's house. They brought sheep and wine, while their wives had put up bread for them to take with them; so they were busy cooking their dinners in the courts].

Meanwhile the suitors were throwing discs or aiming with spears at a mark on the levelled ground in front of Ulysses' house, and were behaving with all their old insolence. Antinous and Eurymachus, who were their ringleaders and much the foremost among them all, were sitting together when Noemon son of Phronius came up and said to Antinous,

"Have we any idea, Antinous, on what day Telemachus returns from Pylos? He has a ship of mine, and I want it, to cross over to Elis: I have twelve brood mares there with yearling mule foals by their side not yet broken in, and I want to bring one of them over here and break him."

They were astounded when they heard this, for they had made sure that Telemachus had not gone to the city of Neleus. They thought he was only away somewhere on the farms, and was with the sheep, or with the swineherd; so Antinous said, "When did he go? Tell me truly, and what young men did he take with him? Were they freemen or his own bondsmen- for he might manage that too? Tell me also, did you let him have the ship of your own free will because he asked you, or did he take it without yourleave?"

"I lent it him," answered Noemon, "what else could I do when a man of his position said he was in a difficulty, and asked me to oblige him? I could not possibly refuse. As for those who went with him they were the best young men we have, and I saw Mentor go on board as captain- or some god who was exactly like him. I cannot understand it, for I saw Mentor here myself yesterday morning, and yet he was then setting out for Pylos."

Noemon then went back to his father's house, but Antinous and Eurymachus were very angry. They told the others to leave off playing, and to come and sit down along with themselves. When they came, Antinous son of Eupeithes spoke in anger. His heart was black with rage, and his eyes flashed fire as he said:

"Good heavens, this voyage of Telemachus is a very serious matter; we had made sure that it would come to nothing, but the young fellow has got away in spite of us, and with a picked crew too. He will be giving us trouble presently; may Jove take him before he is full grown. Find me a ship, therefore, with a crew of twenty men, and I will lie in wait for him in the straits between Ithaca and Samos; he will then rue the day that he set out to try and get news of his father."

Thus did he speak, and the others applauded his saying; they then all of them went inside the buildings.

It was not long ere Penelope came to know what the suitors were plotting; for a man servant, Medon, overheard them from outside the outer court as they were laying their schemes within, and went to tell his mistress. As he crossed the threshold of her room Penelope said: "Medon, what have the suitors sent you here for? Is it to tell the maids to leave their master's business and cook dinner for them? I wish they may neither woo nor dine henceforward, neither here nor anywhere else, but let this be the very last time, for the waste you all make of my son's estate. Did not your fathers tell you when you were children how good Ulysses had been to them- never doing anything high-handed, nor speaking harshly to anybody? Kings may say things sometimes, and they may take a fancy to one man and dislike another, but Ulysses never did an unjust thing by anybody- which shows what bad hearts you have, and that there is no such thing as gratitude left in this world."

Then Medon said, "I wish, Madam, that this were all; but they are plotting something much more dreadful now- may heaven frustrate their design. They are going to try and murder Telemachus as he is coming home from Pylos and Lacedaemon, where he has been to get news of his father."

Then Penelope's heart sank within her, and for a long time she was speechless; her eyes filled with tears, and she could find no utterance. At last, however, she said, "Why did my son leave me? What business had he to go sailing off in ships that make long voyages over the ocean like sea-horses? Does he want to die without leaving any one behind him to keep up his name?"

"I do not know," answered Medon, "whether some god set him on to it, or whether he went on his own impulse to see if he could find out if his father was dead, or alive and on his way home."

Then he went downstairs again, leaving Penelope in an agony of grief. There were plenty of seats in the house, but she. had no heart for sitting on any one of them; she could only fling herself on the floor of her own room and cry; whereon all the maids in the house, both old and young, gathered round her and began to cry too, till at last in a transport of sorrow she exclaimed,

"My dears, heaven has been pleased to try me with more affliction than any other woman of my age and country. First I lost my brave and lion-hearted husband, who had every good quality under heaven, and whose name was great over all Hellas and middle Argos, and now my darling son is at the mercy of the winds and waves, without my having heard one word about his leaving home. You hussies, there was not one of you would so much as think of giving me a call out of my bed, though you all of you very well knew when he was starting. If I had known he meant taking this voyage, he would have had to give it up, no matter how much he was bent upon it, or leave me a corpse behind him- one or other. Now, however, go some of you and call old Dolius, who was given me by my father on my marriage, and who is my gardener. Bid him go at once and tell everything to Laertes, who may be able to hit on some plan for enlisting public sympathy on our side, as against those who are trying to exterminate his own race and that of Ulysses."

Then the dear old nurse Euryclea said, "You may kill me, Madam, or let me live on in your house, whichever you please, but I will tell you the real truth. I knew all about it, and gave him everything he wanted in the way of bread and wine, but he made me take my solemn oath that I would not tell you anything for some ten or twelve days, unless you asked or happened to hear of his having gone, for he did not want you to spoil your beauty by crying. And now, Madam, wash your face, change your dress, and go upstairs with your maids to offer prayers to Minerva, daughter of Aegis-bearing Jove, for she can save him even though he be in the jaws of death. Do not trouble Laertes: he has trouble enough already. Besides, I cannot think that the gods hate die race of the race of the son of Arceisius so much, but there will be a son left to come up after him, and inherit both the house and the fair fields that lie far all round it."

With these words she made her mistress leave off crying, and dried the tears from her eyes. Penelope washed her face, changed her dress, and went upstairs with her maids. She then put some bruised barley into a basket and began praying to Minerva.

"Hear me," she cried, "Daughter of Aegis-bearing Jove, unweariable. If ever Ulysses while he was here burned you fat thigh bones of sheep or heifer, bear it in mind now as in my favour, and save my darling son from the villainy of the suitors."

She cried aloud as she spoke, and the goddess heard her prayer; meanwhile the suitors were clamorous throughout the covered cloister, and one of them said:

"The queen is preparing for her marriage with one or other of us. Little does she dream that her son has now been doomed to die."

This was what they said, but they did not know what was going to happen. Then Antinous said, "Comrades, let there be no loud talking, lest some of it get carried inside. Let us be up and do that in silence, about which we are all of a mind."

He then chose twenty men, and they went down to their. ship and to the sea side; they drew the vessel into the water and got her mast and sails inside her; they bound the oars to the thole-pins with twisted thongs of leather, all in due course, and spread the white sails aloft, while their fine servants brought them their armour. Then they made the ship fast a little way out, came on shore again, got their suppers, and waited till night should fall.

But Penelope lay in her own room upstairs unable to eat or drink, and wondering whether her brave son would escape, or be overpowered by the wicked suitors. Like a lioness caught in the toils with huntsmen hemming her in on every side she thought and thought till she sank into a slumber, and lay on her bed bereft of thought and motion.

Then Minerva bethought her of another matter, and made a vision in the likeness of Penelope's sister Iphthime daughter of Icarius who had married Eumelus and lived in Pherae. She told the vision to go to the house of Ulysses, and to make Penelope leave off crying, so it came into her room by the hole through which the thong went for pulling the door to, and hovered over her head, saying,

"You are asleep, Penelope: the gods who live at ease will not suffer you to weep and be so sad. Your son has done them no wrong, so he will yet come back to you."

Penelope, who was sleeping sweetly at the gates of dreamland, answered, "Sister, why have you come here? You do not come very often, but I suppose that is because you live such a long way off. Am I, then, to leave off crying and refrain from all the sad thoughts that torture me? I, who have lost my brave and lion-hearted husband, who had every good quality under heaven, and whose name was great over all Hellas and middle Argos; and now my darling son has gone off on board of a ship- a foolish fellow who has never been used to roughing it, nor to going about among gatherings of men. I am even more anxious about him than about my husband; I am all in a tremble when I think of him, lest something should happen to him, either from the people among whom he has gone, or by sea, for he has many enemies who are plotting against him, and are bent on killing him before he can return home."

Then the vision said, "Take heart, and be not so much dismayed. There is one gone with him whom many a man would be glad enough to have stand by his side, I mean Minerva; it is she who has compassion upon you, and who has sent me to bear you this message."

"Then," said Penelope, "if you are a god or have been sent here by divine commission, tell me also about that other unhappy one- is he still alive, or is he already dead and in the house of Hades?"

And the vision said, "I shall not tell you for certain whether he is alive or dead, and there is no use in idle conversation."

Then it vanished through the thong-hole of the door and was dissipated into thin air; but Penelope rose from her sleep refreshed and comforted, so vivid had been her dream.

Meantime the suitors went on board and sailed their ways over the sea, intent on murdering Telemachus. Now there is a rocky islet called Asteris, of no great size, in mid channel between Ithaca and Samos, and there is a harbour on either side of it where a ship can lie. Here then the Achaeans placed themselves in ambush.

Book V

And now, as Dawn rose from her couch beside Tithonus- harbinger of light alike to mortals and immortals- the gods met in council and with them, Jove the lord of thunder, who is their king. Thereon Minerva began to tell them of the many sufferings of Ulysses, for she pitied him away there in the house of the nymph Calypso.

"Father Jove," said she, "and all you other gods that live in everlasting bliss, I hope there may never be such a thing as a kind and well-disposed ruler any more, nor one who will govern equitably. I hope they will be all henceforth cruel and unjust, for there is not one of his subjects but has forgotten Ulysses, who ruled them as though he were their father. There he is, lying in great pain in an island where dwells the nymph Calypso, who will not let him go; and he cannot get back to his own country, for he can find neither ships nor sailors to take him over the sea. Furthermore, wicked people are now trying to murder his only son Telemachus, who is coming home from Pylos and Lacedaemon, where he has been to see if he can get news of his father."

"What, my dear, are you talking about?" replied her father, "did you not send him there yourself, because you thought it would help Ulysses to get home and punish the suitors? Besides, you are perfectly able to protect

Telemachus, and to see him safely home again, while the suitors have to come hurry-skurrying back without having killed him."

When he had thus spoken, he said to his son Mercury, "Mercury, you are our messenger, go therefore and tell Calypso we have decreed that poor Ulysses is to return home. He is to be convoyed neither by gods nor men, but after a perilous voyage of twenty days upon a raft he is to reach fertile Scheria, the land of the Phaeacians, who are near of kin to the gods, and will honour him as though he were one of ourselves. They will send him in a ship to his own country, and will give him more bronze and gold and raiment than he would have brought back from Troy, if he had had had all his prize money and had got home without disaster. This is how we have settled that he shall return to his country and his friends."

Thus he spoke, and Mercury, guide and guardian, slayer of Argus, did as he was told. Forthwith he bound on his glittering golden sandals with which he could fly like the wind over land and sea. He took the wand with which he seals men's eyes in sleep or wakes them just as he pleases, and flew holding it in his hand over Pieria; then he swooped down through the firmament till he reached the level of the sea, whose waves he skimmed like a cormorant that flies fishing every hole and corner of the ocean, and drenching its thick plumage in the spray. He flew and flew over many a weary wave, but when at last he got to the island which was his journey's end, he left the sea and went on by land till he came to the cave where the nymph Calypso lived.

He found her at home. There was a large fire burning on the hearth, and one could smell from far the fragrant reek of burning cedar and sandal wood. As for herself, she was busy at her loom, shooting her golden shuttle through the warp and singing beautifully. Round her cave there was a thick wood of alder, poplar, and sweet smelling cypress trees, wherein all kinds of great birds had built their nests- owls, hawks, and chattering sea-crows that occupy their business in the waters. A vine loaded with grapes was trained and grew luxuriantly about the mouth of the cave; there were also four running rills of water in channels cut pretty close together, and turned hither and thither so as to irrigate the beds of violets and luscious herbage over which they flowed. Even a god could not help being charmed with such a lovely spot, so Mercury stood still and looked at it; but when he had admired it sufficiently he went inside the cave.

Calypso knew him at once- for the gods all know each other, no matter how far they live from one another- but Ulysses was not within; he was on the sea-shore as usual, looking out upon the barren ocean with tears in his eyes, groaning and breaking his heart for sorrow. Calypso gave Mercury a seat and said: "Why have you come to see me, Mercury- honoured, and ever welcome- for you do not visit me often? Say what you want; I will do it for be you at once if I can, and if it can be done at all; but come inside, and let me set refreshment before you.

As she spoke she drew a table loaded with ambrosia beside him and mixed him some red nectar, so Mercury ate and drank till he had had enough, and then said:

"We are speaking god and goddess to one another, one another, and you ask me why I have come here, and I will tell you truly as you would have me do. Jove sent me; it was no doing of mine; who could possibly want to come all this way over the sea where there are no cities full of people to offer me sacrifices or choice hecatombs? Nevertheless I had to come, for none of us other gods can cross Jove, nor transgress his orders. He says that you have here the most ill-starred of alf those who fought nine years before the city of King Priam and sailed home in the tenth year after having sacked it. On their way home they sinned against Minerva, who raised both wind and waves against them, so that all his brave companions perished, and he alone was carried hither by wind and tide. Jove says that you are to let this by man go at once, for it is decreed that he shall not perish here, far from his own people, but shall return to his house and country and see his friends again."

Calypso trembled with rage when she heard this, "You gods," she exclaimed, to be ashamed of yourselves. You are always jealous and hate seeing a goddess take a fancy to a mortal man, and live with him in open matrimony. So when rosy-fingered Dawn made love to Orion, you precious gods were all of you furious till Diana went and killed him in Ortygia. So again when Ceres fell in love with Iasion, and yielded to him in a thrice ploughed fallow field, Jove came to hear of it before so long and killed Iasion with his thunder-bolts. And now you are angry with me too because I have a man here. I found the poor creature sitting all alone astride of a keel, for Jove had struck his ship with lightning and sunk it in mid ocean, so that all his crew were drowned, while he himself was driven by wind and waves on to my island. I got fond of him and cherished him, and had set my heart on making him immortal, so that he should never grow old all his days; still I cannot cross Jove, nor bring his counsels to nothing; therefore, if he insists upon it, let the man go beyond the seas again; but I cannot send him anywhere myself for I have neither ships nor men who can take him. Nevertheless I will readily give him such advice, in all good faith, as will be likely to bring him safely to his own country."

"Then send him away," said Mercury, "or Jove will be angry with you and punish you"'

On this he took his leave, and Calypso went out to look for Ulysses, for she had heard Jove's message. She found him sitting upon the beach with his eyes ever filled with tears, and dying of sheer home-sickness; for he had got tired of Calypso, and though he was forced to sleep with her in the cave by night, it was she, not he, that would have it so. As for the day time, he spent it on the rocks and on the sea-shore, weeping, crying aloud for his despair, and always looking out upon the sea. Calypso then went close up to him said:

"My poor fellow, you shall not stay here grieving and fretting your life out any longer. I am going to send you away of my own free will; so go, cut some beams of wood, and make yourself a large raft with an upper deck that it may carry you safely over the sea. I will put bread, wine, and water on board to save you from starving. I will also give you clothes, and will send you a fair wind to take you home, if the gods in heaven so will it- for they know more about these things, and can settle them better than I can."

Ulysses shuddered as he heard her. "Now goddess," he answered, "there is something behind all this; you cannot be really meaning to help me home when you bid me do such a dreadful thing as put to sea on a raft. Not even a well-found ship with a fair wind could venture on such a distant voyage: nothing that you can say or do shall mage me go on board a raft unless you first solemnly swear that you mean me no mischief."

Calypso smiled at this and caressed him with her hand: "You know a great deal," said she, "but you are quite wrong here. May heaven above and earth below be my witnesses, with the waters of the river Styx- and this is the most solemn oath which a blessed god can take- that I mean you no sort of harm, and am only advising you to do exactly what I should do myself in your place. I am dealing with you quite straightforwardly; my heart is not made of iron, and I am very sorry for you."

When she had thus spoken she led the way rapidly before him, and Ulysses followed in her steps; so the pair, goddess and man, went on and on till they came to Calypso's cave, where Ulysses took the seat that Mercury had just left. Calypso set meat and drink before him of the food that mortals eat; but her maids brought ambrosia and nectar for herself, and they laid their hands on the good things that were before them. When they had satisfied themselves with meat and drink, Calypso spoke, saying:

"Ulysses, noble son of Laertes, so you would start home to your own land at once? Good luck go with you, but if you could only know how much suffering is in store for you before you get back to your own country, you would stay where you are, keep house along with me, and let me make you immortal, no matter how anxious you may be to see this wife of yours, of whom you are thinking all the time day after day; yet I flatter myself that at am no whit less tall or well-looking than she is, for it is not to be expected that a mortal woman should compare in beauty with an immortal."

"Goddess," replied Ulysses, "do not be angry with me about this. I am quite aware that my wife Penelope is nothing like so tall or so beautiful as yourself. She is only a woman, whereas you are an immortal. Nevertheless, I want to get home, and can think of nothing else. If some god wrecks me when I am on the sea, I will bear it and make the best of it. I have had infinite trouble both by land and sea already, so let this go with the rest."

Presently the sun set and it became dark, whereon the pair retired into the inner part of the cave and went to bed.

When the child of morning, rosy-fingered Dawn, appeared, Ulysses put on his shirt and cloak, while the goddess wore a dress of a light gossamer fabric, very fine and graceful, with a beautiful golden girdle about her waist and a veil to cover her head. She at once set herself to think how she could speed Ulysses on his way. So she gave him a great bronze axe that suited his hands; it was sharpened on both sides, and had a beautiful olive-wood handle fitted firmly on to it. She also gave him a sharp adze, and then led the way to the far end of the island where the largest trees grew- alder, poplar and pine, that reached the sky- very dry and well seasoned, so as to sail light for him in the water. Then, when she had shown him where the best trees grew, Calypso went home, leaving him to cut them, which he soon finished doing. He cut down twenty trees in all and adzed them smooth, squaring them by rule in good workmanlike fashion. Meanwhile Calypso came back with some augers, so he bored holes with them and fitted the timbers together with bolts and rivets. He made the raft as broad as a skilled shipwright makes the beam of a large vessel, and he filed a deck on top of the ribs, and ran a gunwale all round it. He also made a mast with a yard arm, and a rudder to steer with. He fenced the raft all round with wicker hurdles as a protection against the waves, and then he threw on a quantity of wood. By and by Calypso brought him some linen to make the sails, and he made these too, excellently, making them fast with braces and sheets. Last of all, with the help of levers, he drew the raft down into the water.

In four days he had completed the whole work, and on the fifth Calypso sent him from the island after washing him and giving him some clean clothes.

She gave him a goat skin full of black wine, and another larger one of water; she also gave him a wallet full of provisions, and found him in much good meat. Moreover, she made the wind fair and warm for him, and gladly did Ulysses spread his sail before it, while he sat and guided the raft skilfully by means of the rudder. He never closed his eyes, but kept them fixed on the Pleiads, on late-setting Bootes, and on the Bear- which men also call the wain, and which turns round and round where it is, facing Orion, and alone never dipping into the stream of Oceanus- for Calypso had told him to keep this to his left. Days seven and ten did he sail over the sea, and on the eighteenth the dim outlines of the mountains on the nearest part of the Phaeacian coast appeared, rising like a shield on the horizon.

But King Neptune, who was returning from the Ethiopians, caught sight of Ulysses a long way off, from the mountains of the Solymi. He could see him sailing upon the sea, and it made him very angry, so he wagged his head and muttered to himself, saying, heavens, so the gods have been changing their minds about Ulysses while I was away in Ethiopia, and now he is close to the land of the Phaeacians, where it is decreed that he shall escape from the calamities that have befallen him. Still, he shall have plenty of hardship yet before he has done with it."

Thereon he gathered his clouds together, grasped his trident, stirred it round in the sea, and roused the rage of every wind that blows till earth, sea, and sky were hidden in cloud, and night sprang forth out of the heavens. Winds from East, South, North, and West fell upon him all at the same time, and a tremendous sea got up, so that Ulysses' heart began to fail him. "Alas," he said to himself in his dismay, "what ever will become of me? I am afraid Calypso was right when she said I should have trouble by sea before I got back home. It is all coming true. How black is Jove making heaven with his clouds, and what a sea the winds are raising from every quarter at once. I am now safe to perish. Blest and thrice blest were those Danaans who fell before Troy in the cause of the sons of Atreus. Would that had been killed on the day when the Trojans were pressing me so sorely about the dead body of Achilles, for then I should have had due burial and the Achaeans would have honoured my name; but now it seems that I shall come to a most pitiable end."

As he spoke a sea broke over him with such terrific fury that the raft reeled again, and he was carried overboard a long way off. He let go the helm, and the force of the hurricane was so great that it broke the mast half way up, and both sail and yard went over into the sea. For a long time Ulysses was under water, and it was all he could do to rise to the surface again, for the clothes Calypso had given him weighed him down; but at last he got his head above water and spat out the bitter brine that was running down his face in streams. In spite of all this, however, he did not lose sight of his raft, but swam as fast as he could towards it, got hold of it, and climbed on board again so as to escape drowning. The sea took the raft and tossed it about as Autumn winds whirl thistledown round and round upon a road. It was as though the South, North, East, and West winds were all playing battledore and shuttlecock with it at once.

When he was in this plight, Ino daughter of Cadmus, also called Leucothea, saw him. She had formerly been a mere mortal, but had been since raised to the rank of a marine goddess. Seeing in what great distress Ulysses now was, she had compassion upon him, and, rising like a sea-gull from the waves, took her seat upon the raft.

"My poor good man," said she, "why is Neptune so furiously angry with you?

He is giving you a great deal of trouble, but for all his bluster he will not kill you. You seem to be a sensible person, do then as I bid you; strip, leave your raft to drive before the wind, and swim to the Phaecian coast where better luck awaits you. And here, take my veil and put it round your chest; it is enchanted, and you can come to no harm so long as you wear it. As soon as you touch land take it off, throw it back as far as you can into the sea, and then go away again." With these words she took off her veil and gave it him. Then she dived down again like a sea-gull and vanished beneath the dark blue waters.

But Ulysses did not know what to think. "Alas," he said to himself in his dismay, "this is only some one or other of the gods who is luring me to ruin by advising me to will quit my raft. At any rate I will not do so at present, for the land where she said I should be quit of all troubles seemed to be still a good way off. I know what I will do- I am sure it will be best- no matter what happens I will stick to the raft as long as her timbers hold together, but when the sea breaks her up I will swim for it; I do not see how I can do any better than this."

While he was thus in two minds, Neptune sent a terrible great wave that seemed to rear itself above his head till it broke right over the raft, which then went to pieces as though it were a heap of dry chaff tossed about by a whirlwind. Ulysses got astride of one plank and rode upon it as if he were on horseback; he then took off the clothes Calypso had given him, bound Ino's veil under his arms, and plunged into the sea- meaning to swim on shore. King Neptune watched him as he did so, and wagged his head, muttering to himself and saying, "'There now, swim up and down as you best can till you fall in with well-to-do people. I do not think you will be able to say that I have let you off too lightly." On this he lashed his horses and drove to Aegae where his palace is.

But Minerva resolved to help Ulysses, so she bound the ways of all the winds except one, and made them lie quite still; but she roused a good stiff breeze from the North that should lay the waters till Ulysses reached the land of the Phaeacians where he would be safe.

Thereon he floated about for two nights and two days in the water, with a heavy swell on the sea and death staring him in the face; but when the third day broke, the wind fell and there was a dead calm without so much as a breath of air stirring. As he rose on the swell he looked eagerly ahead, and could see land quite near. Then, as children rejoice when their dear father begins to get better after having for a long time borne sore affliction sent him by some angry spirit, but the gods deliver him from evil, so was Ulysses thankful when he again saw land and trees, and swam on with all his strength that he might once more set foot upon dry ground. When, however, he got within earshot, he began to hear the surf thundering up against the rocks, for the swell still broke against them with a terrific roar. Everything was enveloped in spray; there were no harbours where a ship might ride, nor shelter of any kind, but only headlands, low-lying rocks, and mountain tops.

Ulysses' heart now began to fail him, and he said despairingly to himself, "Alas, Jove has let me see land after swimming so far that I had given up all hope, but I can find no landing place, for the coast is rocky and surf-beaten, the rocks are smooth and rise sheer from the sea, with deep water close under them so that I cannot climb out for want of foothold. I am afraid some great wave will lift me off my legs and dash me against the rocks as I leave the water- which would give me a sorry landing. If, on the other hand, I swim further in search of some shelving beach or harbour, a hurricane may carry me out to sea again sorely against my will, or heaven may send some great monster of the deep to attack me; for Amphitrite breeds many such, and I know that Neptune is very angry with me."

While he was thus in two minds a wave caught him and took him with such force against the rocks that he would have been smashed and torn to pieces if Minerva had not shown him what to do. He caught hold of the rock with both hands and clung to it groaning with pain till the wave retired, so he was saved that time; but presently the wave came on again and carried him back with it far into the sea-tearing his hands as the suckers of a polypus are torn when some one plucks it from its bed, and the stones come up along with it even so did the rocks tear the skin from his strong hands, and then the wave drew him deep down under the water.

Here poor Ulysses would have certainly perished even in spite of his own destiny, if Minerva had not helped him to keep his wits about him. He swam seaward again, beyond reach of the surf that was beating against the land, and at the same time he kept looking towards the shore to see if he could find some haven, or a spit that should take the waves aslant. By and by, as he swam on, he came to the mouth of a river, and here he thought would be the best place, for there were no rocks, and it afforded shelter from the wind. He felt that there was a current, so he prayed inwardly and said:

"Hear me, O King, whoever you may be, and save me from the anger of the sea-god Neptune, for I approach you prayerfully. Any one who has lost his way has at all times a claim even upon the gods, wherefore in my distress I draw near to your stream, and cling to the knees of your riverhood. Have mercy upon me, O king, for I declare myself your suppliant."

Then the god stayed his stream and stilled the waves, making all calm before him, and bringing him safely into the mouth of the river. Here at last Ulysses' knees and strong hands failed him, for the sea had completely broken him. His body was all swollen, and his mouth and nostrils ran down like a river with sea-water, so that he could neither breathe nor speak, and lay swooning from sheer exhaustion; presently, when he had got his breath and came to himself again, he took off the scarf that Ino had given him and threw it back into the salt stream of the river, whereon Ino received it into her hands from the wave that bore it towards her. Then he left the river, laid himself down among the rushes, and kissed the bounteous earth.

"Alas," he cried to himself in his dismay, "what ever will become of me, and how is it all to end? If I stay here upon the river bed through the long watches of the night, I am so exhausted that the bitter cold and damp may make an end of me- for towards sunrise there will be a keen wind blowing from off the river. If, on the other hand, I climb the hill side, find shelter in the woods, and sleep in some thicket, I may escape the cold and have a good night's rest, but some savage beast may take advantage of me and devour me."

In the end he deemed it best to take to the woods, and he found one upon some high ground not far from the water. There he crept beneath two shoots of olive that grew from a single stock- the one an ungrafted sucker, while the other had been grafted. No wind, however squally, could break through the cover they afforded, nor could the sun's rays pierce them, nor the rain get through them, so closely did they grow into one another. Ulysses crept under these and began to make himself a bed to lie on, for there was a great litter of dead leaves lying about- enough to make a covering for two or three men even in hard winter weather. He was glad enough to see this, so he laid himself down and heaped the leaves all round him. Then, as one who lives alone in the country, far from any neighbor, hides a brand as fire-seed in the ashes to save himself from having to get a light elsewhere, even so did Ulysses cover himself up with leaves; and Minerva shed a sweet sleep upon his eyes, closed his eyelids, and made him lose all memories of his sorrows.

Book X

Thence we went on to the Aeoli island where lives Aeolus son of Hippotas, dear to the immortal gods. It is an island that floats (as it were) upon the sea, iron bound with a wall that girds it. Now, Aeolus has six daughters and six lusty sons, so he made the sons marry the daughters, and they all live with their dear father and mother, feasting and enjoying every conceivable kind of luxury. All day long the atmosphere of the house is loaded with the savour of roasting meats till it groans again, yard and all; but by night they sleep on their well-made bedsteads, each with his own wife between the blankets. These were the people among whom we had now come.

"Aeolus entertained me for a whole month asking me questions all the time about Troy, the Argive fleet, and the return of the Achaeans. I told him exactly how everything had happened, and when I said I must go, and asked him to further me on my way, he made no sort of difficulty, but set about doing so at once. Moreover, he flayed me a prime ox-hide to hold the ways of the roaring winds, which he shut up in the hide as in a sack- for Jove had made him captain over the winds, and he could stir or still each one of them according to his own pleasure. He put the sack in the ship and bound the mouth so tightly with a silver thread that not even a breath of a side-wind could blow from any quarter. The West wind which was fair for us did he alone let blow as it chose; but it all came to nothing, for we were lost through our own folly.

"Nine days and nine nights did we sail, and on the tenth day our native land showed on the horizon. We got so close in that we could see the stubble fires burning, and I, being then dead beat, fell into a light sleep, for I had never let the rudder out of my own hands, that we might get home the faster. On this the men fell to talking among themselves, and said I was bringing back gold and silver in the sack that Aeolus had given me. 'Bless my heart,' would one turn to his neighbour, saying, 'how this man gets honoured and makes friends to whatever city or country he may go. See what fine prizes he is taking home from Troy, while we, who have travelled just as far as he has, come back with hands as empty as we set out with- and now Aeolus has given him ever so much more. Quick- let us see what it all is, and how much gold and silver there is in the sack he gave him.'

"Thus they talked and evil counsels prevailed. They loosed the sack, whereupon the wind flew howling forth and raised a storm that carried us weeping out to sea and away from our own country. Then I awoke, and knew not whether to throw myself into the sea or to live on and make the best of it; but I bore it, covered myself up, and lay down in the ship, while the men lamented bitterly as the fierce winds bore our fleet back to the Aeolian island.

"When we reached it we went ashore to take in water, and dined hard by the ships. Immediately after dinner I took a herald and one of my men and went straight to the house of Aeolus, where I found him feasting with his wife and family; so we sat down as suppliants on the threshold. They were astounded when they saw us and said, 'Ulysses, what brings you here? What god has been ill-treating you? We took great pains to further you on your way home to Ithaca, or wherever it was that you wanted to go to.'

"Thus did they speak, but I answered sorrowfully, 'My men have undone me; they, and cruel sleep, have ruined me. My friends, mend me this mischief, for you can if you will.'

"I spoke as movingly as I could, but they said nothing, till their father answered, 'Vilest of mankind, get you gone at once out of the island; him whom heaven hates will I in no wise help. Be off, for you come here as one abhorred of heaven. "And with these words he sent me sorrowing from his door.

"Thence we sailed sadly on till the men were worn out with long and fruitless rowing, for there was no longer any wind to help them. Six days, night and day did we toil, and on the seventh day we reached the rocky stronghold of Lamus- Telepylus, the city of the Laestrygonians, where the shepherd who is driving in his sheep and goats [to be milked] salutes him who is driving out his flock [to feed] and this last answers the salute. In that country a man who could do without sleep might earn double wages, one as a herdsman of cattle, and another as a shepherd, for they work much the same by night as they do by day.

"When we reached the harbour we found it land-locked under steep cliffs, with a narrow entrance between two headlands. My captains took all their ships inside, and made them fast close to one another, for there was never so much as a breath of wind inside, but it was always dead calm. I kept my own ship outside, and moored it to a rock at the very end of the point; then I climbed a high rock to reconnoitre, but could see no sign neither of man nor cattle, only some smoke rising from the ground. So I sent two of my company with an attendant to find out what sort of people the inhabitants were.

"The men when they got on shore followed a level road by which the people draw their firewood from the mountains into the town, till presently they met a young woman who had come outside to fetch water, and who was daughter to a Laestrygonian named Antiphates. She was going to the fountain Artacia from which the people bring in their water, and when my men had come close up to her, they asked her who the king of that country might be, and over what kind of people he ruled; so she directed them to her father's house, but when they got there they found his wife to be a giantess as huge as a mountain, and they were horrified at the sight of her.

"She at once called her husband Antiphates from the place of assembly, and forthwith he set about killing my men. He snatched up one of them, and began to make his dinner off him then and there, whereon the other two ran back to the ships as fast as ever they could. But Antiphates raised a hue and cry after them, and thousands of sturdy Laestrygonians sprang up from every quarter- ogres, not men. They threw vast rocks at us from the cliffs as though they had been mere stones, and I heard the horrid sound of the ships crunching up against one another, and the death cries of my men, as the Laestrygonians speared them like fishes and took them home to eat them. While they were thus killing my men within the harbour I drew my sword, cut the cable of my own ship, and told my men to row with alf their might if they too would not fare like the rest; so they laid out for their lives, and we were thankful enough when we got into open water out of reach of the rocks they hurled at us. As for the others there was not one of them left.

"Thence we sailed sadly on, glad to have escaped death, though we had lost our comrades, and came to the Aeaean island, where Circe lives a great and cunning goddess who is own sister to the magician Aeetes- for they are both children of the sun by Perse, who is daughter to Oceanus. We brought our ship into a safe harbour without a word, for some god guided us thither, and having landed we there for two days and two nights, worn out in body and mind. When the morning of the third day came I took my spear and my sword, and went away from the ship to reconnoitre, and see if I could discover signs of human handiwork, or hear the sound of voices. Climbing to the top of a high look-out I espied the smoke of Circe's house rising upwards amid a dense forest of trees, and when I saw this I doubted whether, having seen the smoke, I would not go on at once and find out more, but in the end I deemed it best to go back to the ship, give the men their dinners, and send some of them instead of going myself.

"When I had nearly got back to the ship some god took pity upon my solitude, and sent a fine antlered stag right into the middle of my path. He was coming down his pasture in the forest to drink of the river, for the heat of the sun drove him, and as he passed I struck him in the middle of the back; the bronze point of the spear went clean through him, and he lay groaning in the dust until the life went out of him. Then I set my foot upon him, drew my spear from the wound, and laid it down; I also gathered rough grass and rushes and twisted them into a fathom or so of good stout rope, with which I bound the four feet of the noble creature together; having so done I hung him round my neck and walked back to the ship leaning upon my spear, for the stag was much too big for me to be able to carry him on my shoulder, steadying him with one hand. As I threw him down in front of the ship, I called the men and spoke cheeringly man by man to each of them. 'Look here my friends,' said I, 'we are not going to die so much before our time after all, and at any rate we will not starve so long as we have got something to eat and drink on board.' On this they uncovered their heads upon the sea shore and admired the stag, for he was indeed a splendid fellow. Then, when they had feasted their eyes upon him sufficiently, they washed their hands and began to cook him for dinner.

"Thus through the livelong day to the going down of the sun we stayed there eating and drinking our fill, but when the sun went down and it came on dark, we camped upon the sea shore. When the child of morning, fingered Dawn, appeared, I called a council and said, 'My friends, we are in very great difficulties; listen therefore to me. We have no idea where the sun either sets or rises, so that we do not even know East from West. I see no way out of it; nevertheless, we must try and find one. We are certainly on an island, for I went as high as I could this morning, and saw the sea reaching all round it to the horizon; it lies low, but towards the middle I saw smoke rising from out of a thick forest of trees.'

"Their hearts sank as they heard me, for they remembered how they had been treated by the Laestrygonian Antiphates, and by the savage ogre Polyphemus. They wept bitterly in their dismay, but there was nothing to be got by crying, so I divided them into two companies and set a captain over each; I gave one company to Eurylochus, while I took command of the other myself. Then we cast lots in a helmet, and the lot fell upon Eurylochus; so he set out with his twenty-two men, and they wept, as also did we who were left behind.

"When they reached Circe's house they found it built of cut stones, on a site that could be seen from far, in the middle of the forest. There were wild mountain wolves and lions prowling all round it- poor bewitched creatures whom she had tamed by her enchantments and drugged into subjection. They did not attack my men, but wagged their great tails, fawned upon them, and rubbed their noses lovingly against them. As hounds crowd round their master when they see him coming from dinner- for they know he will bring them something- even so did these wolves and lions with their great claws fawn upon my men, but the men were terribly frightened at seeing such strange creatures. Presently they reached the gates of the goddess's house, and as they stood there they could hear Circe within, singing most beautifully as she worked at her loom, making a web so fine, so soft, and of such dazzling colours as no one but a goddess could weave. On this Polites, whom I valued and trusted more than any other of my men, said, 'There is some one inside working at a loom and singing most beautifully; the whole place resounds with it, let us call her and see whether she is woman or goddess.'

"They called her and she came down, unfastened the door, and bade them enter. They, thinking no evil, followed her, all except Eurylochus, who suspected mischief and stayed outside. When she had got them into her house, she set them upon benches and seats and mixed them a mess with cheese, honey, meal, and Pramnian but she drugged it with wicked poisons to make them forget their homes, and when they had drunk she turned them into pigs by a stroke of her wand, and shut them up in her pigsties. They were like pigs-head, hair, and all, and they grunted just as pigs do; but their senses were the same as before, and they remembered everything.

"Thus then were they shut up squealing, and Circe threw them some acorns and beech masts such as pigs eat, but Eurylochus hurried back to tell me about the sad fate of our comrades. He was so overcome with dismay that though he tried to speak he could find no words to do so; his eyes filled with tears and he could only sob and sigh, till at last we forced his story out of him, and he told us what had happened to the others.

"'We went,' said he, as you told us, through the forest, and in the middle of it there was a fine house built with cut stones in a place that could be seen from far. There we found a woman, or else she was a goddess, working at her loom and singing sweetly; so the men shouted to her and called her, whereon she at once came down, opened the door, and invited us in. The others did not suspect any mischief so they followed her into the house, but I stayed where I was, for I thought there might be some treachery. From that moment I saw them no more, for not one of them ever came out, though I sat a long time watching for them.'

"Then I took my sword of bronze and slung it over my shoulders; I also took my bow, and told Eurylochus to come back with me and show me the way. But he laid hold of me with both his hands and spoke piteously, saying, 'Sir, do not force me to go with you, but let me stay here, for I know you will not bring one of them back with you, nor even return alive yourself; let us rather see if we cannot escape at any rate with the few that are left us, for we may still save our lives.'

"'Stay where you are, then, 'answered I, 'eating and drinking at the ship, but I must go, for I am most urgently bound to do so.'

"With this I left the ship and went up inland. When I got through the charmed grove, and was near the great house of the enchantress Circe, I met Mercury with his golden wand, disguised as a young man in the hey-day of his youth and beauty with the down just coming upon his face. He came up to me and took my hand within his own, saying, 'My poor unhappy man, whither are you going over this mountain top, alone and without knowing the way? Your men are shut up in Circe's pigsties, like so many wild boars in their lairs. You surely do not fancy that you can set them free? I can tell you that you will never get back and will have to stay there with the rest of them.

But never mind, I will protect you and get you out of your difficulty. Take this herb, which is one of great virtue, and keep it about you when you go to Circe's house, it will be a talisman to you against every kind of mischief.

"'And I will tell you of all the wicked witchcraft that Circe will try to practise upon you. She will mix a mess for you to drink, and she will drug the meal with which she makes it, but she will not be able to charm you, for the virtue of the herb that I shall give you will prevent her spells from working. I will tell you all about it. When Circe strikes you with her wand, draw your sword and spring upon her as though you were goings to kill her. She will then be frightened and will desire you to go to bed with her; on this you must not point blank refuse her, for you want her to set your companions free, and to take good care also of yourself, but you make her swear solemnly by all the blessed that she will plot no further mischief against you, or else when she has got you naked she will unman you and make you fit for nothing.'

"As he spoke he pulled the herb out of the ground an showed me what it was like. The root was black, while the flower was as white as milk; the gods call it Moly, and mortal men cannot uproot it, but the gods can do whatever they like.

"Then Mercury went back to high Olympus passing over the wooded island; but I fared onward to the house of Circe, and my heart was clouded with care as I walked along. When I got to the gates I stood there and called the goddess, and as soon as she heard me she came down, opened the door, and asked me to come in; so I followed her- much troubled in my mind. She set me on a richly decorated seat inlaid with silver, there was a footstool also under my feet, and she mixed a mess in a golden goblet for me to drink; but she drugged it, for she meant me mischief. When she had given it me, and I had drunk it without its charming me, she struck she, struck me with her wand. 'There now,' she cried, 'be off to the pigsty, and make your lair with the rest of them.'

"But I rushed at her with my sword drawn as though I would kill her, whereon she fell with a loud scream, clasped my knees, and spoke piteously, saying, 'Who and whence are you? from what place and people have you come? How can it be that my drugs have no power to charm you? Never yet was any man able to stand so much as a taste of the herb I gave you; you must be spell-proof; surely you can be none other than the bold hero Ulysses, who Mercury always said would come here some day with his ship while on his way home form Troy; so be it then; sheathe your sword and let us go to bed, that we may make friends and learn to trust each other.'

"And I answered, 'Circe, how can you expect me to be friendly with you when you have just been turning all my men into pigs? And now that you have got me here myself, you mean me mischief when you ask me to go to bed with you, and will unman me and make me fit for nothing. I shall certainly not consent to go to bed with you unless you will first take your solemn oath to plot no further harm against me.'

"So she swore at once as I had told her, and when she had completed her oath then I went to bed with her.

"Meanwhile her four servants, who are her housemaids, set about their work. They are the children of the groves and fountains, and of the holy waters that run down into the sea. One of them spread a fair purple cloth over a seat, and laid a carpet underneath it. Another brought tables of silver up to the seats, and set them with baskets of gold. A third mixed some sweet wine with water in a silver bowl and put golden cups upon the tables, while the fourth she brought in water and set it to boil in a large cauldron over a good fire which she had lighted. When the water in the cauldron was boiling, she poured cold into it till it was just as I liked it, and then she set me in a bath and began washing me from the cauldron about the head and shoulders, to take the tire and stiffness out of my limbs. As soon as she had done washing me and anointing me with oil, she arrayed me in a good cloak and shirt and led me to a richly decorated seat inlaid with silver; there was a footstool also under my feet. A maid servant then brought me water in a beautiful golden ewer and poured it into a silver basin for me to wash my hands, and she drew a clean table beside me; an upper servant brought me bread and offered me many things of what there was in the house, and then Circe bade me eat, but I would not, and sat without heeding what was before me, still moody and suspicious.

"When Circe saw me sitting there without eating, and in great grief, she came to me and said, 'Ulysses, why do you sit like that as though you were dumb, gnawing at your own heart, and refusing both meat and drink? Is it that you are still suspicious? You ought not to be, for I have already sworn solemnly that I will not hurt you.'

"And I said, 'Circe, no man with any sense of what is right can think of either eating or drinking in your house until you have set his friends free and let him see them. If you want me to eat and drink, you must free my men and bring them to me that I may see them with my own eyes.'

"When I had said this she went straight through the court with her wand in her hand and opened the pigsty doors. My men came out like so many prime hogs and stood looking at her, but she went about among them and anointed each with a second drug, whereon the bristles that the bad drug had given them fell off, and they became men again, younger than they were before, and much taller and better looking. They knew me at once, seized me each of them by the hand, and wept for joy till the whole house was filled with the sound of their hullabalooing, and Circe herself was so sorry for them that she came up to me and said, 'Ulysses, noble son of Laertes, go back at once to the sea where you have left your ship, and first draw it on to the land. Then, hide all your ship's gear and property in some cave, and come back here with your men.'

"I agreed to this, so I went back to the sea shore, and found the men at the ship weeping and wailing most piteously. When they saw me the silly blubbering fellows began frisking round me as calves break out and gambol round their mothers, when they see them coming home to be milked after they have been feeding all day, and the homestead resounds with their lowing. They seemed as glad to see me as though they had got back to their own rugged Ithaca, where they had been born and bred. 'Sir,' said the affectionate creatures, 'we are as glad to see you back as though we had got safe home to Ithaca; but tell us all about the fate of our comrades.'

"I spoke comfortingly to them and said, 'We must draw our ship on to the land, and hide the ship's gear with all our property in some cave; then come with me all of you as fast as you can to Circe's house, where you will find your comrades eating and drinking in the midst of great abundance.'

"On this the men would have come with me at once, but Eurylochus tried to hold them back and said, 'Alas, poor wretches that we are, what will become of us? Rush not on your ruin by going to the house of Circe, who will turn us all into pigs or wolves or lions, and we shall have to keep guard over her house. Remember how the Cyclops treated us when our comrades went inside his cave, and Ulysses with them. It was all through his sheer folly that those men lost their lives.'

"When I heard him I was in two minds whether or no to draw the keen blade that hung by my sturdy thigh and cut his head off in spite of his being a near relation of my own; but the men interceded for him and said, 'Sir, if it may so be, let this fellow stay here and mind the ship, but take the rest of us with you to Circe's house.'

"On this we all went inland, and Eurylochus was not left behind after all, but came on too, for he was frightened by the severe reprimand that I had given him.

"Meanwhile Circe had been seeing that the men who had been left behind were washed and anointed with olive oil; she had also given them woollen cloaks and shirts, and when we came we found them all comfortably at dinner in her house. As soon as the men saw each other face to face and knew one another, they wept for joy and cried aloud till the whole palace rang again. Thereon Circe came up to me and said, 'Ulysses, noble son of Laertes, tell your men to leave off crying; I know how much you have all of you suffered at sea, and how ill you have fared among cruel savages on the mainland, but that is over now, so stay here, and eat and drink till you are once more as strong and hearty as you were when you left Ithaca; for at present you are weakened both in body and mind; you keep all the time thinking of the hardships- you have suffered during your travels, so that you have no more cheerfulness left in you.'

"Thus did she speak and we assented. We stayed with Circe for a whole twelvemonth feasting upon an untold quantity both of meat and wine. But when the year had passed in the waning of moons and the long days had come round, my men called me apart and said, 'Sir, it is time you began to think about going home, if so be you are to be spared to see your house and native country at all.'

"Thus did they speak and I assented. Thereon through the livelong day to the going down of the sun we feasted our fill on meat and wine, but when the sun went down and it came on dark the men laid themselves down to sleep in the covered cloisters. I, however, after I had got into bed with Circe, besought her by her knees, and the goddess listened to what I had got to say. 'Circe,' said I, 'please to keep the promise you made me about furthering me on my homeward voyage. I want to get back and so do my men, they are always pestering me with their complaints as soon as ever your back is turned.'

"And the goddess answered, 'Ulysses, noble son of Laertes, you shall none of you stay here any longer if you do not want to, but there is another journey which you have got to take before you can sail homewards. You must go to the house of Hades and of dread Proserpine to consult the ghost of the blind Theban prophet Teiresias whose reason is still unshaken. To him alone has Proserpine left his understanding even in death, but the other ghosts flit about aimlessly.'

"I was dismayed when I heard this. I sat up in bed and wept, and would gladly have lived no longer to see the light of the sun, but presently when I was tired of weeping and tossing myself about, I said, 'And who shall guide me upon this voyage- for the house of Hades is a port that no ship can reach.'

"'You will want no guide,' she answered; 'raise you mast, set your white sails, sit quite still, and the North Wind will blow you there of itself. When your ship has traversed the waters of Oceanus, you will reach the fertile shore of Proserpine's country with its groves of tall poplars and willows that shed their fruit untimely; here beach your ship upon the shore of Oceanus, and go straight on to the dark abode of Hades. You will find it near the place where the rivers Pyriphlegethon and Cocytus (which is a branch of the river Styx) flow into Acheron, and you will see a rock near it, just where the two roaring rivers run into one another.

"'When you have reached this spot, as I now tell you, dig a trench a cubit or so in length, breadth, and depth, and pour into it as a drink-offering to all the dead, first, honey mixed with milk, then wine, and in the third place water-sprinkling white barley meal over the whole. Moreover you must offer many prayers to the poor feeble ghosts, and promise them that when you get back to Ithaca you will sacrifice a barren heifer to them, the best you have, and will load the pyre with good things. More particularly you must promise that Teiresias shall have a black sheep all to himself, the finest in all your flocks.

"'When you shall have thus besought the ghosts with your prayers, offer them a ram and a black ewe, bending their heads towards Erebus; but yourself turn away from them as though you would make towards the river. On this, many dead men's ghosts will come to you, and you must tell your men to skin the two sheep that you have just killed, and offer them as a burnt sacrifice with prayers to Hades and to Proserpine. Then draw your sword and sit there, so as to prevent any other poor ghost from coming near the split blood before Teiresias shall have answered your questions. The seer will presently come to you, and will tell you about your voyage- what stages you are to make, and how you are to sail the see so as to reach your home.'

"It was day-break by the time she had done speaking, so she dressed me in my shirt and cloak. As for herself she threw a beautiful light gossamer fabric over her shoulders, fastening it with a golden girdle round her waist, and she covered her head with a mantle. Then I went about among the men everywhere all over the house, and spoke kindly to each of them man by man: 'You must not lie sleeping here any longer,' said I to them, 'we must be going, for Circe has told me all about it.' And this they did as I bade them.

"Even so, however, I did not get them away without misadventure. We had with us a certain youth named Elpenor, not very remarkable for sense or courage, who had got drunk and was lying on the house-top away from the rest of the men, to sleep off his liquor in the cool. When he heard the noise of the men bustling about, he jumped up on a sudden and forgot all about coming down by the main staircase, so he tumbled right off the roof and broke his neck, and his soul went down to the house of Hades.

"When I had got the men together I said to them, 'You think you are about to start home again, but Circe has explained to me that instead of this, we have got to go to the house of Hades and Proserpine to consult the ghost of the Theban prophet Teiresias.'

"The men were broken-hearted as they heard me, and threw themselves on the ground groaning and tearing their hair, but they did not mend matters by crying. When we reached the sea shore, weeping and lamenting our fate, Circe brought the ram and the ewe, and we made them fast hard by the ship. She passed through the midst of us without our knowing it, for who can see the comings and goings of a god, if the god does not wish to be seen?

Book XI

Then, when we had got down to the sea shore we drew our ship into the water and got her mast and sails into her; we also put the sheep on board and took our places, weeping and in great distress of mind. Circe, that great and cunning goddess, sent us a fair wind that blew dead aft and stayed steadily with us keeping our sails all the time well filled; so we did whatever wanted doing to the ship's gear and let her go as the wind and helmsman headed her. All day long her sails were full as she held her course over the sea, but when the sun went down and darkness was over all the earth, we got into the deep waters of the river Oceanus, where lie the land and city of the Cimmerians who live enshrouded in mist and darkness which the rays of the sun never pierce neither at his rising nor as he goes down again out of the heavens, but the poor wretches live in one long melancholy night. When we got there we beached the ship, took the sheep out of her, and went along by the waters of Oceanus till we came to the place of which Circe had told us.

"Here Perimedes and Eurylochus held the victims, while I drew my sword and dug the trench a cubit each way. I made a drink-offering to all the dead, first with honey and milk, then with wine, and thirdly with water, and I sprinkled white barley meal over the whole, praying earnestly to the poor feckless ghosts, and promising them that when I got back to Ithaca I would sacrifice a barren heifer for them, the best I had, and would load the pyre with good things. I also particularly promised that Teiresias should have a black sheep to himself, the best in all my flocks. When I had prayed sufficiently to the dead, I cut the throats of the two sheep and let the blood run into the trench, whereon the ghosts came trooping up from Erebus- brides, young bachelors, old men worn out with toil, maids who had been crossed in love, and brave men who had been killed in battle, with their armour still smirched with blood; they came from every quarter and flitted round the trench with a strange kind of screaming sound that made me turn pale with fear. When I saw them coming I told the men to be quick and flay the carcasses of the two dead sheep and make burnt offerings of them, and at the same time to repeat prayers to Hades and to Proserpine; but I sat where I was with my sword drawn and would not let the poor feckless ghosts come near the blood till Teiresias should have answered my questions.

"The first ghost 'that came was that of my comrade Elpenor, for he had not yet been laid beneath the earth. We had left his body unwaked and unburied in Circe's house, for we had had too much else to do. I was very sorry for him, and cried when I saw him: 'Elpenor,' said I, 'how did you come down here into this gloom and darkness? You have here on foot quicker than I have with my ship.'

"'Sir,' he answered with a groan, 'it was all bad luck, and my own unspeakable drunkenness. I was lying asleep on the top of Circe's house, and never thought of coming down again by the great staircase but fell right off the roof and broke my neck, so my soul down to the house of Hades. And now I beseech you by all those whom you have left behind you, though they are not here, by your wife, by the father who brought you up when you were a child, and by Telemachus who is the one hope of your house, do what I shall now ask you. I know that when you leave this limbo you will again hold your ship for the Aeaean island. Do not go thence leaving me unwaked and unburied behind you, or I may bring heaven's anger upon you; but burn me with whatever armour I have, build a barrow for me on the sea shore, that may tell people in days to come what a poor unlucky fellow I was, and plant over my grave the oar I used to row with when I was yet alive and with my messmates.' And I said, 'My poor fellow, I will do all that you have asked of me.'

"Thus, then, did we sit and hold sad talk with one another, I on the one side of the trench with my sword held over the blood, and the ghost of my comrade saying all this to me from the other side. Then came the ghost of my dead mother Anticlea, daughter to Autolycus. I had left her alive when I set out for Troy and was moved to tears when I saw her, but even so, for all my sorrow I would not let her come near the blood till I had asked my questions of Teiresias.

"Then came also the ghost of Theban Teiresias, with his golden sceptre in his hand. He knew me and said, 'Ulysses, noble son of Laertes, why, poor man, have you left the light of day and come down to visit the dead in this sad place? Stand back from the trench and withdraw your sword that I may drink of the blood and answer your questions truly.'

"So I drew back, and sheathed my sword, whereon when he had drank of the blood he began with his prophecy.

"You want to know,' said he, 'about your return home, but heaven will make this hard for you. I do not think that you will escape the eye of Neptune, who still nurses his bitter grudge against you for having blinded his son. Still, after much suffering you may get home if you can restrain yourself and your companions when your ship reaches the Thrinacian island, where you will find the sheep and cattle belonging to the sun, who sees and gives ear to everything. If you leave these flocks unharmed and think of nothing but of getting home, you may yet after much hardship reach Ithaca; but if you harm them, then I forewarn you of the destruction both of your ship and of your men. Even though you may yourself escape, you will return in bad plight after losing all your men, [in another man's ship, and you will find trouble in your house, which will be overrun by high-handed people, who are devouring your substance under the pretext of paying court and making presents to your wife.

"'When you get home you will take your revenge on these suitors; and after you have killed them by force or fraud in your own house, you must take a well-made oar and carry it on and on, till you come to a country where the people have never heard of the sea and do not even mix salt with their food, nor do they know anything about ships, and oars that are as the wings of a ship. I will give you this certain token which cannot escape your notice. A wayfarer will meet you and will say it must be a winnowing shovel that you have got upon your shoulder; on this you must fix the oar in the ground and sacrifice a ram, a bull, and a boar to Neptune. Then go home and offer hecatombs to an the gods in heaven one after the other. As for yourself, death shall come to you from the sea, and your life shall ebb away very gently when you are full of years and peace of mind, and your people shall bless you. All that I have said will come true].'

"'This,' I answered, 'must be as it may please heaven, but tell me and tell me and tell me true, I see my poor mother's ghost close by us; she is sitting by the blood without saying a word, and though I am her own son she does not remember me and speak to me; tell me, Sir, how I can make her know me.'

"'That,' said he, 'I can soon do Any ghost that you let taste of the blood will talk with you like a reasonable being, but if you do not let them have any blood they will go away again.'

"On this the ghost of Teiresias went back to the house of Hades, for his prophecyings had now been spoken, but I sat still where I was until my mother came up and tasted the blood. Then she knew me at once and spoke fondly to me, saying, 'My son, how did you come down to this abode of darkness while you are still alive? It is a hard thing for the living to see these places, for between us and them there are great and terrible waters, and there is Oceanus, which no man can cross on foot, but he must have a good ship to take him. Are you all this time trying to find your way home from Troy, and have you never yet got back to Ithaca nor seen your wife in your own house?'

"'Mother,' said I, 'I was forced to come here to consult the ghost of the Theban prophet Teiresias. I have never yet been near the Achaean land nor set foot on my native country, and I have had nothing but one long series of misfortunes from the very first day that I set out with Agamemnon for Ilius, the land of noble steeds, to fight the Trojans. But tell me, and tell me true, in what way did you die? Did you have a long illness, or did heaven vouchsafe you a gentle easy passage to eternity? Tell me also about my father, and the son whom I left behind me; is my property still in their hands, or has some one else got hold of it, who thinks that I shall not return to claim it? Tell me again what my wife intends doing, and in what mind she is; does she live with my son and guard my estate securely, or has she made the best match she could and married again?'

"My mother answered, 'Your wife still remains in your house, but she is in great distress of mind and spends her whole time in tears both night and day. No one as yet has got possession of your fine property, and Telemachus still holds your lands undisturbed. He has to entertain largely, as of course he must, considering his position as a magistrate, and how every one invites him; your father remains at his old place in the country and never goes near the town. He has no comfortable bed nor bedding; in the winter he sleeps on the floor in front of the fire with the men and goes about all in rags, but in summer, when the warm weather comes on again, he lies out in the vineyard on a bed of vine leaves thrown anyhow upon the ground. He grieves continually about your never having come home, and suffers more and more as he grows older. As for my own end it was in this wise: heaven did not take me swiftly and painlessly in my own house, nor was I attacked by any illness such as those that generally wear people out and kill them, but my longing to know what you were doing and the force of my affection for you- this it was that was the death of me.'

"Then I tried to find some way of embracing my mother's ghost. Thrice I sprang towards her and tried to clasp her in my arms, but each time she flitted from my embrace as it were a dream or phantom, and being touched to the quick I said to her, 'Mother, why do you not stay still when I would embrace you? If we could throw our arms around one another we might find sad comfort in the sharing of our sorrows even in the house of Hades; does Proserpine want to lay a still further load of grief upon me by mocking me with a phantom only?'

"'My son,' she answered, 'most ill-fated of all mankind, it is not Proserpine that is beguiling you, but all people are like this when they are dead. The sinews no longer hold the flesh and bones together; these perish in the fierceness of consuming fire as soon as life has left the body, and the soul flits away as though it were a dream. Now, however, go back to the light of day as soon as you can, and note all these things that you may tell them to your wife hereafter.'

"Thus did we converse, and anon Proserpine sent up the ghosts of the wives and daughters of all the most famous men. They gathered in crowds about the blood, and I considered how I might question them severally. In the end I deemed that it would be best to draw the keen blade that hung by my sturdy thigh, and keep them from all drinking the blood at once. So they came up one after the other, and each one as I questioned her told me her race and lineage.

"The first I saw was Tyro. She was daughter of Salmoneus and wife of Cretheus the son of Aeolus. She fell in love with the river Enipeus who is much the most beautiful river in the whole world. Once when she was taking a walk by his side as usual, Neptune, disguised as her lover, lay with her at the mouth of the river, and a huge blue wave arched itself like a mountain over them to hide both woman and god, whereon he loosed her virgin girdle and laid her in a deep slumber. When the god had accomplished the deed of love, he took her hand in his own and said, 'Tyro, rejoice in all good will; the embraces of the gods are not fruitless, and you will have fine twins about this time twelve months. Take great care of them. I am Neptune, so now go home, but hold your tongue and do not tell any one.'

"Then he dived under the sea, and she in due course bore Pelias and Neleus, who both of them served Jove with all their might. Pelias was a great breeder of sheep and lived in Iolcus, but the other lived in Pylos. The rest of her children were by Cretheus, namely, Aeson, Pheres, and Amythaon, who was a mighty warrior and charioteer.

"Next to her I saw Antiope, daughter to Asopus, who could boast of having slept in the arms of even Jove himself, and who bore him two sons Amphion and Zethus. These founded Thebes with its seven gates, and built a wall all round it; for strong though they were they could not hold Thebes till they had walled it.

"Then I saw Alcmena, the wife of Amphitryon, who also bore to Jove indomitable Hercules; and Megara who was daughter to great King Creon, and married the redoubtable son of Amphitryon.

"I also saw fair Epicaste mother of king OEdipodes whose awful lot it was to marry her own son without suspecting it. He married her after having killed his father, but the gods proclaimed the whole story to the world; whereon he remained king of Thebes, in great grief for the spite the gods had borne him; but Epicaste went to the house of the mighty jailor Hades, having hanged herself for grief, and the avenging spirits haunted him as for an outraged mother- to his ruing bitterly thereafter.

"Then I saw Chloris, whom Neleus married for her beauty, having given priceless presents for her. She was youngest daughter to Amphion son of Iasus and king of Minyan Orchomenus, and was Queen in Pylos. She bore Nestor, Chromius, and Periclymenus, and she also bore that marvellously lovely woman Pero, who was wooed by all the country round; but Neleus would only give her to him who should raid the cattle of Iphicles from the grazing grounds of Phylace, and this was a hard task. The only man who would undertake to raid them was a certain excellent seer, but the will of heaven was against him, for the rangers of the cattle caught him and put him in prison; nevertheless when a full year had passed and the same season came round again, Iphicles set him at liberty, after he had expounded all the oracles of heaven. Thus, then, was the will of Jove accomplished.

"And I saw Leda the wife of Tyndarus, who bore him two famous sons, Castor breaker of horses, and Pollux the mighty boxer. Both these heroes are lying under the earth, though they are still alive, for by a special dispensation of Jove, they die and come to life again, each one of them every other day throughout all time, and they have the rank of gods.

"After her I saw Iphimedeia wife of Aloeus who boasted the embrace of

Neptune. She bore two sons Otus and Ephialtes, but both were short lived. They were the finest children that were ever born in this world, and the best looking, Orion only excepted; for at nine years old they were nine fathoms high, and measured nine cubits round the chest. They threatened to make war with the gods in Olympus, and tried to set Mount Ossa on the top of Mount Olympus, and Mount Pelion on the top of Ossa, that they might scale heaven itself, and they would have done it too if they had been grown up, but Apollo, son of Leto, killed both of them, before they had got so much as a sign of hair upon their cheeks or chin.

"Then I saw Phaedra, and Procris, and fair Ariadne daughter of the magician Minos, whom Theseus was carrying off from Crete to Athens, but he did not enjoy her, for before he could do so Diana killed her in the island of Dia on account of what Bacchus had said against her.

"I also saw Maera and Clymene and hateful Eriphyle, who sold her own husband for gold. But it would take me all night if I were to name every single one of the wives and daughters of heroes whom I saw, and it is time for me to go to bed, either on board ship with my crew, or here. As for my escort, heaven and yourselves will see to it."

Here he ended, and the guests sat all of them enthralled and speechless throughout the covered cloister. Then Arete said to them:

"What do you think of this man, O Phaecians? Is he not tall and good looking, and is he not Clever? True, he is my own guest, but all of you share in the distinction. Do not he a hurry to send him away, nor niggardly in the presents you make to one who is in such great need, for heaven has blessed all of you with great abundance."

Then spoke the aged hero Echeneus who was one of the oldest men among them, "My friends," said he, "what our august queen has just said to us is both reasonable and to the purpose, therefore be persuaded by it; but the decision whether in word or deed rests ultimately with King Alcinous."

"The thing shall be done," exclaimed Alcinous, "as surely as I still live and reign over the Phaeacians. Our guest is indeed very anxious to get home, still we must persuade him to remain with us until to-morrow, by which time I shall be able to get together the whole sum that I mean to give him. As regards- his escort it will be a matter for you all, and mine above all others as the chief person among you."

And Ulysses answered, "King Alcinous, if you were to bid me to stay here for a whole twelve months, and then speed me on my way, loaded with your noble gifts, I should obey you gladly and it would redound greatly to my advantage, for I should return fuller-handed to my own people, and should thus be more respected and beloved by all who see me when I get back to Ithaca."

"Ulysses," replied Alcinous, "not one of us who sees you has any idea that you are a charlatan or a swindler. I know there are many people going about who tell such plausible stories that it is very hard to see through them, but there is a style about your language which assures me of your good disposition. Moreover you have told the story of your own misfortunes, and those of the Argives, as though you were a practised bard; but tell me, and tell me true, whether you saw any of the mighty heroes who went to Troy at the same time with yourself, and perished there. The evenings are still at their longest, and it is not yet bed time- go on, therefore, with your divine story, for I could stay here listening till to-morrow morning, so long as you will continue to tell us of your adventures."

"Alcinous," answered Ulysses, "there is a time for making speeches, and a time for going to bed; nevertheless, since you so desire, I will not refrain from telling you the still sadder tale of those of my comrades who did not fall fighting with the Trojans, but perished on their return, through the treachery of a wicked woman.

"When Proserpine had dismissed the female ghosts in all directions, the ghost of Agamemnon son of Atreus came sadly up tome, surrounded by those who had perished with him in the house of Aegisthus. As soon as he had tasted the blood he knew me, and weeping bitterly stretched out his arms towards me to embrace me; but he had no strength nor substance any more, and I too wept and pitied him as I beheld him. 'How did you come by your death,' said I, 'King Agamemnon? Did Neptune raise his winds and waves against you when you were at sea, or did your enemies make an end of you on the mainland when you were cattle-lifting or sheep-stealing, or while they were fighting in defence of their wives and city?'

"'Ulysses,' he answered, 'noble son of Laertes, was not lost at sea in any storm of Neptune's raising, nor did my foes despatch me upon the mainland, but Aegisthus and my wicked wife were the death of me between them. He asked me to his house, feasted me, and then butchered me most miserably as though I were a fat beast in a slaughter house, while all around me my comrades were slain like sheep or pigs for the wedding breakfast, or picnic, or gorgeous banquet of some great nobleman. You must have seen numbers of men killed either in a general engagement, or in single combat, but you never saw anything so truly pitiable as the way in which we fell in that cloister, with the mixing-bowl and the loaded tables lying all about, and the ground reeking with our-blood. I heard Priam's daughter Cassandra scream as Clytemnestra killed her close beside me. I lay dying upon the earth with the sword in my body, and raised my hands to kill the slut of a murderess, but she slipped away from me; she would not even close my lips nor my eyes when I was dying, for there is nothing in this world so cruel and so shameless as a woman when she has fallen into such guilt as hers was. Fancy murdering her own husband! I thought I was going to be welcomed home by my children and my servants, but her abominable crime has brought disgrace on herself and all women who shall come after- even on the good ones.'

"And I said, 'In truth Jove has hated the house of Atreus from first to last in the matter of their women's counsels. See how many of us fell for Helen's sake, and now it seems that Clytemnestra hatched mischief against too during your absence.'

"'Be sure, therefore,' continued Agamemnon, 'and not be too friendly even with your own wife. Do not tell her all that you know perfectly well yourself. Tell her a part only, and keep your own counsel about the rest. Not that your wife, Ulysses, is likely to murder you, for Penelope is a very admirable woman, and has an excellent nature. We left her a young bride with an infant at her breast when we set out for Troy. This child no doubt is now grown up happily to man's estate, and he and his father will have a joyful meeting and embrace one another as it is right they should do, whereas my wicked wife did not even allow me the happiness of looking upon my son, but killed me ere I could do so. Furthermore I say- and lay my saying to your heart- do not tell people when you are bringing your ship to Ithaca, but steal a march upon them, for after all this there is no trusting women. But now tell me, and tell me true, can you give me any news of my son Orestes? Is he in Orchomenus, or at Pylos, or is he at

Sparta with Menelaus- for I presume that he is still living.'

"And I said, 'Agamemnon, why do you ask me? I do not know whether your son is alive or dead, and it is not right to talk when one does not know.'

"As we two sat weeping and talking thus sadly with one another the ghost of Achilles came up to us with Patroclus, Antilochus, and Ajax who was the finest and goodliest man of all the Danaans after the son of Peleus. The fleet descendant of Aeacus knew me and spoke piteously, saying, 'Ulysses, noble son of Laertes, what deed of daring will you undertake next, that you venture down to the house of Hades among us silly dead, who are but the ghosts of them that can labour no more?'

"And I said, 'Achilles, son of Peleus, foremost champion of the Achaeans, I came to consult Teiresias, and see if he could advise me about my return home to Ithaca, for I have never yet been able to get near the Achaean land, nor to set foot in my own country, but have been in trouble all the time. As for you, Achilles, no one was ever yet so fortunate as you have been, nor ever will be, for you were adored by all us Argives as long as you were alive, and now that you are here you are a great prince among the dead. Do not, therefore, take it so much to heart even if you are dead.'

"'Say not a word,' he answered, 'in death's favour; I would rather be a paid servant in a poor man's house and be above ground than king of kings among the dead. But give me news about son; is he gone to the wars and will he be a great soldier, or is this not so? Tell me also if you have heard anything about my father Peleus- does he still rule among the Myrmidons, or do they show him no respect throughout Hellas and Phthia now that he is old and his limbs fail him? Could I but stand by his side, in the light of day, with the same strength that I had when I killed the bravest of our foes upon the plain of Troy- could I but be as I then was and go even for a short time to my father's house, any one who tried to do him violence or supersede him would soon me it.'

"'I have heard nothing,' I answered, 'of Peleus, but I can tell you all about your son Neoptolemus, for I took him in my own ship from Scyros with the Achaeans. In our councils of war before Troy he was always first to speak, and his judgement was unerring. Nestor and I were the only two who could surpass him; and when it came to fighting on the plain of Troy, he would never remain with the body of his men, but would dash on far in front, foremost of them all in valour. Many a man did he kill in battle- I cannot name every single one of those whom he slew while fighting on the side of the Argives, but will only say how he killed that valiant hero Eurypylus son of Telephus, who was the handsomest man I ever saw except Memnon; many others also of the Ceteians fell around him by reason of a woman's bribes. Moreover, when all the bravest of the Argives went inside the horse that Epeus had made, and it was left to me to settle when we should either open the door of our ambuscade, or close it, though all the other leaders and chief men among the Danaans were drying their eyes and quaking in every limb, I never once saw him turn pale nor wipe a tear from his cheek; he was all the time urging me to break out from the horse- grasping the handle of his sword and his bronze-shod spear, and breathing fury against the foe. Yet when we had sacked the city of Priam he got his handsome share of the prize money and went on board (such is the fortune of war) without a wound upon him, neither from a thrown spear nor in close combat, for the rage of Mars is a matter of great chance.'

"When I had told him this, the ghost of Achilles strode off across a meadow full of asphodel, exulting over what I had said concerning the prowess of his son.

"The ghosts of other dead men stood near me and told me each his own melancholy tale; but that of Ajax son of Telamon alone held aloof- still angry with me for having won the cause in our dispute about the armour of Achilles. Thetis had offered it as a prize, but the Trojan prisoners and Minerva were the judges. Would that I had never gained the day in such a contest, for it cost the life of Ajax, who was foremost of all the Danaans after the son of Peleus, alike in stature and prowess.

"When I saw him I tried to pacify him and said, 'Ajax, will you not forget and forgive even in death, but must the judgement about that hateful armour still rankle with you? It cost us Argives dear enough to lose such a tower of strength as you were to us. We mourned you as much as we mourned Achilles son of Peleus himself, nor can the blame be laid on anything but on the spite which Jove bore against the Danaans, for it was this that made him counsel your destruction- come hither, therefore, bring your proud spirit into subjection, and hear what I can tell you.'

"He would not answer, but turned away to Erebus and to the other ghosts; nevertheless, I should have made him talk to me in spite of his being so angry, or I should have gone talking to him, only that there were still others among the dead whom I desired to see.

"Then I saw Minos son of Jove with his golden sceptre in his hand sitting in judgement on the dead, and the ghosts were gathered sitting and standing round him in the spacious house of Hades, to learn his sentences upon them.

"After him I saw huge Orion in a meadow full of asphodel driving the ghosts of the wild beasts that he had killed upon the mountains, and he had a great bronze club in his hand, unbreakable for ever and ever.

"And I saw Tityus son of Gaia stretched upon the plain and covering some nine acres of ground. Two vultures on either side of him were digging their beaks into his liver, and he kept on trying to beat them off with his hands, but could not; for he had violated Jove's mistress Leto as she was going through Panopeus on her way to Pytho.

"I saw also the dreadful fate of Tantalus, who stood in a lake that reached his chin; he was dying to quench his thirst, but could never reach the water, for whenever the poor creature stooped to drink, it dried up and vanished, so that there was nothing but dry ground- parched by the spite of heaven. There were tall trees, moreover, that shed their fruit over his head- pears, pomegranates, apples, sweet figs and juicy olives, but whenever the poor creature stretched out his hand to take some, the wind tossed the branches back again to the clouds.

"And I saw Sisyphus at his endless task raising his prodigious stone with both his hands. With hands and feet he' tried to roll it up to the top of the hill, but always, just before he could roll it over on to the other side, its weight would be too much for him, and the pitiless stone would come thundering down again on to the plain. Then he would begin trying to push it up hill again, and the sweat ran off him and the steam rose after him.

"After him I saw mighty Hercules, but it was his phantom only, for he is feasting ever with the immortal gods, and has lovely Hebe to wife, who is daughter of Jove and Juno. The ghosts were screaming round him like scared birds flying all whithers. He looked black as night with his bare bow in his hands and his arrow on the string, glaring around as though ever on the point of taking aim. About his breast there was a wondrous golden belt adorned in the most marvellous fashion with bears, wild boars, and lions with gleaming eyes; there was also war, battle, and death. The man who made that belt, do what he might, would never be able to make another like it. Hercules knew me at once when he saw me, and spoke piteously, saying, my poor Ulysses, noble son of Laertes, are you too leading the same sorry kind of life that I did when I was above ground? I was son of Jove, but I went through an infinity of suffering, for I became bondsman to one who was far beneath me- a low fellow who set me all manner of labours. He once sent me here to fetch the hell-hound- for he did not think he could find anything harder for me than this, but I got the hound out of Hades and brought him to him, for Mercury and Minerva helped me.'

"On this Hercules went down again into the house of Hades, but I stayed where I was in case some other of the mighty dead should come to me. And I should have seen still other of them that are gone before, whom I would fain have seen- Theseus and Pirithous glorious children of the gods, but so many thousands of ghosts came round me and uttered such appalling cries, that I was panic stricken lest Proserpine should send up from the house of Hades the head of that awful monster Gorgon. On this I hastened back to my ship and ordered my men to go on board at once and loose the hawsers; so they embarked and took their places, whereon the ship went down the stream of the river Oceanus. We had to row at first, but presently a fair wind sprang up.

Book XII

After we were clear of the river Oceanus, and had got out into the open sea, we went on till we reached the Aeaean island where there is dawn and sunrise as in other places. We then drew our ship on to the sands and got out of her on to the shore, where we went to sleep and waited till day should break.

"Then, when the child of morning, rosy-fingered Dawn, appeared, I sent some men to Circe's house to fetch the body of Elpenor. We cut firewood from a wood where the headland jutted out into the sea, and after we had wept over him and lamented him we performed his funeral rites. When his body and armour had been burned to ashes, we raised a cairn, set a stone over it, and at the top of the cairn we fixed the oar that he had been used to row with.

"While we were doing all this, Circe, who knew that we had got back from the house of Hades, dressed herself and came to us as fast as she could; and her maid servants came with her bringing us bread, meat, and wine. Then she stood in the midst of us and said, 'You have done a bold thing in going down alive to the house of Hades, and you will have died twice, to other people's once; now, then, stay here for the rest of the day, feast your fill, and go on with your voyage at daybreak tomorrow morning. In the meantime I will tell Ulysses about your course, and will explain everything to him so as to prevent your suffering from misadventure either by land or sea.'

"We agreed to do as she had said, and feasted through the livelong day to the going down of the sun, but when the sun had set and it came on dark, the men laid themselves down to sleep by the stern cables of the ship. Then Circe took me by the hand and bade me be seated away from the others, while she reclined by my side and asked me all about our adventures.

"'So far so good,' said she, when I had ended my story, 'and now pay attention to what I am about to tell you- heaven itself, indeed, will recall it to your recollection. First you will come to the Sirens who enchant all who come near them. If any one unwarily draws in too close and hears the singing of the Sirens, his wife and children will never welcome him home again, for they sit in a green field and warble him to death with the sweetness of their song. There is a great heap of dead men's bones lying all around, with the flesh still rotting off them. Therefore pass these Sirens by, and stop your men's ears with wax that none of them may hear; but if you like you can listen yourself, for you may get the men to bind you as you stand upright on a cross-piece half way up the mast, and they must lash the rope's ends to the mast itself, that you may have the pleasure of listening. If you beg and pray the men to unloose you, then they must bind you faster.

"'When your crew have taken you past these Sirens, I cannot give you coherent directions as to which of two courses you are to take; I will lay the two alternatives before you, and you must consider them for yourself. On the one hand there are some overhanging rocks against which the deep blue waves of Amphitrite beat with terrific fury; the blessed gods call these rocks the Wanderers. Here not even a bird may pass, no, not even the timid doves that bring ambrosia to Father Jove, but the sheer rock always carries off one of them, and Father Jove has to send another to make up their number; no ship that ever yet came to these rocks has got away again, but the waves and whirlwinds of fire are freighted with wreckage and with the bodies of dead men. The only vessel that ever sailed and got through, was the famous Argo on her way from the house of Aetes, and she too would have gone against these great rocks, only that Juno piloted her past them for the love she bore to Jason.

"'Of these two rocks the one reaches heaven and its peak is lost in a dark cloud. This never leaves it, so that the top is never clear not even in summer and early autumn. No man though he had twenty hands and twenty feet could get a foothold on it and climb it, for it runs sheer up, as smooth as though it had been polished. In the middle of it there is a large cavern, looking West and turned towards Erebus; you must take your ship this way, but the cave is so high up that not even the stoutest archer could send an arrow into it. Inside it Scylla sits and yelps with a voice that you might take to be that of a young hound, but in truth she is a dreadful monster and no one- not even a god- could face her without being terror-struck. She has twelve mis-shapen feet, and six necks of the most prodigious length; and at the end of each neck she has a frightful head with three rows of teeth in each, all set very close together, so that they would crunch any one to death in a moment, and she sits deep within her shady cell thrusting out her heads and peering all round the rock, fishing for dolphins or dogfish or any larger monster that she can catch, of the thousands with which Amphitrite teems. No ship ever yet got past her without losing some men, for she shoots out all her heads at once, and carries off a man in each mouth.

"'You will find the other rocks lie lower, but they are so close together that there is not more than a bowshot between them. [A large fig tree in full leaf grows upon it], and under it lies the sucking whirlpool of Charybdis. Three times in the day does she vomit forth her waters, and three times she sucks them down again; see that you be not there when she is sucking, for if you are, Neptune himself could not save you; you must hug the Scylla side and drive ship by as fast as you can, for you had better lose six men than your whole crew.'

"'Is there no way,' said I, 'of escaping Charybdis, and at the same time keeping Scylla off when she is trying to harm my men?'

"'You dare-devil,' replied the goddess, you are always wanting to fight somebody or something; you will not let yourself be beaten even by the immortals. For Scylla is not mortal; moreover she is savage, extreme, rude, cruel and invincible. There is no help for it; your best chance will be to get by her as fast as ever you can, for if you dawdle about her rock while you are putting on your armour, she may catch you with a second cast of her six heads, and snap up another half dozen of your men; so drive your ship past her at full speed, and roar out lustily to Crataiis who is Scylla's dam, bad luck to her; she will then stop her from making a second raid upon you.

"'You will now come to the Thrinacian island, and here you will see many herds of cattle and flocks of sheep belonging to the sun-god- seven herds of cattle and seven flocks of sheep, with fifty head in each flock. They do not breed, nor do they become fewer in number, and they are tended by the goddesses Phaethusa and Lampetie, who are children of the sun-god Hyperion by Neaera. Their mother when she had borne them and had done suckling them sent them to the Thrinacian island, which was a long way off, to live there and look after their father's flocks and herds. If you leave these flocks unharmed, and think of nothing but getting home, you may yet after much hardship reach Ithaca; but if you harm them, then I forewarn you of the destruction both of your ship and of your comrades; and even though you may yourself escape, you will return late, in bad plight, after losing all your men.'

"Here she ended, and dawn enthroned in gold began to show in heaven, whereon she returned inland. I then went on board and told my men to loose the ship from her moorings; so they at once got into her, took their places, and began to smite the grey sea with their oars. Presently the great and cunning goddess Circe befriended us with a fair wind that blew dead aft, and stayed steadily with us, keeping our sails well filled, so we did whatever wanted doing to the ship's gear, and let her go as wind and helmsman headed her.

"Then, being much troubled in mind, I said to my men, 'My friends, it is not right that one or two of us alone should know the prophecies that Circe has made me, I will therefore tell you about them, so that whether we live or die we may do so with our eyes open. First she said we were to keep clear of the Sirens, who sit and sing most beautifully in a field of flowers; but she said I might hear them myself so long as no one else did. Therefore, take me and bind me to the crosspiece half way up the mast; bind me as I stand upright, with a bond so fast that I cannot possibly break away, and lash the rope's ends to the mast itself. If I beg and pray you to set me free, then bind me more tightly still.'

"I had hardly finished telling everything to the men before we reached the island of the two Sirens, for the wind had been very favourable. Then all of a sudden it fell dead calm; there was not a breath of wind nor a ripple upon the water, so the men furled the sails and stowed them; then taking to their oars they whitened the water with the foam they raised in rowing. Meanwhile I look a large wheel of wax and cut it up small with my sword. Then I kneaded the wax in my strong hands till it became soft, which it soon did between the kneading and the rays of the sun-god son of Hyperion. Then I stopped the ears of all my men, and they bound me hands and feet to the mast as I stood upright on the crosspiece; but they went on rowing themselves. When we had got within earshot of the land, and the ship was going at a good rate, the Sirens saw that we were getting in shore and began with their singing.

"'Come here,' they sang, 'renowned Ulysses, honour to the Achaean name, and listen to our two voices. No one ever sailed past us without staying to hear the enchanting sweetness of our song- and he who listens will go on his way not only charmed, but wiser, for we know all the ills that the gods laid upon the Argives and Trojans before Troy, and can tell you everything that is going to happen over the whole world.'

"They sang these words most musically, and as I longed to hear them further I made by frowning to my men that they should set me free; but they quickened their stroke, and Eurylochus and Perimedes bound me with still stronger bonds till we had got out of hearing of the Sirens' voices. Then my men took the wax from their ears and unbound me.

"Immediately after we had got past the island I saw a great wave from which spray was rising, and I heard a loud roaring sound. The men were so frightened that they loosed hold of their oars, for the whole sea resounded with the rushing of the waters, but the ship stayed where it was, for the men had left off rowing. I went round, therefore, and exhorted them man by man not to lose heart.

"'My friends,' said I, 'this is not the first time that we have been in danger, and we are in nothing like so bad a case as when the Cyclops shut us up in his cave; nevertheless, my courage and wise counsel saved us then, and we shall live to look back on all this as well. Now, therefore, let us all do as I say, trust in Jove and row on with might and main. As for you, coxswain, these are your orders; attend to them, for the ship is in your hands; turn her head away from these steaming rapids and hug the rock, or she will give you the slip and be over yonder before you know where you are, and you will be the death of us.'

"So they did as I told them; but I said nothing about the awful monster Scylla, for I knew the men would not on rowing if I did, but would huddle together in the hold. In one thing only did I disobey Circe's strict instructions- I put on my armour. Then seizing two strong spears I took my stand on the ship Is bows, for it was there that I expected first to see the monster of the rock, who was to do my men so much harm; but I could not make her out anywhere, though I strained my eyes with looking the gloomy rock all over and over

"Then we entered the Straits in great fear of mind, for on the one hand was Scylla, and on the other dread Charybdis kept sucking up the salt water. As she vomited it up, it was like the water in a cauldron when it is boiling over upon a great fire, and the spray reached the top of the rocks on either side. When she began to suck again, we could see the water all inside whirling round and round, and it made a deafening sound as it broke against the rocks. We could see the bottom of the whirlpool all black with sand and mud, and the men were at their wit's ends for fear. While we were taken up with this, and were expecting each moment to be our last, Scylla pounced down suddenly upon us and snatched up my six best men. I was looking at once after both ship and men, and in a moment I saw their hands and feet ever so high above me, struggling in the air as Scylla was carrying them off, and I heard them call out my name in one last despairing cry. As a fisherman, seated, spear in hand, upon some jutting rock throws bait into the water to deceive the poor little fishes, and spears them with the ox's horn with which his spear is shod, throwing them gasping on to the land as he catches them one by one- even so did Scylla land these panting creatures on her rock and munch them up at the mouth of her den, while they screamed and stretched out their hands to me in their mortal agony. This was the most sickening sight that I saw throughout all my voyages.

"When we had passed the [Wandering] rocks, with Scylla and terrible Charybdis, we reached the noble island of the sun-god, where were the goodly cattle and sheep belonging to the sun Hyperion. While still at sea in my ship I could bear the cattle lowing as they came home to the yards, and the sheep bleating. Then I remembered what the blind Theban prophet Teiresias had told me, and how carefully Aeaean Circe had warned me to shun the island of the blessed sun-god. So being much troubled I said to the men, 'My men, I know you are hard pressed, but listen while I tell you the prophecy that Teiresias made me, and how carefully Aeaean Circe warned me to shun the island of the blessed sun-god, for it was here, she said, that our worst danger would lie. Head the ship, therefore, away from the island.'

"The men were in despair at this, and Eurylochus at once gave me an insolent answer. 'Ulysses,' said he, 'you are cruel; you are very strong yourself and never get worn out; you seem to be made of iron, and now, though your men are exhausted with toil and want of sleep, you will not let them land and cook themselves a good supper upon this island, but bid them put out to sea and go faring fruitlessly on through the watches of the flying night. It is by night that the winds blow hardest and do so much damage; how can we escape should one of those sudden squalls spring up from South West or West, which so often wreck a vessel when our lords the gods are unpropitious? Now, therefore, let us obey the of night and prepare our supper here hard by the ship; to-morrow morning we will go on board again and put out to sea.'

"Thus spoke Eurylochus, and the men approved his words. I saw that heaven meant us a mischief and said, 'You force me to yield, for you are many against one, but at any rate each one of you must take his solemn oath that if he meet with a herd of cattle or a large flock of sheep, he will not be so mad as to kill a single head of either, but will be satisfied with the food that Circe has given us.'

"They all swore as I bade them, and when they had completed their oath we made the ship fast in a harbour that was near a stream of fresh water, and the men went ashore and cooked their suppers. As soon as they had had enough to eat and drink, they began talking about their poor comrades whom Scylla had snatched up and eaten; this set them weeping and they went on crying till they fell off into a sound sleep.

"In the third watch of the night when the stars had shifted their places, Jove raised a great gale of wind that flew a hurricane so that land and sea were covered with thick clouds, and night sprang forth out of the heavens. When the child of morning, rosy-fingered Dawn, appeared, we brought the ship to land and drew her into a cave wherein the sea-nymphs hold their courts and dances, and I called the men together in council.

"'My friends,' said I, 'we have meat and drink in the ship, let us mind, therefore, and not touch the cattle, or we shall suffer for it; for these cattle and sheep belong to the mighty sun, who sees and gives ear to everything. And again they promised that they would obey.

"For a whole month the wind blew steadily from the South, and there was no other wind, but only South and East. As long as corn and wine held out the men did not touch the cattle when they were hungry; when, however, they had eaten all there was in the ship, they were forced to go further afield, with hook and line, catching birds, and taking whatever they could lay their hands on; for they were starving. One day, therefore, I went up inland that I might pray heaven to show me some means of getting away. When I had gone far enough to be clear of all my men, and had found a place that was well sheltered from the wind, I washed my hands and prayed to all the gods in Olympus till by and by they sent me off into a sweet sleep.

"Meanwhile Eurylochus had been giving evil counsel to the men, 'Listen to me,' said he, 'my poor comrades. All deaths are bad enough but there is none so bad as famine. Why should not we drive in the best of these cows and offer them in sacrifice to the immortal Rods? If we ever get back to Ithaca, we can build a fine temple to the sun-god and enrich it with every kind of ornament; if, however, he is determined to sink our ship out of revenge for these homed cattle, and the other gods are of the same mind, I for one would rather drink salt water once for all and have done with it, than be starved to death by inches in such a desert island as this is.'

"Thus spoke Eurylochus, and the men approved his words. Now the cattle, so fair and goodly, were feeding not far from the ship; the men, therefore drove in the best of them, and they all stood round them saying their prayers, and using young oak-shoots instead of barley-meal, for there was no barley left. When they had done praying they killed the cows and dressed their carcasses; they cut out the thigh bones, wrapped them round in two layers of fat, and set some pieces of raw meat on top of them. They had no wine with which to make drink-offerings over the sacrifice while it was cooking, so they kept pouring on a little water from time to time while the inward meats were being grilled; then, when the thigh bones were burned and they had tasted the inward meats, they cut the rest up small and put the pieces upon the spits.

"By this time my deep sleep had left me, and I turned back to the ship and to the sea shore. As I drew near I began to smell hot roast meat, so I groaned out a prayer to the immortal gods. 'Father Jove,' I exclaimed, 'and all you other gods who live in everlasting bliss, you have done me a cruel mischief by the sleep into which you have sent me; see what fine work these men of mine have been making in my absence.'

"Meanwhile Lampetie went straight off to the sun and told him we had been killing his cows, whereon he flew into a great rage, and said to the immortals, 'Father Jove, and all you other gods who live in everlasting bliss, I must have vengeance on the crew of Ulysses' ship: they have had the insolence to kill my cows, which were the one thing I loved to look upon, whether I was going up heaven or down again. If they do not square accounts with me about my cows, I will go down to Hades and shine there among the dead.'

"'Sun,' said Jove, 'go on shining upon us gods and upon mankind over the fruitful earth. I will shiver their ship into little pieces with a bolt of white lightning as soon as they get out to sea.'

"I was told all this by Calypso, who said she had heard it from the mouth of Mercury.

"As soon as I got down to my ship and to the sea shore I rebuked each one of the men separately, but we could see no way out of it, for the cows were dead already. And indeed the gods began at once to show signs and wonders among us, for the hides of the cattle crawled about, and the joints upon the spits began to low like cows, and the meat, whether cooked or raw, kept on making a noise just as cows do.

"For six days my men kept driving in the best cows and feasting upon them, but when Jove the son of Saturn had added a seventh day, the fury of the gale abated; we therefore went on board, raised our masts, spread sail, and put out to sea. As soon as we were well away from the island, and could see nothing but sky and sea, the son of Saturn raised a black cloud over our ship, and the sea grew dark beneath it. We not get on much further, for in another moment we were caught by a terrific squall from the West that snapped the forestays of the mast so that it fell aft, while all the ship's gear tumbled about at the bottom of the vessel. The mast fell upon the head of the helmsman in the ship's stern, so that the bones of his head were crushed to pieces, and he fell overboard as though he were diving, with no more life left in him.

"Then Jove let fly with his thunderbolts, and the ship went round and round, and was filled with fire and brimstone as the lightning struck it. The men all fell into the sea; they were carried about in the water round the ship, looking like so many sea-gulls, but the god presently deprived them of all chance of getting home again.

"I stuck to the ship till the sea knocked her sides from her keel (which drifted about by itself) and struck the mast out of her in the direction of the keel; but there was a backstay of stout ox-thong still hanging about it, and with this I lashed the mast and keel together, and getting astride of them was carried wherever the winds chose to take me.

"[The gale from the West had now spent its force, and the wind got into the South again, which frightened me lest I should be taken back to the terrible whirlpool of Charybdis. This indeed was what actually happened, for I was borne along by the waves all night, and by sunrise had reacfied the rock of Scylla, and the whirlpool. She was then sucking down the salt sea water, but I was carried aloft toward the fig tree, which I caught hold of and clung on to like a bat. I could not plant my feet anywhere so as to stand securely, for the roots were a long way off and the boughs that overshadowed the whole pool were too high, too vast, and too far apart for me to reach them; so I hung patiently on, waiting till the pool should discharge my mast and raft again- and a very long while it seemed. A juryman is not more glad to get home to supper, after having been long detained in court by troublesome cases, than I was to see my raft beginning to work its way out of the whirlpool again. At last I let go with my hands and feet, and fell heavily into the sea, bard by my raft on to which I then got, and began to row with my hands. As for Scylla, the father of gods and men would not let her get further sight of me- otherwise I should have certainly been lost.]

"Hence I was carried along for nine days till on the tenth night the gods stranded me on the Ogygian island, where dwells the great and powerful goddess Calypso. She took me in and was kind to me, but I need say no more about this, for I told you and your noble wife all about it yesterday, and I hate saying the same thing over and over again."

Book XIII

Thus did he speak, and they all held their peace throughout the covered cloister, enthralled by the charm of his story, till presently Alcinous began to speak.

"Ulysses," said he, "now that you have reached my house I doubt not you will get home without further misadventure no matter how much you have suffered in the past. To you others, however, who come here night after night to drink my choicest wine and listen to my bard, I would insist as follows. Our guest has already packed up the clothes, wrought gold, and other valuables which you have brought for his acceptance; let us now, therefore, present him further, each one of us, with a large tripod and a cauldron. We will recoup ourselves by the levy of a general rate; for private individuals cannot be expected to bear the burden of such a handsome present."

Every one approved of this, and then they went home to bed each in his own abode. When the child of morning, rosy-fingered Dawn, appeared, they hurried down to the ship and brought their cauldrons with them. Alcinous went on board and saw everything so securely stowed under the ship's benches that nothing could break adrift and injure the rowers. Then they went to the house of Alcinous to get dinner, and he sacrificed a bull for them in honour of Jove who is the lord of all. They set the steaks to grill and made an excellent dinner, after which the inspired bard, Demodocus, who was a favourite with every one, sang to them; but Ulysses kept on turning his eyes towards the sun, as though to hasten his setting, for he was longing to be on his way. As one who has been all day ploughing a fallow field with a couple of oxen keeps thinking about his supper and is glad when night comes that he may go and get it, for it is all his legs can do to carry him, even so did Ulysses rejoice when the sun went down, and he at once said to the Phaecians, addressing himself more particularly to King Alcinous:

"Sir, and all of you, farewell. Make your drink-offerings and send me on my way rejoicing, for you have fulfilled my heart's desire by giving me an escort, and making me presents, which heaven grant that I may turn to good account; may I find my admirable wife living in peace among friends, and may you whom I leave behind me give satisfaction to your wives and children; may heaven vouchsafe you every good grace, and may no evil thing come among your people."

Thus did he speak. His hearers all of them approved his saying and agreed that he should have his escort inasmuch as he had spoken reasonably. Alcinous therefore said to his servant, "Pontonous, mix some wine and hand it round to everybody, that we may offer a prayer to father Jove, and speed our guest upon his way."

Pontonous mixed the wine and handed it to every one in turn; the others each from his own seat made a drink-offering to the blessed gods that live in heaven, but Ulysses rose and placed the double cup in the hands of queen Arete.

"Farewell, queen," said he, "henceforward and for ever, till age and death, the common lot of mankind, lay their hands upon you. I now take my leave; be happy in this house with your children, your people, and with king Alcinous."

As he spoke he crossed the threshold, and Alcinous sent a man to conduct him to his ship and to the sea shore. Arete also sent some maid servants with him- one with a clean shirt and cloak, another to carry his strong-box, and a third with corn and wine. When they got to the water side the crew took these things and put them on board, with all the meat and drink; but for Ulysses they spread a rug and a linen sheet on deck that he might sleep soundly in the stern of the ship. Then he too went on board and lay down without a word, but the crew took every man his place and loosed the hawser from the pierced stone to which it had been bound. Thereon, when they began rowing out to sea, Ulysses fell into a deep, sweet, and almost deathlike slumber.

The ship bounded forward on her way as a four in hand chariot flies over the course when the horses feel the whip. Her prow curveted as it were the neck of a stallion, and a great wave of dark blue water seethed in her wake. She held steadily on her course, and even a falcon, swiftest of all birds, could not have kept pace with her. Thus, then, she cut her way through the water. carrying one who was as cunning as the gods, but who was now sleeping peacefully, forgetful of all that he had suffered both on the field of battle and by the waves of the weary sea.

When the bright star that heralds the approach of dawn began to show. the ship drew near to land. Now there is in Ithaca a haven of the old merman Phorcys, which lies between two points that break the line of the sea and shut the harbour in. These shelter it from the storms of wind and sea that rage outside, so that, when once within it, a ship may lie without being even moored.

At the head of this harbour there is a large olive tree, and at no distance a fine overarching cavern sacred to the nymphs who are called Naiads. There are mixing-bowls within it and wine-jars of stone, and the bees hive there. Moreover, there are great looms of stone on which the nymphs weave their robes of sea purple- very curious to see- and at all times there is water within it. It has two entrances, one facing North by which mortals can go down into the cave, while the other comes from the South and is more mysterious; mortals cannot possibly get in by it, it is the way taken by the gods.

Into this harbour, then, they took their ship, for they knew the place, She had so much way upon her that she ran half her own length on to the shore; when, however, they had landed, the first thing they did was to lift Ulysses with his rug and linen sheet out of the ship, and lay him down upon the sand still fast asleep. Then they took out the presents which Minerva had persuaded the Phaeacians to give him when he was setting out on his voyage homewards. They put these all together by the root of the olive tree, away from the road, for fear some passer by might come and steal them before Ulysses awoke; and then they made the best of their way home again.

But Neptune did not forget the threats with which he had already threatened Ulysses, so he took counsel with Jove. “Father Jove,” said he, “I shall no longer be held in any sort of respect among you gods, if mortals like the Phaeacians, who are my own flesh and blood, show such small regard for me. I said I would Ulysses get home when he had suffered sufficiently. I did not say that he should never get home at all, for I knew you had already nodded your head about it, and promised that he should do so; but now they have brought him in a ship fast asleep and have landed him in Ithaca after loading him with more magnificent presents of bronze, gold, and raiment than he would ever have brought back from Troy, if he had had his share of the spoil and got home without misadventure.”

And Jove answered, “What, O Lord of the Earthquake, are you talking about? The gods are by no means wanting in respect for you. It would be monstrous were they to insult one so old and honoured as you are. As regards mortals, however, if any of them is indulging in insolence and treating you disrespectfully, it will always rest with yourself to deal with him as you may think proper, so do just as you please.”

“I should have done so at once,” replied Neptune, “if I were not anxious to avoid anything that might displease you; now, therefore, I should like to wreck the Phaecian ship as it is returning from its escort. This will stop them from escorting people in future; and I should also like to bury their city under a huge mountain.”

“My good friend,” answered Jove, “I should recommend you at the very moment when the people from the city are watching the ship on her way, to turn it into a rock near the land and looking like a ship. This will astonish everybody, and you can then bury their city under the mountain.”

When earth-encircling Neptune heard this he went to Scheria where the Phaecians live, and stayed there till the ship, which was making rapid way, had got close-in. Then he went up to it, turned it into stone, and drove it down with the flat of his hand so as to root it in the ground. After this he went away.

The Phaeacians then began talking among themselves, and one would turn towards his neighbour, saying, “Bless my heart, who is it that can have rooted the ship in the sea just as she was getting into port? We could see the whole of her only moment ago.”

This was how they talked, but they knew nothing about it; and Alcinous said, "I remember now the old prophecy of my father. He said that Neptune would be angry with us for taking every one so safely over the sea, and would one day wreck a Phaeacian ship as it was returning from an escort, and bury our city under a high mountain. This was what my old father used to say, and now it is all coming true. Now therefore let us all do as I say; in the first place we must leave off giving people escorts when they come here, and in the next let us sacrifice twelve picked bulls to Neptune that he may have mercy upon us, and not bury our city under the high mountain." When the people heard this they were afraid and got ready the bulls.

Thus did the chiefs and rulers of the Phaecians to king Neptune, standing round his altar; and at the same time Ulysses woke up once more upon his own soil. He had been so long away that he did not know it again; moreover, Jove's daughter Minerva had made it a foggy day, so that people might not know of his having come, and that she might tell him everything without either his wife or his fellow citizens and friends recognizing him until he had taken his revenge upon the wicked suitors. Everything, therefore, seemed quite different to him- the long straight tracks, the harbours, the precipices, and the goodly trees, appeared all changed as he started up and looked upon his native land. So he smote his thighs with the flat of his hands and cried aloud despairingly.

"Alas," he exclaimed, "among what manner of people am I fallen? Are they savage and uncivilized or hospitable and humane? Where shall I put all this treasure, and which way shall I go? I wish I had stayed over there with the Phaeacians; or I could have gone to some other great chief who would have been good to me and given me an escort. As it is I do not know where to put my treasure, and I cannot leave it here for fear somebody else should get hold of it. In good truth the chiefs and rulers of the Phaeacians have not been dealing fairly by me, and have left me in the wrong country; they said they would take me back to Ithaca and they have not done so: may Jove the protector of suppliants chastise them, for he watches over everybody and punishes those who do wrong. Still, I suppose I must count my goods and see if the crew have gone off with any of them."

He counted his goodly coppers and cauldrons, his gold and all his clothes, but there was nothing missing; still he kept grieving about not being in his own country, and wandered up and down by the shore of the sounding sea bewailing his hard fate. Then Minerva came up to him disguised as a young shepherd of delicate and princely mien, with a good cloak folded double about her shoulders; she had sandals on her comely feet and held a javelin in her hand. Ulysses was glad when he saw her, and went straight up to her.

"My friend," said he, "you are the first person whom I have met with in this country; I salute you, therefore, and beg you to be will disposed towards me. Protect these my goods, and myself too, for I embrace your knees and pray to you as though you were a god. Tell me, then, and tell me truly, what land and country is this? Who are its inhabitants? Am I on an island, or is this the sea board of some continent?"

Minerva answered, "Stranger, you must be very simple, or must have come from somewhere a long way off, not to know what country this is. It is a very celebrated place, and everybody knows it East and West. It is rugged and not a good driving country, but it is by no means a bid island for what there is of it. It grows any quantity of corn and also wine, for it is watered both by rain and dew; it breeds cattle also and goats; all kinds of timber grow here, and there are watering places where the water never runs dry; so, sir, the name of Ithaca is known even as far as Troy, which I understand to be a long way off from this Achaean country."

Ulysses was glad at finding himself, as Minerva told him, in his own country, and he began to answer, but he did not speak the truth, and made up a lying story in the instinctive wiliness of his heart.

"I heard of Ithaca," said he, "when I was in Crete beyond the seas, and now it seems I have reached it with all these treasures. I have left as much more behind me for my children, but am flying because I killed Orsilochus son of Idomeneus, the fleetest runner in Crete. I killed him because he wanted to rob me of the spoils I had got from Troy with so much trouble and danger both on the field of battle and by the waves of the weary sea; he said I had not served his father loyally at Troy as vassal, but had set myself up as an independent ruler, so I lay in wait for him and with one of my followers by the road side, and speared him as he was coming into town from the country. my It was a very dark night and nobody saw us; it was not known, therefore, that I had killed him, but as soon as I had done so I went to a ship and besought the owners, who were Phoenicians, to take me on board and set me in Pylos or in Elis where the Epeans rule, giving them as much spoil as satisfied them. They meant no guile, but the wind drove them off their course, and we sailed on till we came hither by night. It was all we could do to get inside the harbour, and none of us said a word about supper though we wanted it badly, but we all went on shore and lay down just as we were. I was very tired and fell asleep directly, so they took my goods out of the ship, and placed them beside me where I was lying upon the sand. Then they sailed away to Sidonia, and I was left here in great distress of mind."

Such was his story, but Minerva smiled and caressed him with her hand. Then she took the form of a woman, fair, stately, and wise, "He must be indeed a shifty lying fellow," said she, "who could surpass you in all manner of craft even though you had a god for your antagonist. Dare-devil that you are, full of guile, unwearying in deceit, can you not drop your tricks and your instinctive falsehood, even now that you are in your own country again? We will say no more, however, about this, for we can both of us deceive upon occasion- you are the most accomplished counsellor and orator among all mankind, while I for diplomacy and subtlety have no equal among the gods. Did you not know Jove's daughter Minerva- me, who have been ever with you, who kept watch over you in all your troubles, and who made the Phaeacians take so great a liking to you? And now, again, I am come here to talk things over with you, and help you to hide the treasure I made the Phaeacians give you; I want to tell you about the troubles that await you in your own house; you have got to face them, but tell no one, neither man nor woman, that you have come home again. Bear everything, and put up with every man's insolence, without a word."

And Ulysses answered, "A man, goddess, may know a great deal, but you are so constantly changing your appearance that when he meets you it is a hard matter for him to know whether it is you or not. This much, however, I know exceedingly well; you were very kind to me as long as we Achaeans were fighting before Troy, but from the day on which we went on board ship after having sacked the city of Priam, and heaven dispersed us- from that day, Minerva, I saw no more of you, and cannot ever remember your coming to my ship to help me in a difficulty; I had to wander on sick and sorry till the gods delivered me from evil and I reached the city of the Phaeacians, where you encouraged me and took me into the town. And now, I beseech you in your father's name, tell me the truth, for I do not believe I am really back in Ithaca. I am in some other country and you are mocking me and deceiving me in all you have been saying. Tell me then truly, have I really got back to my own country?"

"You are always taking something of that sort into your head," replied Minerva, "and that is why I cannot desert you in your afflictions; you are so plausible, shrewd and shifty. Any one but yourself on returning from so long a voyage would at once have gone home to see his wife and children, but you do not seem to care about asking after them or hearing any news about them till you have exploited your wife, who remains at home vainly grieving for you, and having no peace night or day for the tears she sheds on your behalf. As for my not coming near you, I was never uneasy about you, for I was certain you would get back safely though you would lose all your men, and I did not wish to quarrel with my uncle Neptune, who never forgave you for having blinded his son. I will now, however, point out to you the lie of the land, and you will then perhaps believe me. This is the haven of the old merman Phorcys, and here is the olive tree that grows at the head of it; [near it is the cave sacred to the Naiads;] here too is the overarching cavern in which you have offered many an acceptable hecatomb to the nymphs, and this is the wooded mountain Neritum."

As she spoke the goddess dispersed the mist and the land appeared. Then Ulysses rejoiced at finding himself again in his own land, and kissed the bounteous soil; he lifted up his hands and prayed to the nymphs, saying, "Naiad nymphs, daughters of Jove, I made sure that I was never again to see you, now therefore I greet you with all loving salutations, and I will bring you offerings as in the old days, if Jove's redoubtable daughter will grant me life, and bring my son to manhood."

"Take heart, and do not trouble yourself about that," rejoined Minerva, "let us rather set about stowing your things at once in the cave, where they will be quite safe. Let us see how we can best manage it all."

Therewith she went down into the cave to look for the safest hiding places, while Ulysses brought up all the treasure of gold, bronze, and good clothing which the Phaecians had given him. They stowed everything carefully away, and Minerva set a stone against the door of the cave. Then the two sat down by the root of the great olive, and consulted how to compass the destruction of the wicked suitors.

"Ulysses," said Minerva, "noble son of Laertes, think how you can lay hands on these disreputable people who have been lording it in your house these three years, courting your wife and making wedding presents to her, while she does nothing but lament your absence, giving hope and sending your encouraging messages to every one of them, but meaning the very opposite of all she says'

And Ulysses answered, "In good truth, goddess, it seems I should have come to much the same bad end in my own house as Agamemnon did, if you had not given me such timely information. Advise me how I shall best avenge myself. Stand by my side and put your courage into my heart as on the day when we loosed Troy's fair diadem from her brow. Help me now as you did then, and I will fight three hundred men, if you, goddess, will be with me."

"Trust me for that," said she, "I will not lose sight of you when once we set about it, and I would imagine that some of those who are devouring your substance will then bespatter the pavement with their blood and brains. I will begin by disguising you so that no human being shall know you; I will cover your body with wrinkles; you shall lose all your yellow hair; I will clothe you in a garment that shall fill all who see it with loathing; I will blear your fine eyes for you, and make you an unseemly object in the sight of the suitors, of your wife, and of the son whom you left behind you. Then go at once to the swineherd who is in charge of your pigs; he has been always well affected towards you, and is devoted to Penelope and your son; you will find him feeding his pigs near the rock that is called Raven by the fountain Arethusa, where they are fattening on beechmast and spring water after their manner. Stay with him and find out how things are going, while I proceed to Sparta and see your son, who is with Menelaus at Lacedaemon, where he has gone to try and find out whether you are still alive."

"But why," said Ulysses, "did you not tell him, for you knew all about it? Did you want him too to go sailing about amid all kinds of hardship while others are eating up his estate?"

Minerva answered, "Never mind about him, I sent him that he might be well spoken of for having gone. He is in no sort of difficulty, but is staying quite comfortably with Menelaus, and is surrounded with abundance of every kind. The suitors have put out to sea and are lying in wait for him, for they mean to kill him before he can get home. I do not much think they will succeed, but rather that some of those who are now eating up your estate will first find a grave themselves."

As she spoke Minerva touched him with her wand and covered him with wrinkles, took away all his yellow hair, and withered the flesh over his whole body; she bleared his eyes, which were naturally very fine ones; she changed his clothes and threw an old rag of a wrap about him, and a tunic, tattered, filthy, and begrimed with smoke; she also gave him an undressed deer skin as an outer garment, and furnished him with a staff and a wallet all in holes, with a twisted thong for him to sling it over his shoulder.

When the pair had thus laid their plans they parted, and the goddess went straight to Lacedaemon to fetch Telemachus.

Book XIV

Ulysses now left the haven, and took the rough track up through the wooded country and over the crest of the mountain till he reached the place where Minerva had said that he would find the swineherd, who was the most thrifty servant he had. He found him sitting in front of his hut, which was by the yards that he had built on a site which could be seen from far. He had made them spacious and fair to see, with a free ran for the pigs all round them; he had built them during his master's absence, of stones which he had gathered out of the ground, without saying anything to Penelope or Laertes, and he had fenced them on top with thorn bushes. Outside the yard he had run a strong fence of oaken posts, split, and set pretty close together, while inside lie had built twelve sties near one another for the sows to lie in. There were fifty pigs wallowing in each sty, all of them breeding sows; but the boars slept outside and were much fewer in number, for the suitors kept on eating them, and die swineherd had to send them the best he had continually. There were three hundred and sixty boar pigs, and the herdsman's four hounds, which were as fierce as wolves, slept always with them. The swineherd was at that moment cutting out a pair of sandals from a good stout ox hide. Three of his men were out herding the pigs in one place or another, and he had sent the fourth to town with a boar that he had been forced to send the suitors that they might sacrifice it and have their fill of meat.

When the hounds saw Ulysses they set up a furious barking and flew at him, but Ulysses was cunning enough to sit down and loose his hold of the stick that he had in his hand: still, he would have been torn by them in his own homestead had not the swineherd dropped his ox hide, rushed full speed through the gate of the yard and driven the dogs off by shouting and throwing stones at them. Then he said to Ulysses, "Old man, the dogs were likely to have made short work of you, and then you would have got me into trouble. The gods have given me quite enough worries without that, for I have lost the best of masters, and am in continual grief on his account. I have to attend swine for other people to eat, while he, if he yet lives to see the light of day, is starving in some distant land. But come inside, and when you have had your fill of bread and wine, tell me where you come from, and all about your misfortunes."

On this the swineherd led the way into the hut and bade him sit down. He strewed a good thick bed of rushes upon the floor, and on the top of this he threw the shaggy chamois skin- a great thick one- on which he used to sleep by night. Ulysses was pleased at being made thus welcome, and said "May Jove, sir, and the rest of the gods grant you your heart's desire in return for the kind way in which you have received me."

To this you answered, O swineherd Eumaeus, "Stranger, though a still poorer man should come here, it would not be right for me to insult him, for all strangers and beggars are from Jove. You must take what you can get and be thankful, for servants live in fear when they have young lords for their masters; and this is my misfortune now, for heaven has hindered the return of him who would have been always good to me and given me something of my own- a house, a piece of land, a good looking wife, and all else that a liberal master allows a servant who has worked hard for him, and whose labour the gods have prospered as they have mine in the situation which I hold. If my master had grown old here he would have done great things by me, but he is gone, and I wish that Helen's whole race were utterly destroyed, for she has been the death of many a good man. It was this matter that took my master to Ilius, the land of noble steeds, to fight the Trojans in the cause of kin Agamemnon."

As he spoke he bound his girdle round him and went to the sties where the young sucking pigs were penned. He picked out two which he brought back with him and sacrificed. He singed them, cut them up, and spitted on them; when the meat was cooked he brought it all in and set it before Ulysses, hot and still on the spit, whereon Ulysses sprinkled it over with white barley meal. The swineherd then mixed wine in a bowl of ivy-wood, and taking a seat opposite Ulysses told him to begin.

"Fall to, stranger," said he, "on a dish of servant's pork. The fat pigs have to go to the suitors, who eat them up without shame or scruple; but the blessed gods love not such shameful doings, and respect those who do what is lawful and right. Even the fierce free-booters who go raiding on other people's land, and Jove gives them their spoil- even they, when they have filled their ships and got home again live conscience-stricken, and look fearfully for judgement; but some god seems to have told these people that Ulysses is dead and gone; they will not, therefore, go back to their own homes and make their offers of marriage in the usual way, but waste his estate by force, without fear or stint. Not a day or night comes out of heaven, but they sacrifice not one victim nor two only, and they take the run of his wine, for he was exceedingly rich. No other great man either in Ithaca or on the mainland is as rich as he was; he had as much as twenty men put together. I will tell you what he had. There are twelve herds of cattle upon the mainland, and as many flocks of sheep, there are also twelve droves of pigs, while his own men and hired strangers feed him twelve widely spreading herds of goats. Here in Ithaca he runs even large flocks of goats on the far end of the island, and they are in the charge of excellent goatherds. Each one of these sends the suitors the best goat in the flock every day. As for myself, I am in charge of the pigs that you see here, and I have to keep picking out the best I have and sending it to them."

This was his story, but Ulysses went on eating and drinking ravenously without a word, brooding his revenge. When he had eaten enough and was satisfied, the swineherd took the bowl from which he usually drank, filled it with wine, and gave it to Ulysses, who was pleased, and said as he took it in his hands, "My friend, who was this master of yours that bought you and paid for you, so rich and so powerful as you tell me? You say he perished in the cause of King Agamemnon; tell me who he was, in case I may have met with such a person. Jove and the other gods know, but I may be able to give you news of him, for I have travelled much."

Eumaeus answered, "Old man, no traveller who comes here with news will get Ulysses' wife and son to believe his story. Nevertheless, tramps in want of a lodging keep coming with their mouths full of lies, and not a word of truth; every one who finds his way to Ithaca goes to my mistress and tells her falsehoods, whereon she takes them in, makes much of them, and asks them all manner of questions, crying all the time as women will when they have lost their husbands. And you too, old man, for a shirt and a cloak would doubtless make up a very pretty story. But the wolves and birds of prey have long since torn Ulysses to pieces, or the fishes of the sea have eaten him, and his bones are lying buried deep in sand upon some foreign shore; he is dead and gone, and a bad business it is for all his friends- for me especially; go where I may I shall never find so good a master, not even if I were to go home to my mother and father where I was bred and born. I do not so much care, however, about my parents now, though I should dearly like to see them again in my own country; it is the loss of Ulysses that grieves me most; I cannot speak of him without reverence though he is here no longer, for he was very fond of me, and took such care of me that whereever he may be I shall always honour his memory."

"My friend," replied Ulysses, "you are very positive, and very hard of belief about your master's coming home again, nevertheless I will not merely say, but will swear, that he is coming. Do not give me anything for my news till he has actually come, you may then give me a shirt and cloak of good wear if you will. I am in great want, but I will not take anything at all till then, for I hate a man, even as I hate hell fire, who lets his poverty tempt him into lying. I swear by king Jove, by the rites of hospitality, and by that hearth of Ulysses to which I have now come, that all will surely happen as I have said it will. Ulysses will return in this self same year; with the end of this moon and the beginning of the next he will be here to do vengeance on all those who are ill treating his wife and son."

To this you answered, O swineherd Eumaeus, "Old man, you will neither get paid for bringing good news, nor will Ulysses ever come home; drink you wine in peace, and let us talk about something else. Do not keep on reminding me of all this; it always pains me when any one speaks about my honoured master. As for your oath we will let it alone, but I only wish he may come, as do Penelope, his old father Laertes, and his son Telemachus. I am terribly unhappy too about this same boy of his; he was running up fast into manhood, and bade fare to be no worse man, face and figure, than his father, but some one, either god or man, has been unsettling his mind, so he has gone off to Pylos to try and get news of his father, and the suitors are lying in wait for him as he is coming home, in the hope of leaving the house of Arceisius without a name in Ithaca. But let us say no more about him, and leave him to be taken, or else to escape if the son of Saturn holds his hand over him to protect him. And now, old man, tell me your own story; tell me also, for I want to know, who you are and where you come from. Tell me of your town and parents, what manner of ship you came in, how crew brought you to Ithaca, and from what country they professed to come- for you cannot have come by land."

And Ulysses answered, "I will tell you all about it. If there were meat and wine enough, and we could stay here in the hut with nothing to do but to eat and drink while the others go to their work, I could easily talk on for a whole twelve months without ever finishing the story of the sorrows with which it has pleased heaven to visit me.

"I am by birth a Cretan; my father was a well-to-do man, who had many sons born in marriage, whereas I was the son of a slave whom he had purchased for a concubine; nevertheless, my father Castor son of Hylax (whose lineage I claim, and who was held in the highest honour among the Cretans for his wealth, prosperity, and the valour of his sons) put me on the same level with my brothers who had been born in wedlock. When, however, death took him to the house of Hades, his sons divided his estate and cast lots for their shares, but to me they gave a holding and little else; nevertheless, my valour enabled me to marry into a rich family, for I was not given to bragging, or shirking on the field of battle. It is all over now; still, if you look at the straw you can see what the ear was, for I have had trouble enough and to spare. Mars and Minerva made me doughty in war; when I had picked my men to surprise the enemy with an ambuscade I never gave death so much as a thought, but was the first to leap forward and spear all whom I could overtake. Such was I in battle, but I did not care about farm work, nor the frugal home life of those who would bring up children. My delight was in ships, fighting, javelins, and arrows- things that most men shudder to think of; but one man likes one thing and another another, and this was what I was most naturally inclined to. Before the Achaeans went to Troy, nine times was I in command of men and ships on foreign service, and I amassed much wealth. I had my pick of the spoil in the first instance, and much more was allotted to me later on.

"My house grew apace and I became a great man among the Cretans, but when Jove counselled that terrible expedition, in which so many perished, the people required me and Idomeneus to lead their ships to Troy, and there was no way out of it, for they insisted on our doing so. There we fought for nine whole years, but in the tenth we sacked the city of Priam and sailed home again as heaven dispersed us. Then it was that Jove devised evil against me. I spent but one month happily with my children, wife, and property, and then I conceived the idea of making a descent on Egypt, so I fitted out a fine fleet and manned it. I had nine ships, and the people flocked to fill them. For six days I and my men made feast, and I found them many victims both for sacrifice to the gods and for themselves, but on the seventh day we went on board and set sail from Crete with a fair North wind behind us though we were going down a river. Nothing went ill with any of our ships, and we had no sickness on board, but sat where we were and let the ships go as the wind and steersmen took them. On the fifth day we reached the river Aegyptus; there I stationed my ships in the river, bidding my men stay by them and keep guard over them while I sent out scouts to reconnoitre from every point of vantage.

"But the men disobeyed my orders, took to their own devices, and ravaged the land of the Egyptians, killing the men, and taking their wives and children captive. The alarm was soon carried to the city, and when they heard the war cry, the people came out at daybreak till the plain was filled with horsemen and foot soldiers and with the gleam of armour. Then Jove spread panic among my men, and they would no longer face the enemy, for they found themselves surrounded. The Egyptians killed many of us, and took the rest alive to do forced labour for them. Jove, however, put it in my mind to do thus- and I wish I had died then and there in Egypt instead, for there was much sorrow in store for me- I took off my helmet and shield and dropped my spear from my hand; then I went straight up to the king's chariot, clasped his knees and kissed them, whereon he spared my life, bade me get into his chariot, and took me weeping to his own home. Many made at me with their ashen spears and tried to kil me in their fury, but the king protected me, for he feared the wrath of Jove the protector of strangers, who punishes those who do evil.

"I stayed there for seven years and got together much money among the Egyptians, for they all gave me something; but when it was now going on for eight years there came a certain Phoenician, a cunning rascal, who had already committed all sorts of villainy, and this man talked me over into going with him to Phoenicia, where his house and his possessions lay. I stayed there for a whole twelve months, but at the end of that time when months and days had gone by till the same season had come round again, he set me on board a ship bound for Libya, on a pretence that I was to take a cargo along with him to that place, but really that he might sell me as a slave and take the money I fetched. I suspected his intention, but went on board with him, for I could not help it.

"The ship ran before a fresh North wind till we had reached the sea that lies between Crete and Libya; there, however, Jove counselled their destruction, for as soon as we were well out from Crete and could see nothing but sea and sky, he raised a black cloud over our ship and the sea grew dark beneath it. Then Jove let fly with his thunderbolts and the ship went round and round and was filled with fire and brimstone as the lightning struck it. The men fell all into the sea; they were carried about in the water round the ship looking like so many sea-gulls, but the god presently deprived them of all chance of getting home again. I was all dismayed; Jove, however, sent the ship's mast within my reach, which saved my life, for I clung to it, and drifted before the fury of the gale. Nine days did I drift but in the darkness of the tenth night a great wave bore me on to the Thesprotian coast. There Pheidon king of the Thesprotians entertained me hospitably without charging me anything at all for his son found me when I was nearly dead with cold and fatigue, whereon he raised me by the hand, took me to his father's house and gave me clothes to wear.

"There it was that I heard news of Ulysses, for the king told me he had entertained him, and shown him much hospitality while he was on his homeward journey. He showed me also the treasure of gold, and wrought iron that Ulysses had got together. There was enough to keep his family for ten generations, so much had he left in the house of king Pheidon. But the king said Ulysses had gone to Dodona that he might learn Jove's mind from the god's high oak tree, and know whether after so long an absence he should return to Ithaca openly, or in secret. Moreover the king swore in my presence, making drink-offerings in his own house as he did so, that the ship was by the water side, and the crew found, that should take him to his own country. He sent me off however before Ulysses returned, for there happened to be a Thesprotian ship sailing for the wheat-growing island of Dulichium, and he told those in charge of her to be sure and take me safely to King Acastus.

"These men hatched a plot against me that would have reduced me to the very extreme of misery, for when the ship had got some way out from land they resolved on selling me as a slave. They stripped me of the shirt and cloak that I was wearing, and gave me instead the tattered old clouts in which you now see me; then, towards nightfall, they reached the tilled lands of Ithaca, and there they bound me with a strong rope fast in the ship, while they went on shore to get supper by the sea side. But the gods soon undid my bonds for me, and having drawn my rags over my head I slid down the rudder into the sea, where I struck out and swam till I was well clear of them, and came ashore near a thick wood in which I lay concealed. They were very angry at my having escaped and went searching about for me, till at last they thought it was no further use and went back to their ship. The gods, having hidden me thus easily, then took me to a good man's door- for it seems that I am not to die yet awhile."

To this you answered, O swineherd Eumaeus, "Poor unhappy stranger, I have found the story of your misfortunes extremely interesting, but that part about Ulysses is not right; and you will never get me to believe it. Why should a man like you go about telling lies in this way? I know all about the return of my master. The gods one and all of them detest him, or they would have taken him before Troy, or let him die with friends around him when the days of his fighting were done; for then the Achaeans would have built a mound over his ashes and his son would have been heir to his renown, but now the storm winds have spirited him away we know not whither.

"As for me I live out of the way here with the pigs, and never go to the town unless when Penelope sends for me on the arrival of some news about Ulysses. Then they all sit round and ask questions, both those who grieve over the king's absence, and those who rejoice at it because they can eat up his property without paying for it. For my own part I have never cared about asking anyone else since the time when I was taken in by an Aetolian, who had killed a man and come a long way till at last he reached my station, and I was very kind to him. He said he had seen Ulysses with Idomeneus among the Cretans, refitting his ships which had been damaged in a gale. He said Ulysses would return in the following summer or autumn with his men, and that he would bring back much wealth. And now you, you unfortunate old man, since fate has brought you to my door, do not try to flatter me in this way with vain hopes. It is not for any such reason that I shall treat you kindly, but only out of respect for Jove the god of hospitality, as fearing him and pitying you."

Ulysses answered, "I see that you are of an unbelieving mind; I have given you my oath, and yet you will not credit me; let us then make a bargain, and call all the gods in heaven to witness it. If your master comes home, give me a cloak and shirt of good wear, and send me to Dulichium where I want to go; but if he does not come as I say he will, set your men on to me, and tell them to throw me from yonder precepice, as a warning to tramps not to go about the country telling lies."

"And a pretty figure I should cut then," replied Eumaeus, both now and hereafter, if I were to kill you after receiving you into my hut and showing you hospitality. I should have to say my prayers in good earnest if I did; but it is just supper time and I hope my men will come in directly, that we may cook something savoury for supper."

Thus did they converse, and presently the swineherds came up with the pigs, which were then shut up for the night in their sties, and a tremendous squealing they made as they were being driven into them. But Eumaeus called to his men and said, "Bring in the best pig you have, that I may sacrifice for this stranger, and we will take toll of him ourselves. We have had trouble enough this long time feeding pigs, while others reap the fruit of our labour."

On this he began chopping firewood, while the others brought in a fine fat five year old boar pig, and set it at the altar. Eumaeus did not forget the gods, for he was a man of good principles, so the first thing he did was to cut bristles from the pig's face and throw them into the fire, praying to all the gods as he did so that Ulysses might return home again. Then he clubbed the pig with a billet of oak which he had kept back when he was chopping the firewood, and stunned it, while the others slaughtered and singed it. Then they cut it up, and Eumaeus began by putting raw pieces from each joint on to some of the fat; these he sprinkled with barley meal, and laid upon the embers; they cut the rest of the meat up small, put the pieces upon the spits and roasted them till they were done; when they had taken them off the spits they threw them on to the dresser in a heap. The swineherd, who was a most equitable man, then stood up to give every one his share. He made seven portions; one of these he set apart for Mercury the son of Maia and the nymphs, praying to them as he did so; the others he dealt out to the men man by man. He gave Ulysses some slices cut lengthways down the loin as a mark of especial honour, and Ulysses was much pleased. "I hope, Eumaeus," said he, "that Jove will be as well disposed towards you as I am, for the respect you are showing to an outcast like myself."

To this you answered, O swineherd Eumaeus, "Eat, my good fellow, and enjoy your supper, such as it is. God grants this, and withholds that, just as he thinks right, for he can do whatever he chooses."

As he spoke he cut off the first piece and offered it as a burnt sacrifice to the immortal gods; then he made them a drink-offering, put the cup in the hands of Ulysses, and sat down to his own portion. Mesaulius brought them their bread; the swineherd had bought this man on his own account from among the Taphians during his master's absence, and had paid for him with his own money without saying anything either to his mistress or Laertes. They then laid their hands upon the good things that were before them, and when they had had enough to eat and drink, Mesaulius took away what was left of the bread, and they all went to bed after having made a hearty supper.

Now the night came on stormy and very dark, for there was no moon. It poured without ceasing, and the wind blew strong from the West, which is a wet quarter, so Ulysses thought he would see whether Eumaeus, in the excellent care he took of him, would take off his own cloak and give it him, or make one of his men give him one. "Listen to me," said he, "Eumaeus and the rest of you; when I have said a prayer I will tell you something. It is the wine that makes me talk in this way; wine will make even a wise man fall to singing; it will make him chuckle and dance and say many a word that he had better leave unspoken; still, as I have begun, I will go on. Would that I were still young and strong as when we got up an ambuscade before Troy. Menelaus and Ulysses were the leaders, but I was in command also, for the other two would have it so. When we had come up to the wall of the city we crouched down beneath our armour and lay there under cover of the reeds and thick brush-wood that grew about the swamp. It came on to freeze with a North wind blowing; the snow fell small and fine like hoar frost, and our shields were coated thick with rime. The others had all got cloaks and shirts, and slept comfortably enough with their shields about their shoulders, but I had carelessly left my cloak behind me, not thinking that I should be too cold, and had gone off in nothing but my shirt and shield. When the night was two-thirds through and the stars had shifted their their places, I nudged Ulysses who was close to me with my elbow, and he at once gave me his ear.

"'Ulysses,' said I, 'this cold will be the death of me, for I have no cloak; some god fooled me into setting off with nothing on but my shirt, and I do not know what to do.'

"Ulysses, who was as crafty as he was valiant, hit upon the following plan:

"'Keep still,' said he in a low voice, 'or the others will hear you.' Then he raised his head on his elbow.

"'My friends,' said he, 'I have had a dream from heaven in my sleep. We are a long way from the ships; I wish some one would go down and tell Agamemnon to send us up more men at once.'

"On this Thoas son of Andraemon threw off his cloak and set out running to the ships, whereon I took the cloak and lay in it comfortably enough till morning. Would that I were still young and strong as I was in those days, for then some one of you swineherds would give me a cloak both out of good will and for the respect due to a brave soldier; but now people look down upon me because my clothes are shabby."

And Eumaeus answered, "Old man, you have told us an excellent story, and have said nothing so far but what is quite satisfactory; for the present, therefore, you shall want neither clothing nor anything else that a stranger in distress may reasonably expect, but to-morrow morning you have to shake your own old rags about your body again, for we have not many spare cloaks nor shirts up here, but every man has only one. When Ulysses' son comes home again he will give you both cloak and shirt, and send you wherever you may want to go."

With this he got up and made a bed for Ulysses by throwing some goatskins and sheepskins on the ground in front of the fire. Here Ulysses lay down, and Eumaeus covered him over with a great heavy cloak that he kept for a change in case of extraordinarily bad weather.

Thus did Ulysses sleep, and the young men slept beside him. But the swineherd did not like sleeping away from his pigs, so he got ready to go and Ulysses was glad to see that he looked after his property during his master's absence. First he slung his sword over his brawny shoulders and put on a thick cloak to keep out the wind. He also took the skin of a large and well fed goat, and a javelin in case of attack from men or dogs. Thus equipped he went to his rest where the pigs were camping under an overhanging rock that gave them shelter from the North wind.

But Minerva went to the fair city of Lacedaemon to tell Ulysses' son that he was to return at once. She found him and Pisistratus sleeping in the forecourt of Menelaus's house; Pisistratus was fast asleep, but Telemachus could get no rest all night for thinking of his unhappy father, so Minerva went close up to him and said:

"Telemachus, you should not remain so far away from home any longer, nor leave your property with such dangerous people in your house; they will eat up everything you have among them, and you will have been on a fool's errand. Ask Menelaus to send you home at once if you wish to find your excellent mother still there when you get back. Her father and brothers are already urging her to marry Eurymachus, who has given her more than any of the others, and has been greatly increasing his wedding presents. I hope nothing valuable may have been taken from the house in spite of you, but you know what women are- they always want to do the best they can for the man who marries them, and never give another thought to the children of their first husband, nor to their father either when he is dead and done with. Go home, therefore, and put everything in charge of the most respectable woman servant that you have, until it shall please heaven to send you a wife of your own. Let me tell you also of another matter which you had better attend to. The chief men among the suitors are lying in wait for you in the Strait between

Ithaca and Samos, and they mean to kill you before you can reach home. I do not much think they will succeed; it is more likely that some of those who are now eating up your property will find a grave themselves. Sail night and day, and keep your ship well away from the islands; the god who watches over you and protects you will send you a fair wind. As soon as you get to Ithaca send your ship and men on to the town, but yourself go straight to the swineherd who has charge your pigs; he is well disposed towards you, stay with him, therefore, for the night, and then send him to Penelope to tell her that you have got back safe from Pylos."

Then she went back to Olympus; but Telemachus stirred Pisistratus with his heel to rouse him, and said, "Wake up Pisistratus, and yoke the horses to the chariot, for we must set off home."

But Pisistratus said, "No matter what hurry we are in we cannot drive in the dark. It will be morning soon; wait till Menelaus has brought his presents and put them in the chariot for us; and let him say good-bye to us in the usual way. So long as he lives a guest should never forget a host who has shown him kindness."

As he spoke day began to break, and Menelaus, who had already risen, leaving Helen in bed, came towards them. When Telemachus saw him he put on his shirt as fast as he could, threw a great cloak over his shoulders, and went out to meet him. "Menelaus," said he, "let me go back now to my own country, for I want to get home."

And Menelaus answered, "Telemachus, if you insist on going I will not detain you. not like to see a host either too fond of his guest or too rude to him. Moderation is best in all things, and not letting a man go when he wants to do so is as bad as telling him to go if he would like to stay. One should treat a guest well as long as he is in the house and speed him when he wants to leave it. Wait, then, till I can get your beautiful presents into your chariot, and till you have yourself seen them. I will tell the women to prepare a sufficient dinner for you of what there may be in the house; it will be at once more proper and cheaper for you to get your dinner before setting out on such a long journey. If, moreover, you have a fancy for making a tour in Hellas or in the Peloponnese, I will yoke my horses, and will conduct you myself through all our principal cities. No one will send us away empty handed; every one will give us something- a bronze tripod, a couple of mules, or a gold cup."

"Menelaus," replied Telemachus, "I want to go home at once, for when I came away I left my property without protection, and fear that while looking for my father I shall come to ruin myself, or find that something valuable has been stolen during my absence."

When Menelaus heard this he immediately told his wife and servants to prepare a sufficient dinner from what there might be in the house. At this moment Eteoneus joined him, for he lived close by and had just got up; so Menelaus told him to light the fire and cook some meat, which he at once did. Then Menelaus went down into his fragrant store room, not alone, but Helen went too, with Megapenthes. When he reached the place where the treasures of his house were kept, he selected a double cup, and told his son Megapenthes to bring also a silver mixing-bowl. Meanwhile Helen went to the chest where she kept the lovely dresses which she had made with her own hands, and took out one that was largest and most beautifully enriched with embroidery; it glittered like a star, and lay at the very bottom of the chest. Then they all came back through the house again till they got to Telemachus, and Menelaus said, "Telemachus, may Jove, the mighty husband of Juno, bring you safely home according to your desire. I will now present you with the finest and most precious piece of plate in all my house. It is a mixing-bowl of pure silver, except the rim, which is inlaid with gold, and it is the work of Vulcan. Phaedimus king of the Sidonians made me a present of it in the course of a visit that I paid him while I was on my return home. I should like to give it to you."

With these words he placed the double cup in the hands of Telemachus, while Megapenthes brought the beautiful mixing-bowl and set it before him. Hard by stood lovely Helen with the robe ready in her hand.

"I too, my son," said she, "have something for you as a keepsake from the hand of Helen; it is for your bride to wear upon her wedding day. Till then, get your dear mother to keep it for you; thus may you go back rejoicing to your own country and to your home."

So saying she gave the robe over to him and he received it gladly. Then Pisistratus put the presents into the chariot, and admired them all as he did so. Presently Menelaus took Telemachus and Pisistratus into the house, and they both of them sat down to table. A maid servant brought them water in a beautiful golden ewer, and poured it into a silver basin for them to wash their hands, and she drew a clean table beside them; an upper servant brought them bread and offered them many good things of what there was in the house. Eteoneus carved the meat and gave them each their portions, while Megapenthes poured out the wine. Then they laid their hands upon the good things that were before them, but as soon as they had had had enough to eat and drink Telemachus and Pisistratus yoked the horses, and took their places in the chariot. They drove out through the inner gateway and under the echoing gatehouse of the outer court, and Menelaus came after them with a golden goblet of wine in his right hand that they might make a drink-offering before they set out. He stood in front of the horses and pledged them, saying, "Farewell to both of you; see that you tell Nestor how I have treated you, for he was as kind to me as any father could be while we Achaeans were fighting before Troy."

"We will be sure, sir," answered Telemachus, "to tell him everything as soon as we see him. I wish I were as certain of finding Ulysses returned when I get back to Ithaca, that I might tell him of the very great kindness you have shown me and of the many beautiful presents I am taking with me."

As he was thus speaking a bird flew on his right hand- an eagle with a great white goose in its talons which it had carried off from the farm yard- and all the men and women were running after it and shouting. It came quite close up to them and flew away on their right hands in front of the horses. When they saw it they were glad, and their hearts took comfort within them, whereon Pisistratus said, "Tell me, Menelaus, has heaven sent this omen for us or for you?"

Menelaus was thinking what would be the most proper answer for him to make, but Helen was too quick for him and said, "I will read this matter as heaven has put it in my heart, and as I doubt not that it will come to pass. The eagle came from the mountain where it was bred and has its nest, and in like manner Ulysses, after having travelled far and suffered much, will return to take his revenge- if indeed he is not back already and hatching mischief for the suitors."

"May Jove so grant it," replied Telemachus; "if it should prove to be so, I will make vows to you as though you were a god, even when I am at home."

As he spoke he lashed his horses and they started off at full speed through the town towards the open country. They swayed the yoke upon their necks and travelled the whole day long till the sun set and darkness was over all the land. Then they reached Pherae, where Diocles lived who was son of Ortilochus, the son of Alpheus. There they passed the night and were treated hospitably. When the child of morning, rosy-fingered Dawn, appeared, they again yoked their horses and their places in the chariot. They drove out through the inner gateway and under the echoing gatehouse of the outer court. Then Pisistratus lashed his horses on and they flew forward nothing loath; ere long they came to Pylos, and then Telemachus said:

"Pisistratus, I hope you will promise to do what I am going to ask you. You know our fathers were old friends before us; moreover, we are both of an age, and this journey has brought us together still more closely; do not, therefore, take me past my ship, but leave me there, for if I go to your father's house he will try to keep me in the warmth of his good will towards me, and I must go home at once."

Pisistratus thought how he should do as he was asked, and in the end he deemed it best to turn his horses towards the ship, and put Menelaus's beautiful presents of gold and raiment in the stern of the vessel. Then he said, "Go on board at once and tell your men to do so also before I can reach home to tell my father. I know how obstinate he is, and am sure he will not let you go; he will come down here to fetch you, and he will not go back without you. But he will be very angry."

With this he drove his goodly steeds back to the city of the Pylians and soon reached his home, but Telemachus called the men together and gave his orders. "Now, my men," said he, "get everything in order on board the ship, and let us set out home."

Thus did he speak, and they went on board even as he had said. But as Telemachus was thus busied, praying also and sacrificing to Minerva in the ship's stern, there came to him a man from a distant country, a seer, who was flying from Argos because he had killed a man. He was descended from Melampus, who used to live in Pylos, the land of sheep; he was rich and owned a great house, but he was driven into exile by the great and powerful king Neleus. Neleus seized his goods and held them for a whole year, during which he was a close prisoner in the house of king Phylacus, and in much distress of mind both on account of the daughter of Neleus and because he was haunted by a great sorrow that dread Erinyes had laid upon him. In the end, however, he escaped with his life, drove the cattle from Phylace to Pylos, avenged the wrong that had been done him, and gave the daughter of Neleus to his brother. Then he left the country and went to Argos, where it was ordained that he should reign over much people. There he married, established himself, and had two famous sons Antiphates and Mantius. Antiphates became father of Oicleus, and Oicleus of Amphiaraus, who was dearly loved both by Jove and by Apollo, but he did not live to old age, for he was killed in Thebes by reason of a woman's gifts. His sons were Alcmaeon and Amphilochus. Mantius, the other son of Melampus, was father to Polypheides and Cleitus. Aurora, throned in gold, carried off Cleitus for his beauty's sake, that he might dwell among the immortals, but Apollo made Polypheides the greatest seer in the whole world now that Amphiaraus was dead. He quarrelled with his father and went to live in Hyperesia, where he remained and prophesied for all men.

His son, Theoclymenus, it was who now came up to Telemachus as he was making drink-offerings and praying in his ship. "Friend'" said he, "now that I find you sacrificing in this place, I beseech you by your sacrifices themselves, and by the god to whom you make them, I pray you also by your own head and by those of your followers, tell me the truth and nothing but the truth. Who and whence are you? Tell me also of your town and parents."

Telemachus said, "I will answer you quite truly. I am from Ithaca, and my father is 'Ulysses, as surely as that he ever lived. But he has come to some miserable end. Therefore I have taken this ship and got my crew together to see if I can hear any news of him, for he has been away a long time."

"I too," answered Theoclymenus, am an exile, for I have killed a man of my own race. He has many brothers and kinsmen in Argos, and they have great power among the Argives. I am flying to escape death at their hands, and am thus doomed to be a wanderer on the face of the earth. I am your suppliant; take me, therefore, on board your ship that they may not kill me, for I know they are in pursuit."

"I will not refuse you," replied Telemachus, "if you wish to join us. Come, therefore, and in Ithaca we will treat you hospitably according to what we have."

On this he received Theoclymenus' spear and laid it down on the deck of the ship. He went on board and sat in the stern, bidding Theoclymenus sit beside him; then the men let go the hawsers. Telemachus told them to catch hold of the ropes, and they made all haste to do so. They set the mast in its socket in the cross plank, raised it and made it fast with the forestays, and they hoisted their white sails with sheets of twisted ox hide. Minerva sent them a fair wind that blew fresh and strong to take the ship on her course as fast as possible. Thus then they passed by Crouni and Chalcis.

Presently the sun set and darkness was over all the land. The vessel made a quick pass sage to Pheae and thence on to Elis, where the Epeans rule. Telemachus then headed her for the flying islands, wondering within himself whether he should escape death or should be taken prisoner.

Meanwhile Ulysses and the swineherd were eating their supper in the hut, and the men supped with them. As soon as they had had to eat and drink, Ulysses began trying to prove the swineherd and see whether he would continue to treat him kindly, and ask him to stay on at the station or pack him off to the city; so he said:

"Eumaeus, and all of you, to-morrow I want to go away and begin begging about the town, so as to be no more trouble to you or to your men. Give me your advice therefore, and let me have a good guide to go with me and show me the way. I will go the round of the city begging as I needs must, to see if any one will give me a drink and a piece of bread. I should like also to go to the house of Ulysses and bring news of her husband to queen Penelope. I could then go about among the suitors and see if out of all their abundance they will give me a dinner. I should soon make them an excellent servant in all sorts of ways. Listen and believe when I tell you that by the blessing of Mercury who gives grace and good name to the works of all men, there is no one living who would make a more handy servant than I should- to put fresh wood on the fire, chop fuel, carve, cook, pour out wine, and do all those services that poor men have to do for their betters."

The swineherd was very much disturbed when he heard this. "Heaven help me," he exclaimed, "what ever can have put such a notion as that into your head? If you go near the suitors you will be undone to a certainty, for their pride and insolence reach the very heavens. They would never think of taking a man like you for a servant. Their servants are all young men, well dressed, wearing good cloaks and shirts, with well looking faces and their hair always tidy, the tables are kept quite clean and are loaded with bread, meat, and wine. Stay where you are, then; you are not in anybody's way; I do not mind your being here, no more do any of the others, and when Telemachus comes home he will give you a shirt and cloak and will send you wherever you want to go."

Ulysses answered, "I hope you may be as dear to the gods as you are to me, for having saved me from going about and getting into trouble; there is nothing worse than being always ways on the tramp; still, when men have once got low down in the world they will go through a great deal on behalf of their miserable bellies. Since however you press me to stay here and await the return of Telemachus, tell about Ulysses' mother, and his father whom he left on the threshold of old age when he set out for Troy. Are they still living or are they already dead and in the house of Hades?"

"I will tell you all about them," replied Eumaeus, "Laertes is still living and prays heaven to let him depart peacefully his own house, for he is terribly distressed about the absence of his son, and also about the death of his wife, which grieved him greatly and aged him more than anything else did. She came to an unhappy end through sorrow for her son: may no friend or neighbour who has dealt kindly by me come to such an end as she did. As long as she was still living, though she was always grieving, I used to like seeing her and asking her how she did, for she brought me up along with her daughter Ctimene, the youngest of her children; we were boy and girl together, and she made little difference between us. When, however, we both grew up, they sent Ctimene to Same and received a splendid dowry for her. As for me, my mistress gave me a good shirt and cloak with a pair of sandals for my feet, and sent me off into the country, but she was just as fond of me as ever. This is all over now. Still it has pleased heaven to prosper my work in the situation which I now hold. I have enough to eat and drink, and can find something for any respectable stranger who comes here; but there is no getting a kind word or deed out of my mistress, for the house has fallen into the hands of wicked people. Servants want sometimes to see their mistress and have a talk with her; they like to have something to eat and drink at the house, and something too to take back with them into the country. This is what will keep servants in a good humour."

Ulysses answered, "Then you must have been a very little fellow, Eumaeus, when you were taken so far away from your home and parents. Tell me, and tell me true, was the city in which your father and mother lived sacked and pillaged, or did some enemies carry you off when you were alone tending sheep or cattle, ship you off here, and sell you for whatever your master gave them?"

"Stranger," replied Eumaeus, "as regards your question: sit still, make yourself comfortable, drink your wine, and listen to me. The nights are now at their longest; there is plenty of time both for sleeping and sitting up talking together; you ought not to go to bed till bed time, too much sleep is as bad as too little; if any one of the others wishes to go to bed let him leave us and do so; he can then take my master's pigs out when he has done breakfast in the morning. We two will sit here eating and drinking in the hut, and telling one another stories about our misfortunes; for when a man has suffered much, and been buffeted about in the world, he takes pleasure in recalling the memory of sorrows that have long gone by. As regards your question, then, my tale is as follows:

"You may have heard of an island called Syra that lies over above Ortygia, where the land begins to turn round and look in another direction. It is not very thickly peopled, but the soil is good, with much pasture fit for cattle and sheep, and it abounds with wine and wheat. Dearth never comes there, nor are the people plagued by any sickness, but when they grow old Apollo comes with Diana and kills them with his painless shafts. It contains two communities, and the whole country is divided between these two. My father Ctesius son of Ormenus, a man comparable to the gods, reigned over both.

"Now to this place there came some cunning traders from Phoenicia (for the Phoenicians are great mariners) in a ship which they had freighted with gewgaws of all kinds. There happened to be a Phoenician woman in my father's house, very tall and comely, and an excellent servant; these scoundrels got hold of her one day when she was washing near their ship, seduced her, and cajoled her in ways that no woman can resist, no matter how good she may be by nature. The man who had seduced her asked her who she was and where she came from, and on this she told him her father's name. 'I come from Sidon,' said she, 'and am daughter to Arybas, a man rolling in wealth. One day as I was coming into the town from the country some Taphian pirates seized me and took me here over the sea, where they sold me to the man who owns this house, and he gave them their price for me.'

"The man who had seduced her then said, 'Would you like to come along with us to see the house of your parents and your parents themselves? They are both alive and are said to be well off.'

"'I will do so gladly,' answered she, 'if you men will first swear me a solemn oath that you will do me no harm by the way.'

"They all swore as she told them, and when they had completed their oath the woman said, 'Hush; and if any of your men meets me in the street or at the well, do not let him speak to me, for fear some one should go and tell my master, in which case he would suspect something. He would put me in prison, and would have all of you murdered; keep your own counsel therefore; buy your merchandise as fast as you can, and send me word when you have done loading. I will bring as much gold as I can lay my hands on, and there is something else also that I can do towards paying my fare. I am nurse to the son of the good man of the house, a funny little fellow just able to run about. I will carry him off in your ship, and you will get a great deal of money for him if you take him and sell him in foreign parts.'

"On this she went back to the house. The Phoenicians stayed a whole year till they had loaded their ship with much precious merchandise, and then, when they had got freight enough, they sent to tell the woman. Their messenger, a very cunning fellow, came to my father's house bringing a necklace of gold with amber beads strung among it; and while my mother and the servants had it in their hands admiring it and bargaining about it, he made a sign quietly to the woman and then went back to the ship, whereon she took me by the hand and led me out of the house. In the fore part of the house she saw the tables set with the cups of guests who had been feasting with my father, as being in attendance on him; these were now all gone to a meeting of the public assembly, so she snatched up three cups and carried them off in the bosom of her dress, while I followed her, for I knew no better. The sun was now set, and darkness was over all the land, so we hurried on as fast as we could till we reached the harbour, where the Phoenician ship was lying. When they had got on board they sailed their ways over the sea, taking us with them, and Jove sent then a fair wind; six days did we sail both night and day, but on the seventh day Diana struck the woman and she fell heavily down into the ship's hold as though she were a sea gull alighting on the water; so they threw her overboard to the seals and fishes, and I was left all sorrowful and alone.

Presently the winds and waves took the ship to Ithaca, where Laertes gave sundry of his chattels for me, and thus it was that ever I came to set eyes upon this country."

Ulysses answered, "Eumaeus, I have heard the story of your misfortunes with the most lively interest and pity, but Jove has given you good as well as evil, for in spite of everything you have a good master, who sees that you always have enough to eat and drink; and you lead a good life, whereas I am still going about begging my way from city to city."

Thus did they converse, and they had only a very little time left for sleep, for it was soon daybreak. In the meantime Telemachus and his crew were nearing land, so they loosed the sails, took down the mast, and rowed the ship into the harbour. They cast out their mooring stones and made fast the hawsers; they then got out upon the sea shore, mixed their wine, and got dinner ready. As soon as they had had enough to eat and drink Telemachus said, "Take the ship on to the town, but leave me here, for I want to look after the herdsmen on one of my farms. In the evening, when I have seen all I want, I will come down to the city, and to-morrow morning in return for your trouble I will give you all a good dinner with meat and wine."

Then Theoclymenus said, 'And what, my dear young friend, is to become of me? To whose house, among all your chief men, am I to repair? or shall I go straight to your own house and to your mother?"

"At any other time," replied Telemachus, "I should have bidden you go to my own house, for you would find no want of hospitality; at the present moment, however, you would not be comfortable there, for I shall be away, and my mother will not see you; she does not often show herself even to the suitors, but sits at her loom weaving in an upper chamber, out of their way; but I can tell you a man whose house you can go to- I mean Eurymachus the son of Polybus, who is held in the highest estimation by every one in Ithaca. He is much the best man and the most persistent wooer, of all those who are paying court to my mother and trying to take Ulysses' place. Jove, however, in heaven alone knows whether or no they will come to a bad end before the marriage takes place."

As he was speaking a bird flew by upon his right hand- a hawk, Apollo's messenger. It held a dove in its talons, and the feathers, as it tore them off, fell to the ground midway between Telemachus and the ship. On this Theoclymenus called him apart and caught him by the hand. "Telemachus," said he, "that bird did not fly on your right hand without having been sent there by some god. As soon as I saw it I knew it was an omen; it means that you will remain powerful and that there will be no house in Ithaca more royal than your own."

"I wish it may prove so," answered Telemachus. "If it does, I will show you so much good will and give you so many presents that all who meet you will congratulate you."

Then he said to his friend Piraeus, "Piraeus, son of Clytius, you have throughout shown yourself the most willing to serve me of all those who have accompanied me to Pylos; I wish you would take this stranger to your own house and entertain him hospitably till I can come for him."

And Piraeus answered, "Telemachus, you may stay away as long as you please, but I will look after him for you, and he shall find no lack of hospitality."

As he spoke he went on board, and bade the others do so also and loose the hawsers, so they took their places in the ship. But Telemachus bound on his sandals, and took a long and doughty spear with a head of sharpened bronze from the deck of the ship. Then they loosed the hawsers, thrust the ship off from land, and made on towards the city as they had been told to do, while Telemachus strode on as fast as he could, till he reached the homestead where his countless herds of swine were feeding, and where dwelt the excellent swineherd, who was so devoted a servant to his master.

Book XV

But Minerva went to the fair city of Lacedaemon to tell Ulysses' son that he was to return at once. She found him and Pisistratus sleeping in the forecourt of Menelaus's house; Pisistratus was fast asleep, but Telemachus could get no rest all night for thinking of his unhappy father, so Minerva went close up to him and said:

"Telemachus, you should not remain so far away from home any longer, nor leave your property with such dangerous people in your house; they will eat up everything you have among them, and you will have been on a fool's errand. Ask Menelaus to send you home at once if you wish to find your excellent mother still there when you get back. Her father and brothers are already urging her to marry Eurymachus, who has given her more than any of the others, and has been greatly increasing his wedding presents. I hope nothing valuable may have been taken from the house in spite of you, but you know what women are- they always want to do the best they can for the man who marries them, and never give another thought to the children of their first husband, nor to their father either when he is dead and done with. Go home, therefore, and put everything in charge of the most respectable woman servant that you have, until it shall please heaven to send you a wife of your own. Let me tell you also of another matter which you had better attend to. The chief men among the suitors are lying in wait for you in the Strait between Ithaca and Samos, and they mean to kill you before you can reach home. I do not much think they will succeed; it is more likely that some of those who are now eating up your property will find a grave themselves. Sail night and day, and keep your ship well away from the islands; the god who watches over you and protects you will send you a fair wind. As soon as you get to Ithaca send your ship and men on to the town, but yourself go straight to the swineherd who has charge your pigs; he is well disposed towards you, stay with him, therefore, for the night, and then send him to Penelope to tell her that you have got back safe from Pylos."

Then she went back to Olympus; but Telemachus stirred Pisistratus with his heel to rouse him, and said, "Wake up Pisistratus, and yoke the horses to the chariot, for we must set off home."

But Pisistratus said, "No matter what hurry we are in we cannot drive in the dark. It will be morning soon; wait till Menelaus has brought his presents and put them in the chariot for us; and let him say good-bye to us in the usual way. So long as he lives a guest should never forget a host who has shown him kindness."

As he spoke day began to break, and Menelaus, who had already risen, leaving Helen in bed, came towards them. When Telemachus saw him he put on his shirt as fast as he could, threw a great cloak over his shoulders, and went out to meet him. "Menelaus," said he, "let me go back now to my own country, for I want to get home."

And Menelaus answered, "Telemachus, if you insist on going I will not detain you. not like to see a host either too fond of his guest or too rude to him. Moderation is best in all things, and not letting a man go when he wants to do so is as bad as telling him to go if he would like to stay. One should treat a guest well as long as he is in the house and speed him when he wants to leave it. Wait, then, till I can get your beautiful presents into your chariot, and till you have yourself seen them. I will tell the women to prepare a sufficient dinner for you of what there may be in the house; it will be at once more proper and cheaper for you to get your dinner before setting out on such a long journey. If, moreover, you have a fancy for making a tour in Hellas or in the Peloponnese, I will yoke my horses, and will conduct you myself through all our principal cities. No one will send us away empty handed; every one will give us something- a bronze tripod, a couple of mules, or a gold cup."

"Menelaus," replied Telemachus, "I want to go home at once, for when I came away I left my property without protection, and fear that while looking for my father I shall come to ruin myself, or find that something valuable has been stolen during my absence."

When Menelaus heard this he immediately told his wife and servants to prepare a sufficient dinner from what there might be in the house. At this moment Eteoneus joined him, for he lived close by and had just got up; so Menelaus told him to light the fire and cook some meat, which he at once did. Then Menelaus went down into his fragrant store room, not alone, but Helen went too, with Megapenthes. When he reached the place where the treasures of his house were kept, he selected a double cup, and told his son Megapenthes to bring also a silver mixing-bowl. Meanwhile Helen went to the chest where she kept the lovely dresses which she had made with her own hands, and took out one that was largest and most beautifully enriched with embroidery; it glittered like a star, and lay at the very bottom of the chest. Then they all came back through the house again till they got to Telemachus, and Menelaus said, "Telemachus, may Jove, the mighty husband of Juno, bring you safely home according to your desire. I will now present you with the finest and most precious piece of plate in all my house. It is a mixing-bowl of pure silver, except the rim, which is inlaid with gold, and it is the work of Vulcan. Phaedimus king of the Sidonians made me a present of it in the course of a visit that I paid him while I was on my return home. I should like to give it to you."

With these words he placed the double cup in the hands of Telemachus, while Megapenthes brought the beautiful mixing-bowl and set it before him. Hard by stood lovely Helen with the robe ready in her hand.

"I too, my son," said she, "have something for you as a keepsake from the hand of Helen; it is for your bride to wear upon her wedding day. Till then, get your dear mother to keep it for you; thus may you go back rejoicing to your own country and to your home."

So saying she gave the robe over to him and he received it gladly. Then Pisistratus put the presents into the chariot, and admired them all as he did so. Presently Menelaus took Telemachus and Pisistratus into the house, and they both of them sat down to table. A maid servant brought them water in a beautiful golden ewer, and poured it into a silver basin for them to wash their hands, and she drew a clean table beside them; an upper servant brought them bread and offered them many good things of what there was in the house. Eteoneus carved the meat and gave them each their portions, while Megapenthes poured out the wine. Then they laid their hands upon the good things that were before them, but as soon as they had had had enough to eat and drink Telemachus and Pisistratus yoked the horses, and took their places in the chariot. They drove out through the inner gateway and under the echoing gatehouse of the outer court, and Menelaus came after them with a golden goblet of wine in his right hand that they might make a drink-offering before they set out. He stood in front of the horses and pledged them, saying, "Farewell to both of you; see that you tell Nestor how I have treated you, for he was as kind to me as any father could be while we Achaeans were fighting before Troy."

"We will be sure, sir," answered Telemachus, "to tell him everything as soon as we see him. I wish I were as certain of finding Ulysses returned when I get back to Ithaca, that I might tell him of the very great kindness you have shown me and of the many beautiful presents I am taking with me."

As he was thus speaking a bird flew on his right hand- an eagle with a great white goose in its talons which it had carried off from the farm yard- and all the men and women were running after it and shouting. It came quite close up to them and flew away on their right hands in front of the horses. When they saw it they were glad, and their hearts took comfort within them, whereon Pisistratus said, "Tell me, Menelaus, has heaven sent this omen for us or for you?"

Menelaus was thinking what would be the most proper answer for him to make, but Helen was too quick for him and said, "I will read this matter as heaven has put it in my heart, and as I doubt not that it will come to pass. The eagle came from the mountain where it was bred and has its nest, and in like manner Ulysses, after having travelled far and suffered much, will return to take his revenge- if indeed he is not back already and hatching mischief for the suitors."

"May Jove so grant it," replied Telemachus; "if it should prove to be so, I will make vows to you as though you were a god, even when I am at home."

As he spoke he lashed his horses and they started off at full speed through the town towards the open country. They swayed the yoke upon their necks and travelled the whole day long till the sun set and darkness was over all the land. Then they reached Pherae, where Diocles lived who was son of Ortilochus, the son of Alpheus. There they passed the night and were treated hospitably. When the child of morning, rosy-fingered Dawn, appeared, they again yoked their horses and their places in the chariot. They drove out through the inner gateway and under the echoing gatehouse of the outer court. Then Pisistratus lashed his horses on and they flew forward nothing loath; ere long they came to Pylos, and then Telemachus said:

"Pisistratus, I hope you will promise to do what I am going to ask you. You know our fathers were old friends before us; moreover, we are both of an age, and this journey has brought us together still more closely; do not, therefore, take me past my ship, but leave me there, for if I go to your father's house he will try to keep me in the warmth of his good will towards me, and I must go home at once."

Pisistratus thought how he should do as he was asked, and in the end he deemed it best to turn his horses towards the ship, and put Menelaus's beautiful presents of gold and raiment in the stern of the vessel. Then he said, "Go on board at once and tell your men to do so also before I can reach home to tell my father. I know how obstinate he is, and am sure he will not let you go; he will come down here to fetch you, and he will not go back without you. But he will be very angry."

With this he drove his goodly steeds back to the city of the Pylians and soon reached his home, but Telemachus called the men together and gave his orders. "Now, my men," said he, "get everything in order on board the ship, and let us set out home."

Thus did he speak, and they went on board even as he had said. But as Telemachus was thus busied, praying also and sacrificing to Minerva in the ship's stern, there came to him a man from a distant country, a seer, who was flying from Argos because he had killed a man. He was descended from Melampus, who used to live in Pylos, the land of sheep; he was rich and owned a great house, but he was driven into exile by the great and powerful king Neleus. Neleus seized his goods and held them for a whole year, during which he was a close prisoner in the house of king Phylacus, and in much distress of mind both on account of the daughter of Neleus and because he was haunted by a great sorrow that dread Erinyes had laid upon him. In the end, however, he escaped with his life, drove the cattle from Phylace to Pylos, avenged the wrong that had been done him, and gave the daughter of Neleus to his brother. Then he left the country and went to Argos, where it was ordained that he should reign over much people. There he married, established himself, and had two famous sons Antiphates and Mantius. Antiphates became father of Oicleus, and Oicleus of Amphiaraus, who was dearly loved both by Jove and by Apollo, but he did not live to old age, for he was killed in Thebes by reason of a woman's gifts. His sons were Alcmaeon and Amphilochus. Mantius, the other son of Melampus, was father to Polypheides and Cleitus. Aurora, throned in gold, carried off Cleitus for his beauty's sake, that he might dwell among the immortals, but Apollo made Polypheides the greatest seer in the whole world now that Amphiaraus was dead. He quarrelled with his father and went to live in Hyperesia, where he remained and prophesied for all men.

His son, Theoclymenus, it was who now came up to Telemachus as he was making drink-offerings and praying in his ship. "Friend'" said he, "now that I find you sacrificing in this place, I beseech you by your sacrifices themselves, and by the god to whom you make them, I pray you also by your own head and by those of your followers, tell me the truth and nothing but the truth. Who and whence are you? Tell me also of your town and parents."

Telemachus said, "I will answer you quite truly. I am from Ithaca, and my father is 'Ulysses, as surely as that he ever lived. But he has come to some miserable end. Therefore I have taken this ship and got my crew together to see if I can hear any news of him, for he has been away a long time."

"I too," answered Theoclymenus, am an exile, for I have killed a man of my own race. He has many brothers and kinsmen in Argos, and they have great power among the Argives. I am flying to escape death at their hands, and am thus doomed to be a wanderer on the face of the earth. I am your suppliant; take me, therefore, on board your ship that they may not kill me, for I know they are in pursuit."

"I will not refuse you," replied Telemachus, "if you wish to join us. Come, therefore, and in Ithaca we will treat you hospitably according to what we have."

On this he received Theoclymenus' spear and laid it down on the deck of the ship. He went on board and sat in the stern, bidding Theoclymenus sit beside him; then the men let go the hawsers. Telemachus told them to catch hold of the ropes, and they made all haste to do so. They set the mast in its socket in the cross plank, raised it and made it fast with the forestays, and they hoisted their white sails with sheets of twisted ox hide. Minerva sent them a fair wind that blew fresh and strong to take the ship on her course as fast as possible. Thus then they passed by Crouni and Chalcis.

Presently the sun set and darkness was over all the land. The vessel made a quick pass sage to Pheae and thence on to Elis, where the Epeans rule. Telemachus then headed her for the flying islands, wondering within himself whether he should escape death or should be taken prisoner.

Meanwhile Ulysses and the swineherd were eating their supper in the hut, and the men supped with them. As soon as they had had to eat and drink, Ulysses began trying to prove the swineherd and see whether he would continue to treat him kindly, and ask him to stay on at the station or pack him off to the city; so he said:

"Eumaeus, and all of you, to-morrow I want to go away and begin begging about the town, so as to be no more trouble to you or to your men. Give me your advice therefore, and let me have a good guide to go with me and show me the way. I will go the round of the city begging as I needs must, to see if any one will give me a drink and a piece of bread. I should like also to go to the house of Ulysses and bring news of her husband to queen Penelope. I could then go about among the suitors and see if out of all their abundance they will give me a dinner. I should soon make them an excellent servant in all sorts of ways. Listen and believe when I tell you that by the blessing of Mercury who gives grace and good name to the works of all men, there is no one living who would make a more handy servant than I should- to put fresh wood on the fire, chop fuel, carve, cook, pour out wine, and do all those services that poor men have to do for their betters."

The swineherd was very much disturbed when he heard this. "Heaven help me," he exclaimed, "what ever can have put such a notion as that into your head? If you go near the suitors you will be undone to a certainty, for their pride and insolence reach the very heavens. They would never think of taking a man like you for a servant. Their servants are all young men, well dressed, wearing good cloaks and shirts, with well looking faces and their hair always tidy, the tables are kept quite clean and are loaded with bread, meat, and wine. Stay where you are, then; you are not in anybody's way; I do not mind your being here, no more do any of the others, and when Telemachus comes home he will give you a shirt and cloak and will send you wherever you want to go."

Ulysses answered, "I hope you may be as dear to the gods as you are to me, for having saved me from going about and getting into trouble; there is nothing worse than being always ways on the tramp; still, when men have once got low down in the world they will go through a great deal on behalf of their miserable bellies. Since however you press me to stay here and await the return of Telemachus, tell about Ulysses' mother, and his father whom he left on the threshold of old age when he set out for Troy. Are they still living or are they already dead and in the house of Hades?"

"I will tell you all about them," replied Eumaeus, "Laertes is still living and prays heaven to let him depart peacefully his own house, for he is terribly distressed about the absence of his son, and also about the death of his wife, which grieved him greatly and aged him more than anything else did. She came to an unhappy end through sorrow for her son: may no friend or neighbour who has dealt kindly by me come to such an end as she did. As long as she was still living, though she was always grieving, I used to like seeing her and asking her how she did, for she brought me up along with her daughter Ctimene, the youngest of her children; we were boy and girl together, and she made little difference between us. When, however, we both grew up, they sent Ctimene to Same and received a splendid dowry for her. As for me, my mistress gave me a good shirt and cloak with a pair of sandals for my feet, and sent me off into the country, but she was just as fond of me as ever. This is all over now. Still it has pleased heaven to prosper my work in the situation which I now hold. I have enough to eat and drink, and can find something for any respectable stranger who comes here; but there is no getting a kind word or deed out of my mistress, for the house has fallen into the hands of wicked people. Servants want sometimes to see their mistress and have a talk with her; they like to have something to eat and drink at the house, and something too to take back with them into the country. This is what will keep servants in a good humour."

Ulysses answered, "Then you must have been a very little fellow, Eumaeus, when you were taken so far away from your home and parents. Tell me, and tell me true, was the city in which your father and mother lived sacked and pillaged, or did some enemies carry you off when you were alone tending sheep or cattle, ship you off here, and sell you for whatever your master gave them?"

"Stranger," replied Eumaeus, "as regards your question: sit still, make yourself comfortable, drink your wine, and listen to me. The nights are now at their longest; there is plenty of time both for sleeping and sitting up talking together; you ought not to go to bed till bed time, too much sleep is as bad as too little; if any one of the others wishes to go to bed let him leave us and do so; he can then take my master's pigs out when he has done breakfast in the morning. We two will sit here eating and drinking in the hut, and telling one another stories about our misfortunes; for when a man has suffered much, and been buffeted about in the world, he takes pleasure in recalling the memory of sorrows that have long gone by. As regards your question, then, my tale is as follows:

"You may have heard of an island called Syra that lies over above Ortygia, where the land begins to turn round and look in another direction. It is not very thickly peopled, but the soil is good, with much pasture fit for cattle and sheep, and it abounds with wine and wheat. Dearth never comes there, nor are the people plagued by any sickness, but when they grow old Apollo comes with Diana and kills them with his painless shafts. It contains two communities, and the whole country is divided between these two. My father Ctesius son of Ormenus, a man comparable to the gods, reigned over both.

"Now to this place there came some cunning traders from Phoenicia (for the Phoenicians are great mariners) in a ship which they had freighted with gewgaws of all kinds. There happened to be a Phoenician woman in my father's house, very tall and comely, and an excellent servant; these scoundrels got hold of her one day when she was washing near their ship, seduced her, and cajoled her in ways that no woman can resist, no matter how good she may be by nature. The man who had seduced her asked her who she was and where she came from, and on this she told him her father's name. 'I come from Sidon,' said she, 'and am daughter to Arybas, a man rolling in wealth. One day as I was coming into the town from the country some Taphian pirates seized me and took me here over the sea, where they sold me to the man who owns this house, and he gave them their price for me.'

"The man who had seduced her then said, 'Would you like to come along with us to see the house of your parents and your parents themselves? They are both alive and are said to be well off.'

"'I will do so gladly,' answered she, 'if you men will first swear me a solemn oath that you will do me no harm by the way.'

"They all swore as she told them, and when they had completed their oath the woman said, 'Hush; and if any of your men meets me in the street or at the well, do not let him speak to me, for fear some one should go and tell my master, in which case he would suspect something. He would put me in prison, and would have all of you murdered; keep your own counsel therefore; buy your merchandise as fast as you can, and send me word when you have done loading. I will bring as much gold as I can lay my hands on, and there is something else also that I can do towards paying my fare. I am nurse to the son of the good man of the house, a funny little fellow just able to run about. I will carry him off in your ship, and you will get a great deal of money for him if you take him and sell him in foreign parts.'

"On this she went back to the house. The Phoenicians stayed a whole year till they had loaded their ship with much precious merchandise, and then, when they had got freight enough, they sent to tell the woman. Their messenger, a very cunning fellow, came to my father's house bringing a necklace of gold with amber beads strung among it; and while my mother and the servants had it in their hands admiring it and bargaining about it, he made a sign quietly to the woman and then went back to the ship, whereon she took me by the hand and led me out of the house. In the fore part of the house she saw the tables set with the cups of guests who had been feasting with my father, as being in attendance on him; these were now all gone to a meeting of the public assembly, so she snatched up three cups and carried them off in the bosom of her dress, while I followed her, for I knew no better. The sun was now set, and darkness was over all the land, so we hurried on as fast as we could till we reached the harbour, where the Phoenician ship was lying. When they had got on board they sailed their ways over the sea, taking us with them, and Jove sent then a fair wind; six days did we sail both night and day, but on the seventh day Diana struck the woman and she fell heavily down into the ship's hold as though she were a sea gull alighting on the water; so they threw her overboard to the seals and fishes, and I was left all sorrowful and alone. Presently the winds and waves took the ship to Ithaca, where Laertes gave sundry of his chattels for me, and thus it was that ever I came to set eyes upon this country."

Ulysses answered, "Eumaeus, I have heard the story of your misfortunes with the most lively interest and pity, but Jove has given you good as well as evil, for in spite of everything you have a good master, who sees that you always have enough to eat and drink; and you lead a good life, whereas I am still going about begging my way from city to city."

Thus did they converse, and they had only a very little time left for sleep, for it was soon daybreak. In the meantime Telemachus and his crew were nearing land, so they loosed the sails, took down the mast, and rowed the ship into the harbour. They cast out their mooring stones and made fast the hawsers; they then got out upon the sea shore, mixed their wine, and got dinner ready. As soon as they had had enough to eat and drink Telemachus said, "Take the ship on to the town, but leave me here, for I want to look after the herdsmen on one of my farms. In the evening, when I have seen all I want, I will come down to the city, and to-morrow morning in return for your trouble I will give you all a good dinner with meat and wine."

Then Theoclymenus said, 'And what, my dear young friend, is to become of me? To whose house, among all your chief men, am I to repair? or shall I go straight to your own house and to your mother?"

"At any other time," replied Telemachus, "I should have bidden you go to my own house, for you would find no want of hospitality; at the present moment, however, you would not be comfortable there, for I shall be away, and my mother will not see you; she does not often show herself even to the suitors, but sits at her loom weaving in an upper chamber, out of their way; but I can tell you a man whose house you can go to- I mean Eurymachus the son of Polybus, who is held in the highest estimation by every one in Ithaca. He is much the best man and the most persistent wooer, of all those who are paying court to my mother and trying to take Ulysses' place. Jove, however, in heaven alone knows whether or no they will come to a bad end before the marriage takes place."

As he was speaking a bird flew by upon his right hand- a hawk, Apollo's messenger. It held a dove in its talons, and the feathers, as it tore them off, fell to the ground midway between Telemachus and the ship. On this Theoclymenus called him apart and caught him by the hand. "Telemachus," said he, "that bird did not fly on your right hand without having been sent there by some god. As soon as I saw it I knew it was an omen; it means that you will remain powerful and that there will be no house in Ithaca more royal than your own."

"I wish it may prove so," answered Telemachus. "If it does, I will show you so much good will and give you so many presents that all who meet you will congratulate you."

Then he said to his friend Piraeus, "Piraeus, son of Clytius, you have throughout shown yourself the most willing to serve me of all those who have accompanied me to Pylos; I wish you would take this stranger to your own house and entertain him hospitably till I can come for him."

And Piraeus answered, "Telemachus, you may stay away as long as you please, but I will look after him for you, and he shall find no lack of hospitality."

As he spoke he went on board, and bade the others do so also and loose the hawsers, so they took their places in the ship. But Telemachus bound on his sandals, and took a long and doughty spear with a head of sharpened bronze from the deck of the ship. Then they loosed the hawsers, thrust the ship off from land, and made on towards the city as they had been told to do, while Telemachus strode on as fast as he could, till he reached the homestead where his countless herds of swine were feeding, and where dwelt the excellent swineherd, who was so devoted a servant to his master

Book XVI

Meanwhile Ulysses and the swineherd had lit a fire in the hut and were were getting breakfast ready at daybreak for they had sent the men out with the pigs. When Telemachus came up, the dogs did not bark, but fawned upon him, so Ulysses, hearing the sound of feet and noticing that the dogs did not bark, said to Eumaeus:

"Eumaeus, I hear footsteps; I suppose one of your men or some one of your acquaintance is coming here, for the dogs are fawning urn him and not barking."

The words were hardly out of his mouth before his son stood at the door. Eumaeus sprang to his feet, and the bowls in which he was mixing wine fell from his hands, as he made towards his master. He kissed his head and both his beautiful eyes, and wept for joy. A father could not be more delighted at the return of an only son, the child of his old age, after ten years' absence in a foreign country and after having gone through much hardship. He embraced him, kissed him all over as though he had come back from the dead, and spoke fondly to him saying:

"So you are come, Telemachus, light of my eyes that you are. When I heard you had gone to Pylos I made sure I was never going to see you any more. Come in, my dear child, and sit down, that I may have a good look at you now you are home again; it is not very often you come into the country to see us herdsmen; you stick pretty close to the town generally. I suppose you think it better to keep an eye on what the suitors are doing."

"So be it, old friend," answered Telemachus, "but I am come now because I want to see you, and to learn whether my mother is still at her old home or whether some one else has married her, so that the bed of Ulysses is without bedding and covered with cobwebs."

"She is still at the house," replied Eumaeus, "grieving and breaking her heart, and doing nothing but weep, both night and day continually."

As spoke he took Telemachus' spear, whereon he crossed the stone threshold and came inside. Ulysses rose from his seat to give him place as he entered, but Telemachus checked him; "Sit down, stranger." said he, "I can easily find another seat, and there is one here who will lay it for me."

Ulysses went back to his own place, and Eumaeus strewed some green brushwood on the floor and threw a sheepskin on top of it for Telemachus to sit upon. Then the swineherd brought them platters of cold meat, the remains from what they had eaten the day before, and he filled the bread baskets with bread as fast as he could. He mixed wine also in bowls of ivy-wood, and took his seat facing Ulysses. Then they laid their hands on the good things that were before them, and as soon as they had had enough to eat and drink Telemachus said to Eumaeus, "Old friend, where does this stranger come from? How did his crew bring him to Ithaca, and who were they?-for assuredly he did not come here by land"'

To this you answered, O swineherd Eumaeus, "My son, I will tell you the real truth. He says he is a Cretan, and that he has been a great traveller. At this moment he is running away from a Thesprotian ship, and has refuge at my station, so I will put him into your hands. Do whatever you like with him, only remember that he is your suppliant."

"I am very much distressed," said Telemachus, "by what you have just told me. How can I take this stranger into my house? I am as yet young, and am not strong enough to hold my own if any man attacks me. My mother cannot make up her mind whether to stay where she is and look after the house out of respect for public opinion and the memory of her husband, or whether the time is now come for her to take the best man of those who are wooing her, and the one who will make her the most advantageous offer; still, as the stranger has come to your station I will find him a cloak and shirt of good wear, with a sword and sandals, and will send him wherever he wants to go. Or if you like you can keep him here at the station, and I will send him clothes and food that he may be no burden on you and on your men; but I will not have him go near the suitors, for they are very insolent, and are sure to ill-treat him in a way that would greatly grieve me; no matter how valiant a man may be he can do nothing against numbers, for they will be too strong for him."

Then Ulysses said, "Sir, it is right that I should say something myself. I am much shocked about what you have said about the insolent way in which the suitors are behaving in despite of such a man as you are. Tell me, do you submit to such treatment tamely, or has some god set your people against you? May you not complain of your brothers- for it is to these that a man may look for support, however great his quarrel may be? I wish I were as young as you are and in my present mind; if I were son to Ulysses, or, indeed, Ulysses himself, I would rather some one came and cut my head off, but I would go to the house and be the bane of every one of these men. If they were too many for me- I being single-handed- I would rather die fighting in my own house than see such disgraceful sights day after day, strangers grossly maltreated, and men dragging the women servants about the house in an unseemly way, wine drawn recklessly, and bread wasted all to no purpose for an end that shall never be accomplished."

And Telemachus answered, "I will tell you truly everything. There is no emnity between me and my people, nor can I complain of brothers, to whom a man may look for support however great his quarrel may be. Jove has made us a race of only sons. Laertes was the only son of Arceisius, and Ulysses only son of Laertes. I am myself the only son of Ulysses who left me behind him when he went away, so that I have never been of any use to him. Hence it comes that my house is in the hands of numberless marauders; for the chiefs from all the neighbouring islands, Dulichium, Same, Zacynthus, as also all the principal men of Ithaca itself, are eating up my house under the pretext of paying court to my mother, who will neither say point blank that she will not marry, nor yet bring matters to an end, so they are making havoc of my estate, and before long will do so with myself into the bargain. The issue, however, rests with heaven. But do you, old friend Eumaeus, go at once and tell Penelope that I am safe and have returned from Pylos. Tell it to herself alone, and then come back here without letting any one else know, for there are many who are plotting mischief against me."

"I understand and heed you," replied Eumaeus; "you need instruct me no further, only I am going that way say whether I had not better let poor Laertes know that you are returned. He used to superintend the work on his farm in spite of his bitter sorrow about Ulysses, and he would eat and drink at will along with his servants; but they tell me that from the day on which you set out for Pylos he has neither eaten nor drunk as he ought to do, nor does he look after his farm, but sits weeping and wasting the flesh from off his bones."

"More's the pity," answered Telemachus, "I am sorry for him, but we must leave him to himself just now. If people could have everything their own way, the first thing I should choose would be the return of my father; but go, and give your message; then make haste back again, and do not turn out of your way to tell Laertes. Tell my mother to send one of her women secretly with the news at once, and let him hear it from her."

Thus did he urge the swineherd; Eumaeus, therefore, took his sandals, bound them to his feet, and started for the town. Minerva watched him well off the station, and then came up to it in the form of a woman- fair, stately, and wise. She stood against the side of the entry, and revealed herself to Ulysses, but Telemachus could not see her, and knew not that she was there, for the gods do not let themselves be seen by everybody. Ulysses saw her, and so did the dogs, for they did not bark, but went scared and whining off to the other side of the yards. She nodded her head and motioned to Ulysses with her eyebrows; whereon he left the hut and stood before her outside the main wall of the yards. Then she said to him:

"Ulysses, noble son of Laertes, it is now time for you to tell your son: do not keep him in the dark any longer, but lay your plans for the destruction of the suitors, and then make for the town. I will not be long in joining you, for I too am eager for the fray."

As she spoke she touched him with her golden wand. First she threw a fair clean shirt and cloak about his shoulders; then she made him younger and of more imposing presence; she gave him back his colour, filled out his cheeks, and let his beard become dark again. Then she went away and Ulysses came back inside the hut. His son was astounded when he saw him, and turned his eyes away for fear he might be looking upon a god.

"Stranger," said he, "how suddenly you have changed from what you were a moment or two ago. You are dressed differently and your colour is not the same. Are you some one or other of the gods that live in heaven? If so, be propitious to me till I can make you due sacrifice and offerings of wrought gold. Have mercy upon me."

And Ulysses said, "I am no god, why should you take me for one? I am your father, on whose account you grieve and suffer so much at the hands of lawless men."

As he spoke he kissed his son, and a tear fell from his cheek on to the ground, for he had restrained all tears till now. but Telemachus could not yet believe that it was his father, and said:

"You are not my father, but some god is flattering me with vain hopes that I may grieve the more hereafter; no mortal man could of himself contrive to do as you have been doing, and make yourself old and young at a moment's notice, unless a god were with him. A second ago you were old and all in rags, and now you are like some god come down from heaven."

Ulysses answered, "Telemachus, you ought not to be so immeasurably astonished at my being really here. There is no other Ulysses who will come hereafter. Such as I am, it is I, who after long wandering and much hardship have got home in the twentieth year to my own country. What you wonder at is the work of the redoubtable goddess Minerva, who does with me whatever she will, for she can do what she pleases. At one moment she makes me like a beggar, and the next I am a young man with good clothes on my back; it is an easy matter for the gods who live in heaven to make any man look either rich or poor."

As he spoke he sat down, and Telemachus threw his arms about his father and wept. They were both so much moved that they cried aloud like eagles or vultures with crooked talons that have been robbed of their half fledged young by peasants. Thus piteously did they weep, and the sun would have gone down upon their mourning if Telemachus had not suddenly said, "In what ship, my dear father, did your crew bring you to Ithaca? Of what nation did they declare themselves to be- for you cannot have come by land?"

"I will tell you the truth, my son," replied Ulysses. "It was the Phaeacians who brought me here. They are great sailors, and are in the habit of giving escorts to any one who reaches their coasts. They took me over the sea while I was fast asleep, and landed me in Ithaca, after giving me many presents in bronze, gold, and raiment. These things by heaven's mercy are lying concealed in a cave, and I am now come here on the suggestion of Minerva that we may consult about killing our enemies. First, therefore, give me a list of the suitors, with their number, that I may learn who, and how many, they are. I can then turn the matter over in my mind, and see whether we two can fight the whole body of them ourselves, or whether we must find others to help us."

To this Telemachus answered, "Father, I have always heard of your renown both in the field and in council, but the task you talk of is a very great one: I am awed at the mere thought of it; two men cannot stand against many and brave ones. There are not ten suitors only, nor twice ten, but ten many times over; you shall learn their number at once. There are fifty-two chosen youths from Dulichium, and they have six servants; from Same there are twenty-four; twenty young Achaeans from Zacynthus, and twelve from Ithaca itself, all of them well born. They have with them a servant Medon, a bard, and two men who can carve at table. If we face such numbers as this, you may have bitter cause to rue your coming, and your revenge. See whether you cannot think of some one who would be willing to come and help us."

"Listen to me," replied Ulysses, "and think whether Minerva and her father Jove may seem sufficient, or whether I am to try and find some one else as well."

"Those whom you have named," answered Telemachus, "are a couple of good allies, for though they dwell high up among the clouds they have power over both gods and men."

"These two," continued Ulysses, "will not keep long out of the fray, when the suitors and we join fight in my house. Now, therefore, return home early to-morrow morning, and go about among the suitors as before. Later on the swineherd will bring me to the city disguised as a miserable old beggar. If you see them ill-treating me, steel your heart against my sufferings; even though they drag me feet foremost out of the house, or throw things at me, look on and do nothing beyond gently trying to make them behave more reasonably; but they will not listen to you, for the day of their reckoning is at hand. Furthermore I say, and lay my saying to your heart, when Minerva shall put it in my mind, I will nod my head to you, and on seeing me do this you must collect all the armour that is in the house and hide it in the strong store room. Make some excuse when the suitors ask you why you are removing it; say that you have taken it to be out of the way of the smoke, inasmuch as it is no longer what it was when Ulysses went away, but has become soiled and begrimed with soot. Add to this more particularly that you are afraid Jove may set them on to quarrel over their wine, and that they may do each other some harm which may disgrace both banquet and wooing, for the sight of arms sometimes tempts people to use them. But leave a sword and a spear apiece for yourself and me, and a couple oxhide shields so that we can snatch them up at any moment; Jove and Minerva will then soon quiet these people. There is also another matter; if you are indeed my son and my blood runs in your veins, let no one know that Ulysses is within the house- neither Laertes, nor yet the swineherd, nor any of the servants, nor even Penelope herself. Let you and me exploit the women alone, and let us also make trial of some other of the men servants, to see who is on our side and whose hand is against us."

"Father," replied Telemachus, "you will come to know me by and by, and when you do you will find that I can keep your counsel. I do not think, however, the plan you propose will turn out well for either of us. Think it over. It will take us a long time to go the round of the farms and exploit the men, and all the time the suitors will be wasting your estate with impunity and without compunction. Prove the women by all means, to see who are disloyal and who guiltless, but I am not in favour of going round and trying the men. We can attend to that later on, if you really have some sign from Jove that he will support you."

Thus did they converse, and meanwhile the ship which had brought Telemachus and his crew from Pylos had reached the town of Ithaca. When they had come inside the harbour they drew the ship on to the land; their servants came and took their armour from them, and they left all the presents at the house of Clytius. Then they sent a servant to tell Penelope that Telemachus had gone into the country, but had sent the ship to the town to prevent her from being alarmed and made unhappy. This servant and Eumaeus happened to meet when they were both on the same errand of going to tell Penelope. When they reached the House, the servant stood up and said to the queen in the presence of the waiting women, "Your son, Madam, is now returned from Pylos"; but Eumaeus went close up to Penelope, and said privately that her son had given bidden him tell her. When he had given his message he left the house with its outbuildings and went back to his pigs again.

The suitors were surprised and angry at what had happened, so they went outside the great wall that ran round the outer court, and held a council near the main entrance. Eurymachus, son of Polybus, was the first to speak.

"My friends," said he, "this voyage of Telemachus's is a very serious matter; we had made sure that it would come to nothing. Now, however, let us draw a ship into the water, and get a crew together to send after the others and tell them to come back as fast as they can."

He had hardly done speaking when Amphinomus turned in his place and saw the ship inside the harbour, with the crew lowering her sails, and putting by their oars; so he laughed, and said to the others, "We need not send them any message, for they are here. Some god must have told them, or else they saw the ship go by, and could not overtake her.

On this they rose and went to the water side. The crew then drew the ship on shore; their servants took their armour from them, and they went up in a body to the place of assembly, but they would not let any one old or young sit along with them, and Antinous, son of Eupeithes, spoke first.

"Good heavens," said he, "see how the gods have saved this man from destruction. We kept a succession of scouts upon the headlands all day long, and when the sun was down we never went on shore to sleep, but waited in the ship all night till morning in the hope of capturing and killing him; but some god has conveyed him home in spite of us. Let us consider how we can make an end of him. He must not escape us; our affair is never likely to come off while is alive, for he is very shrewd, and public feeling is by no means all on our side. We must make haste before he can call the Achaeans in assembly; he will lose no time in doing so, for he will be furious with us, and will tell all the world how we plotted to kill him, but failed to take him. The people will not like this when they come to know of it; we must see that they do us no hurt, nor drive us from our own country into exile. Let us try and lay hold of him either on his farm away from the town, or on the road hither. Then we can divide up his property amongst us, and let his mother and the man who marries her have the house. If this does not please you, and you wish Telemachus to live on and hold his father's property, then we must not gather here and eat up his goods in this way, but must make our offers to Penelope each from his own house, and she can marry the man who will give the most for her, and whose lot it is to win her."

They all held their peace until Amphinomus rose to speak. He was the son of Nisus, who was son to king Aretias, and he was foremost among all the suitors from the wheat-growing and well grassed island of Dulichium; his conversation, moreover, was more agreeable to Penelope than that of any of the other for he was a man of good natural disposition. "My friends," said he, speaking to them plainly and in all honestly, "I am not in favour of killing Telemachus. It is a heinous thing to kill one who is of noble blood. Let us first take counsel of the gods, and if the oracles of Jove advise it, I will both help to kill him myself, and will urge everyone else to do so; but if they dissuade us, I would have you hold your hands."

Thus did he speak, and his words pleased them well, so they rose forthwith and went to the house of Ulysses where they took their accustomed seats.

Then Penelope resolved that she would show herself to the suitors. She knew of the plot against Telemachus, for the servant Medon had overheard their counsels and had told her; she went down therefore to the court attended by her maidens, and when she reached the suitors she stood by one of the bearing-posts supporting the roof of the cloister holding a veil before her face, and rebuked Antinous saying:

"Antinous, insolent and wicked schemer, they say you are the best speaker and counsellor of any man your own age in Ithaca, but you are nothing of the kind. Madman, why should you try to compass the death of Telemachus, and take no heed of suppliants, whose witness is Jove himself? It is not right for you to plot thus against one another. Do you not remember how your father fled to this house in fear of the people, who were enraged against him for having gone with some Taphian pirates and plundered the Thesprotians who were at peace with us? They wanted to tear him in pieces and eat up everything he had, but Ulysses stayed their hands although they were infuriated, and now you devour his property without paying for it, and break my heart by his wooing his wife and trying to kill his son. Leave off doing so, and stop the others also."

To this Eurymachus son of Polybus answered, "Take heart, Queen Penelope daughter of Icarius, and do not trouble yourself about these matters. The man is not yet born, nor never will be, who shall lay hands upon your son Telemachus, while I yet live to look upon the face of the earth. I say- and it shall surely be- that my spear shall be reddened with his blood; for many a time has Ulysses taken me on his knees, held wine up to my lips to drink, and put pieces of meat into my hands. Therefore Telemachus is much the dearest friend I have, and has nothing to fear from the hands of us suitors. Of course, if death comes to him from the gods, he cannot escape it." He said this to quiet her, but in reality he was plotting against Telemachus.

Then Penelope went upstairs again and mourned her husband till Minerva shed sleep over her eyes. In the evening Eumaeus got back to Ulysses and his son, who had just sacrificed a young pig of a year old and were ready; helping one another to get supper ready; Minerva therefore came up to Ulysses, turned him into an old man with a stroke of her wand, and clad him in his old clothes again, for fear that the swineherd might recognize him and not keep the secret, but go and tell Penelope.

Telemachus was the first to speak. "So you have got back, Eumaeus," said he. "What is the news of the town? Have the suitors returned, or are they still waiting over yonder, to take me on my way home?"

"I did not think of asking about that," replied Eumaeus, "when I was in the town. I thought I would give my message and come back as soon as I could. I met a man sent by those who had gone with you to Pylos, and he was the first to tell the new your mother, but I can say what I saw with my own eyes; I had just got on to the crest of the hill of Mercury above the town when I saw a ship coming into harbour with a number of men in her. They had many shields and spears, and I thought it was the suitors, but I cannot be sure."

On hearing this Telemachus smiled to his father, but so that Eumaeus could not see him.

Then, when they had finished their work and the meal was ready, they ate it, and every man had his full share so that all were satisfied. As soon as they had had enough to eat and drink, they laid down to rest and enjoyed the boon of sleep.

Book XVII

When the child of morning, rosy-fingered Dawn, appeared, Telemachus bound on his sandals and took a strong spear that suited his hands, for he wanted to go into the city. "Old friend," said he to the swineherd, "I will now go to the town and show myself to my mother, for she will never leave off grieving till she has seen me. As for this unfortunate stranger, take him to the town and let him beg there of any one who will give him a drink and a piece of bread. I have trouble enough of my own, and cannot be burdened with other people. If this makes him angry so much the worse for him, but I like to say what I mean."

Then Ulysses said, "Sir, I do not want to stay here; a beggar can always do better in town than country, for any one who likes can give him something. I am too old to care about remaining here at the beck and call of a master. Therefore let this man do as you have just told him, and take me to the town as soon as I have had a warm by the fire, and the day has got a little heat in it. My clothes are wretchedly thin, and this frosty morning I shall be perished with cold, for you say the city is some way off."

On this Telemachus strode off through the yards, brooding his revenge upon the When he reached home he stood his spear against a bearing-post of the cloister, crossed the stone floor of the cloister itself, and went inside.

Nurse Euryclea saw him long before any one else did. She was putting the fleeces on to the seats, and she burst out crying as she ran up to him; all the other maids came up too, and covered his head and shoulders with their kisses. Penelope came out of her room looking like Diana or Venus, and wept as she flung her arms about her son. She kissed his forehead and both his beautiful eyes, "Light of my eyes," she cried as she spoke fondly to him, "so you are come home again; I made sure I was never going to see you any more. To think of your having gone off to Pylos without saying anything about it or obtaining my consent. But come, tell me what you saw."

"Do not scold me, mother,' answered Telemachus, "nor vex me, seeing what a narrow escape I have had, but wash your face, change your dress, go upstairs with your maids, and promise full and sufficient hecatombs to all the gods if Jove will only grant us our revenge upon the suitors. I must now go to the place of assembly to invite a stranger who has come back with me from Pylos. I sent him on with my crew, and told Piraeus to take him home and look after him till I could come for him myself."

She heeded her son's words, washed her face, changed her dress, and vowed full and sufficient hecatombs to all the gods if they would only vouchsafe her revenge upon the suitors.

Telemachus went through, and out of, the cloisters spear in hand- not alone, for his two fleet dogs went with him. Minerva endowed him with a presence of such divine comeliness that all marvelled at him as he went by, and the suitors gathered round him with fair words in their mouths and malice in their hearts; but he avoided them, and went to sit with Mentor, Antiphus, and Halitherses, old friends of his father's house, and they made him tell them all that had happened to him. Then Piraeus came up with Theoclymenus, whom he had escorted through the town to the place of assembly, whereon Telemachus at once joined them. Piraeus was first to speak: "Telemachus," said he, "I wish you would send some of your women to my house to take awa the presents Menelaus gave you."

"We do not know, Piraeus," answered Telemachus, "what may happen. If the suitors kill me in my own house and divide my property among them, I would rather you had the presents than that any of those people should get hold of them. If on the other hand I manage to kill them, I shall be much obliged if you will kindly bring me my presents."

With these words he took Theoclymenus to his own house. When they got there they laid their cloaks on the benches and seats, went into the baths, and washed themselves. When the maids had washed and anointed them, and had given them cloaks and shirts, they took their seats at table. A maid servant then brought them water in a beautiful golden ewer, and poured it into a silver basin for them to wash their hands; and she drew a clean table beside them. An upper servant brought them bread and offered them many good things of what there was in the house. Opposite them sat Penelope, reclining on a couch by one of the bearing-posts of the cloister, and spinning. Then they laid their hands on the good things that were before them, and as soon as they had had enough to eat and drink Penelope said:

"Telemachus, I shall go upstairs and lie down on that sad couch, which I have not ceased to water with my tears, from the day Ulysses set out for Troy with the sons of Atreus. You failed, however, to make it clear to me before the suitors came back to the house, whether or no you had been able to hear anything about the return of your father."

"I will tell you then truth," replied her son. "We went to Pylos and saw Nestor, who took me to his house and treated me as hospitably as though I were a son of his own who had just returned after a long absence; so also did his sons; but he said he had not heard a word from any human being about Ulysses, whether he was alive or dead. He sent me, therefore, with a chariot and horses to Menelaus. There I saw Helen, for whose sake so many, both Argives and Trojans, were in heaven's wisdom doomed to suffer. Menelaus asked me what it was that had brought me to Lacedaemon, and I told him the whole truth, whereon he said, 'So, then, these cowards would usurp a brave man's bed? A hind might as well lay her new-born young in the lair of a lion, and then go off to feed in the forest or in some grassy dell. The lion, when he comes back to his lair, will make short work with the pair of them, and so will Ulysses with these suitors. By father Jove, Minerva, and Apollo, if Ulysses is still the man that he was when he wrestled with Philomeleides in Lesbos, and threw him so heavily that all the Greeks cheered him- if he is still such, and were to come near these suitors, they would have a short shrift and a sorry wedding. As regards your question, however, I will not prevaricate nor deceive you, but what the old man of the sea told me, so much will I tell you in full. He said he could see Ulysses on an island sorrowing bitterly in the house of the nymph Calypso, who was keeping him prisoner, and he could not reach his home, for he had no ships nor sailors to take him over the sea.' This was what Menelaus told me, and when I had heard his story I came away; the gods then gave me a fair wind and soon brought me safe home again."

With these words he moved the heart of Penelope. Then Theoclymenus said to her:

"Madam, wife of Ulysses, Telemachus does not understand these things; listen therefore to me, for I can divine them surely, and will hide nothing from you. May Jove the king of heaven be my witness, and the rites of hospitality, with that hearth of Ulysses to which I now come, that Ulysses himself is even now in Ithaca, and, either going about the country or staying in one place, is enquiring into all these evil deeds and preparing a day of reckoning for the suitors. I saw an omen when I was on the ship which meant this, and I told Telemachus about it."

"May it be even so," answered Penelope; "if your words come true, you shall have such gifts and such good will from me that all who see you shall congratulate you."

Thus did they converse. Meanwhile the suitors were throwing discs, or aiming with spears at a mark on the levelled ground in front of the house, and behaving with all their old insolence. But when it was now time for dinner, and the flock of sheep and goats had come into the town from all the country round, with their shepherds as usual, then Medon, who was their favourite servant, and who waited upon them at table, said, "Now then, my young masters, you have had enough sport, so come inside that we may get dinner ready. Dinner is not a bad thing, at dinner time."

They left their sports as he told them, and when they were within the house, they laid their cloaks on the benches and seats inside, and then sacrificed some sheep, goats, pigs, and a heifer, all of them fat and well grown. Thus they made ready for their meal. In the meantime Ulysses and the swineherd were about starting for the town, and the swineherd said, "Stranger, I suppose you still want to go to town to-day, as my master said you were to do; for my own part I should have liked you to stay here as a station hand, but I must do as my master tells me, or he will scold me later on, and a scolding from one's master is a very serious thing. Let us then be off, for it is now broad day; it will be night again directly and then you will find it colder."

"I know, and understand you," replied Ulysses; "you need say no more. Let us be going, but if you have a stick ready cut, let me have it to walk with, for you say the road is a very rough one."

As he spoke he threw his shabby old tattered wallet over his shoulders, by the cord from which it hung, and Eumaeus gave him a stick to his liking. The two then started, leaving the station in charge of the dogs and herdsmen who remained behind; the swineherd led the way and his master followed after, looking like some broken-down old tramp as he leaned upon his staff, and his clothes were all in rags. When they had got over the rough steep ground and were nearing the city, they reached the fountain from which the citizens drew their water. This had been made by Ithacus, Neritus, and Polyctor. There was a grove of water-loving poplars planted in a circle all round it, and the clear cold water came down to it from a rock high up, while above the fountain there was an altar to the nymphs, at which all wayfarers used to sacrifice. Here Melanthius son of Dolius overtook them as he was driving down some goats, the best in his flock, for the suitors' dinner, and there were two shepherds with him. When he saw Eumaeus and Ulysses he reviled them with outrageous and unseemly language, which made Ulysses very angry.

"There you go," cried he, "and a precious pair you are. See how heaven brings birds of the same feather to one another. Where, pray, master swineherd, are you taking this poor miserable object? It would make any one sick to see such a creature at table. A fellow like this never won a prize for anything in his life, but will go about rubbing his shoulders against every man's door post, and begging, not for swords and cauldrons like a man, but only for a few scraps not worth begging for. If you would give him to me for a hand on my station, he might do to clean out the folds, or bring a bit of sweet feed to the kids, and he could fatten his thighs as much as he pleased on whey; but he has taken to bad ways and will not go about any kind of work; he will do nothing but beg victuals all the town over, to feed his insatiable belly. I say, therefore and it shall surely be- if he goes near Ulysses' house he will get his head broken by the stools they will fling at him, till they turn him out."

On this, as he passed, he gave Ulysses a kick on the hip out of pure wantonness, but Ulysses stood firm, and did not budge from the path. For a moment he doubted whether or no to fly at Melanthius and kill him with his staff, or fling him to the ground and beat his brains out; he resolved, however, to endure it and keep himself in check, but the swineherd looked straight at Melanthius and rebuked him, lifting up his hands and praying to heaven as he did so.

"Fountain nymphs," he cried, "children of Jove, if ever Ulysses burned you thigh bones covered with fat whether of lambs or kids, grant my prayer that heaven may send him home. He would soon put an end to the swaggering threats with which such men as you go about insulting people-gadding all over the town while your flocks are going to ruin through bad shepherding."

Then Melanthius the goatherd answered, "You ill-conditioned cur, what are you talking about? Some day or other I will put you on board ship and take you to a foreign country, where I can sell you and pocket the money you will fetch. I wish I were as sure that Apollo would strike Telemachus dead this very day, or that the suitors would kill him, as I am that Ulysses will never come home again."

With this he left them to come on at their leisure, while he went quickly forward and soon reached the house of his master. When he got there he went in and took his seat among the suitors opposite Eurymachus, who liked him better than any of the others. The servants brought him a portion of meat, and an upper woman servant set bread before him that he might eat. Presently Ulysses and the swineherd came up to the house and stood by it, amid a sound of music, for Phemius was just beginning to sing to the suitors. Then Ulysses took hold of the swineherd's hand, and said:

"Eumaeus, this house of Ulysses is a very fine place. No matter how far you go you will find few like it. One building keeps following on after another. The outer court has a wall with battlements all round it; the doors are double folding, and of good workmanship; it would be a hard matter to take it by force of arms. I perceive, too, that there are many people banqueting within it, for there is a smell of roast meat, and I hear a sound of music, which the gods have made to go along with feasting."

Then Eumaeus said, "You have perceived aright, as indeed you generally do; but let us think what will be our best course. Will you go inside first and join the suitors, leaving me here behind you, or will you wait here and let me go in first? But do not wait long, or some one may you loitering about outside, and throw something at you. Consider this matter I pray you."

And Ulysses answered, "I understand and heed. Go in first and leave me here where I am. I am quite used to being beaten and having things thrown at me. I have been so much buffeted about in war and by sea that I am case-hardened, and this too may go with the rest. But a man cannot hide away the cravings of a hungry belly; this is an enemy which gives much trouble to all men; it is because of this that ships are fitted out to sail the seas, and to make war upon other people."

As they were thus talking, a dog that had been lying asleep raised his head and pricked up his ears. This was Argos, whom Ulysses had bred before setting out for Troy, but he had never had any work out of him. In the old days he used to be taken out by the young men when they went hunting wild goats, or deer, or hares, but now that his master was gone he was lying neglected on the heaps of mule and cow dung that lay in front of the stable doors till the men should come and draw it away to manure the great close; and he was full of fleas. As soon as he saw Ulysses standing there, he dropped his ears and wagged his tail, but he could not get close up to his master. When Ulysses saw the dog on the other side of the yard, dashed a tear from his eyes without Eumaeus seeing it, and said:

"Eumaeus, what a noble hound that is over yonder on the manure heap: his build is splendid; is he as fine a fellow as he looks, or is he only one of those dogs that come begging about a table, and are kept merely for show?"

"This hound," answered Eumaeus, "belonged to him who has died in a far country. If he were what he was when Ulysses left for Troy, he would soon show you what he could do. There was not a wild beast in the forest that could get away from him when he was once on its tracks. But now he has fallen on evil times, for his master is dead and gone, and the women take no care of him. Servants never do their work when their master's hand is no longer over them, for Jove takes half the goodness out of a man when he makes a slave of him."

As he spoke he went inside the buildings to the cloister where the suitors were, but Argos died as soon as he had recognized his master.

Telemachus saw Eumaeus long before any one else did, and beckoned him to come and sit beside him; so he looked about and saw a seat lying near where the carver sat serving out their portions to the suitors; he picked it up, brought it to Telemachus's table, and sat down opposite him. Then the servant brought him his portion, and gave him bread from the bread-basket.

Immediately afterwards Ulysses came inside, looking like a poor miserable old beggar, leaning on his staff and with his clothes all in rags. He sat down upon the threshold of ash-wood just inside the doors leading from the outer to the inner court, and against a bearing-post of cypress-wood which the carpenter had skillfully planed, and had made to join truly with rule and line. Telemachus took a whole loaf from the bread-basket, with as much meat as he could hold in his two hands, and said to Eumaeus, "Take this to the stranger, and tell him to go the round of the suitors, and beg from them; a beggar must not be shamefaced."

So Eumaeus went up to him and said, "Stranger, Telemachus sends you this, and says you are to go the round of the suitors begging, for beggars must not be shamefaced."

Ulysses answered, "May King Jove grant all happiness to Telemachus, and fulfil the desire of his heart."

Then with both hands he took what Telemachus had sent him, and laid it on the dirty old wallet at his feet. He went on eating it while the bard was singing, and had just finished his dinner as he left off. The suitors applauded the bard, whereon Minerva went up to Ulysses and prompted him to beg pieces of bread from each one of the suitors, that he might see what kind of people they were, and tell the good from the bad; but come what might she was not going to save a single one of them. Ulysses, therefore, went on his round, going from left to right, and stretched out his hands to beg as though he were a real beggar. Some of them pitied him, and were curious about him, asking one another who he was and where he came from; whereon the goatherd Melanthius said, "Suitors of my noble mistress, I can tell you something about him, for I have seen him before. The swineherd brought him here, but I know nothing about the man himself, nor where he comes from."

On this Antinous began to abuse the swineherd. "You precious idiot," he cried, "what have you brought this man to town for? Have we not tramps and beggars enough already to pester us as we sit at meat? Do you think it a small thing that such people gather here to waste your master's property and must you needs bring this man as well?"

And Eumaeus answered, "Antinous, your birth is good but your words evil. It was no doing of mine that he came here. Who is likely to invite a stranger from a foreign country, unless it be one of those who can do public service as a seer, a healer of hurts, a carpenter, or a bard who can charm us with his Such men are welcome all the world over, but no one is likely to ask a beggar who will only worry him. You are always harder on Ulysses' servants than any of the other suitors are, and above all on me, but I do not care so long as Telemachus and Penelope are alive and here."

But Telemachus said, "Hush, do not answer him; Antinous has the bitterest tongue of all the suitors, and he makes the others worse."

Then turning to Antinous he said, "Antinous, you take as much care of my interests as though I were your son. Why should you want to see this stranger turned out of the house? Heaven forbid; take' something and give it him yourself; I do not grudge it; I bid you take it. Never mind my mother, nor any of the other servants in the house; but I know you will not do what I say, for you are more fond of eating things yourself than of giving them to other people."

"What do you mean, Telemachus," replied Antinous, "by this swaggering talk? If all the suitors were to give him as much as I will, he would not come here again for another three months."

As he spoke he drew the stool on which he rested his dainty feet from under the table, and made as though he would throw it at Ulysses, but the other suitors all gave him something, and filled his wallet with bread and meat; he was about, therefore, to go back to the threshold and eat what the suitors had given him, but he first went up to Antinous and said:

"Sir, give me something; you are not, surely, the poorest man here; you seem to be a chief, foremost among them all; therefore you should be the better giver, and I will tell far and wide of your bounty. I too was a rich man once, and had a fine house of my own; in those days I gave to many a tramp such as I now am, no matter who he might be nor what he wanted. I had any number of servants, and all the other things which people have who live well and are accounted wealthy, but it pleased Jove to take all away from me. He sent me with a band of roving robbers to Egypt; it was a long voyage and I was undone by it. I stationed my bade ships in the river Aegyptus, and bade my men stay by them and keep guard over them, while sent out scouts to reconnoitre from every point of vantage.

"But the men disobeyed my orders, took to their own devices, and ravaged the land of the Egyptians, killing the men, and taking their wives and children captives. The alarm was soon carried to the city, and when they heard the war-cry, the people came out at daybreak till the plain was filled with soldiers horse and foot, and with the gleam of armour. Then Jove spread panic among my men, and they would no longer face the enemy, for they found themselves surrounded. The Egyptians killed many of us, and took the rest alive to do forced labour for them; as for myself, they gave me to a friend who met them, to take to Cyprus, Dmetor by name, son of Iasus, who was a great man in Cyprus. Thence I am come hither in a state of great misery."

Then Antinous said, "What god can have sent such a pestilence to plague us during our dinner? Get out, into the open part of the court, or I will give you Egypt and Cyprus over again for your insolence and importunity; you have begged of all the others, and they have given you lavishly, for they have abundance round them, and it is easy to be free with other people's property when there is plenty of it."

On this Ulysses began to move off, and said, "Your looks, my fine sir, are better than your breeding; if you were in your own house you would not spare a poor man so much as a pinch of salt, for though you are in another man's, and surrounded with abundance, you cannot find it in you to give him even a piece of bread."

This made Antinous very angry, and he scowled at him saying, "You shall pay for this before you get clear of the court." With these words he threw a footstool at him, and hit him on the right shoulder-blade near the top of his back. Ulysses stood firm as a rock and the blow did not even stagger him, but he shook his head in silence as he brooded on his revenge. Then he went back to the threshold and sat down there, laying his well-filled wallet at his feet.

"Listen to me," he cried, "you suitors of Queen Penelope, that I may speak even as I am minded. A man knows neither ache nor pain if he gets hit while fighting for his money, or for his sheep or his cattle; and even so Antinous has hit me while in the service of my miserable belly, which is always getting people into trouble. Still, if the poor have gods and avenging deities at all, I pray them that Antinous may come to a bad end before his marriage."

"Sit where you are, and eat your victuals in silence, or be off elsewhere," shouted Antinous. "If you say more I will have you dragged hand and foot through the courts, and the servants shall flay you alive."

The other suitors were much displeased at this, and one of the young men said, "Antinous, you did ill in striking that poor wretch of a tramp: it will be worse for you if he should turn out to be some god- and we know the gods go about disguised in all sorts of ways as people from foreign countries, and travel about the world to see who do amiss and who righteously."

Thus said the suitors, but Antinous paid them no heed. Meanwhile Telemachus was furious about the blow that had been given to his father, and though no tear fell from him, he shook his head in silence and brooded on his revenge.

Now when Penelope heard that the beggar had been struck in the banqueting-cloister, she said before her maids, "Would that Apollo would so strike you, Antinous," and her waiting woman Eurynome answered, "If our prayers were answered not one of the suitors would ever again see the sun rise." Then Penelope said, "Nurse, I hate every single one of them, for they mean nothing but mischief, but I hate Antinous like the darkness of death itself. A poor unfortunate tramp has come begging about the house for sheer want. Every one else has given him something to put in his wallet, but

Antinous has hit him on the right shoulder-blade with a footstool."

Thus did she talk with her maids as she sat in her own room, and in the meantime Ulysses was getting his dinner. Then she called for the swineherd and said, "Eumaeus, go and tell the stranger to come here, I want to see him and ask him some questions. He seems to have travelled much, and he may have seen or heard something of my unhappy husband."

To this you answered, O swineherd Eumaeus, "If these Achaeans, Madam, would only keep quiet, you would be charmed with the history of his adventures. I had him three days and three nights with me in my hut, which was the first place he reached after running away from his ship, and he has not yet completed the story of his misfortunes. If he had been the most heaven-taught minstrel in the whole world, on whose lips all hearers hang entranced, I could not have been more charmed as I sat in my hut and listened to him. He says there is an old friendship between his house and that of Ulysses, and that he comes from Crete where the descendants of Minos live, after having been driven hither and thither by every kind of misfortune; he also declares that he has heard of Ulysses as being alive and near at hand among the Thesprotians, and that he is bringing great wealth home with him."

"Call him here, then," said Penelope, "that I too may hear his story. As for the suitors, let them take their pleasure indoors or out as they will, for they have nothing to fret about. Their corn and wine remain unwasted in their houses with none but servants to consume them, while they keep hanging about our house day after day sacrificing our oxen, sheep, and fat goats for their banquets, and never giving so much as a thought to the quantity of wine they drink. No estate can stand such recklessness, for we have now no Ulysses to protect us. If he were to come again, he and his son would soon have their revenge."

As she spoke Telemachus sneezed so loudly that the whole house resounded with it. Penelope laughed when she heard this, and said to Eumaeus, "Go and call the stranger; did you not hear how my son sneezed just as I was speaking? This can only mean that all the suitors are going to be killed, and that not one of them shall escape. Furthermore I say, and lay my saying to your heart: if I am satisfied that the stranger is speaking the truth I shall give him a shirt and cloak of good wear."

When Eumaeus heard this he went straight to Ulysses and said, "Father stranger, my mistress Penelope, mother of Telemachus, has sent for you; she is in great grief, but she wishes to hear anything you can tell her about her husband, and if she is satisfied that you are speaking the truth, she will give you a shirt and cloak, which are the very things that you are most in want of. As for bread, you can get enough of that to fill your belly, by begging about the town, and letting those give that will."

"I will tell Penelope," answered Ulysses, "nothing but what is strictly true. I know all about her husband, and have been partner with him in affliction, but I am afraid of passing. through this crowd of cruel suitors, for their pride and insolence reach heaven. Just now, moreover, as I was going about the house without doing any harm, a man gave me a blow that hurt me very much, but neither Telemachus nor any one else defended me. Tell Penelope, therefore, to be patient and wait till sundown. Let her give me a seat close up to the fire, for my clothes are worn very thin- you know they are, for you have seen them ever since I first asked you to help me- she can then ask me about the return of her husband."

The swineherd went back when he heard this, and Penelope said as she saw him cross the threshold, "Why do you not bring him here, Eumaeus? Is he afraid that some one will ill-treat him, or is he shy of coming inside the house at all? Beggars should not be shamefaced."

To this you answered, O swineherd Eumaeus, "The stranger is quite reasonable. He is avoiding the suitors, and is only doing what any one else would do. He asks you to wait till sundown, and it will be much better, madam, that you should have him all to yourself, when you can hear him and talk to him as you will."

"The man is no fool," answered Penelope, "it would very likely be as he says, for there are no such abominable people in the whole world as these men are."

When she had done speaking Eumaeus went back to the suitors, for he had explained everything. Then he went up to Telemachus and said in his ear so that none could overhear him, "My dear sir, I will now go back to the pigs, to see after your property and my own business. You will look to what is going on here, but above all be careful to keep out of danger, for there are many who bear you ill will. May Jove bring them to a bad end before they do us a mischief."

"Very well," replied Telemachus, "go home when you have had your dinner, and in the morning come here with the victims we are to sacrifice for the day. Leave the rest to heaven and me."

On this Eumaeus took his seat again, and when he had finished his dinner he left the courts and the cloister with the men at table, and went back to his pigs. As for the suitors, they presently began to amuse themselves with singing and dancing, for it was now getting on towards evening.

Book XVIII

Now there came a certain common tramp who used to go begging all over the city of Ithaca, and was notorious as an incorrigible glutton and drunkard. This man had no strength nor stay in him, but he was a great hulking fellow to look at; his real name, the one his mother gave him, was Arnaeus, but the young men of the place called him Irus, because he used to run errands for any one who would send him. As soon as he came he began to insult Ulysses, and to try and drive him out of his own house.

"Be off, old man," he cried, "from the doorway, or you shall be dragged out neck and heels. Do you not see that they are all giving me the wink, and wanting me to turn you out by force, only I do not like to do so? Get up then, and go of yourself, or we shall come to blows."

Ulysses frowned on him and said, "My friend, I do you no manner of harm; people give you a great deal, but I am not jealous. There is room enough in this doorway for the pair of us, and you need not grudge me things that are not yours to give. You seem to be just such another tramp as myself, but perhaps the gods will give us better luck by and by. Do not, however, talk too much about fighting or you will incense me, and old though I am, I shall cover your mouth and chest with blood. I shall have more peace to-morrow if I do, for you will not come to the house of Ulysses any more."

Irus was very angry and answered, "You filthy glutton, you run on trippingly like an old fish-fag. I have a good mind to lay both hands about you, and knock your teeth out of your head like so many boar's tusks. Get ready, therefore, and let these people here stand by and look on. You will never be able to fight one who is so much younger than yourself."

Thus roundly did they rate one another on the smooth pavement in front of the doorway, and when Antinous saw what was going on he laughed heartily and said to the others, "This is the finest sport that you ever saw; heaven never yet sent anything like it into this house. The stranger and Irus have quarreled and are going to fight, let us set them on to do so at once."

The suitors all came up laughing, and gathered round the two ragged tramps. "Listen to me," said Antinous, "there are some goats' paunches down at the fire, which we have filled with blood and fat, and set aside for supper; he who is victorious and proves himself to be the better man shall have his pick of the lot; he shall be free of our table and we will not allow any other beggar about the house at all."

The others all agreed, but Ulysses, to throw them off the scent, said, "Sirs, an old man like myself, worn out with suffering, cannot hold his own against a young one; but my irrepressible belly urges me on, though I know it can only end in my getting a drubbing. You must swear, however that none of you will give me a foul blow to favour Irus and secure him the victory."

They swore as he told them, and when they had completed their oath Telemachus put in a word and said, "Stranger, if you have a mind to settle with this fellow, you need not be afraid of any one here. Whoever strikes you will have to fight more than one. I am host, and the other chiefs, Antinous and Eurymachus, both of them men of understanding, are of the same mind as I am."

Every one assented, and Ulysses girded his old rags about his loins, thus baring his stalwart thighs, his broad chest and shoulders, and his mighty arms; but Minerva came up to him and made his limbs even stronger still. The suitors were beyond measure astonished, and one would turn towards his neighbour saying, "The stranger has brought such a thigh out of his old rags that there will soon be nothing left of Irus."

Irus began to be very uneasy as he heard them, but the servants girded him by force, and brought him [into the open part of the court] in such a fright that his limbs were all of a tremble. Antinous scolded him and said, "You swaggering bully, you ought never to have been born at all if you are afraid of such an old broken-down creature as this tramp is. I say, therefore- and it shall surely be- if he beats you and proves himself the better man, I shall pack you off on board ship to the mainland and send you to king Echetus, who kills every one that comes near him. He will cut off your nose and ears, and draw out your entrails for the dogs to eat."

This frightened Irus still more, but they brought him into the middle of the court, and the two men raised their hands to fight. Then Ulysses considered whether he should let drive so hard at him as to make an end of him then and there, or whether he should give him a lighter blow that should only knock him down; in the end he deemed it best to give the lighter blow for fear the Achaeans should begin to suspect who he was. Then they began to fight, and Irus hit Ulysses on the right shoulder; but Ulysses gave Irus a blow on the neck under the ear that broke in the bones of his skull, and the blood came gushing out of his mouth; he fell groaning in the dust, gnashing his teeth and kicking on the ground, but the suitors threw up their hands and nearly died of laughter, as Ulysses caught hold of him by the foot and dragged him into the outer court as far as the gate-house. There he propped him up against the wall and put his staff in his hands. "Sit here," said he, "and keep the dogs and pigs off; you are a pitiful creature, and if you try to make yourself king of the beggars any more you shall fare still worse."

Then he threw his dirty old wallet, all tattered and torn, over his shoulder with the cord by which it hung, and went back to sit down upon the threshold; but the suitors went within the cloisters, laughing and saluting him, "May Jove, and all the other gods," said they, 'grant you whatever you want for having put an end to the importunity of this insatiable tramp. We will take him over to the mainland presently, to king Echetus, who kills every one that comes near him."

Ulysses hailed this as of good omen, and Antinous set a great goat's paunch before him filled with blood and fat. Amphinomus took two loaves out of the bread-basket and brought them to him, pledging him as he did so in a golden goblet of wine. "Good luck to you," he said, "father stranger, you are very badly off at present, but I hope you will have better times by and by."

To this Ulysses answered, "Amphinomus, you seem to be a man of good understanding, as indeed you may well be, seeing whose son you are. I have heard your father well spoken of; he is Nisus of Dulichium, a man both brave and wealthy. They tell me you are his son, and you appear to be a considerable person; listen, therefore, and take heed to what I am saying. Man is the vainest of all creatures that have their being upon earth. As long as heaven vouchsafes him health and strength, he thinks that he shall come to no harm hereafter, and even when the blessed gods bring sorrow upon him, he bears it as he needs must, and makes the best of it; for God Almighty gives men their daily minds day by day. I know all about it, for I was a rich man once, and did much wrong in the stubbornness of my pride, and in the confidence that my father and my brothers would support me; therefore let a man fear God in all things always, and take the good that heaven may see fit to send him without vainglory. Consider the infamy of what these suitors are doing; see how they are wasting the estate, and doing dishonour to the wife, of one who is certain to return some day, and that, too, not long hence. Nay, he will be here soon; may heaven send you home quietly first that you may not meet with him in the day of his coming, for once he is here the suitors and he will not part bloodlessly."

With these words he made a drink-offering, and when he had drunk he put the gold cup again into the hands of Amphinomus, who walked away serious and bowing his head, for he foreboded evil. But even so he did not escape destruction, for Minerva had doomed him fall by the hand of Telemachus. So he took his seat again at the place from which he had come.

Then Minerva put it into the mind of Penelope to show herself to the suitors, that she might make them still more enamoured of her, and win still further honour from her son and husband. So she feigned a mocking laugh and said, "Eurynome, I have changed my and have a fancy to show myself to the suitors although I detest them. I should like also to give my son a hint that he had better not have anything more to do with them. They speak fairly enough but they mean mischief."

"My dear child," answered Eurynome, "all that you have said is true, go and tell your son about it, but first wash yourself and anoint your face. Do not go about with your cheeks all covered with tears; it is not right that you should grieve so incessantly; for Telemachus, whom you always prayed that you might live to see with a beard, is already grown up."

"I know, Eurynome," replied Penelope, "that you mean well, but do not try and persuade me to wash and to anoint myself, for heaven robbed me of all my beauty on the day my husband sailed; nevertheless, tell Autonoe and Hippodamia that I want them. They must be with me when I am in the cloister; I am not going among the men alone; it would not be proper for me to do so."

On this the old woman went out of the room to bid the maids go to their mistress. In the meantime Minerva bethought her of another matter, and sent Penelope off into a sweet slumber; so she lay down on her couch and her limbs became heavy with sleep. Then the goddess shed grace and beauty over her that all the Achaeans might admire her. She washed her face with the ambrosial loveliness that Venus wears when she goes dancing with the Graces; she made her taller and of a more commanding figure, while as for her complexion it was whiter than sawn ivory. When Minerva had done all this she went away, whereon the maids came in from the women's room and woke Penelope with the sound of their talking.

"What an exquisitely delicious sleep I have been having," said she, as she passed her hands over her face, "in spite of all my misery. I wish Diana would let me die so sweetly now at this very moment, that I might no longer waste in despair for the loss of my dear husband, who possessed every kind of good quality and was the most distinguished man among the Achaeans."

With these words she came down from her upper room, not alone but attended by two of her maidens, and when she reached the suitors she stood by one of the bearing-posts supporting the roof of the cloister, holding a veil before her face, and with a staid maid servant on either side of her. As they beheld her the suitors were so overpowered and became so desperately enamoured of her, that each one prayed he might win her for his own bed fellow.

"Telemachus," said she, addressing her son, "I fear you are no longer so discreet and well conducted as you used to be. When you were younger you had a greater sense of propriety; now, however, that you are grown up, though a stranger to look at you would take you for the son of a well-to-do father as far as size and good looks go, your conduct is by no means what it should be. What is all this disturbance that has been going on, and how came you to allow a stranger to be so disgracefully ill-treated? What would have happened if he had suffered serious injury while a suppliant in our house? Surely this would have been very discreditable to you."

"I am not surprised, my dear mother, at your displeasure," replied Telemachus, "I understand all about it and know when things are not as they should be, which I could not do when I was younger; I cannot, however, behave with perfect propriety at all times. First one and then another of these wicked people here keeps driving me out of my mind, and I have no one to stand by me. After all, however, this fight between Irus and the stranger did not turn out as the suitors meant it to do, for the stranger got the best of it. I wish Father Jove, Minerva, and Apollo would break the neck of every one of these wooers of yours, some inside the house and some out; and I wish they might all be as limp as Irus is over yonder in the gate of the outer court. See how he nods his head like a drunken man; he has had such a thrashing that he cannot stand on his feet nor get back to his home, wherever that may be, for has no strength left in him."

Thus did they converse. Eurymachus then came up and said, "Queen Penelope, daughter of Icarius, if all the Achaeans in Iasian Argos could see you at this moment, you would have still more suitors in your house by tomorrow morning, for you are the most admirable woman in the whole world both as regards personal beauty and strength of understanding."

To this Penelope replied, "Eurymachus, heaven robbed me of all my beauty whether of face or figure when the Argives set sail for Troy and my dear husband with them. If he were to return and look after my affairs, I should both be more respected and show a better presence to the world. As it is, I am oppressed with care, and with the afflictions which heaven has seen fit to heap upon me. My husband foresaw it all, and when he was leaving home he took my right wrist in his hand- 'Wife, 'he said, 'we shall not all of us come safe home from Troy, for the Trojans fight well both with bow and spear. They are excellent also at fighting from chariots, and nothing decides the issue of a fight sooner than this. I know not, therefore, whether heaven will send me back to you, or whether I may not fall over there at Troy. In the meantime do you look after things here. Take care of my father and mother as at present, and even more so during my absence, but when you see our son growing a beard, then marry whom you will, and leave this your present home. This is what he said and now it is all coming true. A night will come when I shall have to yield myself to a marriage which I detest, for Jove has taken from me all hope of happiness. This further grief, moreover, cuts me to the very heart. You suitors are not wooing me after the custom of my country. When men are courting a woman who they think will be a good wife to them and who is of noble birth, and when they are each trying to win her for himself, they usually bring oxen and sheep to feast the friends of the lady, and they make her magnificent presents, instead of eating up other people's property without paying for it."

This was what she said, and Ulysses was glad when he heard her trying to get presents out of the suitors, and flattering them with fair words which he knew she did not mean.

Then Antinous said, "Queen Penelope, daughter of Icarius, take as many presents as you please from any one who will give them to you; it is not well to refuse a present; but we will not go about our business nor stir from where we are, till you have married the best man among us whoever he may be."

The others applauded what Antinous had said, and each one sent his servant to bring his present. Antinous's man returned with a large and lovely dress most exquisitely embroidered. It had twelve beautifully made brooch pins of pure gold with which to fasten it. Eurymachus immediately brought her a magnificent chain of gold and amber beads that gleamed like sunlight. Eurydamas's two men returned with some earrings fashioned into three brilliant pendants which glistened most beautifully; while king Pisander son of Polyctor gave her a necklace of the rarest workmanship, and every one else brought her a beautiful present of some kind.

Then the queen went back to her room upstairs, and her maids brought the presents after her. Meanwhile the suitors took to singing and dancing, and stayed till evening came. They danced and sang till it grew dark; they then brought in three braziers to give light, and piled them up with chopped firewood very and dry, and they lit torches from them, which the maids held up turn and turn about. Then Ulysses said:

"Maids, servants of Ulysses who has so long been absent, go to the queen inside the house; sit with her and amuse her, or spin, and pick wool. I will hold the light for all these people. They may stay till morning, but shall not beat me, for I can stand a great deal."

The maids looked at one another and laughed, while pretty Melantho began to gibe at him contemptuously. She was daughter to Dolius, but had been brought up by Penelope, who used to give her toys to play with, and looked after her when she was a child; but in spite of all this she showed no consideration for the sorrows of her mistress, and used to misconduct herself with Eurymachus, with whom she was in love.

"Poor wretch," said she, "are you gone clean out of your mind? Go and sleep in some smithy, or place of public gossips, instead of chattering here. Are you not ashamed of opening your mouth before your betters- so many of them too? Has the wine been getting into your head, or do you always babble in this way? You seem to have lost your wits because you beat the tramp Irus; take care that a better man than he does not come and cudgel you about the head till he pack you bleeding out of the house."

"Vixen," replied Ulysses, scowling at her, "I will go and tell Telemachus what you have been saying, and he will have you torn limb from limb."

With these words he scared the women, and they went off into the body of the house. They trembled all aver, for they thought he would do as he said. But Ulysses took his stand near the burning braziers, holding up torches and looking at the people- brooding the while on things that should surely come to pass.

But Minerva would not let the suitors for one moment cease their insolence, for she wanted Ulysses to become even more bitter against them; she therefore set Eurymachus son of Polybus on to gibe at him, which made the others laugh. "Listen to me," said he, "you suitors of Queen Penelope, that I may speak even as I am minded. It is not for nothing that this man has come to the house of Ulysses; I believe the light has not been coming from the torches, but from his own head- for his hair is all gone, every bit of it."

Then turning to Ulysses he said, "Stranger, will you work as a servant, if I send you to the wolds and see that you are well paid? Can you build a stone fence, or plant trees? I will have you fed all the year round, and will find you in shoes and clothing. Will you go, then? Not you; for you have got into bad ways, and do not want to work; you had rather fill your belly by going round the country begging."

"Eurymachus," answered Ulysses, "if you and I were to work one against the other in early summer when the days are at their longest- give me a good scythe, and take another yourself, and let us see which will fast the longer or mow the stronger, from dawn till dark when the mowing grass is about. Or if you will plough against me, let us each take a yoke of tawny oxen, well-mated and of great strength and endurance: turn me into a four acre field, and see whether you or I can drive the straighter furrow. If, again, war were to break out this day, give me a shield, a couple of spears and a helmet fitting well upon my temples- you would find me foremost in the fray, and would cease your gibes about my belly. You are insolent and cruel, and think yourself a great man because you live in a little world, ind that a bad one. If Ulysses comes to his own again, the doors of his house are wide, but you will find them narrow when you try to fly through them."

Eurymachus was furious at all this. He scowled at him and cried, "You wretch, I will soon pay you out for daring to say such things to me, and in public too. Has the wine been getting into your head or do you always babble in this way? You seem to have lost your wits because you beat the tramp Irus. With this he caught hold of a footstool, but Ulysses sought protection at the knees of Amphinomus of Dulichium, for he was afraid. The stool hit the cupbearer on his right hand and knocked him down: the man fell with a cry flat on his back, and his wine-jug fell ringing to the ground. The suitors in the covered cloister were now in an uproar, and one would turn towards his neighbour, saying, "I wish the stranger had gone somewhere else, bad luck to hide, for all the trouble he gives us. We cannot permit such disturbance about a beggar; if such ill counsels are to prevail we shall have no more pleasure at our banquet."

On this Telemachus came forward and said, "Sirs, are you mad? Can you not carry your meat and your liquor decently? Some evil spirit has possessed you. I do not wish to drive any of you away, but you have had your suppers, and the sooner you all go home to bed the better."

The suitors bit their lips and marvelled at the boldness of his speech; but Amphinomus the son of Nisus, who was son to Aretias, said, "Do not let us take offence; it is reasonable, so let us make no answer. Neither let us do violence to the stranger nor to any of Ulysses' servants. Let the cupbearer go round with the drink-offerings, that we may make them and go home to our rest. As for the stranger, let us leave Telemachus to deal with him, for it is to his house that he has come."

Thus did he speak, and his saying pleased them well, so Mulius of Dulichium, servant to Amphinomus, mixed them a bowl of wine and water and handed it round to each of them man by man, whereon they made their drink-offerings to the blessed gods: Then, when they had made their drink-offerings and had drunk each one as he was minded, they took their several ways each of them to his own abode.

Book XIX

Ulysses was left in the cloister, pondering on the means whereby with Minerva's help he might be able to kill the suitors. Presently he said to Telemachus, "Telemachus, we must get the armour together and take it down inside. Make some excuse when the suitors ask you why you have removed it. Say that you have taken it to be out of the way of the smoke, inasmuch as it is no longer what it was when Ulysses went away, but has become soiled and begrimed with soot. Add to this more particularly that you are afraid Jove may set them on to quarrel over their wine, and that they may do each other some harm which may disgrace both banquet and wooing, for the sight of arms sometimes tempts people to use them."

Telemachus approved of what his father had said, so he called nurse Euryclea and said, "Nurse, shut the women up in their room, while I take the armour that my father left behind him down into the store room. No one looks after it now my father is gone, and it has got all smirched with soot during my own boyhood. I want to take it down where the smoke cannot reach it."

"I wish, child," answered Euryclea, "that you would take the management of the house into your own hands altogether, and look after all the property yourself. But who is to go with you and light you to the store room? The maids would have so, but you would not let them.

"The stranger," said Telemachus, "shall show me a light; when people eat my bread they must earn it, no matter where they come from."

Euryclea did as she was told, and bolted the women inside their room. Then Ulysses and his son made all haste to take the helmets, shields, and spears inside; and Minerva went before them with a gold lamp in her hand that shed a soft and brilliant radiance, whereon Telemachus said, "Father, my eyes behold a great marvel: the walls, with the rafters, crossbeams, and the supports on which they rest are all aglow as with a flaming fire. Surely there is some god here who has come down from heaven."

"Hush," answered Ulysses, "hold your peace and ask no questions, for this is the manner of the gods. Get you to your bed, and leave me here to talk with your mother and the maids. Your mother in her grief will ask me all sorts of questions."

On this Telemachus went by torch-light to the other side of the inner court, to the room in which he always slept. There he lay in his bed till morning, while Ulysses was left in the cloister pondering on the means whereby with Minerva's help he might be able to kill the suitors.

Then Penelope came down from her room looking like Venus or Diana, and they set her a seat inlaid with scrolls of silver and ivory near the fire in her accustomed place. It had been made by Icmalius and had a footstool all in one piece with the seat itself; and it was covered with a thick fleece: on this she now sat, and the maids came from the women's room to join her. They set about removing the tables at which the wicked suitors had been dining, and took away the bread that was left, with the cups from which they had drunk. They emptied the embers out of the braziers, and heaped much wood upon them to give both light and heat; but Melantho began to rail at Ulysses a second time and said, "Stranger, do you mean to plague us by hanging about the house all night and spying upon the women? Be off, you wretch, outside, and eat your supper there, or you shall be driven out with a firebrand."

Ulysses scowled at her and answered, "My good woman, why should you be so angry with me? Is it because I am not clean, and my clothes are all in rags, and because I am obliged to go begging about after the manner of tramps and beggars generall? I too was a rich man once, and had a fine house of my own; in those days I gave to many a tramp such as I now am, no matter who he might be nor what he wanted. I had any number of servants, and all the other things which people have who live well and are accounted wealthy, but it pleased Jove to take all away from me; therefore, woman, beware lest you too come to lose that pride and place in which you now wanton above your fellows; have a care lest you get out of favour with your mistress, and lest Ulysses should come home, for there is still a chance that he may do so. Moreover, though he be dead as you think he is, yet by Apollo's will he has left a son behind him, Telemachus, who will note anything done amiss by the maids in the house, for he is now no longer in his boyhood."

Penelope heard what he was saying and scolded the maid, "Impudent baggage, said she, "I see how abominably you are behaving, and you shall smart for it. You knew perfectly well, for I told you myself, that I was going to see the stranger and ask him about my husband, for whose sake I am in such continual sorrow."

Then she said to her head waiting woman Eurynome, "Bring a seat with a fleece upon it, for the stranger to sit upon while he tells his story, and listens to what I have to say. I wish to ask him some questions."

Eurynome brought the seat at once and set a fleece upon it, and as soon as Ulysses had sat down Penelope began by saying, "Stranger, I shall first ask you who and whence are you? Tell me of your town and parents."

"Madam;" answered Ulysses, "who on the face of the whole earth can dare to chide with you? Your fame reaches the firmament of heaven itself; you are like some blameless king, who upholds righteousness, as the monarch over a great and valiant nation: the earth yields its wheat and barley, the trees are loaded with fruit, the ewes bring forth lambs, and the sea abounds with fish by reason of his virtues, and his people do good deeds under him. Nevertheless, as I sit here in your house, ask me some other question and do not seek to know my race and family, or you will recall memories that will yet more increase my sorrow. I am full of heaviness, but I ought not to sit weeping and wailing in another person's house, nor is it well to be thus grieving continually. I shall have one of the servants or even yourself complaining of me, and saying that my eyes swim with tears because I am heavy with wine."

Then Penelope answered, "Stranger, heaven robbed me of all beauty, whether of face or figure, when the Argives set sail for Troy and my dear husband with them. If he were to return and look after my affairs I should be both more respected and should show a better presence to the world. As it is, I am oppressed with care, and with the afflictions which heaven has seen fit to heap upon me. The chiefs from all our islands- Dulichium, Same, and Zacynthus, as also from Ithaca itself, are wooing me against my will and are wasting my estate. I can therefore show no attention to strangers, nor suppliants, nor to people who say that they are skilled artisans, but am all the time brokenhearted about Ulysses. They want me to marry again at once, and I have to invent stratagems in order to deceive them. In the first place heaven put it in my mind to set up a great tambour-frame in my room, and to begin working upon an enormous piece of fine needlework. Then I said to them, 'Sweethearts, Ulysses is indeed dead, still, do not press me to marry again immediately; wait- for I would not have my skill in needlework perish unrecorded- till I have finished making a pall for the hero Laertes, to be ready against the time when death shall take him. He is very rich, and the women of the place will talk if he is laid out without a pall.' This was what I said, and they assented; whereon I used to keep working at my great web all day long, but at night I would unpick the stitches again by torch light. I fooled them in this way for three years without their finding it out, but as time wore on and I was now in my fourth year, in the waning of moons, and many days had been accomplished, those good-for-nothing hussies my maids betrayed me to the suitors, who broke in upon me and caught me; they were very angry with me, so I was forced to finish my work whether I would or no. And now I do not see how I can find any further shift for getting out of this marriage. My parents are putting great pressure upon me, and my son chafes at the ravages the suitors are making upon his estate, for he is now old enough to understand all about it and is perfectly able to look after his own affairs, for heaven has blessed him with an excellent disposition. Still, notwithstanding all this, tell me who you are and where you come from- for you must have had father and mother of some sort; you cannot be the son of an oak or of a rock."

Then Ulysses answered, "madam, wife of Ulysses, since you persist in asking me about my family, I will answer, no matter what it costs me: people must expect to be pained when they have been exiles as long as I have, and suffered as much among as many peoples. Nevertheless, as regards your question I will tell you all you ask. There is a fair and fruitful island in mid-ocean called Crete; it is thickly peopled and there are nine cities in it: the people speak many different languages which overlap one another, for there are Achaeans, brave Eteocretans, Dorians of three-fold race, and noble Pelasgi. There is a great town there, Cnossus, where Minos reigned who every nine years had a conference with Jove himself. Minos was father to Deucalion, whose son I am, for Deucalion had two sons Idomeneus and myself. Idomeneus sailed for Troy, and I, who am the younger, am called Aethon; my brother, however, was at once the older and the more valiant of the two; hence it was in Crete that I saw Ulysses and showed him hospitality, for the winds took him there as he was on his way to Troy, carrying him out of his course from cape Malea and leaving him in Amnisus off the cave of Ilithuia, where the harbours are difficult to enter and he could hardly find shelter from the winds that were then xaging. As soon as he got there he went into the town and asked for Idomeneus, claiming to be his old and valued friend, but Idomeneus had already set sail for Troy some ten or twelve days earlier, so I took him to my own house and showed him every kind of hospitality, for I had abundance of everything. Moreover, I fed the men who were with him with barley meal from the public store, and got subscriptions of wine and oxen for them to sacrifice to their heart's content. They stayed with me twelve days, for there was a gale blowing from the North so strong that one could hardly keep one's feet on land. I suppose some unfriendly god had raised it for them, but on the thirteenth day the wind dropped, and they got away."

Many a plausible tale did Ulysses further tell her, and Penelope wept as she listened, for her heart was melted. As the snow wastes upon the mountain tops when the winds from South East and West have breathed upon it and thawed it till the rivers run bank full with water, even so did her cheeks overflow with tears for the husband who was all the time sitting by her side. Ulysses felt for her and was for her, but he kept his eyes as hard as or iron without letting them so much as quiver, so cunningly did he restrain his tears. Then, when she had relieved herself by weeping, she turned to him again and said: "Now, stranger, I shall put you to the test and see whether or no you really did entertain my husband and his men, as you say you did. Tell me, then, how he was dressed, what kind of a man he was to look at, and so also with his companions."

"Madam," answered Ulysses, "it is such a long time ago that I can hardly say. Twenty years are come and gone since he left my home, and went elsewhither; but I will tell you as well as I can recollect. Ulysses wore a mantle of purple wool, double lined, and it was fastened by a gold brooch with two catches for the pin. On the face of this there was a device that showed a dog holding a spotted fawn between his fore paws, and watching it as it lay panting upon the ground. Every one marvelled at the way in which these things had been done in gold, the dog looking at the fawn, and strangling it, while the fawn was struggling convulsively to escape. As for the shirt that he wore next his skin, it was so soft that it fitted him like the skin of an onion, and glistened in the sunlight to the admiration of all the women who beheld it. Furthermore I say, and lay my saying to your heart, that I do not know whether Ulysses wore these clothes when he left home, or whether one of his companions had given them to him while he was on his voyage; or possibly some one at whose house he was staying made him a present of them, for he was a man of many friends and had few equals among the Achaeans. I myself gave him a sword of bronze and a beautiful purple mantle, double lined, with a shirt that went down to his feet, and I sent him on board his ship with every mark of honour. He had a servant with him, a little older than himself, and I can tell you what he was like; his shoulders were hunched, he was dark, and he had thick curly hair. His name was Eurybates, and Ulysses treated him with greater familiarity than he did any of the others, as being the most like-minded with himself."

Penelope was moved still more deeply as she heard the indisputable proofs that Ulysses laid before her; and when she had again found relief in tears she said to him, "Stranger, I was already disposed to pity you, but henceforth you shall be honoured and made welcome in my house. It was I who gave Ulysses the clothes you speak of. I took them out of the store room and folded them up myself, and I gave him also the gold brooch to wear as an ornament. Alas! I shall never welcome him home again. It was by an ill fate that he ever set out for that detested city whose very name I cannot bring myself even to mention."

Then Ulysses answered, "Madam, wife of Ulysses, do not disfigure yourself further by grieving thus bitterly for your loss, though I can hardly blame you for doing so. A woman who has loved her husband and borne him children, would naturally be grieved at losing him, even though he were a worse man than Ulysses, who they say was like a god. Still, cease your tears and listen to what I can tell I will hide nothing from you, and can say with perfect truth that I have lately heard of Ulysses as being alive and on his way home; he is among the Thesprotians, and is bringing back much valuable treasure that he has begged from one and another of them; but his ship and all his crew were lost as they were leaving the Thrinacian island, for Jove and the sun-god were angry with him because his men had slaughtered the sun-god's cattle, and they were all drowned to a man. But Ulysses stuck to the keel of the ship and was drifted on to the land of the Phaecians, who are near of kin to the immortals, and who treated him as though he had been a god, giving him many presents, and wishing to escort him home safe and sound. In fact Ulysses would have been here long ago, had he not thought better to go from land to land gathering wealth; for there is no man living who is so wily as he is; there is no one can compare with him. Pheidon king of the Thesprotians told me all this, and he swore to me- making drink-offerings in his house as he did so- that the ship was by the water side and the crew found who would take Ulysses to his own country. He sent me off first, for there happened to be a Thesprotian ship sailing for the wheat-growing island of Dulichium, but he showed me all treasure Ulysses had got together, and he had enough lying in the house of king Pheidon to keep his family for ten generations; but the king said Ulysses had gone to Dodona that he might learn Jove's mind from the high oak tree, and know whether after so long an absence he should return to Ithaca openly or in secret. So you may know he is safe and will be here shortly; he is close at hand and cannot remain away from home much longer; nevertheless I will confirm my words with an oath, and call Jove who is the first and mightiest of all gods to witness, as also that hearth of Ulysses to which I have now come, that all I have spoken shall surely come to pass. Ulysses will return in this self same year; with the end of this moon and the beginning of the next he will be here."

"May it be even so," answered Penelope; "if your words come true you shall have such gifts and such good will from me that all who see you shall congratulate you; but I know very well how it will be. Ulysses will not return, neither will you get your escort hence, for so surely as that Ulysses ever was, there are now no longer any such masters in the house as he was, to receive honourable strangers or to further them on their way home. And now, you maids, wash his feet for him, and make him a bed on a couch with rugs and blankets, that he may be warm and quiet till morning. Then, at day break wash him and anoint him again, that he may sit in the cloister and take his meals with Telemachus. It shall be the worse for any one of these hateful people who is uncivil to him; like it or not, he shall have no more to do in this house. For how, sir, shall you be able to learn whether or no I am superior to others of my sex both in goodness of heart and understanding, if I let you dine in my cloisters squalid and ill clad? Men live but for a little season; if they are hard, and deal hardly, people wish them ill so long as they are alive, and speak contemptuously of them when they are dead, but he that is righteous and deals righteously, the people tell of his praise among all lands, and many shall call him blessed."

Ulysses answered, "Madam, I have foresworn rugs and blankets from the day that I left the snowy ranges of Crete to go on shipboard. I will lie as I have lain on many a sleepless night hitherto. Night after night have I passed in any rough sleeping place, and waited for morning. Nor, again, do I like having my feet washed; I shall not let any of the young hussies about your house touch my feet; but, if you have any old and respectable woman who has gone through as much trouble as I have, I will allow her to wash them."

To this Penelope said, "My dear sir, of all the guests who ever yet came to my house there never was one who spoke in all things with such admirable propriety as you do. There happens to be in the house a most respectable old woman- the same who received my poor dear husband in her arms the night he was born, and nursed him in infancy. She is very feeble now, but she shall wash your feet." "Come here," said she, "Euryclea, and wash your master's age-mate; I suppose Ulysses' hands and feet are very much the same now as his are, for trouble ages all of us dreadfully fast."

On these words the old woman covered her face with her hands; she began to weep and made lamentation saying, "My dear child, I cannot think whatever I am to do with you. I am certain no one was ever more god-fearing than yourself, and yet Jove hates you. No one in the whole world ever burned him more thigh bones, nor gave him finer hecatombs when you prayed you might come to a green old age yourself and see your son grow up to take after you; yet see how he has prevented you alone from ever getting back to your own home. I have no doubt the women in some foreign palace which Ulysses has got to are gibing at him as all these sluts here have been gibing you. I do not wonder at your not choosing to let them wash you after the manner in which they have insulted you; I will wash your feet myself gladly enough, as Penelope has said that I am to do so; I will wash them both for Penelope's sake and for your own, for you have raised the most lively feelings of compassion in my mind; and let me say this moreover, which pray attend to; we have had all kinds of strangers in distress come here before now, but I make bold to say that no one ever yet came who was so like Ulysses in figure, voice, and feet as you are."

"Those who have seen us both," answered Ulysses, "have always said we were wonderfully like each other, and now you have noticed it too.

Then the old woman took the cauldron in which she was going to wash his feet, and poured plenty of cold water into it, adding hot till the bath was warm enough. Ulysses sat by the fire, but ere long he turned away from the light, for it occurred to him that when the old woman had hold of his leg she would recognize a certain scar which it bore, whereon the whole truth would come out. And indeed as soon as she began washing her master, she at once knew the scar as one that had been given him by a wild boar when he was hunting on Mount Parnassus with his excellent grandfather Autolycus- who was the most accomplished thief and perjurer in the whole world- and with the sons of Autolycus. Mercury himself had endowed him with this gift, for he used to burn the thigh bones of goats and kids to him, so he took pleasure in his companionship. It happened once that Autolycus had gone to Ithaca and had found the child of his daughter just born. As soon as he had done supper Euryclea set the infant upon his knees and said, you must find a name for your grandson; you greatly wished that you might have one."

'Son-in-law and daughter," replied Autolycus, "call the child thus: I am highly displeased with a large number of people in one place and another, both men and women; so name the child 'Ulysses,' or the child of anger. When he grows up and comes to visit his mother's family on Mount Parnassus, where my possessions lie, I will make him a present and will send him on his way rejoicing."

Ulysses, therefore, went to Parnassus to get the presents from Autolycus, who with his sons shook hands with him and gave him welcome. His grandmother Amphithea threw her arms about him, and kissed his head, and both his beautiful eyes, while Autolycus desired his sons to get dinner ready, and they did as he told them. They brought in a five year old bull, flayed it, made it ready and divided it into joints; these they then cut carefully up into smaller pieces and spitted them; they roasted them sufficiently and served the portions round. Thus through the livelong day to the going down of the sun they feasted, and every man had his full share so that all were satisfied; but when the sun set and it came on dark, they went to bed and enjoyed the boon of sleep.

When the child of morning, rosy-fingered Dawn, appeared, the sons of Autolycus went out with their hounds hunting, and Ulysses went too. They climbed the wooded slopes of Parnassus and soon reached its breezy upland valleys; but as the sun was beginning to beat upon the fields, fresh-risen from the slow still currents of Oceanus, they came to a mountain dell. The dogs were in front searching for the tracks of the beast they were chasing, and after them came the sons of Autolycus, among whom was Ulysses, close behind the dogs, and he had a long spear in his hand. Here was the lair of a huge boar among some thick brushwood, so dense that the wind and rain could not get through it, nor could the sun's rays pierce it, and the ground underneath lay thick with fallen leaves. The boar heard the noise of the men's feet, and the hounds baying on every side as the huntsmen came up to him, so rushed from his lair, raised the bristles on his neck, and stood at bay with fire flashing from his eyes. Ulysses was the first to raise his spear and try to drive it into the brute, but the boar was too quick for him, and charged him sideways, ripping him above the knee with a gash that tore deep though it did not reach the bone. As for the boar, Ulysses hit him on the right shoulder, and the point of the spear went right through him, so that he fell groaning in the dust until the life went out of him. The sons of Autolycus busied themselves with the carcass of the boar, and bound Ulysses' wound; then, after saying a spell to stop the bleeding, they went home as fast as they could. But when Autolycus and his sons had thoroughly healed Ulysses, they made him some splendid presents, and sent him back to Ithaca with much mutual good will. When he got back, his father and mother were rejoiced to see him, and asked him all about it, and how he had hurt himself to get the scar; so he told them how the boar had ripped him when he was out hunting with Autolycus and his sons on Mount Parnassus.

As soon as Euryclea had got the scarred limb in her hands and had well hold of it, she recognized it and dropped the foot at once. The leg fell into the bath, which rang out and was overturned, so that all the water was spilt on the ground; Euryclea's eyes between her joy and her grief filled with tears, and she could not speak, but she caught Ulysses by the beard and said, "My dear child, I am sure you must be Ulysses himself, only I did not know you till I had actually touched and handled you."

As she spoke she looked towards Penelope, as though wanting to tell her that her dear husband was in the house, but Penelope was unable to look in that direction and observe what was going on, for Minerva had diverted her attention; so Ulysses caught Euryclea by the throat with his right hand and with his left drew her close to him, and said, "Nurse, do you wish to be the ruin of me, you who nursed me at your own breast, now that after twenty years of wandering I am at last come to my own home again? Since it has been borne in upon you by heaven to recognize me, hold your tongue, and do not say a word about it any one else in the house, for if you do I tell you- and it shall surely be- that if heaven grants me to take the lives of these suitors, I will not spare you, though you are my own nurse, when I am killing the other women."

"My child," answered Euryclea, "what are you talking about? You know very well that nothing can either bend or break me. I will hold my tongue like a stone or a piece of iron; furthermore let me say, and lay my saying to your heart, when heaven has delivered the suitors into your hand, I will give you a list of the women in the house who have been ill-behaved, and of those who are guiltless."

And Ulysses answered, "Nurse, you ought not to speak in that way; I am well able to form my own opinion about one and all of them; hold your tongue and leave everything to heaven."

As he said this Euryclea left the cloister to fetch some more water, for the first had been all spilt; and when she had washed him and anointed him with oil, Ulysses drew his seat nearer to the fire to warm himself, and hid the scar under his rags. Then Penelope began talking to him and said:

"Stranger, I should like to speak with you briefly about another matter. It is indeed nearly bed time- for those, at least, who can sleep in spite of sorrow. As for myself, heaven has given me a life of such unmeasurable woe, that even by day when I am attending to my duties and looking after the servants, I am still weeping and lamenting during the whole time; then, when night comes, and we all of us go to bed, I lie awake thinking, and my heart comes a prey to the most incessant and cruel tortures. As the dun nightingale, daughter of Pandareus, sings in the early spring from her seat in shadiest covert hid, and with many a plaintive trill pours out the tale how by mishap she killed her own child Itylus, son of king Zethus, even so does my mind toss and turn in its uncertainty whether I ought to stay with my son here, and safeguard my substance, my bondsmen, and the greatness of my house, out of regard to public opinion and the memory of my late husband, or whether it is not now time for me to go with the best of these suitors who are wooing me and making me such magnificent presents. As long as my son was still young, and unable to understand, he would not hear of my leaving my husband's house, but now that he is full grown he begs and prays me to do so, being incensed at the way in which the suitors are eating up his property. Listen, then, to a dream that I have had and interpret it for me if you can. I have twenty geese about the house that eat mash out of a trough, and of which I am exceedingly fond. I dreamed that a great eagle came swooping down from a mountain, and dug his curved beak into the neck of each of them till he had killed them all. Presently he soared off into the sky, and left them lying dead about the yard; whereon I wept in my room till all my maids gathered round me, so piteously was I grieving because the eagle had killed my geese. Then he came back again, and perching on a projecting rafter spoke to me with human voice, and told me to leave off crying. 'Be of good courage,' he said, 'daughter of Icarius; this is no dream, but a vision of good omen that shall surely come to pass. The geese are the suitors, and I am no longer an eagle, but your own husband, who am come back to you, and who will bring these suitors to a disgraceful end.' On this I woke, and when I looked out I saw my geese at the trough eating their mash as usual."

"This dream, Madam," replied Ulysses, "can admit but of one interpretation, for had not Ulysses himself told you how it shall be fulfilled? The death of the suitors is portended, and not one single one of them will escape."

And Penelope answered, "Stranger, dreams are very curious and unaccountable things, and they do not by any means invariably come true. There are two gates through which these unsubstantial fancies proceed; the one is of horn, and the other ivory. Those that come through the gate of ivory are fatuous, but those from the gate of horn mean something to those that see them. I do not think, however, that my own dream came through the gate of horn, though I and my son should be most thankful if it proves to have done so. Furthermore I say- and lay my saying to your heart- the coming dawn will usher in the ill-omened day that is to sever me from the house of Ulysses, for I am about to hold a tournament of axes. My husband used to set up twelve axes in the court, one in front of the other, like the stays upon which a ship is built; he would then go back from them and shoot an arrow through the whole twelve. I shall make the suitors try to do the same thing, and whichever of them can string the bow most easily, and send his arrow through all the twelve axes, him will I follow, and quit this house of my lawful husband, so goodly and so abounding in wealth. But even so, I doubt not that I shall remember it in my dreams."

Then Ulysses answered, "Madam wife of Ulysses, you need not defer your tournament, for Ulysses will return ere ever they can string the bow, handle it how they will, and send their arrows through the iron."

To this Penelope said, "As long, sir, as you will sit here and talk to me, I can have no desire to go to bed. Still, people cannot do permanently without sleep, and heaven has appointed us dwellers on earth a time for all things. I will therefore go upstairs and recline upon that couch which I have never ceased to flood with my tears from the day Ulysses set out for the city with a hateful name."

She then went upstairs to her own room, not alone, but attended by her maidens, and when there, she lamented her dear husband till Minerva shed sweet sleep over her eyelids.

Book XX

Ulysses slept in the cloister upon an undressed bullock's hide, on the top of which he threw several skins of the sheep the suitors had eaten, and Eurynome threw a cloak over him after he had laid himself down. There, then, Ulysses lay wakefully brooding upon the way in which he should kill the suitors; and by and by, the women who had been in the habit of misconducting themselves with them, left the house giggling and laughing with one another. This made Ulysses very angry, and he doubted whether to get up and kill every single one of them then and there, or to let them sleep one more and last time with the suitors. His heart growled within him, and as a bitch with puppies growls and shows her teeth when she sees a stranger, so did his heart growl with anger at the evil deeds that were being done: but he beat his breast and said, "Heart, be still, you had worse than this to bear on the day when the terrible Cyclops ate your brave companions; yet you bore it in silence till your cunning got you safe out of the cave, though you made sure of being killed."

Thus he chided with his heart, and checked it into endurance, but he tossed about as one who turns a paunch full of blood and fat in front of a hot fire, doing it first on one side and then on the other, that he may get it cooked as soon as possible, even so did he turn himself about from side to side, thinking all the time how, single handed as he was, he should contrive to kill so large a body of men as the wicked suitors. But by and by Minerva came down from heaven in the likeness of a woman, and hovered over his head saying, "My poor unhappy man, why do you lie awake in this way? This is your house: your wife is safe inside it, and so is your son who is just such a young man as any father may be proud of."

"Goddess," answered Ulysses, "all that you have said is true, but I am in some doubt as to how I shall be able to kill these wicked suitors single handed, seeing what a number of them there always are. And there is this further difficulty, which is still more considerable. Supposing that with Jove's and your assistance I succeed in killing them, I must ask you to consider where I am to escape to from their avengers when it is all over."

"For shame," replied Minerva, "why, any one else would trust a worse ally than myself, even though that ally were only a mortal and less wise than I am. Am I not a goddess, and have I not protected you throughout in all your troubles? I tell you plainly that even though there were fifty bands of men surrounding us and eager to kill us, you should take all their sheep and cattle, and drive them away with you. But go to sleep; it is a very bad thing to lie awake all night, and you shall be out of your troubles before long."

As she spoke she shed sleep over his eyes, and then went back to Olympus.

While Ulysses was thus yielding himself to a very deep slumber that eased the burden of his sorrows, his admirable wife awoke, and sitting up in her bed began to cry. When she had relieved herself by weeping she prayed to Diana saying, "Great Goddess Diana, daughter of Jove, drive an arrow into my heart and slay me; or let some whirlwind snatch me up and bear me through paths of darkness till it drop me into the mouths of overflowing Oceanus, as it did the daughters of Pandareus. The daughters of Pandareus lost their father and mother, for the gods killed them, so they were left orphans. But Venus took care of them, and fed them on cheese, honey, and sweet wine. Juno taught them to excel all women in beauty of form and understanding; Diana gave them an imposing presence, and Minerva endowed them with every kind of accomplishment; but one day when Venus had gone up to Olympus to see Jove about getting them married (for well does he know both what shall happen and what not happen to every one) the storm winds came and spirited them away to become handmaids to the dread Erinyes. Even so I wish that the gods who live in heaven would hide me from mortal sight, or that fair Diana might strike me, for I would fain go even beneath the sad earth if I might do so still looking towards Ulysses only, and without having to yield myself to a worse man than he was. Besides, no matter how much people may grieve by day, they can put up with it so long as they can sleep at night, for when the eyes are closed in slumber people forget good and ill alike; whereas my misery haunts me even in my dreams. This very night methought there was one lying by my side who was like Ulysses as he was when he went away with his host, and I rejoiced, for I believed that it was no dream, but the very truth itself."

On this the day broke, but Ulysses heard the sound of her weeping, and it puzzled him, for it seemed as though she already knew him and was by his side. Then he gathered up the cloak and the fleeces on which he had lain, and set them on a seat in the cloister, but he took the bullock's hide out into the open. He lifted up his hands to heaven, and prayed, saying "Father Jove, since you have seen fit to bring me over land and sea to my own home after all the afflictions you have laid upon me, give me a sign out of the mouth of some one or other of those who are now waking within the house, and let me have another sign of some kind from outside."

Thus did he pray. Jove heard his prayer and forthwith thundered high up among the from the splendour of Olympus, and Ulysses was glad when he heard it. At the same time within the house, a miller-woman from hard by in the mill room lifted up her voice and gave him another sign. There were twelve miller-women whose business it was to grind wheat and barley which are the staff of life. The others had ground their task and had gone to take their rest, but this one had not yet finished, for she was not so strong as they were, and when she heard the thunder she stopped grinding and gave the sign to her master. "Father Jove," said she, "you who rule over heaven and earth, you have thundered from a clear sky without so much as a cloud in it, and this means something for somebody; grant the prayer, then, of me your poor servant who calls upon you, and let this be the very last day that the suitors dine in the house of Ulysses. They have worn me out with the labour of grinding meal for them, and I hope they may never have another dinner anywhere at all."

Ulysses was glad when he heard the omens conveyed to him by the woman's speech, and by the thunder, for he knew they meant that he should avenge himself on the suitors.

Then the other maids in the house rose and lit the fire on the hearth; Telemachus also rose and put on his clothes. He girded his sword about his shoulder, bound his sandals on his comely feet, and took a doughty spear with a point of sharpened bronze; then he went to the threshold of the cloister and said to Euryclea, "Nurse, did you make the stranger comfortable both as regards bed and board, or did you let him shift for himself?- for my mother, good woman though she is, has a way of paying great attention to second-rate people, and of neglecting others who are in reality much better men."

"Do not find fault child," said Euryclea, "when there is no one to find fault with. The stranger sat and drank his wine as long as he liked: your mother did ask him if he would take any more bread and he said he would not. When he wanted to go to bed she told the servants to make one for him, but he said he was re such wretched outcast that he would not sleep on a bed and under blankets; he insisted on having an undressed bullock's hide and some sheepskins put for him in the cloister and I threw a cloak over him myself."

Then Telemachus went out of the court to the place where the Achaeans were meeting in assembly; he had his spear in his hand, and he was not alone, for his two dogs went with him. But Euryclea called the maids and said, "Come, wake up; set about sweeping the cloisters and sprinkling them with water to lay the dust; put the covers on the seats; wipe down the tables, some of you, with a wet sponge; clean out the mixing-jugs and the cups, and for water from the fountain at once; the suitors will be here directly; they will be here early, for it is a feast day."

Thus did she speak, and they did even as she had said: twenty of them went to the fountain for water, and the others set themselves busily to work about the house. The men who were in attendance on the suitors also came up and began chopping firewood. By and by the women returned from the fountain, and the swineherd came after them with the three best pigs he could pick out. These he let feed about the premises, and then he said good-humouredly to Ulysses, "Stranger, are the suitors treating you any better now, or are they as insolent as ever?"

"May heaven," answered Ulysses, "requite to them the wickedness with which they deal high-handedly in another man's house without any sense of shame."

Thus did they converse; meanwhile Melanthius the goatherd came up, for he too was bringing in his best goats for the suitors' dinner; and he had two shepherds with him. They tied the goats up under the gatehouse, and then Melanthius began gibing at Ulysses. "Are you still here, stranger," said he, "to pester people by begging about the house? Why can you not go elsewhere? You and I shall not come to an understanding before we have given each other a taste of our fists. You beg without any sense of decency: are there not feasts elsewhere among the Achaeans, as well as here?"

Ulysses made no answer, but bowed his head and brooded. Then a third man, Philoetius, joined them, who was bringing in a barren heifer and some goats. These were brought over by the boatmen who are there to take people over when any one comes to them. So Philoetius made his heifer and his goats secure under the gatehouse, and then went up to the swineherd. "Who, Swineherd," said he, "is this stranger that is lately come here? Is he one of your men? What is his family? Where does he come from? Poor fellow, he looks as if he had been some great man, but the gods give sorrow to whom they will- even to kings if it so pleases them

As he spoke he went up to Ulysses and saluted him with his right hand; "Good day to you, father stranger," said he, "you seem to be very poorly off now, but I hope you will have better times by and by. Father Jove, of all gods you are the most malicious. We are your own children, yet you show us no mercy in all our misery and afflictions. A sweat came over me when I saw this man, and my eyes filled with tears, for he reminds me of Ulysses, who I fear is going about in just such rags as this man's are, if indeed he is still among the living. If he is already dead and in the house of Hades, then, alas! for my good master, who made me his stockman when I was quite young among the Cephallenians, and now his cattle are countless; no one could have done better with them than I have, for they have bred like ears of corn; nevertheless I have to keep bringing them in for others to eat, who take no heed of his son though he is in the house, and fear not the wrath of heaven, but are already eager to divide Ulysses' property among them because he has been away so long. I have often thought- only it would not be right while his son is living- of going off with the cattle to some foreign country; bad as this would be, it is still harder to stay here and be ill-treated about other people's herds. My position is intolerable, and I should long since have run away and put myself under the protection of some other chief, only that I believe my poor master will yet return, and send all these suitors flying out of the house."

"Stockman," answered Ulysses, "you seem to be a very well-disposed person, and I can see that you are a man of sense. Therefore I will tell you, and will confirm my words with an oath: by Jove, the chief of all gods, and by that hearth of Ulysses to which I am now come, Ulysses shall return before you leave this place, and if you are so minded you shall see him killing the suitors who are now masters here."

"If Jove were to bring this to pass," replied the stockman, "you should see how I would do my very utmost to help him."

And in like manner Eumaeus prayed that Ulysses might return home.

Thus did they converse. Meanwhile the suitors were hatching a plot to murder Telemachus: but a bird flew near them on their left hand- an eagle with a dove in its talons. On this Amphinomus said, "My friends, this plot of ours to murder Telemachus will not succeed; let us go to dinner instead."

The others assented, so they went inside and laid their cloaks on the benches and seats. They sacrificed the sheep, goats, pigs, and the heifer, and when the inward meats were cooked they served them round. They mixed the wine in the mixing-bowls, and the swineherd gave every man his cup, while Philoetius handed round the bread in the breadbaskets, and Melanthius poured them out their wine. Then they laid their hands upon the good things that were before them.

Telemachus purposely made Ulysses sit in the part of the cloister that was paved with stone; he gave him a shabby-looking seat at a little table to himself, and had his portion of the inward meats brought to him, with his wine in a gold cup. "Sit there," said he, "and drink your wine among the great people. I will put a stop to the gibes and blows of the suitors, for this is no public house, but belongs to Ulysses, and has passed from him to me. Therefore, suitors, keep your hands and your tongues to yourselves, or there will be mischief."

The suitors bit their lips, and marvelled at the boldness of his speech; then Antinous said, "We do not like such language but we will put up with it, for Telemachus is threatening us in good earnest. If Jove had let us we should have put a stop to his brave talk ere now."

Thus spoke Antinous, but Telemachus heeded him not. Meanwhile the heralds were bringing the holy hecatomb through the city, and the Achaeans gathered under the shady grove of Apollo.

Then they roasted the outer meat, drew it off the spits, gave every man his portion, and feasted to their hearts' content; those who waited at table gave Ulysses exactly the same portion as the others had, for Telemachus had told them to do so.

But Minerva would not let the suitors for one moment drop their insolence, for she wanted Ulysses to become still more bitter against them. Now there happened to be among them a ribald fellow, whose name was Ctesippus, and who came from Same. This man, confident in his great wealth, was paying court to the wife of Ulysses, and said to the suitors, "Hear what I have to say. The stranger has already had as large a portion as any one else; this is well, for it is not right nor reasonable to ill-treat any guest of Telemachus who comes here. I will, however, make him a present on my own account, that he may have something to give to the bath-woman, or to some other of Ulysses' servants."

As he spoke he picked up a heifer's foot from the meat-basket in which it lay, and threw it at Ulysses, but Ulysses turned his head a little aside, and avoided it, smiling grimly Sardinian fashion as he did so, and it hit the wall, not him. On this Telemachus spoke fiercely to Ctesippus, "It is a good thing for you," said he, "that the stranger turned his head so that you missed him. If you had hit him I should have run you through with my spear, and your father would have had to see about getting you buried rather than married in this house. So let me have no more unseemly behaviour from any of you, for I am grown up now to the knowledge of good and evil and understand what is going on, instead of being the child that I have been heretofore. I have long seen you killing my sheep and making free with my corn and wine: I have put up with this, for one man is no match for many, but do me no further violence. Still, if you wish to kill me, kill me; I would far rather die than see such disgraceful scenes day after day- guests insulted, and men dragging the women servants about the house in an unseemly way."

They all held their peace till at last Agelaus son of Damastor said, "No one should take offence at what has just been said, nor gainsay it, for it is quite reasonable. Leave off, therefore, ill-treating the stranger, or any one else of the servants who are about the house; I would say, however, a friendly word to Telemachus and his mother, which I trust may commend itself to both. 'As long,' I would say, 'as you had ground for hoping that Ulysses would one day come home, no one could complain of your waiting and suffering the suitors to be in your house. It would have been better that he should have returned, but it is now sufficiently clear that he will never do so; therefore talk all this quietly over with your mother, and tell her to marry the best man, and the one who makes her the most advantageous offer. Thus you will yourself be able to manage your own inheritance, and to eat and drink in peace, while your mother will look after some other man's house, not yours.'"

To this Telemachus answered, "By Jove, Agelaus, and by the sorrows of my unhappy father, who has either perished far from Ithaca, or is wandering in some distant land, I throw no obstacles in the way of my mother's marriage; on the contrary I urge her to choose whomsoever she will, and I will give her numberless gifts into the bargain, but I dare not insist point blank that she shall leave the house against her own wishes. Heaven forbid that I should do this."

Minerva now made the suitors fall to laughing immoderately, and set their wits wandering; but they were laughing with a forced laughter. Their meat became smeared with blood; their eyes filled with tears, and their hearts were heavy with forebodings. Theoclymenus saw this and said, "Unhappy men, what is it that ails you? There is a shroud of darkness drawn over you from head to foot, your cheeks are wet with tears; the air is alive with wailing voices; the walls and roof-beams drip blood; the gate of the cloisters and the court beyond them are full of ghosts trooping down into the night of hell; the sun is blotted out of heaven, and a blighting gloom is over all the land."

Thus did he speak, and they all of them laughed heartily. Eurymachus then said, "This stranger who has lately come here has lost his senses. Servants, turn him out into the streets, since he finds it so dark here."

But Theoclymenus said, "Eurymachus, you need not send any one with me. I have eyes, ears, and a pair of feet of my own, to say nothing of an understanding mind. I will take these out of the house with me, for I see mischief overhanging you, from which not one of you men who are insulting people and plotting ill deeds in the house of Ulysses will be able to escape."

He left the house as he spoke, and went back to Piraeus who gave him welcome, but the suitors kept looking at one another and provoking Telemachus fly laughing at the strangers. One insolent fellow said to him, "Telemachus, you are not happy in your guests; first you have this importunate tramp, who comes begging bread and wine and has no skill for work or for hard fighting, but is perfectly useless, and now here is another fellow who is setting himself up as a prophet. Let me persuade you, for it will be much better, to put them on board ship and send them off to the Sicels to sell for what they will bring."

Telemachus gave him no heed, but sat silently watching his father, expecting every moment that he would begin his attack upon the suitors.

Meanwhile the daughter of Icarius, wise Penelope, had had had a rich seat placed for her facing the court and cloisters, so that she could hear what every one was saying. The dinner indeed had been prepared amid merriment; it had been both good and abundant, for they had sacrificed many victims; but the supper was yet to come, and nothing can be conceived more gruesome than the meal which a goddess and a brave man were soon to lay before them- for they had brought their doom upon themselves.

The End

Understanding the Odyssey

1. Examine the relationships of the gods to the mortals and demi-gods. What do their relationships suggest about the Greeks' religious beliefs?
2. Odysseus constantly puts people to the test. List some of those moments when he does so and what are the results each time he does? What does this say about his character?
3. What are some of the characteristic of the ideal hero? What does Odysseus do that might keep him from being heroic?
4. How do the deities in the Odyssey reflect Greek thought about their gods and goddesses? How responsible are they for what happens to people in Greek Life?

The Iliad

By Homer

WRITTEN 800 B.C.E | TRANSLATED BY SAMUEL BUTLER

Book I

Sing, O goddess, the anger of Achilles son of Peleus, that brought countless ills upon the Achaeans. Many a brave soul did it send hurrying down to Hades, and many a hero did it yield a prey to dogs and vultures, for so were the counsels of Jove fulfilled from the day on which the son of Atreus, king of men, and great Achilles, first fell out with one another.

And which of the gods was it that set them on to quarrel? It was the son of Jove and Leto; for he was angry with the king and sent a pestilence upon the host to plague the people, because the son of Atreus had dishonoured Chryses his priest. Now Chryses had come to the ships of the Achaeans to free his daughter, and had brought with him a great ransom: moreover he bore in his hand the sceptre of Apollo wreathed with a suppliant's wreath and he besought the Achaeans, but most of all the two sons of Atreus, who were their chiefs.

"Sons of Atreus," he cried, "and all other Achaeans, may the gods who dwell in Olympus grant you to sack the city of Priam, and to reach your homes in safety; but free my daughter, and accept a ransom for her, in reverence to Apollo, son of Jove."

On this the rest of the Achaeans with one voice were for respecting the priest and taking the ransom that he offered; but not so Agamemnon, who spoke fiercely to him and sent him roughly away. "Old man," said he, "let me not find you tarrying about our ships, nor yet coming hereafter. Your sceptre of the god and your wreath shall profit you nothing. I will not free her. She shall grow old in my house at Argos far from her own home, busying herself with her loom and visiting my couch; so go, and do not provoke me or it shall be the worse for you."

The old man feared him and obeyed. Not a word he spoke, but went by the shore of the sounding sea and prayed apart to King Apollo whom lovely Leto had borne. "Hear me," he cried, "O god of the silver bow, that protectest Chryse and holy Cilla and rulest Tenedos with thy might, hear me oh thou of Sminthe. If I have ever decked your temple with garlands, or burned your thigh-bones in fat of bulls or goats, grant my prayer, and let your arrows avenge these my tears upon the Danaans."

Thus did he pray, and Apollo heard his prayer. He came down furious from the summits of Olympus, with his bow and his quiver upon his shoulder, and the arrows rattled on his back with the rage that trembled within him. He sat himself down away from the ships with a face as dark as night, and his silver bow rang death as he shot his arrow in the midst of them. First he smote their mules and their hounds, but presently he aimed his shafts at the people themselves, and all day long the pyres of the dead were burning.

For nine whole days he shot his arrows among the people, but upon the tenth day Achilles called them in assembly- moved thereto by Juno, who saw the Achaeans in their death-throes and had compassion upon them. Then, when they were got together, he rose and spoke among them.

"Son of Atreus," said he, "I deem that we should now turn roving home if we would escape destruction, for we are being cut down by war and pestilence at once. Let us ask some priest or prophet, or some reader of dreams (for dreams, too, are of Jove) who can tell us why Phoebus Apollo is so angry, and say whether it is for some vow that we have broken, or hecatomb that we have not offered, and whether he will accept the savour of lambs and goats without blemish, so as to take away the plague from us."

With these words he sat down, and Calchas son of Thestor, wisest of augurs, who knew things past present and to come, rose to speak. He it was who had guided the Achaeans with their fleet to Ilius, through the prophesyings with which Phoebus Apollo had inspired him. With all sincerity and goodwill he addressed them thus:-

"Achilles, loved of heaven, you bid me tell you about the anger of King Apollo, I will therefore do so; but consider first and swear that you will stand by me heartily in word and deed, for I know that I shall offend one who rules the Argives with might, to whom all the Achaeans are in subjection. A plain man cannot stand against the anger of a king, who if he swallow his displeasure now, will yet nurse revenge till he has wreaked it. Consider, therefore, whether or no you will protect me."

And Achilles answered, "Fear not, but speak as it is borne in upon you from heaven, for by Apollo, Calchas, to whom you pray, and whose oracles you reveal to us, not a Danaan at our ships shall lay his hand upon you, while I yet live to look upon the face of the earth- no, not though you name Agamemnon himself, who is by far the foremost of the Achaeans."

Thereon the seer spoke boldly. "The god," he said, "is angry neither about vow nor hecatomb, but for his priest's sake, whom Agamemnon has dishonoured, in that he would not free his daughter nor take a ransom for her; therefore has he sent these evils upon us, and will yet send others. He will not deliver the Danaans from this pestilence till Agamemnon has restored the girl without fee or ransom to her father, and has sent a holy hecatomb to Chryse. Thus we may perhaps appease him."

With these words he sat down, and Agamemnon rose in anger. His heart was black with rage, and his eyes flashed fire as he scowled on Calchas and said, "Seer of evil, you never yet prophesied smooth things concerning me, but have ever loved to foretell that which was evil. You have brought me neither comfort nor performance; and now you come seeing among Danaans, and saying that Apollo has plagued us because I would not take a ransom for this girl, the daughter of Chryses. I have set my heart on keeping her in my own house, for I love her better even than my own wife Clytemnestra, whose peer she is alike in form and feature, in understanding and accomplishments. Still I will give her up if I must, for I would have the people live, not die; but you must find me a prize instead, or I alone among the Argives shall be without one. This is not well; for you behold, all of you, that my prize is to go elsewhither."

And Achilles answered, "Most noble son of Atreus, covetous beyond all mankind, how shall the Achaeans find you another prize? We have no common store from which to take one. Those we took from the cities have been awarded; we cannot disallow the awards that have been made already. Give this girl, therefore, to the god, and if ever Jove grants us to sack the city of Troy we will requite you three and fourfold."

Then Agamemnon said, "Achilles, valiant though you be, you shall not thus outwit me. You shall not overreach and you shall not persuade me. Are you to keep your own prize, while I sit tamely under my loss and give up the girl at your bidding? Let the Achaeans find me a prize in fair exchange to my liking, or I will come and take your own, or that of Ajax or of Ulysses; and he to whomsoever I may come shall rue my coming. But of this we will take thought hereafter; for the present, let us draw a ship into the sea, and find a crew for her expressly; let us put a hecatomb on board, and let us send Chryseis also; further, let some chief man among us be in command, either Ajax, or Idomeneus, or yourself, son of Peleus, mighty warrior that you are, that we may offer sacrifice and appease the anger of the god."

Achilles scowled at him and answered, "You are steeped in insolence and lust of gain. With what heart can any of the Achaeans do your bidding, either on foray or in open fighting? I came not warring here for any ill the Trojans had done me. I have no quarrel with them. They have not raided my cattle nor my horses, nor cut down my harvests on the rich plains of Phthia; for between me and them there is a great space, both mountain and sounding sea. We have followed you, Sir Insolence! for your pleasure, not ours- to gain satisfaction from the Trojans for your shameless self and for Menelaus. You forget this, and threaten to rob me of the prize for which I have toiled, and which the sons of the Achaeans have given me. Never when the Achaeans sack any rich city of the Trojans do I receive so good a prize as you do, though it is my hands that do the better part of the fighting. When the sharing comes, your share is far the largest, and I, forsooth, must go back to my ships, take what I can get and be thankful, when my labour of fighting is done. Now, therefore, I shall go back to Phthia; it will be much better for me to return home with my ships, for I will not stay here dishonoured to gather gold and substance for you."

And Agamemnon answered, "Fly if you will, I shall make you no prayers to stay you. I have others here who will do me honour, and above all Jove, the lord of counsel. There is no king here so hateful to me as you are, for you are ever quarrelsome and ill affected. What though you be brave? Was it not heaven that made you so? Go home, then, with your ships and comrades to lord it over the Myrmidons. I care neither for you nor for your anger; and thus will I do: since Phoebus Apollo is taking Chryseis from me, I shall send her with my ship and my followers, but I shall come to your tent and take your own prize Briseis, that you may learn how much stronger I am than you are, and that another may fear to set himself up as equal or comparable with me."

The son of Peleus was furious, and his heart within his shaggy breast was divided whether to draw his sword, push the others aside, and kill the son of Atreus, or to restrain himself and check his anger. While he was thus in two minds, and was drawing his mighty sword from its scabbard, Minerva came down from heaven (for Juno had sent her in the love she bore to them both), and seized the son of Peleus by his yellow hair, visible to him alone, for of the others no man could see her. Achilles turned in amaze, and by the fire that flashed from her eyes at once knew that she was Minerva. "Why are you here," said he, "daughter of aegis-bearing Jove? To see the pride of Agamemnon, son of Atreus? Let me tell you- and it shall surely be- he shall pay for this insolence with his life."

And Minerva said, "I come from heaven, if you will hear me, to bid you stay your anger. Juno has sent me, who cares for both of you alike. Cease, then, this brawling, and do not draw your sword; rail at him if you will, and your railing will not be vain, for I tell you- and it shall surely be- that you shall hereafter receive gifts three times as splendid by reason of this present insult. Hold, therefore, and obey."

"Goddess," answered Achilles, "however angry a man may be, he must do as you two command him. This will be best, for the gods ever hear the prayers of him who has obeyed them."

He stayed his hand on the silver hilt of his sword, and thrust it back into the scabbard as Minerva bade him. Then she went back to Olympus among the other gods, and to the house of aegis-bearing Jove.

But the son of Peleus again began railing at the son of Atreus, for he was still in a rage. "Wine-bibber," he cried, "with the face of a dog and the heart of a hind, you never dare to go out with the host in fight, nor yet with our chosen men in ambuscade. You shun this as you do death itself. You had rather go round and rob his prizes from any man who contradicts you. You devour your people, for you are king over a feeble folk; otherwise, son of Atreus, henceforward you would insult no man. Therefore I say, and swear it with a great oath- nay, by this my sceptre which shalt sprout neither leaf nor shoot, nor bud anew from the day on which it left its parent stem upon the mountains- for the axe stripped it of leaf and bark, and now the sons of the Achaeans bear it as judges and guardians of the decrees of heaven- so surely and solemnly do I swear that hereafter they shall look fondly for Achilles and shall not find him. In the day of your distress, when your men fall dying by the murderous hand of Hector, you shall not know how to help them, and shall rend your heart with rage for the hour when you offered insult to the bravest of the Achaeans."

With this the son of Peleus dashed his gold-bestudded sceptre on the ground and took his seat, while the son of Atreus was beginning fiercely from his place upon the other side. Then uprose smooth-tongued Nestor, the facile speaker of the Pylians, and the words fell from his lips sweeter than honey. Two generations of men born and bred in Pylos had passed away under his rule, and he was now reigning over the third. With all sincerity and goodwill, therefore, he addressed them thus:-

"Of a truth," he said, "a great sorrow has befallen the Achaean land. Surely Priam with his sons would rejoice, and the Trojans be glad at heart if they could hear this quarrel between you two, who are so excellent in fight and counsel. I am older than either of you; therefore be guided by me. Moreover I have been the familiar friend of men even greater than you are, and they did not disregard my counsels. Never again can I behold such men as Pirithous and Dryas shepherd of his people, or as Caeneus, Exadius, godlike Polyphemus, and Theseus son of Aegeus, peer of the immortals. These were the mightiest men ever born upon this earth: mightiest were they, and when they fought the fiercest tribes of mountain savages they utterly overthrew them. I came from distant Pylos, and went about among them, for they would have me come, and I fought as it was in me to do. Not a man now living could withstand them, but they heard my words, and were persuaded by them. So be it also with yourselves, for this is the more excellent way. Therefore, Agamemnon, though you be strong, take not this girl away, for the sons of the Achaeans have already given her to Achilles; and you, Achilles, strive not further with the king, for no man who by the grace of Jove wields a sceptre has like honour with Agamemnon. You are strong, and have a goddess for your mother; but Agamemnon is stronger than you, for he has more people under him. Son of Atreus, check your anger, I implore you; end this quarrel with Achilles, who in the day of battle is a tower of strength to the Achaeans."

And Agamemnon answered, "Sir, all that you have said is true, but this fellow must needs become our lord and master: he must be lord of all, king of all, and captain of all, and this shall hardly be. Granted that the gods have made him a great warrior, have they also given him the right to speak with railing?"

Achilles interrupted him. "I should be a mean coward," he cried, "were I to give in to you in all things. Order other people about, not me, for I shall obey no longer. Furthermore I say- and lay my saying to your heart- I shall fight neither you nor any man about this girl, for those that take were those also that gave. But of all else that is at my ship you shall carry away nothing by force. Try, that others may see; if you do, my spear shall be reddened with your blood."

When they had quarrelled thus angrily, they rose, and broke up the assembly at the ships of the Achaeans. The son of Peleus went back to his tents and ships with the son of Menoetius and his company, while Agamemnon drew a vessel into the water and chose a crew of twenty oarsmen. He escorted Chryseis on board and sent moreover a hecatomb for the god. And Ulysses went as captain.

These, then, went on board and sailed their ways over the sea. But the son of Atreus bade the people purify themselves; so they purified themselves and cast their filth into the sea. Then they offered hecatombs of bulls and goats without blemish on the sea-shore, and the smoke with the savour of their sacrifice rose curling up towards heaven.

Thus did they busy themselves throughout the host. But Agamemnon did not forget the threat that he had made Achilles, and called his trusty messengers and squires Talthybius and Eurybates. "Go," said he, "to the tent of Achilles, son of Peleus; take Briseis by the hand and bring her hither; if he will not give her I shall come with others and take her- which will press him harder."

He charged them straightly further and dismissed them, whereon they went their way sorrowfully by the seaside, till they came to the tents and ships of the Myrmidons. They found Achilles sitting by his tent and his ships, and ill-pleased he was when he beheld them. They stood fearfully and reverently before him, and never a word did they speak, but he knew them and said, "Welcome, heralds, messengers of gods and men; draw near; my quarrel is not with you but with Agamemnon who has sent you for the girl Briseis. Therefore, Patroclus, bring her and give her to them, but let them be witnesses by the blessed gods, by mortal men, and by the fierceness of Agamemnon's anger, that if ever again there be need of me to save the people from ruin, they shall seek and they shall not find. Agamemnon is mad with rage and knows not how to look before and after that the Achaeans may fight by their ships in safety."

Patroclus did as his dear comrade had bidden him. He brought Briseis from the tent and gave her over to the heralds, who took her with them to the ships of the Achaeans- and the woman was loth to go. Then Achilles went all alone by the side of the hoar sea, weeping and looking out upon the boundless waste of waters. He raised his hands in prayer to his immortal mother, "Mother," he cried, "you bore me doomed to live but for a little season; surely Jove, who thunders from Olympus, might have made that little glorious. It is not so. Agamemnon, son of Atreus, has done me dishonour, and has robbed me of my prize by force."

As he spoke he wept aloud, and his mother heard him where she was sitting in the depths of the sea hard by the old man her father. Forthwith she rose as it were a grey mist out of the waves, sat down before him as he stood weeping, caressed him with her hand, and said, "My son, why are you weeping? What is it that grieves you? Keep it not from me, but tell me, that we may know it together."

Achilles drew a deep sigh and said, "You know it; why tell you what you know well already? We went to Thebe the strong city of Eetion, sacked it, and brought hither the spoil. The sons of the Achaeans shared it duly among themselves, and chose lovely Chryseis as the meed of Agamemnon; but Chryses, priest of Apollo, came to the ships of the Achaeans to free his daughter, and brought with him a great ransom: moreover he bore in his hand the sceptre of Apollo, wreathed with a suppliant's wreath, and he besought the Achaeans, but most of all the two sons of Atreus who were their chiefs.

"On this the rest of the Achaeans with one voice were for respecting the priest and taking the ransom that he offered; but not so Agamemnon, who spoke fiercely to him and sent him roughly away. So he went back in anger, and Apollo, who loved him dearly, heard his prayer. Then the god sent a deadly dart upon the Argives, and the people died thick on one another, for the arrows went everywhither among the wide host of the Achaeans. At last a seer in the fulness of his knowledge declared to us the oracles of Apollo, and I was myself first to say that we should appease him. Whereon the son of Atreus rose in anger, and threatened that which he has since done. The Achaeans are now taking the girl in a ship to Chryse, and sending gifts of sacrifice to the god; but the heralds have just taken from my tent the daughter of Briseus, whom the Achaeans had awarded to myself.

"Help your brave son, therefore, if you are able. Go to Olympus, and if you have ever done him service in word or deed, implore the aid of Jove. Ofttimes in my father's house have I heard you glory in that you alone of the immortals saved the son of Saturn from ruin, when the others, with Juno, Neptune, and Pallas Minerva would have put him in bonds. It was you, goddess, who delivered him by calling to Olympus the hundred-handed monster whom gods call Briareus, but men Aegaeon, for he is stronger even than his father; when therefore he took his seat all-glorious beside the son of Saturn, the other gods were afraid, and did not bind him. Go, then, to him, remind him of all this, clasp his knees, and bid him give succour to the Trojans. Let the Achaeans be hemmed in at the sterns of their ships, and perish on the sea-shore, that they may reap what joy they may of their king, and that Agamemnon may rue his blindness in offering insult to the foremost of the Achaeans."

Thetis wept and answered, "My son, woe is me that I should have borne or suckled you. Would indeed that you had lived your span free from all sorrow at your ships, for it is all too brief; alas, that you should be at once short of life and long of sorrow above your peers: woe, therefore, was the hour in which I bore you; nevertheless I will go to the snowy heights of Olympus, and tell this tale to Jove, if he will hear our prayer: meanwhile stay where you are with your ships, nurse your anger against the Achaeans, and hold aloof from fight. For Jove went yesterday to Oceanus, to a feast among the Ethiopians, and the other gods went with him. He will return to Olympus twelve days hence; I will then go to his mansion paved with bronze and will beseech him; nor do I doubt that I shall be able to persuade him."

On this she left him, still furious at the loss of her that had been taken from him. Meanwhile Ulysses reached Chryse with the hecatomb. When they had come inside the harbour they furled the sails and laid them in the ship's hold; they slackened the forestays, lowered the mast into its place, and rowed the ship to the place where they would have her lie; there they cast out their mooring-stones and made fast the hawsers. They then got out upon the sea-shore and landed the hecatomb for Apollo; Chryseis also left the ship, and Ulysses led her to the altar to deliver her into the hands of her father. "Chryses," said he, "King Agamemnon has sent me to bring you back your child, and to offer sacrifice to Apollo on behalf of the Danaans, that we may propitiate the god, who has now brought sorrow upon the Argives."

So saying he gave the girl over to her father, who received her gladly, and they ranged the holy hecatomb all orderly round the altar of the god. They washed their hands and took up the barley-meal to sprinkle over the victims, while Chryses lifted up his hands and prayed aloud on their behalf. "Hear me," he cried, "O god of the silver bow, that protectest Chryse and holy Cilla, and rulest Tenedos with thy might. Even as thou didst hear me aforetime when I prayed, and didst press hardly upon the Achaeans, so hear me yet again, and stay this fearful pestilence from the Danaans."

Thus did he pray, and Apollo heard his prayer. When they had done praying and sprinkling the barley-meal, they drew back the heads of the victims and killed and flayed them. They cut out the thigh-bones, wrapped them round in two layers of fat, set some pieces of raw meat on the top of them, and then Chryses laid them on the wood fire and poured wine over them, while the young men stood near him with five-pronged spits in their hands. When the thigh-bones were burned and they had tasted the inward meats, they cut the rest up small, put the pieces upon the spits, roasted them till they were done, and drew them off: then, when they had finished their work and the feast was ready, they ate it, and every man had his full share, so that all were satisfied. As soon as they had had enough to eat and drink, pages filled the mixing-bowl with wine and water and handed it round, after giving every man his drink-offering.

Thus all day long the young men worshipped the god with song, hymning him and chaunting the joyous paean, and the god took pleasure in their voices; but when the sun went down, and it came on dark, they laid themselves down to sleep by the stern cables of the ship, and when the child of morning, rosy-fingered Dawn, appeared they again set sail for the host of the Achaeans. Apollo sent them a fair wind, so they raised their mast and hoisted their white sails aloft. As the sail bellied with the wind the ship flew through the deep blue water, and the foam hissed against her bows as she sped onward. When they reached the wide-stretching host of the Achaeans, they drew the vessel ashore, high and dry upon the sands, set her strong props beneath her, and went their ways to their own tents and ships.

But Achilles abode at his ships and nursed his anger. He went not to the honourable assembly, and sallied not forth to fight, but gnawed at his own heart, pining for battle and the war-cry.

Now after twelve days the immortal gods came back in a body to Olympus, and Jove led the way. Thetis was not unmindful of the charge her son had laid upon her, so she rose from under the sea and went through great heaven with early morning to Olympus, where she found the mighty son of Saturn sitting all alone upon its topmost ridges. She sat herself down before him, and with her left hand seized his knees, while with her right she caught him under the chin, and besought him, saying-

"Father Jove, if I ever did you service in word or deed among the immortals, hear my prayer, and do honour to my son, whose life is to be cut short so early. King Agamemnon has dishonoured him by taking his prize and keeping her. Honour him then yourself, Olympian lord of counsel, and grant victory to the Trojans, till the Achaeans give my son his due and load him with riches in requital."

Jove sat for a while silent, and without a word, but Thetis still kept firm hold of his knees, and besought him a second time. "Incline your head," said she, "and promise me surely, or else deny me- for you have nothing to fear- that I may learn how greatly you disdain me."

At this Jove was much troubled and answered, "I shall have trouble if you set me quarrelling with Juno, for she will provoke me with her taunting speeches; even now she is always railing at me before the other gods and accusing me of giving aid to the Trojans. Go back now, lest she should find out. I will consider the matter, and will bring it about as wish. See, I incline my head that you believe me. This is the most solemn that I can give to any god. I never recall my word, or deceive, or fail to do what I say, when I have nodded my head."

As he spoke the son of Saturn bowed his dark brows, and the ambrosial locks swayed on his immortal head, till vast Olympus reeled.

When the pair had thus laid their plans, they parted- Jove to his house, while the goddess quitted the splendour of Olympus, and plunged into the depths of the sea. The gods rose from their seats, before the coming of their sire. Not one of them dared to remain sitting, but all stood up as he came among them. There, then, he took his seat. But Juno, when she saw him, knew that he and the old merman's daughter, silver-footed Thetis, had been hatching mischief, so she at once began to upbraid him. "Trickster," she cried, "which of the gods have you been taking into your counsels now? You are always settling matters in secret behind my back, and have never yet told me, if you could help it, one word of your intentions."

"Juno," replied the sire of gods and men, "you must not expect to be informed of all my counsels. You are my wife, but you would find it hard to understand them. When it is proper for you to hear, there is no one, god or man, who will be told sooner, but when I mean to keep a matter to myself, you must not pry nor ask questions."

"Dread son of Saturn," answered Juno, "what are you talking about? I? Pry and ask questions? Never. I let you have your own way in everything. Still, I have a strong misgiving that the old merman's daughter Thetis has been talking you over, for she was with you and had hold of your knees this self-same morning. I believe, therefore, that you have been promising her to give glory to Achilles, and to kill much people at the ships of the Achaeans."

"Wife," said Jove, "I can do nothing but you suspect me and find it out. You will take nothing by it, for I shall only dislike you the more, and it will go harder with you. Granted that it is as you say; I mean to have it so; sit down and hold your tongue as I bid you for if I once begin to lay my hands about you, though all heaven were on your side it would profit you nothing."

On this Juno was frightened, so she curbed her stubborn will and sat down in silence. But the heavenly beings were disquieted throughout the house of Jove, till the cunning workman Vulcan began to try and pacify his mother Juno. "It will be intolerable," said he, "if you two fall to wrangling and setting heaven in an uproar about a pack of mortals. If such ill counsels are to prevail, we shall have no pleasure at our banquet. Let me then advise my mother- and she must herself know that it will be better- to make friends with my dear father Jove, lest he again scold her and disturb our feast. If the Olympian Thunderer wants to hurl us all from our seats, he can do so, for he is far the strongest, so give him fair words, and he will then soon be in a good humour with us."

As he spoke, he took a double cup of nectar, and placed it in his mother's hand. "Cheer up, my dear mother," said he, "and make the best of it. I love you dearly, and should be very sorry to see you get a thrashing; however grieved I might be, I could not help for there is no standing against Jove. Once before when I was trying to help you, he caught me by the foot and flung me from the heavenly threshold. All day long from morn till eve, was I falling, till at sunset I came to ground in the island of Lemnos, and there I lay, with very little life left in me, till the Sintians came and tended me."

Juno smiled at this, and as she smiled she took the cup from her son's hands. Then Vulcan drew sweet nectar from the mixing-bowl, and served it round among the gods, going from left to right; and the blessed gods laughed out a loud applause as they saw him ing bustling about the heavenly mansion.

Thus through the livelong day to the going down of the sun they feasted, and every one had his full share, so that all were satisfied. Apollo struck his lyre, and the Muses lifted up their sweet voices, calling and answering one another. But when the sun's glorious light had faded, they went home to bed, each in his own abode, which lame Vulcan with his consummate skill had fashioned for them. So Jove, the Olympian Lord of Thunder, hied him to the bed in which he always slept; and when he had got on to it he went to sleep, with Juno of the golden throne by his

Book VI

The fight between Trojans and Achaeans was now left to rage as it would, and the tide of war surged hither and thither over the plain as they aimed their bronze-shod spears at one another between the streams of Simois and Xanthus.

First, Ajax son of Telamon, tower of strength to the Achaeans, broke a phalanx of the Trojans, and came to the assistance of his comrades by killing Acamas son of Eussorus, the best man among the Thracians, being both brave and of great stature. The spear struck the projecting peak of his helmet: its bronze point then went through his forehead into the brain, and darkness veiled his eyes.

Then Diomed killed Axylus son of Teuthranus, a rich man who lived in the strong city of Arisbe, and was beloved by all men; for he had a house by the roadside, and entertained every one who passed; howbeit not one of his guests stood before him to save his life, and Diomed killed both him and his squire Calesius, who was then his charioteer- so the pair passed beneath the earth.

Euryalus killed Dresus and Opheltius, and then went in pursuit of Aesepus and Pedasus, whom the naiad nymph Abarbarea had borne to noble Bucolion. Bucolion was eldest son to Laomedon, but he was a bastard. While tending his sheep he had converse with the nymph, and she conceived twin sons; these the son of Mecisteus now slew, and he stripped the armour from their shoulders. Polypoetes then killed Astyalus, Ulysses Pidytes of Percote, and Teucer Aretaon. Ablerus fell by the spear of Nestor's son Antilochus, and Agamemnon, king of men, killed Elatus who dwelt in Pedasus by the banks of the river Satnioeis. Leitus killed Phylacus as he was flying, and Eurypylus slew Melanthus.

Then Menelaus of the loud war-cry took Adrestus alive, for his horses ran into a tamarisk bush, as they were flying wildly over the plain, and broke the pole from the car; they went on towards the city along with the others in full flight, but Adrestus rolled out, and fell in the dust flat on his face by the wheel of his chariot; Menelaus came up to him spear in hand, but Adrestus caught him by the knees begging for his life. "Take me alive," he cried, "son of Atreus, and you shall have a full ransom for me: my father is rich and has much treasure of gold, bronze, and wrought iron laid by in his house. From this store he will give you a large ransom should he hear of my being alive and at the ships of the Achaeans."

Thus did he plead, and Menelaus was for yielding and giving him to a squire to take to the ships of the Achaeans, but Agamemnon came running up to him and rebuked him. "My good Menelaus," said he, "this is no time for giving quarter. Has, then, your house fared so well at the hands of the Trojans? Let us not spare a single one of them- not even the child unborn and in its mother's womb; let not a man of them be left alive, but let all in Ilius perish, unheeded and forgotten."

Thus did he speak, and his brother was persuaded by him, for his words were just. Menelaus, therefore, thrust Adrestus from him, whereon King Agamemnon struck him in the flank, and he fell: then the son of Atreus planted his foot upon his breast to draw his spear from the body.

Meanwhile Nestor shouted to the Argives, saying, "My friends, Danaan warriors, servants of Mars, let no man lag that he may spoil the dead, and bring back much booty to the ships. Let us kill as many as we can; the bodies will lie upon the plain, and you can despoil them later at your leisure."

With these words he put heart and soul into them all. And now the Trojans would have been routed and driven back into Ilius, had not Priam's son Helenus, wisest of augurs, said to Hector and Aeneas, "Hector and Aeneas, you two are the mainstays of the Trojans and Lycians, for you are foremost at all times, alike in fight and counsel; hold your ground here, and go about among the host to rally them in front of the gates, or they will fling themselves into the arms of their wives, to the great joy of our foes. Then, when you have put heart into all our companies, we will stand firm here and fight the Danaans however hard they press us, for there is nothing else to be done. Meanwhile do you, Hector, go to the city and tell our mother what is happening. Tell her to bid the matrons gather at the temple of Minerva in the acropolis; let her then take her key and open the doors of the sacred building; there, upon the knees of Minerva, let her lay the largest, fairest robe she has in her house- the one she sets most store by; let her, moreover, promise to sacrifice twelve yearling heifers that have never yet felt the goad, in the temple of the goddess, if she will take pity on the town, with the wives and little ones of the Trojans, and keep the son of Tydeus from falling on the goodly city of Ilius; for he fights with fury and fills men's souls with panic. I hold him mightiest of them all; we did not fear even their great champion Achilles, son of a goddess though he be, as we do this man: his rage is beyond all bounds, and there is none can vie with him in prowess"

Hector did as his brother bade him. He sprang from his chariot, and went about everywhere among the host, brandishing his spears, urging the men on to fight, and raising the dread cry of battle. Thereon they rallied and again faced the Achaeans, who gave ground and ceased their murderous onset, for they deemed that some one of the immortals had come down from starry heaven to help the Trojans, so strangely had they rallied. And Hector shouted to the Trojans, "Trojans and allies, be men, my friends, and fight with might and main, while I go to Ilius and tell the old men of our council and our wives to pray to the gods and vow hecatombs in their honour."

With this he went his way, and the black rim of hide that went round his shield beat against his neck and his ancles.

Then Glaucus son of Hippolochus, and the son of Tydeus went into the open space between the hosts to fight in single combat. When they were close up to one another Diomed of the loud war-cry was the first to speak. "Who, my good sir," said he, "who are you among men? I have never seen you in battle until now, but you are daring beyond all others if you abide my onset. Woe to those fathers whose sons face my might. If, however, you are one of the immortals and have come down from heaven, I will not fight you; for even valiant Lycurgus, son of Dryas, did not live long when he took to fighting with the gods. He it was that drove the nursing women who were in charge of frenzied Bacchus through the land of Nysa, and they flung their thyrsi on the ground as murderous Lycurgus beat them with his oxgoad. Bacchus himself plunged terror-stricken into the sea, and Thetis took him to her bosom to comfort him, for he was scared by the fury with which the man reviled him. Thereon the gods who live at ease were angry with Lycurgus and the son of Saturn struck him blind, nor did he live much longer after he had become hateful to the immortals. Therefore I will not fight with the blessed gods; but if you are of them that eat the fruit of the ground, draw near and meet your doom."

And the son of Hippolochus answered, son of Tydeus, why ask me of my lineage? Men come and go as leaves year by year upon the trees. Those of autumn the wind sheds upon the ground, but when spring returns the forest buds forth with fresh vines. Even so is it with the generations of mankind, the new spring up as the old are passing away. If, then, you would learn my descent, it is one that is well known to many. There is a city in the heart of Argos, pasture land of horses, called Ephyra, where Sisyphus lived, who was the craftiest of all mankind. He was the son of Aeolus, and had a son named Glaucus, who was father to Bellerophon, whom heaven endowed with the most surpassing comeliness and beauty. But Proetus devised his ruin, and being stronger than he, drove him from the land of the Argives, over which Jove had made him ruler. For Antea, wife of Proetus, lusted after him, and would have had him lie with her in secret; but Bellerophon was an honourable man and would not, so she told lies about him to Proteus. 'Proetus,' said she, 'kill Bellerophon or die, for he would have had converse with me against my will.' The king was angered, but shrank from killing Bellerophon, so he sent him to Lycia with lying letters of introduction, written on a folded tablet, and containing much ill against the bearer. He bade Bellerophon show these letters to his father-in-law, to the end that he might thus perish; Bellerophon therefore went to Lycia, and the gods convoyed him safely.

"When he reached the river Xanthus, which is in Lycia, the king received him with all goodwill, feasted him nine days, and killed nine heifers in his honour, but when rosy-fingered morning appeared upon the tenth day, he questioned him and desired to see the letter from his son-in-law Proetus. When he had received the wicked letter he first commanded Bellerophon to kill that savage monster, the Chimaera, who was not a human being, but a goddess, for she had the head of a lion and the tail of a serpent, while her body was that of a goat, and she breathed forth flames of fire; but Bellerophon slew her, for he was guided by signs from heaven. He next fought the far-famed Solymi, and this, he said, was the hardest of all his battles. Thirdly, he killed the Amazons, women who were the peers of men, and as he was returning thence the king devised yet another plan for his destruction; he picked the bravest warriors in all Lycia, and placed them in ambuscade, but not a man ever came back, for Bellerophon killed every one of them. Then the king knew that he must be the valiant offspring of a god, so he kept him in Lycia, gave him his daughter in marriage, and made him of equal honour in the kingdom with himself; and the Lycians gave him a piece of land, the best in all the country, fair with vineyards and tilled fields, to have and to hold.

"The king's daughter bore Bellerophon three children, Isander, Hippolochus, and Laodameia. Jove, the lord of counsel, lay with Laodameia, and she bore him noble Sarpedon; but when Bellerophon came to be hated by all the gods, he wandered all desolate and dismayed upon the Alean plain, gnawing at his own heart, and shunning the path of man. Mars, insatiate of battle, killed his son Isander while he was fighting the Solymi; his daughter was killed by Diana of the golden reins, for she was angered with her; but Hippolochus was father to myself, and when he sent me to Troy he urged me again and again to fight ever among the foremost and outvie my peers, so as not to shame the blood of my fathers who were the noblest in Ephyra and in all Lycia. This, then, is the descent I claim."

Thus did he speak, and the heart of Diomed was glad. He planted his spear in the ground, and spoke to him with friendly words. "Then," he said, you are an old friend of my father's house. Great Oeneus once entertained Bellerophon for twenty days, and the two exchanged presents. Oeneus gave a belt rich with purple, and Bellerophon a double cup, which I left at home when I set out for Troy. I do not remember Tydeus, for he was taken from us while I was yet a child, when the army of the Achaeans was cut to pieces before Thebes. Henceforth, however, I must be your host in middle Argos, and you mine in Lycia, if I should ever go there; let us avoid one another's spears even during a general engagement; there are many noble Trojans and allies whom I can kill, if I overtake them and heaven delivers them into my hand; so again with yourself, there are many Achaeans whose lives you may take if you can; we two, then, will exchange armour, that all present may know of the old ties that subsist between us."

With these words they sprang from their chariots, grasped one another's hands, and plighted friendship. But the son of Saturn made Glaucus take leave of his wits, for he exchanged golden armour for bronze, the worth of a hundred head of cattle for the worth of nine.

Now when Hector reached the Scaean gates and the oak tree, the wives and daughters of the Trojans came running towards him to ask after their sons, brothers, kinsmen, and husbands: he told them to set about praying to the gods, and many were made sorrowful as they heard him.

Presently he reached the splendid palace of King Priam, adorned with colonnades of hewn stone. In it there were fifty bedchambers- all of hewn stone- built near one another, where the sons of Priam slept, each with his wedded wife. Opposite these, on the other side the courtyard, there were twelve upper rooms also of hewn stone for Priam's daughters, built near one another, where his sons-in-law slept with their wives. When Hector got there, his fond mother came up to him with Laodice the fairest of her daughters. She took his hand within her own and said, "My son, why have you left the battle to come hither? Are the Achaeans, woe betide them, pressing you hard about the city that you have thought fit to come and uplift your hands to Jove from the citadel? Wait till I can bring you wine that you may make offering to Jove and to the other immortals, and may then drink and be refreshed. Wine gives a man fresh strength when he is wearied, as you now are with fighting on behalf of your kinsmen."

And Hector answered, "Honoured mother, bring no wine, lest you unman me and I forget my strength. I dare not make a drink-offering to Jove with unwashed hands; one who is bespattered with blood and filth may not pray to the son of Saturn. Get the matrons together, and go with offerings to the temple of Minerva driver of the spoil; there, upon the knees of Minerva, lay the largest and fairest robe you have in your house- the one you set most store by; promise, moreover, to sacrifice twelve yearling heifers that have never yet felt the goad, in the temple of the goddess if she will take pity on the town, with the wives and little ones of the Trojans, and keep the son of Tydeus from off the goodly city of Ilius, for he fights with fury, and fills men's souls with panic. Go, then, to the temple of Minerva, while I seek Paris and exhort him, if he will hear my words. Would that the earth might open her jaws and swallow him, for Jove bred him to be the bane of the Trojans, and of Priam and Priam's sons. Could I but see him go down into the house of Hades, my heart would forget its heaviness."

His mother went into the house and called her waiting-women who gathered the matrons throughout the city. She then went down into her fragrant store-room, where her embroidered robes were kept, the work of Sidonian women, whom Alexandrus had brought over from Sidon when he sailed the seas upon that voyage during which he carried off Helen. Hecuba took out the largest robe, and the one that was most beautifully enriched with embroidery, as an offering to Minerva: it glittered like a star, and lay at the very bottom of the chest. With this she went on her way and many matrons with her.

When they reached the temple of Minerva, lovely Theano, daughter of Cisseus and wife of Antenor, opened the doors, for the Trojans had made her priestess of Minerva. The women lifted up their hands to the goddess with a loud cry, and Theano took the robe to lay it upon the knees of Minerva, praying the while to the daughter of great Jove. "Holy Minerva," she cried, "protectress of our city, mighty goddess, break the spear of Diomed and lay him low before the Scaean gates. Do this, and we will sacrifice twelve heifers that have never yet known the goad, in your temple, if you will have pity upon the town, with the wives and little ones If the Trojans." Thus she prayed, but Pallas Minerva granted not her prayer.

While they were thus praying to the daughter of great Jove, Hector went to the fair house of Alexandrus, which he had built for him by the foremost builders in the land. They had built him his house, storehouse, and courtyard near those of Priam and Hector on the acropolis. Here Hector entered, with a spear eleven cubits long in his hand; the bronze point gleamed in front of him, and was fastened to the shaft of the spear by a ring of gold. He found Alexandrus within the house, busied about his armour, his shield and cuirass, and handling his curved bow; there, too, sat Argive Helen with her women, setting them their several tasks; and as Hector saw him he rebuked him with words of scorn. "Sir," said he, "you do ill to nurse this rancour; the people perish fighting round this our town; you would yourself chide one whom you saw shirking his part in the combat. Up then, or ere long the city will be in a blaze."

And Alexandrus answered, "Hector, your rebuke is just; listen therefore, and believe me when I tell you that I am not here so much through rancour or ill-will towards the Trojans, as from a desire to indulge my grief. My wife was even now gently urging me to battle, and I hold it better that I should go, for victory is ever fickle. Wait, then, while I put on my armour, or go first and I will follow. I shall be sure to overtake you."

Hector made no answer, but Helen tried to soothe him. "Brother," said she, "to my abhorred and sinful self, would that a whirlwind had caught me up on the day my mother brought me forth, and had borne me to some mountain or to the waves of the roaring sea that should have swept me away ere this mischief had come about. But, since the gods have devised these evils, would, at any rate, that I had been wife to a better man- to one who could smart under dishonour and men's evil speeches. This fellow was never yet to be depended upon, nor never will be, and he will surely reap what he has sown. Still, brother, come in and rest upon this seat, for it is you who bear the brunt of that toil that has been caused by my hateful self and by the sin of Alexandrus- both of whom Jove has doomed to be a theme of song among those that shall be born hereafter."

And Hector answered, "Bid me not be seated, Helen, for all the goodwill you bear me. I cannot stay. I am in haste to help the Trojans, who miss me greatly when I am not among them; but urge your husband, and of his own self also let him make haste to overtake me before I am out of the city. I must go home to see my household, my wife and my little son, for I know not whether I shall ever again return to them, or whether the gods will cause me to fill by the hands of the Achaeans."

Then Hector left her, and forthwith was at his own house. He did not find Andromache, for she was on the wall with her child and one of her maids, weeping bitterly. Seeing, then, that she was not within, he stood on the threshold of the women's rooms and said, "Women, tell me, and tell me true, where did Andromache go when she left the house? Was it to my sisters, or to my brothers' wives? or is she at the temple of Minerva where the other women are propitiating the awful goddess?"

His good housekeeper answered, "Hector, since you bid me tell you truly, she did not go to your sisters nor to your brothers' wives, nor yet to the temple of Minerva, where the other women are propitiating the awful goddess, but she is on the high wall of Ilius, for she had heard the Trojans were being hard pressed, and that the Achaeans were in great force: she went to the wall in frenzied haste, and the nurse went with her carrying the child."

Hector hurried from the house when she had done speaking, and went down the streets by the same way that he had come. When he had gone through the city and had reached the Scaean gates through which he would go out on to the plain, his wife came running towards him, Andromache, daughter of great Eetion who ruled in Thebe under the wooded slopes of Mt. Placus, and was king of the Cilicians. His daughter had married Hector, and now came to meet him with a nurse who carried his little child in her bosom- a mere babe. Hector's darling son, and lovely as a star. Hector had named him Scamandrius, but the people called him Astyanax, for his father stood alone as chief guardian of Ilius. Hector smiled as he looked upon the boy, but he did not speak, and Andromache stood by him weeping and taking his hand in her own. "Dear husband," said she, "your valour will bring you to destruction; think on your infant son, and on my hapless self who ere long shall be your widow- for the Achaeans will set upon you in a body and kill you. It would be better for me, should I lose you, to lie dead and buried, for I shall have nothing left to comfort me when you are gone, save only sorrow. I have neither father nor mother now. Achilles slew my father when he sacked Thebe the goodly city of the Cilicians. He slew him, but did not for very shame despoil him; when he had burned him in his wondrous armour, he raised a barrow over his ashes and the mountain nymphs, daughters of aegis-bearing Jove, planted a grove of elms about his tomb. I had seven brothers in my father's house, but on the same day they all went within the house of Hades. Achilles killed them as they were with their sheep and cattle. My mother- her who had been queen of all the land under Mt. Placus- he brought hither with the spoil, and freed her for a great sum, but the archer- queen Diana took her in the house of your father. Nay- Hector- you who to me are father, mother, brother, and dear husband- have mercy upon me; stay here upon this wall; make not your child fatherless, and your wife a widow; as for the host, place them near the fig-tree, where the city can be best scaled, and the wall is weakest. Thrice have the bravest of them come thither and assailed it, under the two Ajaxes, Idomeneus, the sons of Atreus, and the brave son of Tydeus, either of their own bidding, or because some soothsayer had told them."

And Hector answered, "Wife, I too have thought upon all this, but with what face should I look upon the Trojans, men or women, if I shirked battle like a coward? I cannot do so: I know nothing save to fight bravely in the forefront of the Trojan host and win renown alike for my father and myself. Well do I know that the day will surely come when mighty Ilius shall be destroyed with Priam and Priam's people, but I grieve for none of these- not even for Hecuba, nor King Priam, nor for my brothers many and brave who may fall in the dust before their foes- for none of these do I grieve as for yourself when the day shall come on which some one of the Achaeans shall rob you for ever of your freedom, and bear you weeping away. It may be that you will have to ply the loom in Argos at the bidding of a mistress, or to fetch water from the springs Messeis or Hypereia, treated brutally by some cruel task-master; then will one say who sees you weeping, 'She was wife to Hector, the bravest warrior among the Trojans during the war before Ilius.' On this your tears will break forth anew for him who would have put away the day of captivity from you. May I lie dead under the barrow that is heaped over my body ere I hear your cry as they carry you into bondage."

He stretched his arms towards his child, but the boy cried and nestled in his nurse's bosom, scared at the sight of his father's armour, and at the horse-hair plume that nodded fiercely from his helmet. His father and mother laughed to see him, but Hector took the helmet from his head and laid it all gleaming upon the ground. Then he took his darling child, kissed him, and dandled him in his arms, praying over him the while to Jove and to all the gods. "Jove," he cried, "grant that this my child may be even as myself, chief among the Trojans; let him be not less excellent in strength, and let him rule Ilius with his might. Then may one say of him as he comes from battle, 'The son is far better than the father.' May he bring back the blood-stained spoils of him whom he has laid low, and let his mother's heart be glad.'"

With this he laid the child again in the arms of his wife, who took him to her own soft bosom, smiling through her tears. As her husband watched her his heart yearned towards her and he caressed her fondly, saying, "My own wife, do not take these things too bitterly to heart. No one can hurry me down to Hades before my time, but if a man's hour is come, be he brave or be he coward, there is no escape for him when he has once been born. Go, then, within the house, and busy yourself with your daily duties, your loom, your distaff, and the ordering of your servants; for war is man's matter, and mine above all others of them that have been born in Ilius."

He took his plumed helmet from the ground, and his wife went back again to her house, weeping bitterly and often looking back towards him. When she reached her home she found her maidens within, and bade them all join in her lament; so they mourned Hector in his own house though he was yet alive, for they deemed that they should never see him return safe from battle, and from the furious hands of the Achaeans.

Paris did not remain long in his house. He donned his goodly armour overlaid with bronze, and hasted through the city as fast as his feet could take him. As a horse, stabled and fed, breaks loose and gallops gloriously over the plain to the place where he is wont to bathe in the fair-flowing river- he holds his head high, and his mane streams upon his shoulders as he exults in his strength and flies like the wind to the haunts and feeding ground of the mares- even so went forth Paris from high Pergamus, gleaming like sunlight in his armour, and he laughed aloud as he sped swiftly on his way. Forthwith he came upon his brother Hector, who was then turning away from the place where he had held converse with his wife, and he was himself the first to speak. "Sir," said he, "I fear that I have kept you waiting when you are in haste, and have not come as quickly as you bade me."

"My good brother," answered Hector, you fight bravely, and no man with any justice can make light of your doings in battle. But you are careless and wilfully remiss. It grieves me to the heart to hear the ill that the Trojans speak about you, for they have suffered much on your account. Let us be going, and we will make things right hereafter, should Jove vouchsafe us to set the cup of our deliverance before ever-living gods of heaven in our own homes, when we have chased the Achaeans from Troy."

Book VIII

Now when Morning, clad in her robe of saffron, had begun to suffuse light over the earth, Jove called the gods in council on the topmost crest of serrated Olympus. Then he spoke and all the other gods gave ear. "Hear me," said he, "gods and goddesses, that I may speak even as I am minded. Let none of you neither goddess nor god try to cross me, but obey me every one of you that I may bring this matter to an end. If I see anyone acting apart and helping either Trojans or Danaans, he shall be beaten inordinately ere he come back again to Olympus; or I will hurl him down into dark Tartarus far into the deepest pit under the earth, where the gates are iron and the floor bronze, as far beneath Hades as heaven is high above the earth, that you may learn how much the mightiest I am among you. Try me and find out for yourselves. Hangs me a golden chain from heaven, and lay hold of it all of you, gods and goddesses together- tug as you will, you will not drag Jove the supreme counsellor from heaven to earth; but were I to pull at it myself I should draw you up with earth and sea into the bargain, then would I bind the chain about some pinnacle of Olympus and leave you all dangling in the mid firmament. So far am I above all others either of gods or men."

They were frightened and all of them of held their peace, for he had spoken masterfully; but at last Minerva answered, "Father, son of Saturn, king of kings, we all know that your might is not to be gainsaid, but we are also sorry for the Danaan warriors, who are perishing and coming to a bad end. We will, however, since you so bid us, refrain from actual fighting, but we will make serviceable suggestions to the Argives that they may not all of them perish in your displeasure."

Jove smiled at her and answered, "Take heart, my child, Trito-born; I am not really in earnest, and I wish to be kind to you."

With this he yoked his fleet horses, with hoofs of bronze and manes of glittering gold. He girded himself also with gold about the body, seized his gold whip and took his seat in his chariot. Thereon he lashed his horses and they flew forward nothing loth midway twixt earth and starry heaven. After a while he reached many-fountained Ida, mother of wild beasts, and Gargarus, where are his grove and fragrant altar. There the father of gods and men stayed his horses, took them from the chariot, and hid them in a thick cloud; then he took his seat all glorious upon the topmost crests, looking down upon the city of Troy and the ships of the Achaeans.

The Achaeans took their morning meal hastily at the ships, and afterwards put on their armour. The Trojans on the other hand likewise armed themselves throughout the city, fewer in numbers but nevertheless eager perforce to do battle for their wives and children. All the gates were flung wide open, and horse and foot sallied forth with the tramp as of a great multitude.

When they were got together in one place, shield clashed with shield, and spear with spear, in the conflict of mail-clad men. Mighty was the din as the bossed shields pressed hard on one another- death- cry and shout of triumph of slain and slayers, and the earth ran red with blood.

Now so long as the day waxed and it was still morning their weapons beat against one another, and the people fell, but when the sun had reached mid-heaven, the sire of all balanced his golden scales, and put two fates of death within them, one for the Trojans and the other for the Achaeans. He took the balance by the middle, and when he lifted it up the day of the Achaeans sank; the death-fraught scale of the Achaeans settled down upon the ground, while that of the Trojans rose heavenwards. Then he thundered aloud from Ida, and sent the glare of his lightning upon the Achaeans; when they saw this, pale fear fell upon them and they were sore afraid.

Idomeneus dared not stay nor yet Agamemnon, nor did the two Ajaxes, servants of Mars, hold their ground. Nestor knight of Gerene alone stood firm, bulwark of the Achaeans, not of his own will, but one of his horses was disabled. Alexandrus husband of lovely Helen had hit it with an arrow just on the top of its head where the mane begins to grow away from the skull, a very deadly place. The horse bounded in his anguish as the arrow pierced his brain, and his struggles threw others into confusion. The old man instantly began cutting the traces with his sword, but Hector's fleet horses bore down upon him through the rout with their bold charioteer, even Hector himself, and the old man would have perished there and then had not Diomed been quick to mark, and with a loud cry called Ulysses to help him.

"Ulysses," he cried, "noble son of Laertes where are you flying to, with your back turned like a coward? See that you are not struck with a spear between the shoulders. Stay here and help me to defend Nestor from this man's furious onset."

Ulysses would not give ear, but sped onward to the ships of the Achaeans, and the son of Tydeus flinging himself alone into the thick of the fight took his stand before the horses of the son of Neleus. "Sir," said he, "these young warriors are pressing you hard, your force is spent, and age is heavy upon you, your squire is naught, and your horses are slow to move. Mount my chariot and see what the horses of Tros can do- how cleverly they can scud hither and thither over the plain either in flight or in pursuit. I took them from the hero Aeneas. Let our squires attend to your own steeds, but let us drive mine straight at the Trojans, that Hector may learn how furiously I too can wield my spear."

Nestor knight of Gerene hearkened to his words. Thereon the doughty squires, Sthenelus and kind-hearted Eurymedon, saw to Nestor's horses, while the two both mounted Diomed's chariot. Nestor took the reins in his hands and lashed the horses on; they were soon close up with Hector, and the son of Tydeus aimed a spear at him as he was charging full speed towards them. He missed him, but struck his charioteer and squire Eniopeus son of noble Thebaeus in the breast by the nipple while the reins were in his hands, so that he died there and then, and the horses swerved as he fell headlong from the chariot. Hector was greatly grieved at the loss of his charioteer, but let him lie for all his sorrow, while he went in quest of another driver; nor did his steeds have to go long without one, for he presently found brave Archeptolemus the son of Iphitus, and made him get up behind the horses, giving the reins into his hand.

All had then been lost and no help for it, for they would have been penned up in Ilius like sheep, had not the sire of gods and men been quick to mark, and hurled a fiery flaming thunderbolt which fell just in front of Diomed's horses with a flare of burning brimstone. The horses were frightened and tried to back beneath the car, while the reins dropped from Nestor's hands. Then he was afraid and said to Diomed, "Son of Tydeus, turn your horses in flight; see you not that the hand of Jove is against you? To-day he vouchsafes victory to Hector; to-morrow, if it so please him, he will again grant it to ourselves; no man, however brave, may thwart the purpose of Jove, for he is far stronger than any."

Diomed answered, "All that you have said is true; there is a grief however which pierces me to the very heart, for Hector will talk among the Trojans and say, 'The son of Tydeus fled before me to the ships.' This is the vaunt he will make, and may earth then swallow me."

"Son of Tydeus," replied Nestor, "what mean you? Though Hector say that you are a coward the Trojans and Dardanians will not believe him, nor yet the wives of the mighty warriors whom you have laid low."

So saying he turned the horses back through the thick of the battle, and with a cry that rent the air the Trojans and Hector rained their darts after them. Hector shouted to him and said, "Son of Tydeus, the Danaans have done you honour hitherto as regards your place at table, the meals they give you, and the filling of your cup with wine. Henceforth they will despise you, for you are become no better than a woman. Be off, girl and coward that you are, you shall not scale our walls through any Hinching upon my part; neither shall you carry off our wives in your ships, for I shall kill you with my own hand."

The son of Tydeus was in two minds whether or no to turn his horses round again and fight him. Thrice did he doubt, and thrice did Jove thunder from the heights of. Ida in token to the Trojans that he would turn the battle in their favour. Hector then shouted to them and said, "Trojans, Lycians, and Dardanians, lovers of close fighting, be men, my friends, and fight with might and with main; I see that Jove is minded to vouchsafe victory and great glory to myself, while he will deal destruction upon the Danaans. Fools, for having thought of building this weak and worthless wall. It shall not stay my fury; my horses will spring lightly over their trench, and when I am at their ships forget not to bring me fire that I may burn them, while I slaughter the Argives who will be all dazed and bewildered by the smoke."

Then he cried to his horses, "Xanthus and Podargus, and you Aethon and goodly Lampus, pay me for your keep now and for all the honey-sweet corn with which Andromache daughter of great Eetion has fed you, and for she has mixed wine and water for you to drink whenever you would, before doing so even for me who am her own husband. Haste in pursuit, that we may take the shield of Nestor, the fame of which ascends to heaven, for it is of solid gold, arm-rods and all, and that we may strip from the shoulders of Diomed. the cuirass which Vulcan made him. Could we take these two things, the Achaeans would set sail in their ships this self-same night."

Thus did he vaunt, but Queen Juno made high Olympus quake as she shook with rage upon her throne. Then said she to the mighty god of Neptune, "What now, wide ruling lord of the earthquake? Can you find no compassion in your heart for the dying Danaans, who bring you many a welcome offering to Helice and to Aegae? Wish them well then. If all of us who are with the Danaans were to drive the Trojans back and keep Jove from helping them, he would have to sit there sulking alone on Ida."

King Neptune was greatly troubled and answered, "Juno, rash of tongue, what are you talking about? We other gods must not set ourselves against Jove, for he is far stronger than we are."

Thus did they converse; but the whole space enclosed by the ditch, from the ships even to the wall, was filled with horses and warriors, who were pent up there by Hector son of Priam, now that the hand of Jove was with him. He would even have set fire to the ships and burned them, had not Queen Juno put it into the mind of Agamemnon, to bestir himself and to encourage the Achaeans. To this end he went round the ships and tents carrying a great purple cloak, and took his stand by the huge black hull of Ulysses' ship, which was middlemost of all; it was from this place that his voice would carry farthest, on the one hand towards the tents of Ajax son of Telamon, and on the other towards those of Achilles- for these two heroes, well assured of their own strength, had valorously drawn up their ships at the two ends of the line. From this spot then, with a voice that could be heard afar, he shouted to the Danaans, saying, "Argives, shame on you cowardly creatures, brave in semblance only; where are now our vaunts that we should prove victorious- the vaunts we made so vaingloriously in Lemnos, when we ate the flesh of horned cattle and filled our mixing-bowls to the brim? You vowed that you would each of you stand against a hundred or two hundred men, and now you prove no match even for one- for Hector, who will be ere long setting our ships in a blaze. Father Jove, did you ever so ruin a great king and rob him so utterly of his greatness? yet, when to my sorrow I was coming hither, I never let my ship pass your altars without offering the fat and thigh-bones of heifers upon every one of them, so eager was I to sack the city of Troy. Vouchsafe me then this prayer- suffer us to escape at any rate with our lives, and let not the Achaeans be so utterly vanquished by the Trojans."

Thus did he pray, and father Jove pitying his tears vouchsafed him that his people should live, not die; forthwith he sent them an eagle, most unfailingly portentous of all birds, with a young fawn in its talons; the eagle dropped the fawn by the altar on which the Achaeans sacrificed to Jove the lord of omens; When, therefore, the people saw that the bird had come from Jove, they sprang more fiercely upon the Trojans and fought more boldly.

There was no man of all the many Danaans who could then boast that he had driven his horses over the trench and gone forth to fight sooner than the son of Tydeus; long before any one else could do so he slew an armed warrior of the Trojans, Agelaus the son of Phradmon. He had turned his horses in flight, but the spear struck him in the back midway between his shoulders and went right through his chest, and his armour rang rattling round him as he fell forward from his chariot.

After him came Agamemnon and Menelaus, sons of Atreus, the two Ajaxes clothed in valour as with a garment, Idomeneus and his companion in arms Meriones, peer of murderous Mars, and Eurypylus the brave son of Euaemon. Ninth came Teucer with his bow, and took his place under cover of the shield of Ajax son of Telamon. When Ajax lifted his shield Teucer would peer round, and when he had hit any one in the throng, the man would fall dead; then Teucer would hie back to Ajax as a child to its mother, and again duck down under his shield.

Which of the Trojans did brave Teucer first kill? Orsilochus, and then Ormenus and Ophelestes, Daetor, Chromius, and godlike Lycophontes, Amopaon son of Polyaemon, and Melanippus. these in turn did he lay low upon the earth, and King Agamemnon was glad when he saw him making havoc of the Trojans with his mighty bow. He went up to him and said, "Teucer, man after my own heart, son of Telamon, captain among the host, shoot on, and be at once the saving of the Danaans and the glory of your father Telamon, who brought you up and took care of you in his own house when you were a child, bastard though you were. Cover him with glory though he is far off; I will promise and I will assuredly perform; if aegis-bearing Jove and Minerva grant me to sack the city of Ilius, you shall have the next best meed of honour after my own- a tripod, or two horses with their chariot, or a woman who shall go up into your bed."

And Teucer answered, "Most noble son of Atreus, you need not urge me; from the moment we began to drive them back to Ilius, I have never ceased so far as in me lies to look out for men whom I can shoot and kill; I have shot eight barbed shafts, and all of them have been buried in the flesh of warlike youths, but this mad dog I cannot hit."

As he spoke he aimed another arrow straight at Hector, for he was bent on hitting him; nevertheless he missed him, and the arrow hit Priam's brave son Gorgythion in the breast. His mother, fair Castianeira, lovely as a goddess, had been married from Aesyme, and now he bowed his head as a garden poppy in full bloom when it is weighed down by showers in spring- even thus heavy bowed his head beneath the weight of his helmet.

Again he aimed at Hector, for he was longing to hit him, and again his arrow missed, for Apollo turned it aside; but he hit Hector's brave charioteer Archeptolemus in the breast, by the nipple, as he was driving furiously into the fight. The horses swerved aside as he fell headlong from the chariot, and there was no life left in him. Hector was greatly grieved at the loss of his charioteer, but for all his sorrow he let him lie where he fell, and bade his brother Cebriones, who was hard by, take the reins. Cebriones did as he had said. Hector thereon with a loud cry sprang from his chariot to the ground, and seizing a great stone made straight for Teucer with intent kill him. Teucer had just taken an arrow from his quiver and had laid it upon the bow-string, but Hector struck him with the jagged stone as he was taking aim and drawing the string to his shoulder; he hit him just where the collar-bone divides the neck from the chest, a very deadly place, and broke the sinew of his arm so that his wrist was less, and the bow dropped from his hand as he fell forward on his knees. Ajax saw that his brother had fallen, and running towards him bestrode him and sheltered him with his shield. Meanwhile his two trusty squires, Mecisteus son of Echius, and Alastor, came up and bore him to the ships groaning in his great pain.

Jove now again put heart into the Trojans, and they drove the Achaeans to their deep trench with Hector in all his glory at their head. As a hound grips a wild boar or lion in flank or buttock when he gives him chase, and watches warily for his wheeling, even so did Hector follow close upon the Achaeans, ever killing the hindmost as they rushed panic-stricken onwards. When they had fled through the set stakes and trench and many Achaeans had been laid low at the hands of the Trojans, they halted at their ships, calling upon one another and praying every man instantly as they lifted up their hands to the gods; but Hector wheeled his horses this way and that, his eyes glaring like those of Gorgo or murderous Mars.

Juno when she saw them had pity upon them, and at once said to Minerva, "Alas, child of aegis-bearing Jove, shall you and I take no more thought for the dying Danaans, though it be the last time we ever do so? See how they perish and come to a bad end before the onset of but a single man. Hector the son of Priam rages with intolerable fury, and has already done great mischief."

Minerva answered, "Would, indeed, this fellow might die in his own land, and fall by the hands of the Achaeans; but my father Jove is mad with spleen, ever foiling me, ever headstrong and unjust. He forgets how often I saved his son when he was worn out by the labours Eurystheus had laid on him. He would weep till his cry came up to heaven, and then Jove would send me down to help him; if I had had the sense to foresee all this, when Eurystheus sent him to the house of Hades, to fetch the hell-hound from Erebus, he would never have come back alive out of the deep waters of the river Styx. And now Jove hates me, while he lets Thetis have her way because she kissed his knees and took hold of his beard, when she was begging him to do honour to Achilles. I shall know what to do next time he begins calling me his grey-eyed darling. Get our horses ready, while I go within the house of aegis-bearing Jove and put on my armour; we shall then find out whether Priam's son Hector will be glad to meet us in the highways of battle, or whether the Trojans will glut hounds and vultures with the fat of their flesh as they he dead by the ships of the Achaeans."

Thus did she speak and white-armed Juno, daughter of great Saturn, obeyed her words; she set about harnessing her gold-bedizened steeds, while Minerva daughter of aegis-bearing Jove flung her richly vesture, made with her own hands, on to the threshold of her father, and donned the shirt of Jove, arming herself for battle. Then she stepped into her flaming chariot, and grasped the spear so stout and sturdy and strong with which she quells the ranks of heroes who have displeased her. Juno lashed her horses, and the gates of heaven bellowed as they flew open of their own accord- gates over which the Hours preside, in whose hands are heaven and Olympus, either to open the dense cloud that hides them or to close it. Through these the goddesses drove their obedient steeds.

But father Jove when he saw them from Ida was very angry, and sent winged Iris with a message to them. "Go," said he, "fleet Iris, turn them back, and see that they do not come near me, for if we come to fighting there will be mischief. This is what I say, and this is what I mean to do. I will lame their horses for them; I will hurl them from their chariot, and will break it in pieces. It will take them all ten years to heal the wounds my lightning shall inflict upon them; my grey-eyed daughter will then learn what quarrelling with her father means. I am less surprised and angry with Juno, for whatever I say she always contradicts me."

With this Iris went her way, fleet as the wind, from the heights of Ida to the lofty summits of Olympus. She met the goddesses at the outer gates of its many valleys and gave them her message. "What," said she, "are you about? Are you mad? The son of Saturn forbids going. This is what he says, and this is he means to do, he will lame your horses for you, he will hurl you from your chariot, and will break it in pieces. It will take you all ten years to heal the wounds his lightning will inflict upon you, that you may learn, grey-eyed goddess, what quarrelling with your father means. He is less hurt and angry with Juno, for whatever he says she always contradicts him but you, bold bold hussy, will you really dare to raise your huge spear in defiance of Jove?"

With this she left them, and Juno said to Minerva, "Of a truth, child of aegis-bearing Jove, I am not for fighting men's battles further in defiance of Jove. Let them live or die as luck will have it, and let Jove mete out his judgements upon the Trojans and Danaans according to his own pleasure."

She turned her steeds; the Hours presently unyoked them, made them fast to their ambrosial mangers, and leaned the chariot against the end wall of the courtyard. The two goddesses then sat down upon their golden thrones, amid the company of the other gods; but they were very angry.

Presently father Jove drove his chariot to Olympus, and entered the assembly of gods. The mighty lord of the earthquake unyoked his horses for him, set the car upon its stand, and threw a cloth over it. Jove then sat down upon his golden throne and Olympus reeled beneath him. Minerva and Juno sat alone, apart from Jove, and neither spoke nor asked him questions, but Jove knew what they meant, and said, "Minerva and Juno, why are you so angry? Are you fatigued with killing so many of your dear friends the Trojans? Be this as it may, such is the might of my hands that all the gods in Olympus cannot turn me; you were both of you trembling all over ere ever you saw the fight and its terrible doings. I tell you therefore-and it would have surely been-I should have struck you with lighting, and your chariots would never have brought you back again to Olympus."

Minerva and Juno groaned in spirit as they sat side by side and brooded mischief for the Trojans. Minerva sat silent without a word, for she was in a furious passion and bitterly incensed against her father; but Juno could not contain herself and said, "What, dread son of Saturn, are you talking about? We know how great your power is, nevertheless we have compassion upon the Danaan warriors who are perishing and coming to a bad end. We will, however, since you so bid us, refrain from actual fighting, but we will make serviceable suggestions to the Argives, that they may not all of them perish in your displeasure."

And Jove answered, "To-morrow morning, Juno, if you choose to do so, you will see the son of Saturn destroying large numbers of the Argives, for fierce Hector shall not cease fighting till he has roused the son of Peleus when they are fighting in dire straits at their ships' sterns about the body of Patroclus. Like it or no, this is how it is decreed; for aught I care, you may go to the lowest depths beneath earth and sea, where Iapetus and Saturn dwell in lone Tartarus with neither ray of light nor breath of wind to cheer them. You may go on and on till you get there, and I shall not care one whit for your displeasure; you are the greatest vixen living."

Juno made him no answer. The sun's glorious orb now sank into Oceanus and drew down night over the land. Sorry indeed were the Trojans when light failed them, but welcome and thrice prayed for did darkness fall upon the Achaeans.

Then Hector led the Trojans back from the ships, and held a council on the open space near the river, where there was a spot ear corpses. They left their chariots and sat down on the ground to hear the speech he made them. He grasped a spear eleven cubits long, the bronze point of which gleamed in front of it, while the ring round the spear-head was of gold Spear in hand he spoke. "Hear me," said he, "Trojans, Dardanians, and allies. I deemed but now that I should destroy the ships and all the Achaeans with them ere I went back to Ilius, but darkness came on too soon. It was this alone that saved them and their ships upon the seashore. Now, therefore, let us obey the behests of night, and prepare our suppers. Take your horses out of their chariots and give them their feeds of corn; then make speed to bring sheep and cattle from the city; bring wine also and corn for your horses and gather much wood, that from dark till dawn we may burn watchfires whose flare may reach to heaven. For the Achaeans may try to fly beyond the sea by night, and they must not embark scatheless and unmolested; many a man among them must take a dart with him to nurse at home, hit with spear or arrow as he is leaping on board his ship, that others may fear to bring war and weeping upon the Trojans. Moreover let the heralds tell it about the city that the growing youths and grey-bearded men are to camp upon its heaven-built walls. Let the women each of them light a great fire in her house, and let watch be safely kept lest the town be entered by surprise while the host is outside. See to it, brave Trojans, as I have said, and let this suffice for the moment; at daybreak I will instruct you further. I pray in hope to Jove and to the gods that we may then drive those fate-sped hounds from our land, for 'tis the fates that have borne them and their ships hither. This night, therefore, let us keep watch, but with early morning let us put on our armour and rouse fierce war at the ships of the Achaeans; I shall then know whether brave Diomed the son of Tydeus will drive me back from the ships to the wall, or whether I shall myself slay him and carry off his bloodstained spoils. To-morrow let him show his mettle, abide my spear if he dare. I ween that at break of day, he shall be among the first to fall and many another of his comrades round him. Would that I were as sure of being immortal and never growing old, and of being worshipped like Minerva and Apollo, as I am that this day will bring evil to the Argives."

Thus spoke Hector and the Trojans shouted applause. They took their sweating steeds from under the yoke, and made them fast each by his own chariot. They made haste to bring sheep and cattle from the city, they brought wine also and corn from their houses and gathered much wood. They then offered unblemished hecatombs to the immortals, and the wind carried the sweet savour of sacrifice to heaven- but the blessed gods partook not thereof, for they bitterly hated Ilius with Priam and Priam's people. Thus high in hope they sat through the livelong night by the highways of war, and many a watchfire did they kindle. As when the stars shine clear, and the moon is bright- there is not a breath of air, not a peak nor glade nor jutting headland but it stands out in the ineffable radiance that breaks from the serene of heaven; the stars can all of them be told and the heart of the shepherd is glad- even thus shone the watchfires of the Trojans before Ilius midway between the ships and the river Xanthus. A thousand camp-fires gleamed upon the plain, and in the glow of each there sat fifty men, while the horses, champing oats and corn beside their chariots, waited till dawn should come.

Book IX

Thus did the Trojans watch. But Panic, comrade of blood-stained Rout, had taken fast hold of the Achaeans and their princes were all of them in despair. As when the two winds that blow from Thrace- the north and the northwest- spring up of a sudden and rouse the fury of the main- in a moment the dark waves uprear their heads and scatter their sea-wrack in all directions- even thus troubled were the hearts of the Achaeans.

The son of Atreus in dismay bade the heralds call the people to a council man by man, but not to cry the matter aloud; he made haste also himself to call them, and they sat sorry at heart in their assembly. Agamemnon shed tears as it were a running stream or cataract on the side of some sheer cliff; and thus, with many a heavy sigh he spoke to the Achaeans. "My friends," said he, "princes and councillors of the Argives, the hand of heaven has been laid heavily upon me. Cruel Jove gave me his solemn promise that I should sack the city of Troy before returning, but he has played me false, and is now bidding me go ingloriously back to Argos with the loss of much people. Such is the will of Jove, who has laid many a proud city in the dust as he will yet lay others, for his power is above all. Now, therefore, let us all do as I say and sail back to our own country, for we shall not take Troy."

Thus he spoke, and the sons of the Achaeans for a long while sat sorrowful there, but they all held their peace, till at last Diomed of the loud battle-cry made answer saying, "Son of Atreus, I will chide your folly, as is my right in council. Be not then aggrieved that I should do so. In the first place you attacked me before all the Danaans and said that I was a coward and no soldier. The Argives young and old know that you did so. But the son of scheming Saturn endowed you by halves only. He gave you honour as the chief ruler over us, but valour, which is the highest both right and might he did not give you. Sir, think you that the sons of the Achaeans are indeed as unwarlike and cowardly as you say they are? If your own mind is set upon going home- go- the way is open to you; the many ships that followed you from Mycene stand ranged upon the seashore; but the rest of us stay here till we have sacked Troy. Nay though these too should turn homeward with their ships, Sthenelus and myself will still fight on till we reach the goal of Ilius, for for heaven was with us when we came."

The sons of the Achaeans shouted applause at the words of Diomed, and presently Nestor rose to speak. "Son of Tydeus," said he, "in war your prowess is beyond question, and in council you excel all who are of your own years; no one of the Achaeans can make light of what you say nor gainsay it, but you have not yet come to the end of the whole matter. You are still young- you might be the youngest of my own children- still you have spoken wisely and have counselled the chief of the Achaeans not without discretion; nevertheless I am older than you and I will tell you every" thing; therefore let no man, not even King Agamemnon, disregard my saying, for he that foments civil discord is a clanless, hearthless outlaw.

"Now, however, let us obey the behests of night and get our suppers, but let the sentinels every man of them camp by the trench that is without the wall. I am giving these instructions to the young men; when they have been attended to, do you, son of Atreus, give your orders, for you are the most royal among us all. Prepare a feast for your councillors; it is right and reasonable that you should do so; there is abundance of wine in your tents, which the ships of the Achaeans bring from Thrace daily. You have everything at your disposal wherewith to entertain guests, and you have many subjects. When many are got together, you can be guided by him whose counsel is wisest- and sorely do we need shrewd and prudent counsel, for the foe has lit his watchfires hard by our ships. Who can be other than dismayed? This night will either be the ruin of our host, or save it."

Thus did he speak, and they did even as he had said. The sentinels went out in their armour under command of Nestor's son Thrasymedes, a captain of the host, and of the bold warriors Ascalaphus and Ialmenus: there were also Meriones, Aphareus and Deipyrus, and the son of Creion, noble Lycomedes. There were seven captains of the sentinels, and with each there went a hundred youths armed with long spears: they took their places midway between the trench and the wall, and when they had done so they lit their fires and got every man his supper.

The son of Atreus then bade many councillors of the Achaeans to his quarters prepared a great feast in their honour. They laid their hands on the good things that were before them, and as soon as they had enough to eat and drink, old Nestor, whose counsel was ever truest, was the first to lay his mind before them. He, therefore, with all sincerity and goodwill addressed them thus.

"With yourself, most noble son of Atreus, king of men, Agamemnon, will I both begin my speech and end it, for you are king over much people. Jove, moreover, has vouchsafed you to wield the sceptre and to uphold righteousness, that you may take thought for your people under you; therefore it behooves you above all others both to speak and to give ear, and to out the counsel of another who shall have been minded to speak wisely. All turns on you and on your commands, therefore I will say what I think will be best. No man will be of a truer mind than that which has been mine from the hour when you, sir, angered Achilles by taking the girl Briseis from his tent against my judgment. I urged you not to do so, but you yielded to your own pride, and dishonoured a hero whom heaven itself had honoured- for you still hold the prize that had been awarded to him. Now, however, let us think how we may appease him, both with presents and fair speeches that may conciliate him."

And King Agamemnon answered, "Sir, you have reproved my folly justly. I was wrong. I own it. One whom heaven befriends is in himself a host, and Jove has shown that he befriends this man by destroying much people of the Achaeans. I was blinded with passion and yielded to my worser mind; therefore I will make amends, and will give him great gifts by way of atonement. I will tell them in the presence of you all. I will give him seven tripods that have never yet been on the fire, and ten talents of gold. I will give him twenty iron cauldrons and twelve strong horses that have won races and carried off prizes. Rich, indeed, both in land and gold is he that has as many prizes as my horses have won me. I will give him seven excellent workwomen, Lesbians, whom I chose for myself when he took Lesbos- all of surpassing beauty. I will give him these, and with them her whom I erewhile took from him, the daughter of Briseus; and I swear a great oath that I never went up into her couch, nor have been with her after the manner of men and women.

"All these things will I give him now down, and if hereafter the gods vouchsafe me to sack the city of Priam, let him come when we Achaeans are dividing the spoil, and load his ship with gold and bronze to his liking; furthermore let him take twenty Trojan women, the loveliest after Helen herself. Then, when we reach Achaean Argos, wealthiest of all lands, he shall be my son-in-law and I will show him like honour with my own dear son Orestes, who is being nurtured in all abundance. I have three daughters, Chrysothemis, Laodice, and lphianassa, let him take the one of his choice, freely and without gifts of wooing, to the house of Peleus; I will add such dower to boot as no man ever yet gave his daughter, and will give him seven well established cities, Cardamyle, Enope, and Hire, where there is grass; holy Pherae and the rich meadows of Anthea; Aepea also, and the vine-clad slopes of Pedasus, all near the sea, and on the borders of sandy Pylos. The men that dwell there are rich in cattle and sheep; they will honour him with gifts as though he were a god, and be obedient to his comfortable ordinances. All this will I do if he will now forgo his anger. Let him then yieldit is only Hades who is utterly ruthless and unyielding- and hence he is of all gods the one most hateful to mankind. Moreover I am older and more royal than himself. Therefore, let him now obey me."

Then Nestor answered, "Most noble son of Atreus, king of men, Agamemnon. The gifts you offer are no small ones, let us then send chosen messengers, who may go to the tent of Achilles son of Peleus without delay. Let those go whom I shall name. Let Phoenix, dear to Jove, lead the way; let Ajax and Ulysses follow, and let the heralds Odius and Eurybates go with them. Now bring water for our hands, and bid all keep silence while we pray to Jove the son of Saturn, if so be that he may have mercy upon us."

Thus did he speak, and his saying pleased them well. Men-servants poured water over the hands of the guests, while pages filled the mixing-bowls with wine and water, and handed it round after giving every man his drink-offering; then, when they had made their offerings, and had drunk each as much as he was minded, the envoys set out from the tent of Agamemnon son of Atreus; and Nestor, looking first to one and then to another, but most especially at Ulysses, was instant with them that they should prevail with the noble son of Peleus.

They went their way by the shore of the sounding sea, and prayed earnestly to earth-encircling Neptune that the high spirit of the son of Aeacus might incline favourably towards them. When they reached the ships and tents of the Myrmidons, they found Achilles playing on a lyre, fair, of cunning workmanship, and its cross-bar was of silver. It was part of the spoils which he had taken when he sacked the city of Eetion, and he was now diverting himself with it and singing the feats of heroes. He was alone with Patroclus, who sat opposite to him and said nothing, waiting till he should cease singing. Ulysses and Ajax now came in- Ulysses leading the way -and stood before him. Achilles sprang from his seat with the lyre still in his hand, and Patroclus, when he saw the strangers, rose also. Achilles then greeted them saying, "All hail and welcome- you must come upon some great matter, you, who for all my anger are still dearest to me of the Achaeans."

With this he led them forward, and bade them sit on seats covered with purple rugs; then he said to Patroclus who was close by him, "Son of Menoetius, set a larger bowl upon the table, mix less water with the wine, and give every man his cup, for these are very dear friends, who are now under my roof."

Patroclus did as his comrade bade him; he set the chopping-block in front of the fire, and on it he laid the loin of a sheep, the loin also of a goat, and the chine of a fat hog. Automedon held the meat while Achilles chopped it; he then sliced the pieces and put them on spits while the son of Menoetius made the fire burn high. When the flame had died down, he spread the embers, laid the spits on top of them, lifting them up and setting them upon the spit-racks; and he sprinkled them with salt. When the meat was roasted, he set it on platters, and handed bread round the table in fair baskets, while Achilles dealt them their portions. Then Achilles took his seat facing Ulysses against the opposite wall, and bade his comrade Patroclus offer sacrifice to the gods; so he cast the offerings into the fire, and they laid their hands upon the good things that were before them. As soon as they had had enough to eat and drink, Ajax made a sign to Phoenix, and when he saw this, Ulysses filled his cup with wine and pledged Achilles.

"Hail," said he, "Achilles, we have had no scant of good cheer, neither in the tent of Agamemnon, nor yet here; there has been plenty to eat and drink, but our thought turns upon no such matter. Sir, we are in the face of great disaster, and without your help know not whether we shall save our fleet or lose it. The Trojans and their allies have camped hard by our ships and by the wall; they have lit watchfires throughout their host and deem that nothing can now prevent them from falling on our fleet. Jove, moreover, has sent his lightnings on their right; Hector, in all his glory, rages like a maniac; confident that Jove is with him he fears neither god nor man, but is gone raving mad, and prays for the approach of day. He vows that he will hew the high sterns of our ships in pieces, set fire to their hulls, and make havoc of the Achaeans while they are dazed and smothered in smoke; I much fear that heaven will make good his boasting, and it will prove our lot to perish at Troy far from our home in Argos. Up, then, and late though it be, save the sons of the Achaeans who faint before the fury of the Trojans. You will repent bitterly hereafter if you do not, for when the harm is done there will be no curing it; consider ere it be too late, and save the Danaans from destruction.

"My good friend, when your father Peleus sent you from Phthia to Agamemnon, did he not charge you saying, 'Son, Minerva and Juno will make you strong if they choose, but check your high temper, for the better part is in goodwill. Eschew vain quarrelling, and the Achaeans old and young will respect you more for doing so.' These were his words, but you have forgotten them. Even now, however, be appeased, and put away your anger from you. Agamemnon will make you great amends if you will forgive him; listen, and I will tell you what he has said in his tent that he will give you. He will give you seven tripods that have never yet been on the fire, and ten talents of gold; twenty iron cauldrons, and twelve strong horses that have won races and carried off prizes. Rich indeed both in land and gold is he who has as many prizes as these horses have won for Agamemnon. Moreover he will give you seven excellent workwomen, Lesbians, whom he chose for himself, when you took Lesbos- all of surpassing beauty. He will give you these, and with them her whom he erewhile took from you, the daughter of Briseus, and he will swear a great oath, he has never gone up into her couch nor been with her after the manner of men and women. All these things will he give you now down, and if hereafter the gods vouchsafe him to sack the city of Priam, you can come when we Achaeans are dividing the spoil, and load your ship with gold and bronze to your liking. You can take twenty Trojan women, the loveliest after Helen herself. Then, when we reach Achaean Argos, wealthiest of all lands, you shall be his son-in-law, and he will show you like honour with his own dear son Orestes, who is being nurtured in all abundance. Agamemnon has three daughters, Chrysothemis, Laodice, and Iphianassa; you may take the one of your choice, freely and without gifts of wooing, to the house of Peleus; he will add such dower to boot as no man ever yet gave his daughter, and will give you seven well-established cities, Cardamyle, Enope, and Hire where there is grass; holy Pheras and the rich meadows of Anthea; Aepea also, and the vine-clad slopes of Pedasus, all near the sea, and on the borders of sandy Pylos. The men that dwell there are rich in cattle and sheep; they will honour you with gifts as though were a god, and be obedient to your comfortable ordinances. All this will he do if you will now forgo your anger. Moreover, though you hate both him and his gifts with all your heart, yet pity the rest of the Achaeans who are being harassed in all their host; they will honour you as a god, and you will earn great glory at their hands. You might even kill Hector; he will come within your reach, for he is infatuated, and declares that not a Danaan whom the ships have brought can hold his own against him."

Achilles answered, "Ulysses, noble son of Laertes, I should give you formal notice plainly and in all fixity of purpose that there be no more of this cajoling, from whatsoever quarter it may come. Him do I hate even as the gates of hell who says one thing while he hides another in his heart; therefore I will say what I mean. I will be appeased neither by Agamemnon son of Atreus nor by any other of the Danaans, for I see that I have no thanks for all my fighting. He that fights fares no better than he that does not; coward and hero are held in equal honour, and death deals like measure to him who works and him who is idle. I have taken nothing by all my hardships- with my life ever in my hand; as a bird when she has found a morsel takes it to her nestlings, and herself fares hardly, even so man a long night have I been wakeful, and many a bloody battle have I waged by day against those who were fighting for their women. With my ships I have taken twelve cities, and eleven round about Troy have I stormed with my men by land; I took great store of wealth from every one of them, but I gave all up to Agamemnon son of Atreus. He stayed where he was by his ships, yet of what came to him he gave little, and kept much himself.

"Nevertheless he did distribute some meeds of honour among the chieftains and kings, and these have them still; from me alone of the Achaeans did he take the woman in whom I delighted- let him keep her and sleep with her. Why, pray, must the Argives needs fight the Trojans? What made the son of Atreus gather the host and bring them? Was it not for the sake of Helen? Are the sons of Atreus the only men in the world who love their wives? Any man of common right feeling will love and cherish her who is his own, as I this woman, with my whole heart, though she was but a fruitling of my spear. Agamemnon has taken her from me; he has played me false; I know him; let him tempt me no further, for he shall not move me. Let him look to you, Ulysses, and to the other princes to save his ships from burning. He has done much without me already. He has built a wall; he has dug a trench deep and wide all round it, and he has planted it within with stakes; but even so he stays not the murderous might of Hector. So long as I fought the Achaeans Hector suffered not the battle range far from the city walls; he would come to the Scaean gates and to the oak tree, but no further. Once he stayed to meet me and hardly did he escape my onset: now, however, since I am in no mood to fight him, I will to-morrow offer sacrifice to Jove and to all the gods; I will draw my ships into the water and then victual them duly; to-morrow morning, if you care to look, you will see my ships on the Hellespont, and my men rowing out to sea with might and main. If great Neptune vouchsafes me a fair passage, in three days I shall be in Phthia. I have much there that I left behind me when I came here to my sorrow, and I shall bring back still further store of gold, of red copper, of fair women, and of iron, my share of the spoils that we have taken; but one prize, he who gave has insolently taken away. Tell him all as I now bid you, and tell him in public that the Achaeans may hate him and beware of him should he think that he can yet dupe others for his effrontery never fails him.

"As for me, hound that he is, he dares not look me in the face. I will take no counsel with him, and will undertake nothing in common with him. He has wronged me and deceived me enough, he shall not cozen me further; let him go his own way, for Jove has robbed him of his reason. I loathe his presents, and for himself care not one straw. He may offer me ten or even twenty times what he has now done, nay- not though it be all that he has in the world, both now or ever shall have; he may promise me the wealth of Orchomenus or of Egyptian Thebes, which is the richest city in the whole world, for it has a hundred gates through each of which two hundred men may drive at once with their chariots and horses; he may offer me gifts as the sands of the sea or the dust of the plain in multitude, but even so he shall not move me till I have been revenged in full for the bitter wrong he has done me. I will not marry his daughter; she may be fair as Venus, and skilful as Minerva, but I will have none of her: let another take her, who may be a good match for her and who rules a larger kingdom. If the gods spare me to return home, Peleus will find me a wife; there are Achaean women in Hellas and Phthia, daughters of kings that have cities under them; of these I can take whom I will and marry her. Many a time was I minded when at home in Phthia to woo and wed a woman who would make me a suitable wife, and to enjoy the riches of my old father Peleus. My life is more to me than all the wealth of Ilius while it was yet at peace before the Achaeans went there, or than all the treasure that lies on the stone floor of Apollo's temple beneath the cliffs of Pytho. Cattle and sheep are to be had for harrying, and a man buy both tripods and horses if he wants them, but when his life has once left him it can neither be bought nor harried back again.

"My mother Thetis tells me that there are two ways in which I may meet my end. If I stay here and fight, I shall not return alive but my name will live for ever: whereas if I go home my name will die, but it will be long ere death shall take me. To the rest of you, then, I say, 'Go home, for you will not take Ilius.' Jove has held his hand over her to protect her, and her people have taken heart. Go, therefore, as in duty bound, and tell the princes of the Achaeans the message that I have sent them; tell them to find some other plan for the saving of their ships and people, for so long as my displeasure lasts the one that they have now hit upon may not be. As for Phoenix, let him sleep here that he may sail with me in the morning if he so will. But I will not take him by force."

They all held their peace, dismayed at the sternness with which he had denied them, till presently the old knight Phoenix in his great fear for the ships of the Achaeans, burst into tears and said, "Noble Achilles, if you are now minded to return, and in the fierceness of your anger will do nothing to save the ships from burning, how, my son, can I remain here without you? Your father Peleus bade me go with you when he sent you as a mere lad from Phthia to Agamemnon. You knew nothing neither of war nor of the arts whereby men make their mark in council, and he sent me with you to train you in all excellence of speech and action. Therefore, my son, I will not stay here without you- no, not though heaven itself vouchsafe to strip my years from off me, and make me young as I was when I first left Hellas the land of fair women. I was then flying the anger of father Amyntor, son of Ormenus, who was furious with me in the matter of his concubine, of whom he was enamoured to the wronging of his wife my mother. My mother, therefore, prayed me without ceasing to lie with the woman myself, that so she hate my father, and in the course of time I yielded. But my father soon came to know, and cursed me bitterly, calling the dread Erinyes to witness. He prayed that no son of mine might ever sit upon knees- and the gods, Jove of the world below and awful Proserpine, fulfilled his curse. I took counsel to kill him, but some god stayed my rashness and bade me think on men's evil tongues and how I should be branded as the murderer of my father: nevertheless I could not bear to stay in my father's house with him so bitter a against me. My cousins and clansmen came about me, and pressed me sorely to remain; many a sheep and many an ox did they slaughter, and many a fat hog did they set down to roast before the fire; many a jar, too, did they broach of my father's wine. Nine whole nights did they set a guard over me taking it in turns to watch, and they kept a fire always burning, both in the cloister of the outer court and in the inner court at the doors of the room wherein I lay; but when the darkness of the tenth night came, I broke through the closed doors of my room, and climbed the wall of the outer court after passing quickly and unperceived through the men on guard and the women servants. I then fled through Hellas till I came to fertile Phthia, mother of sheep, and to King Peleus, who made me welcome and treated me as a father treats an only son who will be heir to all his wealth. He made me rich and set me over much people, establishing me on the borders of Phthia where I was chief ruler over the Dolopians.

"It was I, Achilles, who had the making of you; I loved you with all my heart: for you would eat neither at home nor when you had gone out elsewhere, till I had first set you upon my knees, cut up the dainty morsel that you were to eat, and held the wine-cup to your lips. Many a time have you slobbered your wine in baby helplessness over my shirt; I had infinite trouble with you, but I knew that heaven had vouchsafed me no offspring of my own, and I made a son of you, Achilles, that in my hour of need you might protect me. Now, therefore, I say battle with your pride and beat it; cherish not your anger for ever; the might and majesty of heaven are more than ours, but even heaven may be appeased; and if a man has sinned he prays the gods, and reconciles them to himself by his piteous cries and by frankincense, with drink-offerings and the savour of burnt sacrifice. For prayers are as daughters to great Jove; halt, wrinkled, with eyes askance, they follow in the footsteps of sin, who, being fierce and fleet of foot, leaves them far behind him, and ever baneful to mankind outstrips them even to the ends of the world; but nevertheless the prayers come hobbling and healing after. If a man has pity upon these daughters of Jove when they draw near him, they will bless him and hear him too when he is praying; but if he deny them and will not listen to them, they go to Jove the son of Saturn and pray that he may presently fall into sin- to his ruing bitterly hereafter. Therefore, Achilles, give these daughters of Jove due reverence, and bow before them as all good men will bow. Were not the son of Atreus offering you gifts and promising others later- if he were still furious and implacable- I am not he that would bid you throw off your anger and help the Achaeans, no matter how great their need; but he is giving much now, and more hereafter; he has sent his captains to urge his suit, and has chosen those who of all the Argives are most acceptable to you; make not then their words and their coming to be of none effect. Your anger has been righteous so far. We have heard in song how heroes of old time quarrelled when they were roused to fury, but still they could be won by gifts, and fair words could soothe them.

"I have an old story in my mind- a very old one- but you are all friends and I will tell it. The Curetes and the Aetolians were fighting and killing one another round Calydon- the Aetolians defending the city and the Curetes trying to destroy it. For Diana of the golden throne was angry and did them hurt because Oeneus had not offered her his harvest first-fruits. The other gods had all been feasted with hecatombs, but to the daughter of great Jove alone he had made no sacrifice. He had forgotten her, or somehow or other it had escaped him, and this was a grievous sin. Thereon the archer goddess in her displeasure sent a prodigious creature against him- a savage wild boar with great white tusks that did much harm to his orchard lands, uprooting apple-trees in full bloom and throwing them to the ground. But Meleager son of Oeneus got huntsmen and hounds from many cities and killed it- for it was so monstrous that not a few were needed, and many a man did it stretch upon his funeral pyre. On this the goddess set the Curetes and the Aetolians fighting furiously about the head and skin of the boar.

"So long as Meleager was in the field things went badly with the Curetes, and for all their numbers they could not hold their ground under the city walls; but in the course of time Meleager was angered as even a wise man will sometimes be. He was incensed with his mother Althaea, and therefore stayed at home with his wedded wife fair Cleopatra, who was daughter of Marpessa daughter of Euenus, and of Ides the man then living. He it was who took his bow and faced King Apollo himself for fair Marpessa's sake; her father and mother then named her Alcyone, because her mother had mourned with the plaintive strains of the halcyon-bird when Phoebus Apollo had carried her off. Meleager, then, stayed at home with Cleopatra, nursing the anger which he felt by reason of his mother's curses. His mother, grieving for the death of her brother, prayed the gods, and beat the earth with her hands, calling upon Hades and on awful Proserpine; she went down upon her knees and her bosom was wet with tears as she prayed that they would kill her son- and Erinys that walks in darkness and knows no ruth heard her from Erebus.

"Then was heard the din of battle about the gates of Calydon, and the dull thump of the battering against their walls. Thereon the elders of the Aetolians besought Meleager; they sent the chiefest of their priests, and begged him to come out and help them, promising him a great reward. They bade him choose fifty plough-gates, the most fertile in the plain of Calydon, the one-half vineyard and the other open plough-land. The old warrior Oeneus implored him, standing at the threshold of his room and beating the doors in supplication. His sisters and his mother herself besought him sore, but he the more refused them; those of his comrades who were nearest and dearest to him also prayed him, but they could not move him till the foe was battering at the very doors of his chamber, and the Curetes had scaled the walls and were setting fire to the city. Then at last his sorrowing wife detailed the horrors that befall those whose city is taken; she reminded him how the men are slain, and the city is given over to the flames, while the women and children are carried into captivity; when he heard all this, his heart was touched, and he donned his armour to go forth. Thus of his own inward motion he saved the city of the Aetolians; but they now gave him nothing of those rich rewards that they had offered earlier, and though he saved the city he took nothing by it. Be not then, my son, thus minded; let not heaven lure you into any such course. When the ships are burning it will be a harder matter to save them. Take the gifts, and go, for the Achaeans will then honour you as a god; whereas if you fight without taking them, you may beat the battle back, but you will not be held in like honour."

And Achilles answered, "Phoenix, old friend and father, I have no need of such honour. I have honour from Jove himself, which will abide with me at my ships while I have breath in my body, and my limbs are strong. I say further- and lay my saying to your heart- vex me no more with this weeping and lamentation, all in the cause of the son of Atreus. Love him so well, and you may lose the love I bear you. You ought to help me rather in troubling those that trouble me; be king as much as I am, and share like honour with myself; the others shall take my answer; stay here yourself and sleep comfortably in your bed; at daybreak we will consider whether to remain or go."

On this she nodded quietly to Patroclus as a sign that he was to prepare a bed for Phoenix, and that the others should take their leave. Ajax son of Telamon then said, "Ulysses, noble son of Laertes, let us be gone, for I see that our journey is vain. We must now take our answer, unwelcome though it be, to the Danaans who are waiting to receive it. Achilles is savage and remorseless; he is cruel, and cares nothing for the love his comrades lavished upon him more than on all the others. He is implacable- and yet if a man's brother or son has been slain he will accept a fine by way of amends from him that killed him, and the wrong-doer having paid in full remains in peace among his own people; but as for you, Achilles, the gods have put a wicked unforgiving spirit in your heart, and this, all about one single girl, whereas we now offer you the seven best we have, and much else into the bargain. Be then of a more gracious mind, respect the hospitality of your own roof. We are with you as messengers from the host of the Danaans, and would fain he held nearest and dearest to yourself of all the Achaeans."

"Ajax," replied Achilles, "noble son of Telamon, you have spoken much to my liking, but my blood boils when I think it all over, and remember how the son of Atreus treated me with contumely as though I were some vile tramp, and that too in the presence of the Argives. Go, then, and deliver your message; say that I will have no concern with fighting till Hector, son of noble Priam, reaches the tents of the Myrmidons in his murderous course, and flings fire upon their ships. For all his lust of battle, I take it he will be held in check when he is at my own tent and ship."

On this they took every man his double cup, made their drink-offerings, and went back to the ships, Ulysses leading the way. But Patroclus told his men and the maid-servants to make ready a comfortable bed for Phoenix; they therefore did so with sheepskins, a rug, and a sheet of fine linen. The old man then laid himself down and waited till morning came. But Achilles slept in an inner room, and beside him the daughter of Phorbas lovely Diomede, whom he had carried off from Lesbos. Patroclus lay on the other side of the room, and with him fair Iphis whom Achilles had given him when he took Scyros the city of Enyeus.

When the envoys reached the tents of the son of Atreus, the Achaeans rose, pledged them in cups of gold, and began to question them. King Agamemnon was the first to do so. Tell me, Ulysses," said he, "will he save the ships from burning, or did be refuse, and is he still furious?"

Ulysses answered, "Most noble son of Atreus, king of men, Agamemnon, Achilles will not be calmed, but is more fiercely angry than ever, and spurns both you and your gifts. He bids you take counsel with the Achaeans to save the ships and host as you best may; as for himself, he said that at daybreak he should draw his ships into the water. He said further that he should advise every one to sail home likewise, for that you will not reach the goal of Ilius. 'Jove,' he said, 'has laid his hand over the city to protect it, and the people have taken heart.' This is what he said, and the others who were with me can tell you the same story- Ajax and the two heralds, men, both of them, who may be trusted. The old man Phoenix stayed where he was to sleep, for so Achilles would have it, that he might go home with him in the morning if he so would; but he will not take him by force."

They all held their peace, sitting for a long time silent and dejected, by reason of the sternness with which Achilles had refused them, till presently Diomed said, "Most noble son of Atreus, king of men, Agamemnon, you ought not to have sued the son of Peleus nor offered him gifts. He is proud enough as it is, and you have encouraged him in his pride am further. Let him stay or go as he will. He will fight later when he is in the humour, and heaven puts it in his mind to do so. Now, therefore, let us all do as I say; we have eaten and drunk our fill, let us then take our rest, for in rest there is both strength and stay. But when fair rosy-fingered morn appears, forthwith bring out your host and your horsemen in front of the ships, urging them on, and yourself fighting among the foremost."

Thus he spoke, and the other chieftains approved his words. They then made their drink-offerings and went every man to his own tent, where they laid down to rest and enjoyed the boon of sleep.

Book XVI

Thus did they fight about the ship of Protesilaus. Then Patroclus drew near to Achilles with tears welling from his eyes, as from some spring whose crystal stream falls over the ledges of a high precipice. When Achilles saw him thus weeping he was sorry for him and said, "Why, Patroclus, do you stand there weeping like some silly child that comes running to her mother, and begs to be taken up and carried- she catches hold of her mother's dress to stay her though she is in a hurry, and looks tearfully up until her mother carries her- even such tears, Patroclus, are you now shedding. Have you anything to say to the Myrmidons or to myself? or have you had news from Phthia which you alone know? They tell me Menoetius son of Actor is still alive, as also Peleus son of Aeacus, among the Myrmidons- men whose loss we two should bitterly deplore; or are you grieving about the Argives and the way in which they are being killed at the ships, throu their own high-handed doings? Do not hide anything from me but tell me that both of us may know about it."

Then, O knight Patroclus, with a deep sigh you answered, "Achilles, son of Peleus, foremost champion of the Achaeans, do not be angry, but I weep for the disaster that has now befallen the Argives. All those who have been their champions so far are lying at the ships, wounded by sword or spear. Brave Diomed son of Tydeus has been hit with a spear, while famed Ulysses and Agamemnon have received sword-wounds; Eurypylus again has been struck with an arrow in the thigh; skilled apothecaries are attending to these heroes, and healing them of their wounds; are you still, O Achilles, so inexorable? May it never be my lot to nurse such a passion as you have done, to the baning of your own good name. Who in future story will speak well of you unless you now save the Argives from ruin? You know no pity; knight Peleus was not your father nor Thetis your mother, but the grey sea bore you and the sheer cliffs begot you, so cruel and remorseless are you. If however you are kept back through knowledge of some oracle, or if your mother Thetis has told you something from the mouth of Jove, at least send me and the Myrmidons with me, if I may bring deliverance to the Danaans. Let me moreover wear your armour; the Trojans may thus mistake me for you and quit the field, so that the hard-pressed sons of the Achaeans may have breathing time- which while they are fighting may hardly be. We who are fresh might soon drive tired men back from our ships and tents to their own city."

He knew not what he was asking, nor that he was suing for his own destruction. Achilles was deeply moved and answered, "What, noble Patroclus, are you saying? I know no prophesyings which I am heeding, nor has my mother told me anything from the mouth of Jove, but I am cut to the very heart that one of my own rank should dare to rob me because he is more powerful than I am. This, after all that I have gone through, is more than I can endure. The girl whom the sons of the Achaeans chose for me, whom I won as the fruit of my spear on having sacked a city- her has King Agamemnon taken from me as though I were some common vagrant. Still, let bygones be bygones: no man may keep his anger for ever; I said I would not relent till battle and the cry of war had reached my own ships; nevertheless, now gird my armour about your shoulders, and lead the Myrmidons to battle, for the dark cloud of Trojans has burst furiously over our fleet; the Argives are driven back on to the beach, cooped within a narrow space, and the whole people of Troy has taken heart to sally out against them, because they see not the visor of my helmet gleaming near them. Had they seen this, there would not have been a creek nor grip that had not been filled with their dead as they fled back again.

And so it would have been, if only King Agamemnon had dealt fairly by me. As it is the Trojans have beset our host. Diomed son of Tydeus no longer wields his spear to defend the Danaans, neither have I heard the voice of the son of Atreus coming from his hated head, whereas that of murderous Hector rings in my cars as he gives orders to the Trojans, who triumph over the Achaeans and fill the whole plain with their cry of battle. But even so, Patroclus, fall upon them and save the fleet, lest the Trojans fire it and prevent us from being able to return. Do, however, as I now bid you, that you may win me great honour from all the Danaans, and that they may restore the girl to me again and give me rich gifts into the bargain. When you have driven the Trojans from the ships, come back again. Though Juno's thundering husband should put triumph within your reach, do not fight the Trojans further in my absence, or you will rob me of glory that should be mine. And do not for lust of battle go on killing the Trojans nor lead the Achaeans on to Ilius, lest one of the ever-living gods from Olympus attack you- for Phoebus Apollo loves them well: return when you have freed the ships from peril, and let others wage war upon the plain. Would, by father Jove, Minerva, and Apollo, that not a single man of all the Trojans might be left alive, nor yet of the Argives, but that we two might be alone left to tear aside the mantle that veils the brow of Troy."

Thus did they converse. But Ajax could no longer hold his ground for the shower of darts that rained upon him; the will of Jove and the javelins of the Trojans were too much for him; the helmet that gleamed about his temples rang with the continuous clatter of the missiles that kept pouring on to it and on to the cheek-pieces that protected his face. Moreover his left shoulder was tired with having held his shield so long, yet for all this, let fly at him as they would, they could not make him give ground. He could hardly draw his breath, the sweat rained from every pore of his body, he had not a moment's respite, and on all sides he was beset by danger upon danger.

And now, tell me, O Muses that hold your mansions on Olympus, how fire was thrown upon the ships of the Achaeans. Hector came close up and let drive with his great sword at the ashen spear of Ajax. He cut it clean in two just behind where the point was fastened on to the shaft of the spear. Ajax, therefore, had now nothing but a headless spear, while the bronze point flew some way off and came ringing down on to the ground. Ajax knew the hand of heaven in this, and was dismayed at seeing that Jove had now left him utterly defenceless and was willing victory for the Trojans. Therefore he drew back, and the Trojans flung fire upon the ship which was at once wrapped in flame.

The fire was now flaring about the ship's stern, whereon Achilles smote his two thighs and said to Patroclus, "Up, noble knight, for I see the glare of hostile fire at our fleet; up, lest they destroy our ships, and there be no way by which we may retreat. Gird on your armour at once while I call our people together."

As he spoke Patroclus put on his armour. First he greaved his legs with greaves of good make, and fitted with ancle-clasps of silver; after this he donned the cuirass of the son of Aeacus, richly inlaid and studded. He hung his silver-studded sword of bronze about his shoulders, and then his mighty shield. On his comely head he set his helmet, well wrought, with a crest of horse-hair that nodded menacingly above it. He grasped two redoubtable spears that suited his hands, but he did not take the spear of noble Achilles, so stout and strong, for none other of the Achaeans could wield it, though Achilles could do so easily. This was the ashen spear from Mount Pelion, which Chiron had cut upon a mountain top and had given to Peleus, wherewith to deal out death among heroes. He bade Automedon yoke his horses with all speed, for he was the man whom he held in honour next after Achilles, and on whose support in battle he could rely most firmly. Automedon therefore yoked the fleet horses Xanthus and Balius, steeds that could fly like the wind: these were they whom the harpy Podarge bore to the west wind, as she was grazing in a meadow by the waters of the river Oceanus. In the side traces he set the noble horse Pedasus, whom Achilles had brought away with him when he sacked the city of Eetion, and who, mortal steed though he was, could take his place along with those that were immortal.

Meanwhile Achilles went about everywhere among the tents, and bade his Myrmidons put on their armour. Even as fierce ravening wolves that are feasting upon a homed stag which they have killed upon the mountains, and their jaws are red with blood- they go in a pack to lap water from the clear spring with their long thin tongues; and they reek of blood and slaughter; they know not what fear is, for it is hunger drives them- even so did the leaders and counsellors of the Myrmidons gather round the good squire of the fleet descendant of Aeacus, and among them stood Achilles himself cheering on both men and horses.

Fifty ships had noble Achilles brought to Troy, and in each there was a crew of fifty oarsmen. Over these he set five captains whom he could trust, while he was himself commander over them all. Menesthius of the gleaming corslet, son to the river Spercheius that streams from heaven, was captain of the first company. Fair Polydora daughter of Peleus bore him to ever-flowing Spercheius- a woman mated with a god- but he was called son of Borus son of Perieres, with whom his mother was living as his wedded wife, and who gave great wealth to gain her. The second company was led by noble Eudorus, son to an unwedded woman. Polymele, daughter of Phylas the graceful dancer, bore him; the mighty slayer of Argos was enamoured of her as he saw her among the singing women at a dance held in honour of Diana the rushing huntress of the golden arrows; he therefore- Mercury, giver of all good- went with her into an upper chamber, and lay with her in secret, whereon she bore him a noble son Eudorus, singularly fleet of foot and in fight valiant. When Ilithuia goddess of the pains of child-birth brought him to the light of day, and he saw the face of the sun, mighty Echecles son of Actor took the mother to wife, and gave great wealth to gain her, but her father Phylas brought the child up, and took care of him, doting as fondly upon him as though he were his own son. The third company was led by Pisander son of Maemalus, the finest spearman among all the Myrmidons next to Achilles' own comrade Patroclus. The old knight Phoenix was captain of the fourth company, and Alcimedon, noble son of Laerceus of the fifth.

When Achilles had chosen his men and had stationed them all with their captains, he charged them straitly saying, "Myrmidons, remember your threats against the Trojans while you were at the ships in the time of my anger, and you were all complaining of me. 'Cruel son of Peleus,' you would say, 'your mother must have suckled you on gall, so ruthless are you. You keep us here at the ships against our will; if you are so relentless it were better we went home over the sea.' Often have you gathered and thus chided with me. The hour is now come for those high feats of arms that you have so long been pining for, therefore keep high hearts each one of you to do battle with the Trojans."

With these words he put heart and soul into them all, and they serried their companies yet more closely when they heard the of their king. As the stones which a builder sets in the wall of some high house which is to give shelter from the winds- even so closely were the helmets and bossed shields set against one another. Shield pressed on shield, helm on helm, and man on man; so close were they that the horse-hair plumes on the gleaming ridges of their helmets touched each other as they bent their heads.

In front of them all two men put on their armour- Patroclus and Automedon- two men, with but one mind to lead the Myrmidons. Then Achilles went inside his tent and opened the lid of the strong chest which silver-footed Thetis had given him to take on board ship, and which she had filled with shirts, cloaks to keep out the cold, and good thick rugs. In this chest he had a cup of rare workmanship, from which no man but himself might drink, nor would he make offering from it to any other god save only to father Jove. He took the cup from the chest and cleansed it with sulphur; this done he rinsed it clean water, and after he had washed his hands he drew wine. Then he stood in the middle of the court and prayed, looking towards heaven, and making his drink-offering of wine; nor was he unseen of Jove whose joy is in thunder. "King Jove," he cried, "lord of Dodona, god of the Pelasgi, who dwellest afar, you who hold wintry Dodona in your sway, where your prophets the Selli dwell around you with their feet unwashed and their couches made upon the ground- if you heard me when I prayed to you aforetime, and did me honour while you sent disaster on the Achaeans, vouchsafe me now the fulfilment of yet this further prayer. I shall stay here where my ships are lying, but I shall send my comrade into battle at the head of many Myrmidons. Grant, O all-seeing Jove, that victory may go with him; put your courage into his heart that Hector may learn whether my squire is man enough to fight alone, or whether his might is only then so indomitable when I myself enter the turmoil of war. Afterwards when he has chased the fight and the cry of battle from the ships, grant that he may return unharmed, with his armour and his comrades, fighters in close combat."

Thus did he pray, and all-counselling Jove heard his prayer. Part of it he did indeed vouchsafe him- but not the whole. He granted that Patroclus should thrust back war and battle from the ships, but refused to let him come safely out of the fight.

When he had made his drink-offering and had thus prayed, Achilles went inside his tent and put back the cup into his chest.

Then he again came out, for he still loved to look upon the fierce fight that raged between the Trojans and Achaeans.

Meanwhile the armed band that was about Patroclus marched on till they sprang high in hope upon the Trojans. They came swarming out like wasps whose nests are by the roadside, and whom silly children love to tease, whereon any one who happens to be passing may get stung- or again, if a wayfarer going along the road vexes them by accident, every wasp will come flying out in a fury to defend his little ones- even with such rage and courage did the Myrmidons swarm from their ships, and their cry of battle rose heavenwards. Patroclus called out to his men at the top of his voice, "Myrmidons, followers of Achilles son of Peleus, be men my friends, fight with might and with main, that we may win glory for the son of Peleus, who is far the foremost man at the ships of the Argives- he, and his close fighting followers. The son of Atreus King Agamemnon will thus learn his folly in showing no respect to the bravest of the Achaeans."

With these words he put heart and soul into them all, and they fell in a body upon the Trojans. The ships rang again with the cry which the Achaeans raised, and when the Trojans saw the brave son of Menoetius and his squire all gleaming in their armour, they were daunted and their battalions were thrown into confusion, for they thought the fleet son of Peleus must now have put aside his anger, and have been reconciled to Agamemnon; every one, therefore, looked round about to see whither he might fly for safety.

Patroclus first aimed a spear into the middle of the press where men were packed most closely, by the stern of the ship of Protesilaus. He hit Pyraechmes who had led his Paeonian horsemen from the Amydon and the broad waters of the river Axius; the spear struck him on the right shoulder, and with a groan he fell backwards in the dust; on this his men were thrown into confusion, for by killing their leader, who was the finest soldier among them, Patroclus struck panic into them all. He thus drove them from the ship and quenched the fire that was then blazing- leaving the half-burnt ship to lie where it was. The Trojans were now driven back with a shout that rent the skies, while the Danaans poured after them from their ships, shouting also without ceasing. As when Jove, gatherer of the thunder-cloud, spreads a dense canopy on the top of some lofty mountain, and all the peaks, the jutting headlands, and forest glades show out in the great light that flashes from the bursting heavens, even so when the Danaans had now driven back the fire from their ships, they took breath for a little while; but the fury of the fight was not yet over, for the Trojans were not driven back in utter rout, but still gave battle, and were ousted from their ground only by sheer fighting.

The fight then became more scattered, and the chieftains killed one another when and how they could. The valiant son of Menoetius first drove his spear into the thigh of Areilycus just as he was turning round; the point went clean through, and broke the bone so that he fell forward. Meanwhile Menelaus struck Thoas in the chest, where it was exposed near the rim of his shield, and he fell dead. The son of Phyleus saw Amphiclus about to attack him, and ere he could do so took aim at the upper part of his thigh, where the muscles are thicker than in any other part; the spear tore through all the sinews of the leg, and his eyes were closed in darkness. Of the sons of Nestor one, Antilochus, speared Atymnius, driving the point of the spear through his throat, and down he fell. Maris then sprang on Antilochus in hand-to-hand fight to avenge his brother, and bestrode the body spear in hand; but valiant Thrasymedes was too quick for him, and in a moment had struck him in the shoulder ere he could deal his blow; his aim was true, and the spear severed all the muscles at the root of his arm, and tore them right down to the bone, so he fell heavily to the ground and his eyes were closed in darkness. Thus did these two noble comrades of Sarpedon go down to Erebus slain by the two sons of Nestor; they were the warrior sons of Amisodorus, who had reared the invincible Chimaera, to the bane of many. Ajax son of Oileus sprang on Cleobulus and took him alive as he was entangled in the crush; but he killed him then and there by a sword-blow on the neck. The sword reeked with his blood, while dark death and the strong hand of fate gripped him and closed his eyes.

Peneleos and Lycon now met in close fight, for they had missed each other with their spears. They had both thrown without effect, so now they drew their swords. Lycon struck the plumed crest of Peneleos' helmet but his sword broke at the hilt, while Peneleos smote Lycon on the neck under the ear. The blade sank so deep that the head was held on by nothing but the skin, and there was no more life left in him. Meriones gave chase to Acamas on foot and caught him up just as he was about to mount his chariot; he drove a spear through his right shoulder so that he fell headlong from the car, and his eyes were closed in darkness. Idomeneus speared Erymas in the mouth; the bronze point of the spear went clean through it beneath the brain, crashing in among the white bones and smashing them up. His teeth were all of them knocked out and the blood came gushing in a stream from both his eyes; it also came gurgling up from his mouth and nostrils, and the darkness of death enfolded him round about.

Thus did these chieftains of the Danaans each of them kill his man. As ravening wolves seize on kids or lambs, fastening on them when they are alone on the hillsides and have strayed from the main flock through the carelessness of the shepherd- and when the wolves see this they pounce upon them at once because they cannot defend themselves- even so did the Danaans now fall on the Trojans, who fled with ill-omened cries in their panic and had no more fight left in them.

Meanwhile great Ajax kept on trying to drive a spear into Hector, but Hector was so skilful that he held his broad shoulders well under cover of his ox-hide shield, ever on the look-out for the whizzing of the arrows and the heavy thud of the spears. He well knew that the fortunes of the day had changed, but still stood his ground and tried to protect his comrades.

As when a cloud goes up into heaven from Olympus, rising out of a clear sky when Jove is brewing a gale- even with such panic stricken rout did the Trojans now fly, and there was no order in their going. Hector's fleet horses bore him and his armour out of the fight, and he left the Trojan host penned in by the deep trench against their will. Many a yoke of horses snapped the pole of their chariots in the trench and left their master's car behind them. Patroclus gave chase, calling impetuously on the Danaans and full of fury against the Trojans, who, being now no longer in a body, filled all the ways with their cries of panic and rout; the air was darkened with the clouds of dust they raised, and the horses strained every nerve in their flight from the tents and ships towards the city.

Patroclus kept on heading his horses wherever he saw most men flying in confusion, cheering on his men the while. Chariots were being smashed in all directions, and many a man came tumbling down from his own car to fall beneath the wheels of that of Patroclus, whose immortal steeds, given by the gods to Peleus, sprang over the trench at a bound as they sped onward. He was intent on trying to get near Hector, for he had set his heart on spearing him, but Hector's horses were now hurrying him away. As the whole dark earth bows before some tempest on an autumn day when Jove rains his hardest to punish men for giving crooked judgement in their courts, and arriving justice therefrom without heed to the decrees of heaven- all the rivers run full and the torrents tear many a new channel as they roar headlong from the mountains to the dark sea, and it fares ill with the works of men- even such was the stress and strain of the Trojan horses in their flight.

Patroclus now cut off the battalions that were nearest to him and drove them back to the ships. They were doing their best to reach the city, but he would not Yet them, and bore down on them between the river and the ships and wall. Many a fallen comrade did he then avenge. First he hit Pronous with a spear on the chest where it was exposed near the rim of his shield, and he fell heavily to the ground. Next he sprang on Thestor son of Enops, who was sitting all huddled up in his chariot, for he had lost his head and the reins had been torn out of his hands. Patroclus went up to him and drove a spear into his right jaw; he thus hooked him by the teeth and the spear pulled him over the rim of his car, as one who sits at the end of some jutting rock and draws a strong fish out of the sea with a hook and a line- even so with his spear did he pull Thestor all gaping from his chariot; he then threw him down on his face and he died while falling. On this, as Erylaus was on to attack him, he struck him full on the head with a stone, and his brains were all battered inside his helmet, whereon he fell headlong to the ground and the pangs of death took hold upon him. Then he laid low, one after the other, Erymas, Amphoterus, Epaltes, Tlepolemus, Echius son of Damastor, Pyris, lpheus, Euippus and Polymelus son of Argeas.

Now when Sarpedon saw his comrades, men who wore ungirdled tunics, being overcome by Patroclus son of Menoetius, he rebuked the Lycians saying. "Shame on you, where are you flying to? Show your mettle; I will myself meet this man in fight and learn who it is that is so masterful; he has done us much hurt, and has stretched many a brave man upon the ground."

He sprang from his chariot as he spoke, and Patroclus, when he saw this, leaped on to the ground also. The two then rushed at one another with loud cries like eagle-beaked crook-taloned vultures that scream and tear at one another in some high mountain fastness.

The son of scheming Saturn looked down upon them in pity and said to Juno who was his wife and sister, "Alas, that it should be the lot of Sarpedon whom I love so dearly to perish by the hand of Patroclus. I am in two minds whether to catch him up out of the fight and set him down safe and sound in the fertile land of Lycia, or to let him now fall by the hand of the son of Menoetius."

And Juno answered, "Most dread son of Saturn, what is this that you are saying? Would you snatch a mortal man, whose doom has long been fated, out of the jaws of death? Do as you will, but we shall not all of us be of your mind. I say further, and lay my saying to your heart, that if you send Sarpedon safely to his own home, some other of the gods will be also wanting to escort his son out of battle, for there are many sons of gods fighting round the city of Troy, and you will make every one jealous. If, however, you are fond of him and pity him, let him indeed fall by the hand of Patroclus, but as soon as the life is gone out of him, send Death and sweet Sleep to bear him off the field and take him to the broad lands of Lycia, where his brothers and his kinsmen will bury him with mound and pillar, in due honour to the dead."

The sire of gods and men assented, but he shed a rain of blood upon the earth in honour of his son whom Patroclus was about to kill on the rich plain of Troy far from his home.

When they were now come close to one another Patroclus struck Thrasydemus, the brave squire of Sarpedon, in the lower part of the belly, and killed him. Sarpedon then aimed a spear at Patroclus and missed him, but he struck the horse Pedasus in the right shoulder, and it screamed aloud as it lay, groaning in the dust until the life went out of it. The other two horses began to plunge; the pole of the chariot cracked and they got entangled in the reins through the fall of the horse that was yoked along with them; but Automedon knew what to do; without the loss of a moment he drew the keen blade that hung by his sturdy thigh and cut the third horse adrift; whereon the other two righted themselves, and pulling hard at the reins again went together into battle.

Sarpedon now took a second aim at Patroclus, and again missed him, the point of the spear passed over his left shoulder without hitting him. Patroclus then aimed in his turn, and the spear sped not from his hand in vain, for he hit Sarpedon just where the midriff surrounds the ever-beating heart. He fell like some oak or silver poplar or tall pine to which woodmen have laid their axes upon the mountains to make timber for ship-building- even so did he lie stretched at full length in front of his chariot and horses, moaning and clutching at the blood-stained dust. As when a lion springs with a bound upon a herd of cattle and fastens on a great black bull which dies bellowing in its clutches- even so did the leader of the Lycian warriors struggle in death as he fell by the hand of Patroclus. He called on his trusty comrade and said, "Glaucus, my brother, hero among heroes, put forth all your strength, fight with might and main, now if ever quit yourself like a valiant soldier. First go about among the Lycian captains and bid them fight for Sarpedon; then yourself also do battle to save my armour from being taken. My name will haunt you henceforth and for ever if the Achaeans rob me of my armour now that I have fallen at their ships. Do your very utmost and call all my people together."

Death closed his eyes as he spoke. Patroclus planted his heel on his breast and drew the spear from his body, whereon his senses came out along with it, and he drew out both spear-point and Sarpedon's soul at the same time. Hard by the Myrmidons held his snorting steeds, who were wild with panic at finding themselves deserted by their lords.

Glaucus was overcome with grief when he heard what Sarpedon said, for he could not help him. He had to support his arm with his other hand, being in great pain through the wound which Teucer's arrow had given him when Teucer was defending the wall as he, Glaucus, was assailing it. Therefore he prayed to far-darting Apollo saying, "Hear me O king from your seat, may be in the rich land of Lycia, or may be in Troy, for in all places you can hear the prayer of one who is in distress, as I now am. I have a grievous wound; my hand is aching with pain, there is no staunching the blood, and my whole arm drags by reason of my hurt, so that I cannot grasp my sword nor go among my foes and fight them, thou our prince, Jove's son Sarpedon, is slain. Jove defended not his son, do you, therefore, O king, heal me of my wound, ease my pain and grant me strength both to cheer on the Lycians and to fight along with them round the body of him who has fallen."

Thus did he pray, and Apollo heard his prayer. He eased his pain, staunched the black blood from the wound, and gave him new strength. Glaucus perceived this, and was thankful that the mighty god had answered his prayer; forthwith, therefore, he went among the Lycian captains, and bade them come to fight about the body of Sarpedon. From these he strode on among the Trojans to Polydamas son of Panthous and Agenor; he then went in search of Aeneas and Hector, and when he had found them he said, "Hector, you have utterly forgotten your allies, who languish here for your sake far from friends and home while you do nothing to support them. Sarpedon leader of the Lycian warriors has fallen- he who was at once the right and might of Lycia; Mars has laid him low by the spear of Patroclus. Stand by him, my friends, and suffer not the Myrmidons to strip him of his armour, nor to treat his body with contumely in revenge for all the Danaans whom we have speared at the ships."

As he spoke the Trojans were plunged in extreme and ungovernable grief; for Sarpedon, alien though he was, had been one of the main stays of their city, both as having much people with him, and himself the foremost among them all. Led by Hector, who was infuriated by the fall of Sarpedon, they made instantly for the Danaans with all their might, while the undaunted spirit of Patroclus son of Menoetius cheered on the Achaeans. First he spoke to the two Ajaxes, men who needed no bidding. "Ajaxes," said he, "may it now please you to show youselves the men you have always been, or even better- Sarpedon is fallen- he who was first to overleap the wall of the Achaeans; let us take the body and outrage it; let us strip the armour from his shoulders, and kill his comrades if they try to rescue his body."

He spoke to men who of themselves were full eager; both sides, therefore, the Trojans and Lycians on the one hand, and the Myrmidons and Achaeans on the other, strengthened their battalions, and fought desperately about the body of Sarpedon, shouting fiercely the while. Mighty was the din of their armour as they came together, and Jove shed a thick darkness over the fight, to increase the of the battle over the body of his son.

At first the Trojans made some headway against the Achaeans, for one of the best men among the Myrmidons was killed, Epeigeus, son of noble Agacles who had erewhile been king in the good city of Budeum; but presently, having killed a valiant kinsman of his own, he took refuge with Peleus and Thetis, who sent him to Ilius the land of noble steeds to fight the Trojans under Achilles. Hector now struck him on the head with a stone just as he had caught hold of the body, and his brains inside his helmet were all battered in, so that he fell face foremost upon the body of Sarpedon, and there died. Patroclus was enraged by the death of his comrade, and sped through the front ranks as swiftly as a hawk that swoops down on a flock of daws or starlings. Even so swiftly, O noble knight Patroclus, did you make straight for the Lycians and Trojans to avenge your comrade. Forthwith he struck Sthenelaus the son of Ithaemenes on the neck with a stone, and broke the tendons that join it to the head and spine. On this Hector and the front rank of his men gave ground. As far as a man can throw a javelin when competing for some prize, or even in battle- so far did the Trojans now retreat before the Achaeans. Glaucus, captain of the Lycians, was the first to rally them, by killing Bathycles son of Chalcon who lived in Hellas and was the richest man among the Myrmidons. Glaucus turned round suddenly, just as Bathycles who was pursuing him was about to lay hold of him, and drove his spear right into the middle of his chest, whereon he fell heavily to the ground, and the fall of so good a man filled the Achaeans with dismay, while the Trojans were exultant, and came up in a body round the corpse. Nevertheless the Achaeans, mindful of their prowess, bore straight down upon them.

Meriones then killed a helmed warrior of the Trojans, Laogonus son of Onetor, who was priest of Jove of Mt. Ida, and was honoured by the people as though he were a god. Meriones struck him under the jaw and ear, so that life went out of him and the darkness of death laid hold upon him. Aeneas then aimed a spear at Meriones, hoping to hit him under the shield as he was advancing, but Meriones saw it coming and stooped forward to avoid it, whereon the spear flew past him and the point stuck in the ground, while the butt-end went on quivering till Mars robbed it of its force. The spear, therefore, sped from Aeneas's hand in vain and fell quivering to the ground. Aeneas was angry and said, "Meriones, you are a good dancer, but if I had hit you my spear would soon have made an end of you."

And Meriones answered, "Aeneas, for all your bravery, you will not be able to make an end of every one who comes against you. You are only a mortal like myself, and if I were to hit you in the middle of your shield with my spear, however strong and self-confident you may be, I should soon vanquish you, and you would yield your life to Hades of the noble steeds."

On this the son of Menoetius rebuked him and said, "Meriones, hero though you be, you should not speak thus; taunting speeches, my good friend, will not make the Trojans draw away from the dead body; some of them must go under ground first; blows for battle, and words for council; fight, therefore, and say nothing."

He led the way as he spoke and the hero went forward with him. As the sound of woodcutters in some forest glade upon the mountains- and the thud of their axes is heard afar- even such a din now rose from earth-clash of bronze armour and of good ox-hide shields, as men smote each other with their swords and spears pointed at both ends. A man had need of good eyesight now to know Sarpedon, so covered was he from head to foot with spears and blood and dust. Men swarmed about the body, as flies that buzz round the full milk-pails in spring when they are brimming with milk- even so did they gather round Sarpedon; nor did Jove turn his keen eyes away for one moment from the fight, but kept looking at it all the time, for he was settling how best to kill Patroclus, and considering whether Hector should be allowed to end him now in the fight round the body of Sarpedon, and strip him of his armour, or whether he should let him give yet further trouble to the Trojans. In the end, he deemed it best that the brave squire of Achilles son of Peleus should drive Hector and the Trojans back towards the city and take the lives of many. First, therefore, he made Hector turn fainthearted, whereon he mounted his chariot and fled, bidding the other Trojans fly also, for he saw that the scales of Jove had turned against him. Neither would the brave Lycians stand firm; they were dismayed when they saw their king lying struck to the heart amid a heap of corpses- for when the son of Saturn made the fight wax hot many had fallen above him. The Achaeans, therefore stripped the gleaming armour from his shoulders and the brave son of Menoetius gave it to his men to take to the ships. Then Jove lord of the storm-cloud said to Apollo, "Dear Phoebus, go, I pray you, and take Sarpedon out of range of the weapons; cleanse the black blood from off him, and then bear him a long way off where you may wash him in the river, anoint him with ambrosia, and clothe him in immortal raiment; this done, commit him to the arms of the two fleet messengers, Death, and Sleep, who will carry him straightway to the rich land of Lycia, where his brothers and kinsmen will inter him, and will raise both mound and pillar to his memory, in due honour to the dead."

Thus he spoke. Apollo obeyed his father's saying, and came down from the heights of Ida into the thick of the fight; forthwith he took Sarpedon out of range of the weapons, and then bore him a long way off, where he washed him in the river, anointed him with ambrosia and clothed him in immortal raiment; this done, he committed him to the arms of the two fleet messengers, Death, and Sleep, who presently set him down in the rich land of Lycia.

Meanwhile Patroclus, with many a shout to his horses and to Automedon, pursued the Trojans and Lycians in the pride and foolishness of his heart. Had he but obeyed the bidding of the son of Peleus, he would have, escaped death and have been scatheless; but the counsels of Jove pass man's understanding; he will put even a brave man to flight and snatch victory from his grasp, or again he will set him on to fight, as he now did when he put a high spirit into the heart of Patroclus.

Who then first, and who last, was slain by you, O Patroclus, when the gods had now called you to meet your doom? First Adrestus, Autonous, Echeclus, Perimus the son of Megas, Epistor and Melanippus; after these he killed Elasus, Mulius, and Pylartes. These he slew, but the rest saved themselves by flight.

The sons of the Achaeans would now have taken Troy by the hands of Patroclus, for his spear flew in all directions, had not Phoebus Apollo taken his stand upon the wall to defeat his purpose and to aid the Trojans. Thrice did Patroclus charge at an angle of the high wall, and thrice did Apollo beat him back, striking his shield with his own immortal hands. When Patroclus was coming on like a god for yet a fourth time, Apollo shouted to him with an awful voice and said, "Draw back, noble Patroclus, it is not your lot to sack the city of the Trojan chieftains, nor yet will it be that of Achilles who is a far better man than you are." On hearing this, Patroclus withdrew to some distance and avoided the anger of Apollo.

Meanwhile Hector was waiting with his horses inside the Scaean gates, in doubt whether to drive out again and go on fighting, or to call the army inside the gates. As he was thus doubting Phoebus Apollo drew near him in the likeness of a young and lusty warrior Asius, who was Hector's uncle, being own brother to Hecuba, and son of Dymas who lived in Phrygia by the waters of the river Sangarius; in his likeness Jove's son Apollo now spoke to Hector saying, "Hector, why have you left off fighting? It is ill done of you. If I were as much better a man than you, as I am worse, you should soon rue your slackness. Drive straight towards Patroclus, if so be that Apollo may grant you a triumph over him, and you may rull him."

With this the god went back into the hurly-burly, and Hector bade Cebriones drive again into the fight. Apollo passed in among them, and struck panic into the Argives, while he gave triumph to Hector and the Trojans. Hector let the other Danaans alone and killed no man, but drove straight at Patroclus. Patroclus then sprang from his chariot to the ground, with a spear in his left hand, and in his right a jagged stone as large as his hand could hold. He stood still and threw it, nor did it go far without hitting some one; the cast was not in vain, for the stone struck Cebriones, Hector's charioteer, a bastard son of Priam, as he held the reins in his hands. The stone hit him on the forehead and drove his brows into his head for the bone was smashed, and his eyes fell to the ground at his feet. He dropped dead from his chariot as though he were diving, and there was no more life left in him. Over him did you then vaunt, O knight Patroclus, saying, "Bless my heart, how active he is, and how well he dives. If we had been at sea this fellow would have dived from the ship's side and brought up as many oysters as the whole crew could stomach, even in rough water, for he has dived beautifully off his chariot on to the ground. It seems, then, that there are divers also among the Trojans."

As he spoke he flung himself on Cebriones with the spring, as it were, of a lion that while attacking a stockyard is himself struck in the chest, and his courage is his own bane- even so furiously, O Patroclus, did you then spring upon Cebriones. Hector sprang also from his chariot to the ground. The pair then fought over the body of Cebriones. As two lions fight fiercely on some high mountain over the body of a stag that they have killed, even so did these two mighty warriors, Patroclus son of Menoetius and brave Hector, hack and hew at one another over the corpse of Cebriones. Hector would not let him go when he had once got him by the head, while Patroclus kept fast hold of his feet, and a fierce fight raged between the other Danaans and Trojans. As the east and south wind buffet one another when they beat upon some dense forest on the mountains- there is beech and ash and spreading cornel; the to of the trees roar as they beat on one another, and one can hear the boughs cracking and breaking- even so did the Trojans and Achaeans spring upon one another and lay about each other, and neither side would give way. Many a pointed spear fell to ground and many a winged arrow sped from its bow-string about the body of Cebriones; many a great stone, moreover, beat on many a shield as they fought around his body, but there he lay in the whirling clouds of dust, all huge and hugely, heedless of his driving now.

So long as the sun was still high in mid-heaven the weapons of either side were alike deadly, and the people fell; but when he went down towards the time when men loose their oxen, the Achaeans proved to be beyond all forecast stronger, so that they drew Cebriones out of range of the darts and tumult of the Trojans, and stripped the armour from his shoulders. Then

Patroclus sprang like Mars with fierce intent and a terrific shout upon the Trojans, and thrice did he kill nine men; but as he was coming on like a god for a time, then, O Patroclus, was the hour of your end approaching, for Phoebus fought you in fell earnest. Patroclus did not see him as he moved about in the crush, for he was enshrouded in thick darkness, and the god struck him from behind on his back and his broad shoulders with the flat of his hand, so that his eyes turned dizzy. Phoebus Apollo beat the helmet from off his head, and it rolled rattling off under the horses' feet, where its horse-hair plumes were all begrimed with dust and blood. Never indeed had that helmet fared so before, for it had served to protect the head and comely forehead of the godlike hero Achilles. Now, however, Zeus delivered it over to be worn by Hector. Nevertheless the end of Hector also was near. The bronze-shod spear, so great and so strong, was broken in the hand of Patroclus, while his shield that covered him from head to foot fell to the ground as did also the band that held it, and Apollo undid the fastenings of his corslet.

On this his mind became clouded; his limbs failed him, and he stood as one dazed; whereon Euphorbus son of Panthous a Dardanian, the best spearman of his time, as also the finest horseman and fleetest runner, came behind him and struck him in the back with a spear, midway between the shoulders. This man as soon as ever he had come up with his chariot had dismounted twenty men, so proficient was he in all the arts of war- he it was, O knight Patroclus, that first drove a weapon into you, but he did not quite overpower you. Euphorbus then ran back into the crowd, after drawing his ashen spear out of the wound; he would not stand firm and wait for Patroclus, unarmed though he now was, to attack him; but Patroclus unnerved, alike by the blow the god had given him and by the spear-wound, drew back under cover of his men in fear for his life. Hector on this, seeing him to be wounded and giving ground, forced his way through the ranks, and when close up with him struck him in the lower part of the belly with a spear, driving the bronze point right through it, so that he fell heavily to the ground to the great of the Achaeans. As when a lion has fought some fierce wild-boar and worsted him- the two fight furiously upon the mountains over some little fountain at which they would both drink, and the lion has beaten the boar till he can hardly breathe- even so did Hector son of Priam take the life of the brave son of Menoetius who had killed so many, striking him from close at hand, and vaunting over him the while. "Patroclus," said he, "you deemed that you should sack our city, rob our Trojan women of their freedom, and carry them off in your ships to your own country. Fool; Hector and his fleet horses were ever straining their utmost to defend them. I am foremost of all the Trojan warriors to stave the day of bondage from off them; as for you, vultures shall devour you here. Poor wretch, Achilles with all his bravery availed you nothing; and yet I ween when you left him he charged you straitly saying, 'Come not back to the ships, knight Patroclus, till you have rent the bloodstained shirt of murderous Hector about his body. Thus I ween did he charge you, and your fool's heart answered him 'yea' within you."

Then, as the life ebbed out of you, you answered, O knight Patroclus: "Hector, vaunt as you will, for Jove the son of Saturn and Apollo have vouchsafed you victory; it is they who have vanquished me so easily, and they who have stripped the armour from my shoulders; had twenty such men as you attacked me, all of them would have fallen before my spear. Fate and the son of Leto have overpowered me, and among mortal men Euphorbus; you are yourself third only in the killing of me. I say further, and lay my saying to your heart, you too shall live but for a little season; death and the day of your doom are close upon you, and they will lay you low by the hand of Achilles son of Aeacus."

When he had thus spoken his eyes were closed in death, his soul left his body and flitted down to the house of Hades, mourning its sad fate and bidding farewell to the youth and vigor of its manhood. Dead though he was, Hector still spoke to him saying, "Patroclus, why should you thus foretell my doom? Who knows but Achilles, son of lovely Thetis, may be smitten by my spear and die before me?"

As he spoke he drew the bronze spear from the wound, planting his foot upon the body, which he thrust off and let lie on its back. He then went spear in hand after Automedon, squire of the fleet descendant of Aeacus, for he longed to lay him low, but the immortal steeds which the gods had given as a rich gift to Peleus bore him swiftly from the field.

Book XVII

Brave Menelaus son of Atreus now came to know that Patroclus had fallen, and made his way through the front ranks clad in full armour to bestride him. As a cow stands lowing over her first calf, even so did yellow-haired Menelaus bestride Patroclus. He held his round shield and his spear in front of him, resolute to kill any who should dare face him. But the son of Panthous had also noted the body, and came up to Menelaus saying, "Menelaus, son of Atreus, draw back, leave the body, and let the bloodstained spoils be. I was first of the Trojans and their brave allies to drive my spear into Patroclus, let me, therefore, have my full glory among the Trojans, or I will take aim and kill you."

To this Menelaus answered in great anger "By father Jove, boasting is an ill thing. The pard is not more bold, nor the lion nor savage wild-boar, which is fiercest and most dauntless of all creatures, than are the proud sons of Panthous. Yet Hyperenor did not see out the days of his youth when he made light of me and withstood me, deeming me the meanest soldier among the Danaans. His own feet never bore him back to gladden his wife and parents. Even so shall I make an end of you too, if you withstand me; get you back into the crowd and do not face me, or it shall be worse for you. Even a fool may be wise after the event."

Euphorbus would not listen, and said, "Now indeed, Menelaus, shall you pay for the death of my brother over whom you vaunted, and whose wife you widowed in her bridal chamber, while you brought grief unspeakable on his parents. I shall comfort these poor people if I bring your head and armour and place them in the hands of Panthous and noble Phrontis. The time is come when this matter shall be fought out and settled, for me or against me."

As he spoke he struck Menelaus full on the shield, but the spear did not go through, for the shield turned its point. Menelaus then took aim, praying to father Jove as he did so; Euphorbus was drawing back, and Menelaus struck him about the roots of his throat, leaning his whole weight on the spear, so as to drive it home. The point went clean through his neck, and his armour rang rattling round him as he fell heavily to the ground. His hair which was like that of the Graces, and his locks so deftly bound in bands of silver and gold, were all bedrabbled with blood. As one who has grown a fine young olive tree in a clear space where there is abundance of water- the plant is full of promise, and though the winds beat upon it from every quarter it puts forth its white blossoms till the blasts of some fierce hurricane sweep down upon it and level it with the ground- even so did Menelaus strip the fair youth Euphorbus of his armour after he had slain him. Or as some fierce lion upon the mountains in the pride of his strength fastens on the finest heifer in a herd as it is feeding-first he breaks her neck with his strong jaws, and then gorges on her blood and entrails; dogs and shepherds raise a hue and cry against him, but they stand aloof and will not come close to him, for they are pale with fear- even so no one had the courage to face valiant Menelaus. The son of Atreus would have then carried off the armour of the son of Panthous with ease, had not Phoebus Apollo been angry, and in the guise of Mentes chief of the Cicons incited Hector to attack him. "Hector," said he, "you are now going after the horses of the noble son of Aeacus, but you will not take them; they cannot be kept in hand and driven by mortal man, save only by Achilles, who is son to an immortal mother. Meanwhile Menelaus son of Atreus has bestridden the body of Patroclus and killed the noblest of the Trojans, Euphorbus son of Panthous, so that he can fight no more."

The god then went back into the toil and turmoil, but the soul of Hector was darkened with a cloud of grief; he looked along the ranks and saw Euphorbus lying on the ground with the blood still flowing from his wound, and Menelaus stripping him of his armour. On this he made his way to the front like a flame of fire, clad in his gleaming armour, and crying with a loud voice. When the son of Atreus heard him, he said to himself in his dismay, "Alas! what shall I do? I may not let the Trojans take the armour of Patroclus who has fallen fighting on my behalf, lest some Danaan who sees me should cry shame upon me. Still if for my honour's sake I fight Hector and the Trojans single-handed, they will prove too many for me, for Hector is bringing them up in force. Why, however, should I thus hesitate? When a man fights in despite of heaven with one whom a god befriends, he will soon rue it. Let no Danaan think ill of me if I give place to Hector, for the hand of heaven is with him. Yet, if I could find Ajax, the two of us would fight Hector and heaven too, if we might only save the body of Patroclus for Achilles son of Peleus. This, of many evils would be the least."

While he was thus in two minds, the Trojans came up to him with Hector at their head; he therefore drew back and left the body, turning about like some bearded lion who is being chased by dogs and men from a stockyard with spears and hue and cry, whereon he is daunted and slinks sulkily off- even so did Menelaus son of Atreus turn and leave the body of Patroclus. When among the body of his men, he looked around for mighty Ajax son of Telamon, and presently saw him on the extreme left of the fight, cheering on his men and exhorting them to keep on fighting, for Phoebus Apollo had spread a great panic among them. He ran up to him and said, "Ajax, my good friend, come with me at once to dead Patroclus, if so be that we may take the body to Achilles- as for his armour, Hector already has it."

These words stirred the heart of Ajax, and he made his way among the front ranks, Menelaus going with him. Hector had stripped Patroclus of his armour, and was dragging him away to cut off his head and take the body to fling before the dogs of Troy. But Ajax came up with his shield like wall before him, on which Hector withdrew under shelter of his men, and sprang on to his chariot, giving the armour over to the Trojans to take to the city, as a great trophy for himself; Ajax, therefore, covered the body of Patroclus with his broad shield and bestrode him; as a lion stands over his whelps if hunters have come upon him in a forest when he is with his little ones- in the pride and fierceness of his strength he draws his knit brows down till they cover his eyes- even so did Ajax bestride the body of Patroclus, and by his side stood Menelaus son of Atreus, nursing great sorrow in his heart.

Then Glaucus son of Hippolochus looked fiercely at Hector and rebuked him sternly. "Hector," said he, "you make a brave show, but in fight you are sadly wanting. A runaway like yourself has no claim to so great a reputation. Think how you may now save your town and citadel by the hands of your own people born in Ilius; for you will get no Lycians to fight for you, seeing what thanks they have had for their incessant hardships. Are you likely, sir, to do anything to help a man of less note, after leaving Sarpedon, who was at once your guest and comrade in arms, to be the spoil and prey of the Danaans? So long as he lived he did good service both to your city and yourself; yet you had no stomach to save his body from the dogs. If the Lycians will listen to me, they will go home and leave Troy to its fate. If the Trojans had any of that daring fearless spirit which lays hold of men who are fighting for their country and harassing those who would attack it, we should soon bear off Patroclus into Ilius. Could we get this dead man away and bring him into the city of Priam, the Argives would readily give up the armour of Sarpedon, and we should get his body to boot. For he whose squire has been now killed is the foremost man at the ships of the Achaeans- he and his close-fighting followers. Nevertheless you dared not make a stand against Ajax, nor face him, eye to eye, with battle all round you, for he is a braver man than you are."

Hector scowled at him and answered, "Glaucus, you should know better. I have held you so far as a man of more understanding than any in all Lycia, but now I despise you for saying that I am afraid of Ajax. I fear neither battle nor the din of chariots, but Jove's will is stronger than ours; Jove at one time makes even a strong man draw back and snatches victory from his grasp, while at another he will set him on to fight. Come hither then, my friend, stand by me and see indeed whether I shall play the coward the whole day through as you say, or whether I shall not stay some even of the boldest Danaans from fighting round the body of Patroclus."

As he spoke he called loudly on the Trojans saying, "Trojans, Lycians, and Dardanians, fighters in close combat, be men, my friends, and fight might and main, while I put on the goodly armour of Achilles, which I took when I killed Patroclus."

With this Hector left the fight, and ran full speed after his men who were taking the armour of Achilles to Troy, but had not yet got far. Standing for a while apart from the woeful fight, he changed his armour. His own he sent to the strong city of Ilius and to the Trojans, while he put on the immortal armour of the son of Peleus, which the gods had given to Peleus, who in his age gave it to his son; but the son did not grow old in his father's armour.

When Jove, lord of the storm-cloud, saw Hector standing aloof and arming himself in the armour of the son of Peleus, he wagged his head and muttered to himself saying, "A! poor wretch, you arm in the armour of a hero, before whom many another trembles, and you reck nothing of the doom that is already close upon you. You have killed his comrade so brave and strong, but it was not well that you should strip the armour from his head and shoulders. I do indeed endow you with great might now, but as against this you shall not return from battle to lay the armour of the son of Peleus before Andromache."

The son of Saturn bowed his portentous brows, and Hector fitted the armour to his body, while terrible Mars entered into him, and filled his whole body with might and valour. With a shout he strode in among the allies, and his armour flashed about him so that he seemed to all of them like the great son of Peleus himself. He went about among them and cheered them on- Mesthles, Glaucus, Medon, Thersilochus, Asteropaeus, Deisenor and Hippothous, Phorcys, Chromius and Ennomus the augur. All these did he exhort saying, "Hear me, allies from other cities who are here in your thousands, it was not in order to have a crowd about me that I called you hither each from his several city, but that with heart and soul you might defend the wives and little ones of the Trojans from the fierce Achaeans. For this do I oppress my people with your food and the presents that make you rich. Therefore turn, and charge at the foe, to stand or fall as is the game of war; whoever shall bring Patroclus, dead though he be, into the hands of the Trojans, and shall make Ajax give way before him, I will give him one half of the spoils while I keep the other. He will thus share like honour with myself."

When he had thus spoken they charged full weight upon the Danaans with their spears held out before them, and the hopes of each ran high that he should force Ajax son of Telamon to yield up the body- fools that they were, for he was about to take the lives of many. Then Ajax said to Menelaus, "My good friend Menelaus, you and I shall hardly come out of this fight alive. I am less concerned for the body of Patroclus, who will shortly become meat for the dogs and vultures of Troy, than for the safety of my own head and yours. Hector has wrapped us round in a storm of battle from every quarter, and our destruction seems now certain. Call then upon the princes of the Danaans if there is any who can hear us."

Menelaus did as he said, and shouted to the Danaans for help at the top of his voice. "My friends," he cried, "princes and counsellors of the Argives, all you who with Agamemnon and Menelaus drink at the public cost, and give orders each to his own people as Jove vouchsafes him power and glory, the fight is so thick about me that I cannot distinguish you severally; come on, therefore, every man unbidden, and think it shame that Patroclus should become meat and morsel for Trojan hounds."

Fleet Ajax son of Oileus heard him and was first to force his way through the fight and run to help him. Next came Idomeneus and Meriones his esquire, peer of murderous Mars. As for the others that came into the fight after these, who of his own self could name them?

The Trojans with Hector at their head charged in a body. As a great wave that comes thundering in at the mouth of some heaven-born river, and the rocks that jut into the sea ring with the roar of the breakers that beat and buffet them- even with such a roar did the Trojans come on; but the Achaeans in singleness of heart stood firm about the son of Menoetius, and fenced him with their bronze shields. Jove, moreover, hid the brightness of their helmets in a thick cloud, for he had borne no grudge against the son of Menoetius while he was still alive and squire to the descendant of Aeacus; therefore he was loth to let him fall a prey to the dogs of his foes the Trojans, and urged his comrades on to defend him.

At first the Trojans drove the Achaeans back, and they withdrew from the dead man daunted. The Trojans did not succeed in killing any one, nevertheless they drew the body away. But the Achaeans did not lose it long, for Ajax, foremost of all the Danaans after the son of Peleus alike in stature and prowess, quickly rallied them and made towards the front like a wild boar upon the mountains when he stands at bay in the forest glades and routs the hounds and lusty youths that have attacked him- even so did Ajax son of Telamon passing easily in among the phalanxes of the Trojans, disperse those who had bestridden Patroclus and were most bent on winning glory by dragging him off to their city. At this moment Hippothous brave son of the Pelasgian Lethus, in his zeal for Hector and the Trojans, was dragging the body off by the foot through the press of the fight, having bound a strap round the sinews near the ancle; but a mischief soon befell him from which none of those could save him who would have gladly done so, for the son of Telamon sprang forward and smote him on his bronze-cheeked helmet. The plumed headpiece broke about the point of the weapon, struck at once by the spear and by the strong hand of Ajax, so that the bloody brain came oozing out through the crest-socket. His strength then failed him and he let Patroclus' foot drop from his hand, as he fell full length dead upon the body; thus he died far from the fertile land of Larissa, and never repaid his parents the cost of bringing him up, for his life was cut short early by the spear of mighty Ajax. Hector then took aim at Ajax with a spear, but he saw it coming and just managed to avoid it; the spear passed on and struck Schedius son of noble Iphitus, captain of the Phoceans, who dwelt in famed Panopeus and reigned over much people; it struck him under the middle of the collar-bone the bronze point went right through him, coming out at the bottom of his shoulder-blade, and his armour rang rattling round him as he fell heavily to the ground. Ajax in his turn struck noble Phorcys son of Phaenops in the middle of the belly as he was bestriding Hippothous, and broke the plate of his cuirass; whereon the spear tore out his entrails and he clutched the ground in his palm as he fell to earth. Hector and those who were in the front rank then gave ground, while the Argives raised a loud cry of triumph, and drew off the bodies of Phorcys and Hippothous which they stripped presently of their armour.

The Trojans would now have been worsted by the brave Achaeans and driven back to Ilius through their own cowardice, while the Argives, so great was their courage and endurance, would have achieved a triumph even against the will of Jove, if Apollo had not roused Aeneas, in the likeness of Periphas son of Epytus, an attendant who had grown old in the service of Aeneas' aged father, and was at all times devoted to him. In his likeness, then, Apollo said, "Aeneas, can you not manage, even though heaven be against us, to save high Ilius? I have known men, whose numbers, courage, and self-reliance have saved their people in spite of Jove, whereas in this case he would much rather give victory to us than to the Danaans, if you would only fight instead of being so terribly afraid."

Aeneas knew Apollo when he looked straight at him, and shouted to Hector saying, "Hector and all other Trojans and allies, shame on us if we are beaten by the Achaeans and driven back to Ilius through our own cowardice. A god has just come up to me and told me that Jove the supreme disposer will be with us. Therefore let us make for the Danaans, that it may go hard with them ere they bear away dead Patroclus to the ships."

As he spoke he sprang out far in front of the others, who then rallied and again faced the Achaeans. Aeneas speared Leiocritus son of Arisbas, a valiant follower of Lycomedes, and Lycomedes was moved with pity as he saw him fall; he therefore went close up, and speared Apisaon son of Hippasus shepherd of his people in the liver under the midriff, so that he died; he had come from fertile Paeonia and was the best man of them all after Asteropaeus. Asteropaeus flew forward to avenge him and attack the Danaans, but this might no longer be, inasmuch as those about Patroclus were well covered by their shields, and held their spears in front of them, for Ajax had given them strict orders that no man was either to give ground, or to stand out before the others, but all were to hold well together about the body and fight hand to hand. Thus did huge Ajax bid them, and the earth ran red with blood as the corpses fell thick on one another alike on the side of the Trojans and allies, and on that of the Danaans; for these last, too, fought no bloodless fight though many fewer of them perished, through the care they took to defend and stand by one another.

Thus did they fight as it were a flaming fire; it seemed as though it had gone hard even with the sun and moon, for they were hidden over all that part where the bravest heroes were fighting about the dead son of Menoetius, whereas the other Danaans and Achaeans fought at their ease in full daylight with brilliant sunshine all round them, and there was not a cloud to be seen neither on plain nor mountain. These last moreover would rest for a while and leave off fighting, for they were some distance apart and beyond the range of one another's weapons, whereas those who were in the thick of the fray suffered both from battle and darkness. All the best of them were being worn out by the great weight of their armour, but the two valiant heroes, Thrasymedes and Antilochus, had not yet heard of the death of Patroclus, and believed him to be still alive and leading the van against the Trojans; they were keeping themselves in reserve against the death or rout of their own comrades, for so Nestor had ordered when he sent them from the ships into battle.

Thus through the livelong day did they wage fierce war, and the sweat of their toil rained ever on their legs under them, and on their hands and eyes, as they fought over the squire of the fleet son of Peleus. It was as when a man gives a great ox-hide all drenched in fat to his men, and bids them stretch it; whereon they stand round it in a ring and tug till the moisture leaves it, and the fat soaks in for the many that pull at it, and it is well stretched- even so did the two sides tug the dead body hither and thither within the compass of but a little space- the Trojans steadfastly set on drag ing it into Ilius, while the Achaeans were no less so on taking it to their ships; and fierce was the fight between them. Not Mars himself the lord of hosts, nor yet Minerva, even in their fullest fury could make light of such a battle.

Such fearful turmoil of men and horses did Jove on that day ordain round the body of Patroclus. Meanwhile Achilles did not know that he had fallen, for the fight was under the wall of Troy a long way off the ships. He had no idea, therefore, that Patroclus was dead, and deemed that he would return alive as soon as he had gone close up to the gates. He knew that he was not to sack the city neither with nor without himself, for his mother had often told him this when he had sat alone with her, and she had informed him of the counsels of great Jove. Now, however, she had not told him how great a disaster had befallen him in the death of the one who was far dearest to him of all his comrades.

The others still kept on charging one another round the body with their pointed spears and killing each other. Then would one say, "My friends, we can never again show our faces at the ships- better, and greatly better, that earth should open and swallow us here in this place, than that we should let the Trojans have the triumph of bearing off Patroclus to their city."

The Trojans also on their part spoke to one another saying, "Friends, though we fall to a man beside this body, let none shrink from fighting." With such words did they exhort each other. They fought and fought, and an iron clank rose through the void air to the brazen vault of heaven. The horses of the descendant of Aeacus stood out of the fight and wept when they heard that their driver had been laid low by the hand of murderous Hector. Automedon, valiant son of Diores, lashed them again and again; many a time did he speak kindly to them, and many a time did he upbraid them, but they would neither go back to the ships by the waters of the broad Hellespont, nor yet into battle among the Achaeans; they stood with their chariot stock still, as a pillar set over the tomb of some dead man or woman, and bowed their heads to the ground. Hot tears fell from their eyes as they mourned the loss of their charioteer, and their noble manes drooped all wet from under the yokestraps on either side the yoke.

The son of Saturn saw them and took pity upon their sorrow. He wagged his head, and muttered to himself, saying, "Poor things, why did we give you to King Peleus who is a mortal, while you are yourselves ageless and immortal? Was it that you might share the sorrows that befall mankind? for of all creatures that live and move upon the earth there is none so pitiable as he is- still, Hector son of Priam shall drive neither you nor your chariot. I will not have it. It is enough that he should have the armour over which he vaunts so vainly. Furthermore I will give you strength of heart and limb to bear Automedon safely to the ships from battle, for I shall let the Trojans triumph still further, and go on killing till they reach the ships; whereon night shall fall and darkness overshadow the land."

As he spoke he breathed heart and strength into the horses so that they shook the dust from out of their manes, and bore their chariot swiftly into the fight that raged between Trojans and Achaeans. Behind them fought Automedon full of sorrow for his comrade, as a vulture amid a flock of geese. In and out, and here and there, full speed he dashed amid the throng of the Trojans, but for all the fury of his pursuit he killed no man, for he could not wield his spear and keep his horses in hand when alone in the chariot; at last, however, a comrade, Alcimedon, son of Laerces son of Haemon caught sight of him and came up behind his chariot. "Automedon," said he, "what god has put this folly into your heart and robbed you of your right mind, that you fight the Trojans in the front rank single-handed? He who was your comrade is slain, and Hector plumes himself on being armed in the armour of the descendant of Aeacus."

Automedon son of Diores answered, "Alcimedon, there is no one else who can control and guide the immortal steeds so well as you can, save only Patroclus- while he was alive- peer of gods in counsel. Take then the whip and reins, while I go down from the car and fight.

Alcimedon sprang on to the chariot, and caught up the whip and reins, while Automedon leaped from off the car. When Hector saw him he said to Aeneas who was near him, "Aeneas, counsellor of the mail-clad Trojans, I see the steeds of the fleet son of Aeacus come into battle with weak hands to drive them. I am sure, if you think well, that we might take them; they will not dare face us if we both attack them."

The valiant son of Anchises was of the same mind, and the pair went right on, with their shoulders covered under shields of tough dry ox-hide, overlaid with much bronze. Chromius and Aretus went also with them, and their hearts beat high with hope that they might kill the men and capture the horses- fools that they were, for they were not to return scatheless from their meeting with Automedon, who prayed to father Jove and was forthwith filled with courage and strength abounding. He turned to his trusty comrade Alcimedon and said, "Alcimedon, keep your horses so close up that I may feel their breath upon my back; I doubt that we shall not stay Hector son of Priam till he has killed us and mounted behind the horses; he will then either spread panic among the ranks of the Achaeans, or himself be killed among the foremost."

On this he cried out to the two Ajaxes and Menelaus, "Ajaxes captains of the Argives, and Menelaus, give the dead body over to them that are best able to defend it, and come to the rescue of us living; for Hector and Aeneas who are the two best men among the Trojans, are pressing us hard in the full tide of war. Nevertheless the issue lies on the lap of heaven, I will therefore hurl my spear and leave the rest to Jove."

He poised and hurled as he spoke, whereon the spear struck the round shield of Aretus, and went right through it for the shield stayed it not, so that it was driven through his belt into the lower part of his belly. As when some sturdy youth, axe in hand, deals his blow behind the horns of an ox and severs the tendons at the back of its neck so that it springs forward and then drops, even so did Aretus give one bound and then fall on his back the spear quivering in his body till it made an end of him. Hector then aimed a spear at Automedon but he saw it coming and stooped forward to avoid it, so that it flew past him and the point stuck in the ground, while the butt-end went on quivering till Mars robbed it of its force. They would then have fought hand to hand with swords had not the two Ajaxes forced their way through the crowd when they heard their comrade calling, and parted them for all their fury- for Hector, Aeneas, and Chromius were afraid and drew back, leaving Aretus to lie there struck to the heart. Automedon, peer of fleet Mars, then stripped him of his armour and vaunted over him saying, "I have done little to assuage my sorrow for the son of Menoetius, for the man I have killed is not so good as he was."

As he spoke he took the blood-stained spoils and laid them upon his chariot; then he mounted the car with his hands and feet all steeped in gore as a lion that has been gorging upon a bull.

And now the fierce groanful fight again raged about Patroclus, for Minerva came down from heaven and roused its fury by the command of far-seeing Jove, who had changed his mind and sent her to encourage the Danaans. As when Jove bends his bright bow in heaven in token to mankind either of war or of the chill storms that stay men from their labour and plague the flocks- even so, wrapped in such radiant raiment, did Minerva go in among the host and speak man by man to each. First she took the form and voice of Phoenix and spoke to Menelaus son of Atreus, who was standing near her. "Menelaus," said she, "it will be shame and dishonour to you, if dogs tear the noble comrade of Achilles under the walls of Troy. Therefore be staunch, and urge your men to be so also."

Menelaus answered, "Phoenix, my good old friend, may Minerva vouchsafe me strength and keep the darts from off me, for so shall I stand by Patroclus and defend him; his death has gone to my heart, but Hector is as a raging fire and deals his blows without ceasing, for Jove is now granting him a time of triumph."

Minerva was pleased at his having named herself before any of the other gods. Therefore she put strength into his knees and shoulders, and made him as bold as a fly, which, though driven off will yet come again and bite if it can, so dearly does it love man's blood- even so bold as this did she make him as he stood over Patroclus and threw his spear. Now there was among the Trojans a man named Podes, son of Eetion, who was both rich and valiant. Hector held him in the highest honour for he was his comrade and boon companion; the spear of Menelaus struck this man in the girdle just as he had turned in flight, and went right through him. Whereon he fell heavily forward, and Menelaus son of Atreus drew off his body from the Trojans into the ranks of his own people.

Apollo then went up to Hector and spurred him on to fight, in the likeness of Phaenops son of Asius who lived in Abydos and was the most favoured of all Hector's guests. In his likeness Apollo said, "Hector, who of the Achaeans will fear you henceforward now that you have quailed before Menelaus who has ever been rated poorly as a soldier? Yet he has now got a corpse away from the Trojans single-handed, and has slain your own true comrade, a man brave among the foremost, Podes son of Eetion.

A dark cloud of grief fell upon Hector as he heard, and he made his way to the front clad in full armour. Thereon the son of Saturn seized his bright tasselled aegis, and veiled Ida in cloud: he sent forth his lightnings and his thunders, and as he shook his aegis he gave victory to the Trojans and routed the Achaeans.

The panic was begun by Peneleos the Boeotian, for while keeping his face turned ever towards the foe he had been hit with a spear on the upper part of the shoulder; a spear thrown by Polydamas had grazed the top of the bone, for Polydamas had come up to him and struck him from close at hand. Then Hector in close combat struck Leitus son of noble Alectryon in the hand by the wrist, and disabled him from fighting further. He looked about him in dismay, knowing that never again should he wield spear in battle with the Trojans. While Hector was in pursuit of Leitus, Idomeneus struck him on the breastplate over his chest near the nipple; but the spear broke in the shaft, and the Trojans cheered aloud. Hector then aimed at Idomeneus son of Deucalion as he was standing on his chariot, and very narrowly missed him, but the spear hit Coiranus, a follower and charioteer of Meriones who had come with him from Lyctus. Idomeneus had left the ships on foot and would have afforded a great triumph to the Trojans if Coiranus had not driven quickly up to him, he therefore brought life and rescue to Idomeneus, but himself fell by the hand of murderous Hector. For Hector hit him on the jaw under the ear; the end of the spear drove out his teeth and cut his tongue in two pieces, so that he fell from his chariot and let the reins fall to the ground. Meriones gathered them up from the ground and took them into his own hands, then he said to Idomeneus, "Lay on, till you get back to the ships, for you must see that the day is no longer ours."

On this Idomeneus lashed the horses to the ships, for fear had taken hold upon him.

Ajax and Menelaus noted how Jove had turned the scale in favour of the Trojans, and Ajax was first to speak. "Alas," said he, "even a fool may see that father Jove is helping the Trojans. All their weapons strike home; no matter whether it be a brave man or a coward that hurls them, Jove speeds all alike, whereas ours fall each one of them without effect. What, then, will be best both as regards rescuing the body, and our return to the joy of our friends who will be grieving as they look hitherwards; for they will make sure that nothing can now check the terrible hands of Hector, and that he will fling himself upon our ships. I wish that some one would go and tell the son of Peleus at once, for I do not think he can have yet heard the sad news that the dearest of his friends has fallen. But I can see not a man among the Achaeans to send, for they and their chariots are alike hidden in darkness. O father Jove, lift this cloud from over the sons of the Achaeans; make heaven serene, and let us see; if you will that we perish, let us fall at any rate by daylight."

Father Jove heard him and had compassion upon his tears. Forthwith he chased away the cloud of darkness, so that the sun shone out and all the fighting was revealed. Ajax then said to Menelaus, "Look, Menelaus, and if Antilochus son of Nestor be still living, send him at once to tell Achilles that by far the dearest to him of all his comrades has fallen."

Menelaus heeded his words and went his way as a lion from a stockyard- the lion is tired of attacking the men and hounds, who keep watch the whole night through and will not let him feast on the fat of their herd. In his lust of meat he makes straight at them but in vain, for darts from strong hands assail him, and burning brands which daunt him for all his hunger, so in the morning he slinks sulkily away- even so did Menelaus sorely against his will leave

Patroclus, in great fear lest the Achaeans should be driven back in rout and let him fall into the hands of the foe. He charged Meriones and the two Ajaxes straitly saying, "Ajaxes and Meriones, leaders of the Argives, now indeed remember how good Patroclus was; he was ever courteous while alive, bear it in mind now that he is dead."

With this Menelaus left them, looking round him as keenly as an eagle, whose sight they say is keener than that of any other bird- however high he may be in the heavens, not a hare that runs can escape him by crouching under bush or thicket, for he will swoop down upon it and make an end of it- even so, O Menelaus, did your keen eyes range round the mighty host of your followers to see if you could find the son of Nestor still alive. Presently Menelaus saw him on the extreme left of the battle cheering on his men and exhorting them to fight boldly. Menelaus went up to him and said, "Antilochus, come here and listen to sad news, which I would indeed were untrue. You must see with your own eyes that heaven is heaping calamity upon the Danaans, and giving victory to the Trojans. Patroclus has fallen, who was the bravest of the Achaeans, and sorely will the Danaans miss him. Run instantly to the ships and tell Achilles, that he may come to rescue the body and bear it to the ships. As for the armour, Hector already has it."

Antilochus was struck with horror. For a long time he was speechless; his eyes filled with tears and he could find no utterance, but he did as Menelaus had said, and set off running as soon as he had given his armour to a comrade, Laodocus, who was wheeling his horses round, close beside him.

Thus, then, did he run weeping from the field, to carry the bad news to Achilles son of Peleus. Nor were you, O Menelaus, minded to succour his harassed comrades, when Antilochus had left the Pylians- and greatly did they miss him- but he sent them noble Thrasymedes, and himself went back to Patroclus. He came running up to the two Ajaxes and said, "I have sent Antilochus to the ships to tell Achilles, but rage against Hector as he may, he cannot come, for he cannot fight without armour. What then will be our best plan both as regards rescuing the dead, and our own escape from death amid the battle-cries of the Trojans?"

Ajax answered, "Menelaus, you have said well: do you, then, and Meriones stoop down, raise the body, and bear it out of the fray, while we two behind you keep off Hector and the Trojans, one in heart as in name, and long used to fighting side by side with one another."

On this Menelaus and Meriones took the dead man in their arms and lifted him high aloft with a great effort. The Trojan host raised a hue and cry behind them when they saw the Achaeans bearing the body away, and flew after them like hounds attacking a wounded boar at the loo of a band of young huntsmen. For a while the hounds fly at him as though they would tear him in pieces, but now and again he turns on them in a fury, scaring and scattering them in all directions- even so did the Trojans for a while charge in a body, striking with sword and with spears pointed ai both the ends, but when the two Ajaxes faced them and stood at bay, they would turn pale and no man dared press on to fight further about the dead.

In this wise did the two heroes strain every nerve to bear the body to the ships out of the fight. The battle raged round them like fierce flames that when once kindled spread like wildfire over a city, and the houses fall in the glare of its burning- even such was the roar and tramp of men and horses that pursued them as they bore Patroclus from the field. Or as mules that put forth all their strength to draw some beam or great piece of ship's timber down a rough mountain-track, and they pant and sweat as they, go even so did Menelaus and pant and sweat as they bore the body of Patroclus. Behind them the two Ajaxes held stoutly out. As some wooded mountain-spur that stretches across a plain will turn water and check the flow even of a great river, nor is there any stream strong enough to break through it- even so did the two Ajaxes face the Trojans and stern the tide of their fighting though they kept pouring on towards them and foremost among them all was Aeneas son of Anchises with valiant Hector. As a flock of daws or starlings fall to screaming and chattering when they see a falcon, foe to i'll small birds, come soaring near them, even so did the Achaean youth raise a babel of cries as they fled before Aeneas and Hector, unmindful of their former prowess. In the rout of the Danaans much goodly armour fell round about the trench, and of fighting there was no end.

Book XXVI

The assembly now broke up and the people went their ways each to his own ship. There they made ready their supper, and then bethought them of the blessed boon of sleep; but Achilles still wept for thinking of his dear comrade, and sleep, before whom all things bow, could take no hold upon him. This way and that did he turn as he yearned after the might and manfulness of Patroclus; he thought of all they had done together, and all they had gone through both on the field of battle and on the waves of the weary sea. As he dwelt on these things he wept bitterly and lay now on his side, now on his back, and now face downwards, till at last he rose and went out as one distraught to wander upon the seashore. Then, when he saw dawn breaking over beach and sea, he yoked his horses to his chariot, and bound the body of Hector behind it that he might drag it about. Thrice did he drag it round the tomb of the son of Menoetius, and then went back into his tent, leaving the body on the ground full length and with its face downwards. But Apollo would not suffer it to be disfigured, for he pitied the man, dead though he now was; therefore he shielded him with his golden aegis continually, that he might take no hurt while Achilles was dragging him.

Thus shamefully did Achilles in his fury dishonour Hector; but the blessed gods looked down in pity from heaven, and urged Mercury, slayer of Argus, to steal the body. All were of this mind save only Juno, Neptune, and Jove's grey-eyed daughter, who persisted in the hate which they had ever borne towards Ilius with Priam and his people; for they forgave not the wrong done them by Alexandrus in disdaining the goddesses who came to him when he was in his sheepyards, and preferring her who had offered him a wanton to his ruin.

When, therefore, the morning of the twelfth day had now come, Phoebus Apollo spoke among the immortals saying, "You gods ought to be ashamed of yourselves; you are cruel and hard-hearted. Did not Hector burn you thigh-bones of heifers and of unblemished goats? And now dare you not rescue even his dead body, for his wife to look upon, with his mother and child, his father Priam, and his people, who would forthwith commit him to the flames, and give him his due funeral rites? So, then, you would all be on the side of mad Achilles, who knows neither right nor ruth? He is like some savage lion that in the pride of his great strength and daring springs upon men's flocks and gorges on them. Even so has Achilles flung aside all pity, and all that conscience which at once so greatly banes yet greatly boons him that will heed it. man may lose one far dearer than Achilles has lost- a son, it may be, or a brother born from his own mother's womb; yet when he has mourned him and wept over him he will let him bide, for it takes much sorrow to kill a man;

whereas Achilles, now that he has slain noble Hector, drags him behind his chariot round the tomb of his comrade. It were better of him, and for him, that he should not do so, for brave though he be we gods may take it ill that he should vent his fury upon dead clay."

Juno spoke up in a rage. "This were well," she cried, "O lord of the silver bow, if you would give like honour to Hector and to Achilles; but Hector was mortal and suckled at a woman's breast, whereas Achilles is the offspring of a goddess whom I myself reared and brought up. I married her to Peleus, who is above measure dear to the immortals; you gods came all of you to her wedding; you feasted along with them yourself and brought your lyre- false, and fond of low company, that you have ever been."

Then said Jove, "Juno, be not so bitter. Their honour shall not be equal, but of all that dwell in Ilius, Hector was dearest to the gods, as also to myself, for his offerings never failed me. Never was my altar stinted of its dues, nor of the drink-offerings and savour of sacrifice which we claim of right. I shall therefore permit the body of mighty Hector to be stolen; and yet this may hardly be without Achilles coming to know it, for his mother keeps night and day beside him. Let some one of you, therefore, send Thetis to me, and I will impart my counsel to her, namely that Achilles is to accept a ransom from Priam, and give up the body."

On this Iris fleet as the wind went forth to carry his message. Down she plunged into the dark sea midway between Samos and rocky Imbrus; the waters hissed as they closed over her, and she sank into the bottom as the lead at the end of an ox-horn, that is sped to carry death to fishes. She found Thetis sitting in a great cave with the other sea-goddesses gathered round her; there she sat in the midst of them weeping for her noble son who was to fall far from his own land, on the rich plains of Troy. Iris went up to her and said, "Rise Thetis; Jove, whose counsels fail not, bids you come to him." And Thetis answered, "Why does the mighty god so bid me? I am in great grief, and shrink from going in and out among the immortals. Still, I will go, and the word that he may speak shall not be spoken in vain."

The goddess took her dark veil, than which there can be no robe more sombre, and went forth with fleet Iris leading the way before her. The waves of the sea opened them a path, and when they reached the shore they flew up into the heavens, where they found the all-seeing son of Saturn with the blessed gods that live for ever assembled near him. Minerva gave up her seat to her, and she sat down by the side of father Jove. Juno then placed a fair golden cup in her hand, and spoke to her in words of comfort, whereon Thetis drank and gave her back the cup; and the sire of gods and men was the first to speak.

"So, goddess," said he, "for all your sorrow, and the grief that I well know reigns ever in your heart, you have come hither to Olympus, and I will tell you why I have sent for you. This nine days past the immortals have been quarrelling about Achilles waster of cities and the body of Hector. The gods would have Mercury slayer of Argus steal the body, but in furtherance of our peace and amity henceforward, I will concede such honour to your son as I will now tell you. Go, then, to the host and lay these commands upon him; say that the gods are angry with him, and that I am myself more angry than them all, in that he keeps Hector at the ships and will not give him up. He may thus fear me and let the body go. At the same time I will send Iris to great Priam to bid him go to the ships of the Achaeans, and ransom his son, taking with him such gifts for Achilles as may give him satisfaction.

Silver-footed Thetis did as the god had told her, and forthwith down she darted from the topmost summits of Olympus. She went to her son's tents where she found him grieving bitterly, while his trusty comrades round him were busy preparing their morning meal, for which they had killed a great woolly sheep. His mother sat down beside him and caressed him with her hand saying, "My son, how long will you keep on thus grieving and making moan? You are gnawing at your own heart, and think neither of food nor of woman's embraces; and yet these too were well, for you have no long time to live, and death with the strong hand of fate are already close beside you. Now, therefore, heed what I say, for I come as a messenger from Jove; he says that the gods are angry with you, and himself more angry than them all, in that you keep Hector at the ships and will not give him up. Therefore let him go, and accept a ransom for his body."

And Achilles answered, "So be it. If Olympian Jove of his own motion thus commands me, let him that brings the ransom bear the body away."

Thus did mother and son talk together at the ships in long discourse with one another. Meanwhile the son of Saturn sent Iris to the strong city of Ilius. "Go," said he, "fleet Iris, from the mansions of Olympus, and tell King Priam in Ilius, that he is to go to the ships of the Achaeans and free the body of his dear son. He is to take such gifts with him as shall give satisfaction to Achilles, and he is to go alone, with no other Trojan, save only some honoured servant who may drive his mules and waggon, and bring back the body of him whom noble Achilles has slain. Let him have no thought nor fear of death in his heart, for we will send the slayer of Argus to escort him, and bring him within the tent of Achilles. Achilles will not kill him nor let another do so, for he will take heed to his ways and sin not, and he will entreat a suppliant with all honourable courtesy."

On this Iris, fleet as the wind, sped forth to deliver her message. She went to Priam's house, and found weeping and lamentation therein. His sons were seated round their father in the outer courtyard, and their raiment was wet with tears: the old man sat in the midst of them with his mantle wrapped close about his body, and his head and neck all covered with the filth which he had clutched as he lay grovelling in the mire. His daughters and his sons' wives went wailing about the house, as they thought of the many and brave men who lay dead, slain by the Argives. The messenger of Jove stood by Priam and spoke softly to him, but fear fell upon him as she did so. "Take heart," she said, "Priam offspring of Dardanus, take heart and fear not. I bring no evil tidings, but am minded well towards you. I come as a messenger from Jove, who though he be not near, takes thought for you and pities you. The lord of Olympus bids you go and ransom noble Hector, and take with you such gifts as shall give satisfaction to Achilles. You are to go alone, with no Trojan, save only some honoured servant who may drive your mules and waggon, and bring back to the city the body of him whom noble Achilles has slain. You are to have no thought, nor fear of death, for Jove will send the slayer of Argus to escort you. When he has brought you within Achilles' tent, Achilles will not kill you nor let another do so, for he will take heed to his ways and sin not, and he will entreat a suppliant with all honourable courtesy."

Iris went her way when she had thus spoken, and Priam told his sons to get a mule-waggon ready, and to make the body of the waggon fast upon the top of its bed. Then he went down into his fragrant store-room, high-vaulted, and made of cedar-wood, where his many treasures were kept, and he called Hecuba his wife. "Wife," said he, "a messenger has come to me from Olympus, and has told me to go to the ships of the Achaeans to ransom my dear son, taking with me such gifts as shall give satisfaction to Achilles. What think you of this matter? for my own part I am greatly moved to pass through the of the Achaeans and go to their ships."

His wife cried aloud as she heard him, and said, "Alas, what has become of that judgement for which you have been ever famous both among strangers and your own people? How can you venture alone to the ships of the Achaeans, and look into the face of him who has slain so many of your brave sons? You must have iron courage, for if the cruel savage sees you and lays hold on you, he will know neither respect nor pity. Let us then weep Hector from afar here in our own house, for when I gave him birth the threads of overruling fate were spun for him that dogs should eat his flesh far from his parents, in the house of that terrible man on whose liver I would fain fasten and devour it. Thus would I avenge my son, who showed no cowardice when Achilles slew him, and thought neither of Right nor of avoiding battle as he stood in defence of Trojan men and Trojan women."

Then Priam said, "I would go, do not therefore stay me nor be as a bird of ill omen in my house, for you will not move me. Had it been some mortal man who had sent me some prophet or priest who divines from sacrifice- I should have deemed him false and have given him no heed; but now I have heard the goddess and seen her face to face, therefore I will go and her saying shall not be in vain. If it be my fate to die at the ships of the Achaeans even so would I have it; let Achilles slay me, if I may but first have taken my son in my arms and mourned him to my heart's comforting."

So saying he lifted the lids of his chests, and took out twelve goodly vestments. He took also twelve cloaks of single fold, twelve rugs, twelve fair mantles, and an equal number of shirts. He weighed out ten talents of gold, and brought moreover two burnished tripods, four cauldrons, and a very beautiful cup which the Thracians had given him when he had gone to them on an embassy; it was very precious, but he grudged not even this, so eager was he to ransom the body of his son. Then he chased all the Trojans from the court and rebuked them with words of anger. "Out," he cried, "shame and disgrace to me that you are. Have you no grief in your own homes that you are come to plague me here? Is it a small thing, think you, that the son of Saturn has sent this sorrow upon me, to lose the bravest of my sons? Nay, you shall prove it in person, for now he is gone the Achaeans will have easier work in killing you. As for me, let me go down within the house of Hades, ere mine eyes behold the sacking and wasting of the city."

He drove the men away with his staff, and they went forth as the old man sped them. Then he called to his sons, upbraiding Helenus, Paris, noble Agathon, Pammon, Antiphonus, Polites of the loud battle-cry, Deiphobus, Hippothous, and Dius. These nine did the old man call near him. "Come to me at once," he cried, "worthless sons who do me shame; would that you had all been killed at the ships rather than Hector. Miserable man that I am, I have had the bravest sons in all Troy- noble Nestor, Troilus the dauntless charioteer, and Hector who was a god among men, so that one would have thought he was son to an immortal- yet there is not one of them left. Mars has slain them and those of whom I am ashamed are alone left me. Liars, and light of foot, heroes of the dance, robbers of lambs and kids from your own people, why do you not get a waggon ready for me at once, and put all these things upon it that I may set out on my way?"

Thus did he speak, and they feared the rebuke of their father. They brought out a strong mule-waggon, newly made, and set the body of the waggon fast on its bed. They took the mule-yoke from the peg on which it hung, a yoke of boxwood with a knob on the top of it and rings for the reins to go through. Then they brought a yoke-band eleven cubits long, to bind the yoke to the pole; they bound it on at the far end of the pole, and put the ring over the upright pin making it fast with three turns of the band on either side the knob, and bending the thong of the yoke beneath it. This done, they brought from the store-chamber the rich ransom that was to purchase the body of Hector, and they set it all orderly on the waggon; then they yoked the strong harness-mules which the Mysians had on a time given as a goodly present to Priam; but for Priam himself they yoked horses which the old king had bred, and kept for own use.

Thus heedfully did Priam and his servant see to the yolking of their cars at the palace. Then Hecuba came to them all sorrowful, with a golden goblet of wine in her right hand, that they might make a drink-offering before they set out. She stood in front of the horses and said, "Take this, make a drink-offering to father Jove, and since you are minded to go to the ships in spite of me, pray that you may come safely back from the hands of your enemies. Pray to the son of Saturn lord of the whirlwind, who sits on Ida and looks down over all Troy, pray him to send his swift messenger on your right hand, the bird of omen which is strongest and most dear to him of all birds, that you may see it with your own eyes and trust it as you go forth to the ships of the Danaans. If all-seeing Jove will not send you this messenger, however set upon it you may be, I would not have you go to the ships of the Argives."

And Priam answered, "Wife, I will do as you desire me; it is well to lift hands in prayer to Jove, if so be he may have mercy upon me."

With this the old man bade the serving-woman pour pure water over his hands, and the woman came, bearing the water in a bowl. He washed his hands and took the cup from his wife; then he made the drink-offering and prayed, standing in the middle of the courtyard and turning his eyes to heaven. "Father Jove," he said, "that rulest from Ida, most glorious and most great, grant that I may be received kindly and compassionately in the tents of Achilles; and send your swift messenger upon my right hand, the bird of omen which is strongest and most dear to you of all birds, that I may see it with my own eyes and trust it as I go forth to the ships of the Danaans."

So did he pray, and Jove the lord of counsel heard his prayer. Forthwith he sent an eagle, the most unerring portent of all birds that fly, the dusky hunter that men also call the Black Eagle. His wings were spread abroad on either side as wide as the well-made and well-bolted door of a rich man's chamber. He came to them flying over the city upon their right hands, and when they saw him they were glad and their hearts took comfort within them. The old man made haste to mount his chariot, and drove out through the inner gateway and under the echoing gatehouse of the outer court. Before him went the mules drawing the four-wheeled waggon, and driven by wise Idaeus; behind these were the horses, which the old man lashed with his whip and drove swiftly through the city, while his friends followed after, wailing and lamenting for him as though he were on his road to death. As soon as they had come down from the city and had reached the plain, his sons and sons-in-law who had followed him went back to Ilius.

But Priam and Idaeus as they showed out upon the plain did not escape the ken of all-seeing Jove, who looked down upon the old man and pitied him; then he spoke to his son Mercury and said, "Mercury, for it is you who are the most disposed to escort men on their way, and to hear those whom you will hear, go, and so conduct Priam to the ships of the Achaeans that no other of the

Danaans shall see him nor take note of him until he reach the son of Peleus."

Thus he spoke and Mercury, guide and guardian, slayer of Argus, did as he was told. Forthwith he bound on his glittering golden sandals with which he could fly like the wind over land and sea; he took the wand with which he seals men's eyes in sleep, or wakes them just as he pleases, and flew holding it in his hand till he came to Troy and to the Hellespont. To look at, he was like a young man of noble birth in the hey-day of his youth and beauty with the down just coming upon his face.

Now when Priam and Idaeus had driven past the great tomb of Ilius, they stayed their mules and horses that they might drink in the river, for the shades of night were falling, when, therefore, Idaeus saw Mercury standing near them he said to Priam, "Take heed, descendant of Dardanus; here is matter which demands consideration. I see a man who I think will presently fall upon us; let us fly with our horses, or at least embrace his knees and implore him to take compassion upon us?

When he heard this the old man's heart failed him, and he was in great fear; he stayed where he was as one dazed, and the hair stood on end over his whole body; but the bringer of good luck came up to him and took him by the hand, saying, "Whither, father, are you thus driving your mules and horses in the dead of night when other men are asleep? Are you not afraid of the fierce Achaeans who are hard by you, so cruel and relentless? Should some one of them see you bearing so much treasure through the darkness of the flying night, what would not your state then be? You are no longer young, and he who is with you is too old to protect you from those who would attack you. For myself, I will do you no harm, and I will defend you from any one else, for you remind me of my own father."

And Priam answered, "It is indeed as you say, my dear son; nevertheless some god has held his hand over me, in that he has sent such a wayfarer as yourself to meet me so Opportunely; you are so comely in mien and figure, and your judgement is so excellent that you must come of blessed parents."

Then said the slayer of Argus, guide and guardian, "Sir, all that you have said is right; but tell me and tell me true, are you taking this rich treasure to send it to a foreign people where it may be safe, or are you all leaving strong Ilius in dismay now that your son has fallen who was the bravest man among you and was never lacking in battle with the Achaeans?"

And Priam said, "Wo are you, my friend, and who are your parents, that you speak so truly about the fate of my unhappy son?"

The slayer of Argus, guide and guardian, answered him, "Sir, you would prove me, that you question me about noble Hector. Many a time have I set eyes upon him in battle when he was driving the Argives to their ships and putting them to the sword. We stood still and marvelled, for Achilles in his anger with the son of Atreus suffered us not to fight. I am his squire, and came with him in the same ship. I am a Myrmidon, and my father's name is Polyctor: he is a rich man and about as old as you are; he has six sons besides myself, and I am the seventh. We cast lots, and it fell upon me to sail hither with Achilles. I am now come from the ships on to the plain, for with daybreak the Achaeans will set battle in array about the city. They chafe at doing nothing, and are so eager that their princes cannot hold them back."

Then answered Priam, "If you are indeed the squire of Achilles son of Peleus, tell me now the Whole truth. Is my son still at the ships, or has Achilles hewn him limb from limb, and given him to his hounds?"

"Sir," replied the slayer of Argus, guide and guardian, "neither hounds nor vultures have yet devoured him; he is still just lying at the tents by the ship of Achilles, and though it is now twelve days that he has lain there, his flesh is not wasted nor have the worms eaten him although they feed on warriors. At daybreak Achilles drags him cruelly round the sepulchre of his dear comrade, but it does him no hurt. You should come yourself and see how he lies fresh as dew, with the blood all washed away, and his wounds every one of them closed though many pierced him with their spears. Such care have the blessed gods taken of your brave son, for he was dear to them beyond all measure."

The old man was comforted as he heard him and said, "My son, see what a good thing it is to have made due offerings to the immortals; for as sure as that he was born my son never forgot the gods that hold Olympus, and now they requite it to him even in death. Accept therefore at my hands this goodly chalice; guard me and with heaven's help guide me till I come to the tent of the son of Peleus."

Then answered the slayer of Argus, guide and guardian, "Sir, you are tempting me and playing upon my youth, but you shall not move me, for you are offering me presents without the knowledge of Achilles whom I fear and hold it great guiltless to defraud, lest some evil presently befall me; but as your guide I would go with you even to Argos itself, and would guard you so carefully whether by sea or land, that no one should attack you through making light of him who was with you."

The bringer of good luck then sprang on to the chariot, and seizing the whip and reins he breathed fresh spirit into the mules and horses. When they reached the trench and the wall that was before the ships, those who were on guard had just been getting their suppers, and the slayer of Argus threw them all into a deep sleep. Then he drew back the bolts to open the gates, and took Priam inside with the treasure he had upon his waggon. Ere long they came to the lofty dwelling of the son of Peleus for which the Myrmidons had cut pine and which they had built for their king; when they had built it they thatched it with coarse tussock-grass which they had mown out on the plain, and all round it they made a large courtyard, which was fenced with stakes set close together. The gate was barred with a single bolt of pine which it took three men to force into its place, and three to draw back so as to open the gate, but Achilles could draw it by himself. Mercury opened the gate for the old man, and brought in the treasure that he was taking with him for the son of Peleus. Then he sprang from the chariot on to the ground and said, "Sir, it is I, immortal Mercury, that am come with you, for my father sent me to escort you. I will now leave you, and will not enter into the presence of Achilles, for it might anger him that a god should befriend mortal men thus openly. Go you within, and embrace the knees of the son of Peleus: beseech him by his father, his lovely mother, and his son; thus you may move him."

With these words Mercury went back to high Olympus. Priam sprang from his chariot to the ground, leaving Idaeus where he was, in charge of the mules and horses. The old man went straight into the house where Achilles, loved of the gods, was sitting. There he found him with his men seated at a distance from him: only two, the hero Automedon, and Alcimus of the race of Mars, were busy in attendance about his person, for he had but just done eating and drinking, and the table was still there. King Priam entered without their seeing him, and going right up to Achilles he clasped his knees and kissed the dread murderous hands that had slain so many of his sons.

As when some cruel spite has befallen a man that he should have killed some one in his own country, and must fly to a great man's protection in a land of strangers, and all marvel who see him, even so did Achilles marvel as he beheld Priam. The others looked one to another and marvelled also, but Priam besought Achilles saying, "Think of your father, O Achilles like unto the gods, who is such even as I am, on the sad threshold of old age. It may be that those who dwell near him harass him, and there is none to keep war and ruin from him. Yet when he hears of you being still alive, he is glad, and his days are full of hope that he shall see his dear son come home to him from Troy; but I, wretched man that I am, had the bravest in all Troy for my sons, and there is not one of them left. I had fifty sons when the Achaeans came here; nineteen of them were from a single womb, and the others were borne to me by the women of my household. The greater part of them has fierce Mars laid low, and Hector, him who was alone left, him who was the guardian of the city and ourselves, him have you lately slain; therefore I am now come to the ships of the Achaeans to ransom his body from you with a great ransom. Fear, O Achilles, the wrath of heaven; think on your own father and have compassion upon me, who am the more pitiable, for I have steeled myself as no man yet has ever steeled himself before me, and have raised to my lips the hand of him who slew my son."

Thus spoke Priam, and the heart of Achilles yearned as he bethought him of his father. He took the old man's hand and moved him gently away. The two wept bitterly- Priam, as he lay at Achilles' feet, weeping for Hector, and Achilles now for his father and now for Patroclous, till the house was filled with their lamentation. But when Achilles was now sated with grief and had unburthened the bitterness of his sorrow, he left his seat and raised the old man by the hand, in pity for his white hair and beard; then he said, "Unhappy man, you have indeed been greatly daring; how could you venture to come alone to the ships of the Achaeans, and enter the presence of him who has slain so many of your brave sons? You must have iron courage: sit now upon this seat, and for all our grief we will hide our sorrows in our hearts, for weeping will not avail us. The immortals know no care, yet the lot they spin for man is full of sorrow; on the floor of Jove's palace there stand two urns, the one filled with evil gifts, and the other with good ones. He for whom Jove the lord of thunder mixes the gifts he sends, will meet now with good and now with evil fortune; but he to whom Jove sends none but evil gifts will be pointed at by the finger of scorn, the hand of famine will pursue him to the ends of the world, and he will go up and down the face of the earth, respected neither by gods nor men. Even so did it befall Peleus; the gods endowed him with all good things from his birth upwards, for he reigned over the Myrmidons excelling all men in prosperity and wealth, and mortal though he was they gave him a goddess for his bride. But even on him too did heaven send misfortune, for there is no race of royal children born to him in his house, save one son who is doomed to die all untimely; nor may I take care of him now that he is growing old, for I must stay here at Troy to be the bane of you and your children. And you too, O Priam, I have heard that you were aforetime happy. They say that in wealth and plenitude of offspring you surpassed all that is in Lesbos, the realm of Makar to the northward, Phrygia that is more inland, and those that dwell upon the great Hellespont; but from the day when the dwellers in heaven sent this evil upon you, war and slaughter have been about your city continually. Bear up against it, and let there be some intervals in your sorrow. Mourn as you may for your brave son, you will take nothing by it. You cannot raise him from the dead, ere you do so yet another sorrow shall befall you."

And Priam answered, "O king, bid me not be seated, while Hector is still lying uncared for in your tents, but accept the great ransom which I have brought you, and give him to me at once that I may look upon him. May you prosper with the ransom and reach your own land in safety, seeing that you have suffered me to live and to look upon the light of the sun."

Achilles looked at him sternly and said, "Vex me, sir, no longer; I am of myself minded to give up the body of Hector. My mother, daughter of the old man of the sea, came to me from Jove to bid me deliver it to you. Moreover I know well, O Priam, and you cannot hide it, that some god has brought you to the ships of the Achaeans, for else, no man however strong and in his prime would dare to come to our host; he could neither pass our guard unseen, nor draw the bolt of my gates thus easily; therefore, provoke me no further, lest I sin against the word of Jove, and suffer you not, suppliant though you are, within my tents."

The old man feared him and obeyed. Then the son of Peleus sprang like a lion through the door of his house, not alone, but with him went his two squires Automedon and Alcimus who were closer to him than any others of his comrades now that Patroclus was no more. These unyoked the horses and mules, and bade Priam's herald and attendant be seated within the house. They lifted the ransom for Hector's body from the waggon. but they left two mantles and a goodly shirt, that Achilles might wrap the body in them when he gave it to be taken home. Then he called to his servants and ordered them to wash the body and anoint it, but he first took it to a place where Priam should not see it, lest if he did so, he should break out in the bitterness of his grief, and enrage Achilles, who might then kill him and sin against the word of Jove. When the servants had washed the body and anointed it, and had wrapped it in a fair shirt and mantle, Achilles himself lifted it on to a bier, and he and his men then laid it on the waggon. He cried aloud as he did so and called on the name of his dear comrade, "Be not angry with me, Patroclus," he said, "if you hear even in the house of Hades that I have given Hector to his father for a ransom. It has been no unworthy one, and I will share it equitably with you."

Achilles then went back into the tent and took his place on the richly inlaid seat from which he had risen, by the wall that was at right angles to the one against which Priam was sitting. "Sir," he said, "your son is now laid upon his bier and is ransomed according to desire; you shall look upon him when you him away at daybreak; for the present let us prepare our supper. Even lovely Niobe had to think about eating, though her twelve children- six daughters and six lusty sons- had been all slain in her house. Apollo killed the sons with arrows from his silver bow, to punish Niobe, and Diana slew the daughters, because Niobe had vaunted herself against Leto; she said Leto had borne two children only, whereas she had herself borne many- whereon the two killed the many. Nine days did they lie weltering, and there was none to bury them, for the son of Saturn turned the people into stone; but on the tenth day the gods in heaven themselves buried them, and Niobe then took food, being worn out with weeping. They say that somewhere among the rocks on the mountain pastures of Sipylus, where the nymphs live that haunt the river Achelous, there, they say, she lives in stone and still nurses the sorrows sent upon her by the hand of heaven. Therefore, noble sir, let us two now take food; you can weep for your dear son hereafter as you are bearing him back to Ilius- and many a tear will he cost you."

With this Achilles sprang from his seat and killed a sheep of silvery whiteness, which his followers skinned and made ready all in due order. They cut the meat carefully up into smaller pieces, spitted them, and drew them off again when they were well roasted. Automedon brought bread in fair baskets and served it round the table, while Achilles dealt out the meat, and they laid their hands on the good things that were before them. As soon as they had had enough to eat and drink, Priam, descendant of Dardanus, marvelled at the strength and beauty of Achilles for he was as a god to see, and Achilles marvelled at Priam as he listened to him and looked upon his noble presence. When they had gazed their fill Priam spoke first. "And now, O king," he said, "take me to my couch that we may lie down and enjoy the blessed boon of sleep. Never once have my eyes been closed from the day your hands took the life of my son; I have grovelled without ceasing in the mire of my stable-yard, making moan and brooding over my countless sorrows. Now, moreover, I have eaten bread and drunk wine; hitherto I have tasted nothing."

As he spoke Achilles told his men and the women-servants to set beds in the room that was in the gatehouse, and make them with good red rugs, and spread coverlets on the top of them with woollen cloaks for Priam and Idaeus to wear. So the maids went out carrying a torch and got the two beds ready in all haste. Then Achilles said laughingly to Priam, "Dear sir, you shall lie outside, lest some counsellor of those who in due course keep coming to advise with me should see you here in the darkness of the flying night, and tell it to Agamemnon. This might cause delay in the delivery of the body. And now tell me and tell me true, for how many days would you celebrate the funeral rites of noble Hector? Tell me, that I may hold aloof from war and restrain the host."

And Priam answered, "Since, then, you suffer me to bury my noble son with all due rites, do thus, Achilles, and I shall be grateful. You know how we are pent up within our city; it is far for us to fetch wood from the mountain, and the people live in fear. Nine days, therefore, will we mourn Hector in my house; on the tenth day we will bury him and there shall be a public feast in his honour; on the eleventh we will build a mound over his ashes, and on the twelfth, if there be need, we will fight."

And Achilles answered, "All, King Priam, shall be as you have said. I will stay our fighting for as long a time as you have named."

As he spoke he laid his hand on the old man's right wrist, in token that he should have no fear; thus then did Priam and his attendant sleep there in the forecourt, full of thought, while Achilles lay in an inner room of the house, with fair Briseis by his side.

And now both gods and mortals were fast asleep through the livelong night, but upon Mercury alone, the bringer of good luck, sleep could take no hold for he was thinking all the time how to get King Priam away from the ships without his being seen by the strong force of sentinels. He hovered therefore over Priam's head and said, "Sir, now that Achilles has spared your life, you seem to have no fear about sleeping in the thick of your foes. You have paid a great ransom, and have received the body of your son; were you still alive and a prisoner the sons whom you have left at home would have to give three times as much to free you; and so it would be if Agamemnon and the other Achaeans were to know of your being here."

When he heard this the old man was afraid and roused his servant. Mercury then yoked their horses and mules, and drove them quickly through the host so that no man perceived them. When they came to the ford of eddying Xanthus, begotten of immortal Jove, Mercury went back to high Olympus, and dawn in robe of saffron began to break over all the land. Priam and Idaeus then drove on toward the city lamenting and making moan, and the mules drew the body of Hector. No one neither man nor woman saw them, till Cassandra, fair as golden Venus standing on Pergamus, caught sight of her dear father in his chariot, and his servant that was the city's herald with him. Then she saw him that was lying upon the bier, drawn by the mules, and with a loud cry she went about the city saying, "Come hither Trojans, men and women, and look on Hector; if ever you rejoiced to see him coming from battle when he was alive, look now on him that was the glory of our city and all our people."

At this there was not man nor woman left in the city, so great a sorrow had possessed them. Hard by the gates they met Priam as he was bringing in the body. Hector's wife and his mother were the first to mourn him: they flew towards the waggon and laid their hands upon his head, while the crowd stood weeping round them. They would have stayed before the gates, weeping and lamenting the livelong day to the going down of the sun, had not Priam spoken to them from the chariot and said, "Make way for the mules to pass you. Afterwards when I have taken the body home you shall have your fill of weeping."

On this the people stood asunder, and made a way for the waggon. When they had borne the body within the house they laid it upon a bed and seated minstrels round it to lead the dirge, whereon the women joined in the sad music of their lament. Foremost among them all Andromache led their wailing as she clasped the head of mighty Hector in her embrace. "Husband," she cried, "you have died young, and leave me in your house a widow; he of whom we are the ill-starred parents is still a mere child, and I fear he may not reach manhood. Ere he can do so our city will be razed and overthrown, for you who watched over it are no more- you who were its saviour, the guardian of our wives and children. Our women will be carried away captives to the ships, and I among them; while you, my child, who will be with me will be put to some unseemly tasks, working for a cruel master. Or, may be, some Achaean will hurl you (O miserable death) from our walls, to avenge some brother, son, or father whom Hector slew; many of them have indeed bitten the dust at his hands, for your father's hand in battle was no light one. Therefore do the people mourn him. You have left, O Hector, sorrow unutterable to your parents, and my own grief is greatest of all, for you did not stretch forth your arms and embrace me as you lay dying, nor say to me any words that might have lived with me in my tears night and day for evermore."

Bitterly did she weep the while, and the women joined in her lament. Hecuba in her turn took up the strains of woe. "Hector," she cried, "dearest to me of all my children. So long as you were alive the gods loved you well, and even in death they have not been utterly unmindful of you; for when Achilles took any other of my sons, he would sell him beyond the seas, to Samos Imbrus or rugged Lemnos; and when he had slain you too with his sword, many a time did he drag you round the sepulchre of his comrade- though this could not give him life- yet here you lie all fresh as dew, and comely as one whom Apollo has slain with his painless shafts."

Thus did she too speak through her tears with bitter moan, and then Helen for a third time took up the strain of lamentation. "Hector," said she, "dearest of all my brothers-in-law-for I am wife to Alexandrus who brought me hither to Troy- would that I had died ere he did so- twenty years are come and gone since I left my home and came from over the sea, but I have never heard one word of insult or unkindness from you. When another would chide with me, as it might be one of your brothers or sisters or of your brothers' wives, or my mother-in-law- for Priam was as kind to me as though he were my own father- you would rebuke and check them with words of gentleness and goodwill. Therefore my tears flow both for you and for my unhappy self, for there is no one else in Troy who is kind to me, but all shrink and shudder as they go by me."

She wept as she spoke and the vast crowd that was gathered round her joined in her lament. Then King Priam spoke to them saying, "Bring wood, O Trojans, to the city, and fear no cunning ambush of the Argives, for Achilles when he dismissed me from the ships gave me his word that they should not attack us until the morning of the twelfth day."

Forthwith they yoked their oxen and mules and gathered together before the city. Nine days long did they bring in great heaps wood, and on the morning of the tenth day with many tears they took trave Hector forth, laid his dead body upon the summit of the pile, and set the fire thereto. Then when the child of morning rosy-fingered dawn appeared on the eleventh day, the people again assembled, round the pyre of mighty Hector. When they were got together, they first quenched the fire with wine wherever it was burning, and then his brothers and comrades with many a bitter tear gathered his white bones, wrapped them in soft robes of purple, and laid them in a golden urn, which they placed in a grave and covered over with large stones set close together. Then they built a barrow hurriedly over it keeping guard on every side lest the Achaeans should attack them before they had finished. When they had heaped up the barrow they went back again into the city, and being well assembled they held high feast in the house of Priam their king.

Thus, then, did they celebrate the funeral of Hector tamer of horses.

THE END

Interpreting the Iliad

1. Discuss how the gods interact with man. Who benefits the most from these encounters?
2. Is peace impossible? What would it take for both sides to win?
3. Are there any distinctions drawn between heroic words and deeds?
4. What are the symbolisms and functions is the objects possessed by the gods? (Hephaestus' shield, for example)
5. Is there a place for women in the heroic culture?

The Aeneid

By Virgil

WRITTEN 19 B.C.E | TRANSLATED BY JOHN DRYDEN

Book I

Arms, and the man I sing, who, forc'd by fate,
And haughty Juno's unrelenting hate,
Expell'd and exil'd, left the Trojan shore.
Long labors, both by sea and land, he bore,
And in the doubtful war, before he won
The Latian realm, and built the destin'd town;
His banish'd gods restor'd to rites divine,
And settled sure succession in his line,
From whence the race of Alban fathers come,
And the long glories of majestic Rome.
O Muse! the causes and the crimes relate;
What goddess was provok'd, and whence her hate;
For what offense the Queen of Heav'n began
To persecute so brave, so just a man;
Involv'd his anxious life in endless cares,
Expos'd to wants, and hurried into wars!
Can heav'nly minds such high resentment show,
Or exercise their spite in human woe?
Against the Tiber's mouth, but far away,
An ancient town was seated on the sea;
A Tyrian colony; the people made
Stout for the war, and studious of their trade:
Carthage the name; belov'd by Juno more
Than her own Argos, or the Samian shore.
Here stood her chariot; here, if Heav'n were kind,
The seat of awful empire she design'd.
Yet she had heard an ancient rumor fly,
(Long cited by the people of the sky,)
That times to come should see the Trojan race
Her Carthage ruin, and her tow'rs deface;
Nor thus confin'd, the yoke of sov'reign sway
Should on the necks of all the nations lay.
She ponder'd this, and fear'd it was in fate;
Nor could forget the war she wag'd of late
For conqu'ring Greece against the Trojan state.
Besides, long causes working in her mind,
And secret seeds of envy, lay behind;
Deep graven in her heart the doom remain'd
Of partial Paris, and her form disdain'd;
The grace bestow'd on ravish'd Ganymed,
Electra's glories, and her injur'd bed.
Each was a cause alone; and all combin'd
To kindle vengeance in her haughty mind.
For this, far distant from the Latian coast
She drove the remnants of the Trojan host;
And sev'n long years th' unhappy wand'ring train
Were toss'd by storms, and scatter'd thro' the main.
Such time, such toil, requir'd the Roman name,
Such length of labor for so vast a frame.
Now scarce the Trojan fleet, with sails and oars,
Had left behind the fair Sicilian shores,
Ent'ring with cheerful shouts the wat'ry reign,
And plowing frothy furrows in the main;

When, lab'ring still with endless discontent,
The Queen of Heav'n did thus her fury vent:
"Then am I vanquish'd? must I yield?" said she,
"And must the Trojans reign in Italy?
So Fate will have it, and Jove adds his force;
Nor can my pow'r divert their happy course.
Could angry Pallas, with revengeful spleen,
The Grecian navy burn, and drown the men?
She, for the fault of one offending foe,
The bolts of Jove himself presum'd to throw:
With whirlwinds from beneath she toss'd the ship,
And bare expos'd the bosom of the deep;
Then, as an eagle gripes the trembling game,
The wretch, yet hissing with her father's flame,
She strongly seiz'd, and with a burning wound
Transfix'd, and naked, on a rock she bound.
But I, who walk in awful state above,
The majesty of heav'n, the sister wife of Jove,
For length of years my fruitless force employ
Against the thin remains of ruin'd Troy!
What nations now to Juno's pow'r will pray,
Or off'rings on my slighted altars lay?"
Thus rag'd the goddess; and, with fury fraught.
The restless regions of the storms she sought,
Where, in a spacious cave of living stone,
The tyrant Aeolus, from his airy throne,
With pow'r imperial curbs the struggling winds,
And sounding tempests in dark prisons binds.
This way and that th' impatient captives tend,
And, pressing for release, the mountains rend.
High in his hall th' undaunted monarch stands,
And shakes his scepter, and their rage commands;
Which did he not, their unresisted sway
Would sweep the world before them in their way;
Earth, air, and seas thro' empty space would roll,
And heav'n would fly before the driving soul.
In fear of this, the Father of the Gods
Confin'd their fury to those dark abodes,
And lock'd 'em safe within, oppress'd with mountain loads;
Impos'd a king, with arbitrary sway,
To loose their fetters, or their force allay.
To whom the suppliant queen her pray'rs address'd,
And thus the tenor of her suit express'd:
"O Aeolus! for to thee the King of Heav'n
The pow'r of tempests and of winds has giv'n;
Thy force alone their fury can restrain,
And smooth the waves, or swell the troubled main-
A race of wand'ring slaves, abhorr'd by me,
With prosp'rous passage cut the Tuscan sea;
To fruitful Italy their course they steer,
And for their vanquish'd gods design new temples there.
Raise all thy winds; with night involve the skies;
Sink or disperse my fatal enemies.
Twice sev'n, the charming daughters of the main,
Around my person wait, and bear my train:

Succeed my wish, and second my design;
The fairest, Deiopeia, shall be thine,
And make thee father of a happy line."
To this the god: "'T is yours, O queen, to will
The work which duty binds me to fulfil.
These airy kingdoms, and this wide command,
Are all the presents of your bounteous hand:
Yours is my sov'reign's grace; and, as your guest,
I sit with gods at their celestial feast;
Raise tempests at your pleasure, or subdue;
Dispose of empire, which I hold from you."
He said, and hurl'd against the mountain side
His quiv'ring spear, and all the god applied.
The raging winds rush thro' the hollow wound,
And dance aloft in air, and skim along the ground;
Then, settling on the sea, the surges sweep,
Raise liquid mountains, and disclose the deep.
South, East, and West with mix'd confusion roar,
And roll the foaming billows to the shore.
The cables crack; the sailors' fearful cries
Ascend; and sable night involves the skies;
And heav'n itself is ravish'd from their eyes.
Loud peals of thunder from the poles ensue;
Then flashing fires the transient light renew;
The face of things a frightful image bears,
And present death in various forms appears.
Struck with unusual fright, the Trojan chief,
With lifted hands and eyes, invokes relief;
And, "Thrice and four times happy those," he cried,
"That under Ilian walls before their parents died!
Tydides, bravest of the Grecian train!
Why could not I by that strong arm be slain,
And lie by noble Hector on the plain,
Or great Sarpedon, in those bloody fields
Where Simois rolls the bodies and the shields
Of heroes, whose dismember'd hands yet bear
The dart aloft, and clench the pointed spear!"
Thus while the pious prince his fate bewails,
Fierce Boreas drove against his flying sails,
And rent the sheets; the raging billows rise,
And mount the tossing vessels to the skies:
Nor can the shiv'ring oars sustain the blow;
The galley gives her side, and turns her prow;
While those astern, descending down the steep,
Thro' gaping waves behold the boiling deep.
Three ships were hurried by the southern blast,
And on the secret shelves with fury cast.
Those hidden rocks th' Ausonian sailors knew:
They call'd them Altars, when they rose in view,
And show'd their spacious backs above the flood.
Three more fierce Eurus, in his angry mood,
Dash'd on the shallows of the moving sand,
And in mid ocean left them moor'd aland.
Orontes' bark, that bore the Lycian crew,
(A horrid sight!) ev'n in the hero's view,

From stem to stern by waves was overborne:
The trembling pilot, from his rudder torn,
Was headlong hurl'd; thrice round the ship was toss'd,
Then bulg'd at once, and in the deep was lost;
And here and there above the waves were seen
Arms, pictures, precious goods, and floating men.
The stoutest vessel to the storm gave way,
And suck'd thro' loosen'd planks the rushing sea.
Ilioneus was her chief: Alethes old,
Achates faithful, Abas young and bold,
Endur'd not less; their ships, with gaping seams,
Admit the deluge of the briny streams.
Meantime imperial Neptune heard the sound
Of raging billows breaking on the ground.
Displeas'd, and fearing for his wat'ry reign,
He rear'd his awful head above the main,
Serene in majesty; then roll'd his eyes
Around the space of earth, and seas, and skies.
He saw the Trojan fleet dispers'd, distress'd,
By stormy winds and wintry heav'n oppress'd.
Full well the god his sister's envy knew,
And what her aims and what her arts pursue.
He summon'd Eurus and the western blast,
And first an angry glance on both he cast;
Then thus rebuk'd: "Audacious winds! from whence
This bold attempt, this rebel insolence?
Is it for you to ravage seas and land,
Unauthoriz'd by my supreme command?
To raise such mountains on the troubled main?
Whom I- but first 't is fit the billows to restrain;
And then you shall be taught obedience to my reign.
Hence! to your lord my royal mandate bear-
The realms of ocean and the fields of air
Are mine, not his. By fatal lot to me
The liquid empire fell, and trident of the sea.
His pow'r to hollow caverns is confin'd:
There let him reign, the jailer of the wind,
With hoarse commands his breathing subjects call,
And boast and bluster in his empty hall."
He spoke; and, while he spoke, he smooth'd the sea,
Dispell'd the darkness, and restor'd the day.
Cymothoe, Triton, and the sea-green train
Of beauteous nymphs, the daughters of the main,
Clear from the rocks the vessels with their hands:
The god himself with ready trident stands,
And opes the deep, and spreads the moving sands;
Then heaves them off the shoals. Where'er he guides
His finny coursers and in triumph rides,
The waves unruffle and the sea subsides.
As, when in tumults rise th' ignoble crowd,
Mad are their motions, and their tongues are loud;
And stones and brands in rattling volleys fly,
And all the rustic arms that fury can supply:
If then some grave and pious man appear,
They hush their noise, and lend a list'ning ear;

He soothes with sober words their angry mood,
And quenches their innate desire of blood:
So, when the Father of the Flood appears,
And o'er the seas his sov'reign trident rears,
Their fury falls: he skims the liquid plains,
High on his chariot, and, with loosen'd reins,
Majestic moves along, and awful peace maintains.
The weary Trojans ply their shatter'd oars
To nearest land, and make the Libyan shores.
Within a long recess there lies a bay:
An island shades it from the rolling sea,
And forms a port secure for ships to ride;
Broke by the jutting land, on either side,
In double streams the briny waters glide.
Betwixt two rows of rocks a sylvan scene
Appears above, and groves for ever green:
A grot is form'd beneath, with mossy seats,
To rest the Nereids, and exclude the heats.
Down thro' the crannies of the living walls
The crystal streams descend in murm'ring falls:
No haulsers need to bind the vessels here,
Nor bearded anchors; for no storms they fear.
Sev'n ships within this happy harbor meet,
The thin remainders of the scatter'd fleet.
The Trojans, worn with toils, and spent with woes,
Leap on the welcome land, and seek their wish'd repose.
First, good Achates, with repeated strokes
Of clashing flints, their hidden fire provokes:
Short flame succeeds; a bed of wither'd leaves
The dying sparkles in their fall receives:
Caught into life, in fiery fumes they rise,
And, fed with stronger food, invade the skies.
The Trojans, dropping wet, or stand around
The cheerful blaze, or lie along the ground:
Some dry their corn, infected with the brine,
Then grind with marbles, and prepare to dine.
Aeneas climbs the mountain's airy brow,
And takes a prospect of the seas below,
If Capys thence, or Antheus he could spy,
Or see the streamers of Caicus fly.
No vessels were in view; but, on the plain,
Three beamy stags command a lordly train
Of branching heads: the more ignoble throng
Attend their stately steps, and slowly graze along.
He stood; and, while secure they fed below,
He took the quiver and the trusty bow
Achates us'd to bear: the leaders first
He laid along, and then the vulgar pierc'd;
Nor ceas'd his arrows, till the shady plain
Sev'n mighty bodies with their blood distain.
For the sev'n ships he made an equal share,
And to the port return'd, triumphant from the war.
The jars of gen'rous wine (Acestes' gift,
When his Trinacrian shores the navy left)
He set abroach, and for the feast prepar'd,

In equal portions with the ven'son shar'd.
Thus while he dealt it round, the pious chief
With cheerful words allay'd the common grief:
"Endure, and conquer! Jove will soon dispose
To future good our past and present woes.
With me, the rocks of Scylla you have tried;
Th' inhuman Cyclops and his den defied.
What greater ills hereafter can you bear?
Resume your courage and dismiss your care,
An hour will come, with pleasure to relate
Your sorrows past, as benefits of Fate.
Thro' various hazards and events, we move
To Latium and the realms foredoom'd by Jove.
Call'd to the seat (the promise of the skies)
Where Trojan kingdoms once again may rise,
Endure the hardships of your present state;
Live, and reserve yourselves for better fate."
These words he spoke, but spoke not from his heart;
His outward smiles conceal'd his inward smart.
The jolly crew, unmindful of the past,
The quarry share, their plenteous dinner haste.
Some strip the skin; some portion out the spoil;
The limbs, yet trembling, in the caldrons boil;
Some on the fire the reeking entrails broil.
Stretch'd on the grassy turf, at ease they dine,
Restore their strength with meat, and cheer their souls with wine.
Their hunger thus appeas'd, their care attends
The doubtful fortune of their absent friends:
Alternate hopes and fears their minds possess,
Whether to deem 'em dead, or in distress.
Above the rest, Aeneas mourns the fate
Of brave Orontes, and th' uncertain state
Of Gyas, Lycus, and of Amycus.
The day, but not their sorrows, ended thus.
When, from aloft, almighty Jove surveys
Earth, air, and shores, and navigable seas,
At length on Libyan realms he fix'd his eyes-
Whom, pond'ring thus on human miseries,
When Venus saw, she with a lowly look,
Not free from tears, her heav'nly sire bespoke:
"O King of Gods and Men! whose awful hand
Disperses thunder on the seas and land,
Disposing all with absolute command;
How could my pious son thy pow'r incense?
Or what, alas! is vanish'd Troy's offense?
Our hope of Italy not only lost,
On various seas by various tempests toss'd,
But shut from ev'ry shore, and barr'd from ev'ry coast.
You promis'd once, a progeny divine
Of Romans, rising from the Trojan line,
In after times should hold the world in awe,
And to the land and ocean give the law.
How is your doom revers'd, which eas'd my care
When Troy was ruin'd in that cruel war?
Then fates to fates I could oppose; but now,

When Fortune still pursues her former blow,
What can I hope? What worse can still succeed?
What end of labors has your will decreed?
Antenor, from the midst of Grecian hosts,
Could pass secure, and pierce th' Illyrian coasts,
Where, rolling down the steep, Timavus raves
And thro' nine channels disembogues his waves.
At length he founded Padua's happy seat,
And gave his Trojans a secure retreat;
There fix'd their arms, and there renew'd their name,
And there in quiet rules, and crown'd with fame.
But we, descended from your sacred line,
Entitled to your heav'n and rites divine,
Are banish'd earth; and, for the wrath of one,
Remov'd from Latium and the promis'd throne.
Are these our scepters? these our due rewards?
And is it thus that Jove his plighted faith regards?"
To whom the Father of th' immortal race,
Smiling with that serene indulgent face,
With which he drives the clouds and clears the skies,
First gave a holy kiss; then thus replies:
"Daughter, dismiss thy fears; to thy desire
The fates of thine are fix'd, and stand entire.
Thou shalt behold thy wish'd Lavinian walls;
And, ripe for heav'n, when fate Aeneas calls,
Then shalt thou bear him up, sublime, to me:
No councils have revers'd my firm decree.
And, lest new fears disturb thy happy state,
Know, I have search'd the mystic rolls of Fate:
Thy son (nor is th' appointed season far)
In Italy shall wage successful war,
Shall tame fierce nations in the bloody field,
And sov'reign laws impose, and cities build,
Till, after ev'ry foe subdued, the sun
Thrice thro' the signs his annual race shall run:
This is his time prefix'd. Ascanius then,
Now call'd Iulus, shall begin his reign.
He thirty rolling years the crown shall wear,
Then from Lavinium shall the seat transfer,
And, with hard labor, Alba Longa build.
The throne with his succession shall be fill'd
Three hundred circuits more: then shall be seen
Ilia the fair, a priestess and a queen,
Who, full of Mars, in time, with kindly throes,
Shall at a birth two goodly boys disclose.
The royal babes a tawny wolf shall drain:
Then Romulus his grandsire's throne shall gain,
Of martial tow'rs the founder shall become,
The people Romans call, the city Rome.
To them no bounds of empire I assign,
Nor term of years to their immortal line.
Ev'n haughty Juno, who, with endless broils,
Earth, seas, and heav'n, and Jove himself turmoils;
At length aton'd, her friendly pow'r shall join,
To cherish and advance the Trojan line.

The subject world shall Rome's dominion own,
And, prostrate, shall adore the nation of the gown.
An age is ripening in revolving fate
When Troy shall overturn the Grecian state,
And sweet revenge her conqu'ring sons shall call,
To crush the people that conspir'd her fall.
Then Caesar from the Julian stock shall rise,
Whose empire ocean, and whose fame the skies
Alone shall bound; whom, fraught with eastern spoils,
Our heav'n, the just reward of human toils,
Securely shall repay with rites divine;
And incense shall ascend before his sacred shrine.
Then dire debate and impious war shall cease,
And the stern age be soften'd into peace:
Then banish'd Faith shall once again return,
And Vestal fires in hallow'd temples burn;
And Remus with Quirinus shall sustain
The righteous laws, and fraud and force restrain.
Janus himself before his fane shall wait,
And keep the dreadful issues of his gate,
With bolts and iron bars: within remains
Imprison'd Fury, bound in brazen chains;
High on a trophy rais'd, of useless arms,
He sits, and threats the world with vain alarms."
He said, and sent Cyllenius with command
To free the ports, and ope the Punic land
To Trojan guests; lest, ignorant of fate,
The queen might force them from her town and state.
Down from the steep of heav'n Cyllenius flies,
And cleaves with all his wings the yielding skies.
Soon on the Libyan shore descends the god,
Performs his message, and displays his rod:
The surly murmurs of the people cease;
And, as the fates requir'd, they give the peace:
The queen herself suspends the rigid laws,
The Trojans pities, and protects their cause.
Meantime, in shades of night Aeneas lies:
Care seiz'd his soul, and sleep forsook his eyes.
But, when the sun restor'd the cheerful day,
He rose, the coast and country to survey,
Anxious and eager to discover more.
It look'd a wild uncultivated shore;
But, whether humankind, or beasts alone
Possess'd the new-found region, was unknown.
Beneath a ledge of rocks his fleet he hides:
Tall trees surround the mountain's shady sides;
The bending brow above a safe retreat provides.
Arm'd with two pointed darts, he leaves his friends,
And true Achates on his steps attends.
Lo! in the deep recesses of the wood,
Before his eyes his goddess mother stood:
A huntress in her habit and her mien;
Her dress a maid, her air confess'd a queen.
Bare were her knees, and knots her garments bind;
Loose was her hair, and wanton'd in the wind;

Her hand sustain'd a bow; her quiver hung behind.
She seem'd a virgin of the Spartan blood:
With such array Harpalyce bestrode
Her Thracian courser and outstripp'd the rapid flood.
"Ho, strangers! have you lately seen," she said,
"One of my sisters, like myself array'd,
Who cross'd the lawn, or in the forest stray'd?
A painted quiver at her back she bore;
Varied with spots, a lynx's hide she wore;
And at full cry pursued the tusky boar."
Thus Venus: thus her son replied again:
"None of your sisters have we heard or seen,
O virgin! or what other name you bear
Above that style- O more than mortal fair!
Your voice and mien celestial birth betray!
If, as you seem, the sister of the day,
Or one at least of chaste Diana's train,
Let not an humble suppliant sue in vain;
But tell a stranger, long in tempests toss'd,
What earth we tread, and who commands the coast?
Then on your name shall wretched mortals call,
And offer'd victims at your altars fall."
"I dare not," she replied, "assume the name
Of goddess, or celestial honors claim:
For Tyrian virgins bows and quivers bear,
And purple buskins o'er their ankles wear.
Know, gentle youth, in Libyan lands you are-
A people rude in peace, and rough in war.
The rising city, which from far you see,
Is Carthage, and a Tyrian colony.
Phoenician Dido rules the growing state,
Who fled from Tyre, to shun her brother's hate.
Great were her wrongs, her story full of fate;
Which I will sum in short. Sichaeus, known
For wealth, and brother to the Punic throne,
Possess'd fair Dido's bed; and either heart
At once was wounded with an equal dart.
Her father gave her, yet a spotless maid;
Pygmalion then the Tyrian scepter sway'd:
One who condemn'd divine and human laws.
Then strife ensued, and cursed gold the cause.
The monarch, blinded with desire of wealth,
With steel invades his brother's life by stealth;
Before the sacred altar made him bleed,
And long from her conceal'd the cruel deed.
Some tale, some new pretense, he daily coin'd,
To soothe his sister, and delude her mind.
At length, in dead of night, the ghost appears
Of her unhappy lord: the specter stares,
And, with erected eyes, his bloody bosom bares.
The cruel altars and his fate he tells,
And the dire secret of his house reveals,
Then warns the widow, with her household gods,
To seek a refuge in remote abodes.
Last, to support her in so long a way,

He shows her where his hidden treasure lay.
Admonish'd thus, and seiz'd with mortal fright,
The queen provides companions of her flight:
They meet, and all combine to leave the state,
Who hate the tyrant, or who fear his hate.
They seize a fleet, which ready rigg'd they find;
Nor is Pygmalion's treasure left behind.
The vessels, heavy laden, put to sea
With prosp'rous winds; a woman leads the way.
I know not, if by stress of weather driv'n,
Or was their fatal course dispos'd by Heav'n;
At last they landed, where from far your eyes
May view the turrets of new Carthage rise;
There bought a space of ground, which (Byrsa call'd,
From the bull's hide) they first inclos'd, and wall'd.
But whence are you? what country claims your birth?
What seek you, strangers, on our Libyan earth?"
To whom, with sorrow streaming from his eyes,
And deeply sighing, thus her son replies:
"Could you with patience hear, or I relate,
O nymph, the tedious annals of our fate!
Thro' such a train of woes if I should run,
The day would sooner than the tale be done!
From ancient Troy, by force expell'd, we came-
If you by chance have heard the Trojan name.
On various seas by various tempests toss'd,
At length we landed on your Libyan coast.
The good Aeneas am I call'd- a name,
While Fortune favor'd, not unknown to fame.
My household gods, companions of my woes,
With pious care I rescued from our foes.
To fruitful Italy my course was bent;
And from the King of Heav'n is my descent.
With twice ten sail I cross'd the Phrygian sea;
Fate and my mother goddess led my way.
Scarce sev'n, the thin remainders of my fleet,
From storms preserv'd, within your harbor meet.
Myself distress'd, an exile, and unknown,
Debarr'd from Europe, and from Asia thrown,
In Libyan desarts wander thus alone."
His tender parent could no longer bear;
But, interposing, sought to soothe his care.
"Whoe'er you are- not unbelov'd by Heav'n,
Since on our friendly shore your ships are driv'n-
Have courage: to the gods permit the rest,
And to the queen expose your just request.
Now take this earnest of success, for more:
Your scatter'd fleet is join'd upon the shore;
The winds are chang'd, your friends from danger free;
Or I renounce my skill in augury.
Twelve swans behold in beauteous order move,
And stoop with closing pinions from above;
Whom late the bird of Jove had driv'n along,
And thro' the clouds pursued the scatt'ring throng:
Now, all united in a goodly team,

They skim the ground, and seek the quiet stream.
As they, with joy returning, clap their wings,
And ride the circuit of the skies in rings;
Not otherwise your ships, and ev'ry friend,
Already hold the port, or with swift sails descend.
No more advice is needful; but pursue
The path before you, and the town in view."
Thus having said, she turn'd, and made appear
Her neck refulgent, and dishevel'd hair,
Which, flowing from her shoulders, reach'd the ground.
And widely spread ambrosial scents around:
In length of train descends her sweeping gown;
And, by her graceful walk, the Queen of Love is known.
The prince pursued the parting deity
With words like these: "Ah! whither do you fly?
Unkind and cruel! to deceive your son
In borrow'd shapes, and his embrace to shun;
Never to bless my sight, but thus unknown;
And still to speak in accents not your own."
Against the goddess these complaints he made,
But took the path, and her commands obey'd.
They march, obscure; for Venus kindly shrouds
With mists their persons, and involves in clouds,
That, thus unseen, their passage none might stay,
Or force to tell the causes of their way.
This part perform'd, the goddess flies sublime
To visit Paphos and her native clime;
Where garlands, ever green and ever fair,
With vows are offer'd, and with solemn pray'r:
A hundred altars in her temple smoke;
A thousand bleeding hearts her pow'r invoke.
They climb the next ascent, and, looking down,
Now at a nearer distance view the town.
The prince with wonder sees the stately tow'rs,
Which late were huts and shepherds' homely bow'rs,
The gates and streets; and hears, from ev'ry part,
The noise and busy concourse of the mart.
The toiling Tyrians on each other call
To ply their labor: some extend the wall;
Some build the citadel; the brawny throng
Or dig, or push unwieldly stones along.
Some for their dwellings choose a spot of ground,
Which, first design'd, with ditches they surround.
Some laws ordain; and some attend the choice
Of holy senates, and elect by voice.
Here some design a mole, while others there
Lay deep foundations for a theater;
From marble quarries mighty columns hew,
For ornaments of scenes, and future view.
Such is their toil, and such their busy pains,
As exercise the bees in flow'ry plains,
When winter past, and summer scarce begun,
Invites them forth to labor in the sun;
Some lead their youth abroad, while some condense
Their liquid store, and some in cells dispense;

Some at the gate stand ready to receive
The golden burthen, and their friends relieve;
All with united force, combine to drive
The lazy drones from the laborious hive:
With envy stung, they view each other's deeds;
The fragrant work with diligence proceeds.
"Thrice happy you, whose walls already rise!"
Aeneas said, and view'd, with lifted eyes,
Their lofty tow'rs; then, entiring at the gate,
Conceal'd in clouds (prodigious to relate)
He mix'd, unmark'd, among the busy throng,
Borne by the tide, and pass'd unseen along.
Full in the center of the town there stood,
Thick set with trees, a venerable wood.
The Tyrians, landing near this holy ground,
And digging here, a prosp'rous omen found:
From under earth a courser's head they drew,
Their growth and future fortune to foreshew.
This fated sign their foundress Juno gave,
Of a soil fruitful, and a people brave.
Sidonian Dido here with solemn state
Did Juno's temple build, and consecrate,
Enrich'd with gifts, and with a golden shrine;
But more the goddess made the place divine.
On brazen steps the marble threshold rose,
And brazen plates the cedar beams inclose:
The rafters are with brazen cov'rings crown'd;
The lofty doors on brazen hinges sound.
What first Aeneas this place beheld,
Reviv'd his courage, and his fear expell'd.
For while, expecting there the queen, he rais'd
His wond'ring eyes, and round the temple gaz'd,
Admir'd the fortune of the rising town,
The striving artists, and their arts' renown;
He saw, in order painted on the wall,
Whatever did unhappy Troy befall:
The wars that fame around the world had blown,
All to the life, and ev'ry leader known.
There Agamemnon, Priam here, he spies,
And fierce Achilles, who both kings defies.
He stopp'd, and weeping said: "O friend! ev'n here
The monuments of Trojan woes appear!
Our known disasters fill ev'n foreign lands:
See there, where old unhappy Priam stands!
Ev'n the mute walls relate the warrior's fame,
And Trojan griefs the Tyrians' pity claim."
He said (his tears a ready passage find),
Devouring what he saw so well design'd,
And with an empty picture fed his mind:
For there he saw the fainting Grecians yield,
And here the trembling Trojans quit the field,
Pursued by fierce Achilles thro' the plain,
On his high chariot driving o'er the slain.
The tents of Rhesus next his grief renew,
By their white sails betray'd to nightly view;

And wakeful Diomede, whose cruel sword
The sentries slew, nor spar'd their slumb'ring lord,
Then took the fiery steeds, ere yet the food
Of Troy they taste, or drink the Xanthian flood.
Elsewhere he saw where Troilus defied
Achilles, and unequal combat tried;
Then, where the boy disarm'd, with loosen'd reins,
Was by his horses hurried o'er the plains,
Hung by the neck and hair, and dragg'd around:
The hostile spear, yet sticking in his wound,
With tracks of blood inscrib'd the dusty ground.
Meantime the Trojan dames, oppress'd with woe,
To Pallas' fane in long procession go,
In hopes to reconcile their heav'nly foe.
They weep, they beat their breasts, they rend their hair,
And rich embroider'd vests for presents bear;
But the stern goddess stands unmov'd with pray'r.
Thrice round the Trojan walls Achilles drew
The corpse of Hector, whom in fight he slew.
Here Priam sues; and there, for sums of gold,
The lifeless body of his son is sold.
So sad an object, and so well express'd,
Drew sighs and groans from the griev'd hero's breast,
To see the figure of his lifeless friend,
And his old sire his helpless hand extend.
Himself he saw amidst the Grecian train,
Mix'd in the bloody battle on the plain;
And swarthy Memnon in his arms he knew,
His pompous ensigns, and his Indian crew.
Penthisilea there, with haughty grace,
Leads to the wars an Amazonian race:
In their right hands a pointed dart they wield;
The left, for ward, sustains the lunar shield.
Athwart her breast a golden belt she throws,
Amidst the press alone provokes a thousand foes,
And dares her maiden arms to manly force oppose.
Thus while the Trojan prince employs his eyes,
Fix'd on the walls with wonder and surprise,
The beauteous Dido, with a num'rous train
And pomp of guards, ascends the sacred fane.
Such on Eurotas' banks, or Cynthus' height,
Diana seems; and so she charms the sight,
When in the dance the graceful goddess leads
The choir of nymphs, and overtops their heads:
Known by her quiver, and her lofty mien,
She walks majestic, and she looks their queen;
Latona sees her shine above the rest,
And feeds with secret joy her silent breast.
Such Dido was; with such becoming state,
Amidst the crowd, she walks serenely great.
Their labor to her future sway she speeds,
And passing with a gracious glance proceeds;
Then mounts the throne, high plac'd before the shrine:
In crowds around, the swarming people join.
She takes petitions, and dispenses laws,

Hears and determines ev'ry private cause;
Their tasks in equal portions she divides,
And, where unequal, there by lots decides.
Another way by chance Aeneas bends
His eyes, and unexpected sees his friends,
Antheus, Sergestus grave, Cloanthus strong,
And at their backs a mighty Trojan throng,
Whom late the tempest on the billows toss'd,
And widely scatter'd on another coast.
The prince, unseen, surpris'd with wonder stands,
And longs, with joyful haste, to join their hands;
But, doubtful of the wish'd event, he stays,
And from the hollow cloud his friends surveys,
Impatient till they told their present state,
And where they left their ships, and what their fate,
And why they came, and what was their request;
For these were sent, commission'd by the rest,
To sue for leave to land their sickly men,
And gain admission to the gracious queen.
Ent'ring, with cries they fill'd the holy fane;
Then thus, with lowly voice, Ilioneus began:
"O queen! indulg'd by favor of the gods
To found an empire in these new abodes,
To build a town, with statutes to restrain
The wild inhabitants beneath thy reign,
We wretched Trojans, toss'd on ev'ry shore,
From sea to sea, thy clemency implore.
Forbid the fires our shipping to deface!
Receive th' unhappy fugitives to grace,
And spare the remnant of a pious race!
We come not with design of wasteful prey,
To drive the country, force the swains away:
Nor such our strength, nor such is our desire;
The vanquish'd dare not to such thoughts aspire.
A land there is, Hesperia nam'd of old;
The soil is fruitful, and the men are bold-
Th' Oenotrians held it once- by common fame
Now call'd Italia, from the leader's name.
To that sweet region was our voyage bent,
When winds and ev'ry warring element
Disturb'd our course, and, far from sight of land,
Cast our torn vessels on the moving sand:
The sea came on; the South, with mighty roar,
Dispers'd and dash'd the rest upon the rocky shore.
Those few you see escap'd the Storm, and fear,
Unless you interpose, a shipwreck here.
What men, what monsters, what inhuman race,
What laws, what barb'rous customs of the place,
Shut up a desart shore to drowning men,
And drive us to the cruel seas again?
If our hard fortune no compassion draws,
Nor hospitable rights, nor human laws,
The gods are just, and will revenge our cause.
Aeneas was our prince: a juster lord,
Or nobler warrior, never drew a sword;

Observant of the right, religious of his word.
If yet he lives, and draws this vital air,
Nor we, his friends, of safety shall despair;
Nor you, great queen, these offices repent,
Which he will equal, and perhaps augment.
We want not cities, nor Sicilian coasts,
Where King Acestes Trojan lineage boasts.
Permit our ships a shelter on your shores,
Refitted from your woods with planks and oars,
That, if our prince be safe, we may renew
Our destin'd course, and Italy pursue.
But if, O best of men, the Fates ordain
That thou art swallow'd in the Libyan main,
And if our young Iulus be no more,
Dismiss our navy from your friendly shore,
That we to good Acestes may return,
And with our friends our common losses mourn."
Thus spoke Ilioneus: the Trojan crew
With cries and clamors his request renew.
The modest queen a while, with downcast eyes,
Ponder'd the speech; then briefly thus replies:
"Trojans, dismiss your fears; my cruel fate,
And doubts attending an unsettled state,
Force me to guard my coast from foreign foes.
Who has not heard the story of your woes,
The name and fortune of your native place,
The fame and valor of the Phrygian race?
We Tyrians are not so devoid of sense,
Nor so remote from Phoebus' influence.
Whether to Latian shores your course is bent,
Or, driv'n by tempests from your first intent,
You seek the good Acestes' government,
Your men shall be receiv'd, your fleet repair'd,
And sail, with ships of convoy for your guard:
Or, would you stay, and join your friendly pow'rs
To raise and to defend the Tyrian tow'rs,
My wealth, my city, and myself are yours.
And would to Heav'n, the Storm, you felt, would bring
On Carthaginian coasts your wand'ring king.
My people shall, by my command, explore
The ports and creeks of ev'ry winding shore,
And towns, and wilds, and shady woods, in quest
Of so renown'd and so desir'd a guest."
Rais'd in his mind the Trojan hero stood,
And long'd to break from out his ambient cloud:
Achates found it, and thus urg'd his way:
"From whence, O goddess-born, this long delay?
What more can you desire, your welcome sure,
Your fleet in safety, and your friends secure?
One only wants; and him we saw in vain
Oppose the Storm, and swallow'd in the main.
Orontes in his fate our forfeit paid;
The rest agrees with what your mother said."
Scarce had he spoken, when the cloud gave way,
The mists flew upward and dissolv'd in day.

The Trojan chief appear'd in open sight,
August in visage, and serenely bright.
His mother goddess, with her hands divine,
Had form'd his curling locks, and made his temples shine,
And giv'n his rolling eyes a sparkling grace,
And breath'd a youthful vigor on his face;
Like polish'd ivory, beauteous to behold,
Or Parian marble, when enchas'd in gold:
Thus radiant from the circling cloud he broke,
And thus with manly modesty he spoke:
"He whom you seek am I; by tempests toss'd,
And sav'd from shipwreck on your Libyan coast;
Presenting, gracious queen, before your throne,
A prince that owes his life to you alone.
Fair majesty, the refuge and redress
Of those whom fate pursues, and wants oppress,
You, who your pious offices employ
To save the relics of abandon'd Troy;
Receive the shipwreck'd on your friendly shore,
With hospitable rites relieve the poor;
Associate in your town a wand'ring train,
And strangers in your palace entertain:
What thanks can wretched fugitives return,
Who, scatter'd thro' the world, in exile mourn?
The gods, if gods to goodness are inclin'd;
If acts of mercy touch their heav'nly mind,
And, more than all the gods, your gen'rous heart.
Conscious of worth, requite its own desert!
In you this age is happy, and this earth,
And parents more than mortal gave you birth.
While rolling rivers into seas shall run,
And round the space of heav'n the radiant sun;
While trees the mountain tops with shades supply,
Your honor, name, and praise shall never die.
Whate'er abode my fortune has assign'd,
Your image shall be present in my mind."
Thus having said, he turn'd with pious haste,
And joyful his expecting friends embrac'd:
With his right hand Ilioneus was grac'd,
Serestus with his left; then to his breast
Cloanthus and the noble Gyas press'd;
And so by turns descended to the rest.
The Tyrian queen stood fix'd upon his face,
Pleas'd with his motions, ravish'd with his grace;
Admir'd his fortunes, more admir'd the man;
Then recollected stood, and thus began:
"What fate, O goddess-born; what angry pow'rs
Have cast you shipwrack'd on our barren shores?
Are you the great Aeneas, known to fame,
Who from celestial seed your lineage claim?
The same Aeneas whom fair Venus bore
To fam'd Anchises on th' Idaean shore?
It calls into my mind, tho' then a child,
When Teucer came, from Salamis exil'd,
And sought my father's aid, to be restor'd:

My father Belus then with fire and sword
Invaded Cyprus, made the region bare,
And, conqu'ring, finish'd the successful war.
From him the Trojan siege I understood,
The Grecian chiefs, and your illustrious blood.
Your foe himself the Dardan valor prais'd,
And his own ancestry from Trojans rais'd.
Enter, my noble guest, and you shall find,
If not a costly welcome, yet a kind:
For I myself, like you, have been distress'd,
Till Heav'n afforded me this place of rest;
Like you, an alien in a land unknown,
I learn to pity woes so like my own."
She said, and to the palace led her guest;
Then offer'd incense, and proclaim'd a feast.
Nor yet less careful for her absent friends,
Twice ten fat oxen to the ships she sends;
Besides a hundred boars, a hundred lambs,
With bleating cries, attend their milky dams;
And jars of gen'rous wine and spacious bowls
She gives, to cheer the sailors' drooping souls.
Now purple hangings clothe the palace walls,
And sumptuous feasts are made in splendid halls:
On Tyrian carpets, richly wrought, they dine;
With loads of massy plate the sideboards shine,
And antique vases, all of gold emboss'd
(The gold itself inferior to the cost),
Of curious work, where on the sides were seen
The fights and figures of illustrious men,
From their first founder to the present queen.
The good Aeneas, paternal care
Iulus' absence could no longer bear,
Dispatch'd Achates to the ships in haste,
To give a glad relation of the past,
And, fraught with precious gifts, to bring the boy,
Snatch'd from the ruins of unhappy Troy:
A robe of tissue, stiff with golden wire;
An upper vest, once Helen's rich attire,
From Argos by the fam'd adultress brought,
With golden flow'rs and winding foliage wrought,
Her mother Leda's present, when she came
To ruin Troy and set the world on flame;
The scepter Priam's eldest daughter bore,
Her orient necklace, and the crown she wore
Of double texture, glorious to behold,
One order set with gems, and one with gold.
Instructed thus, the wise Achates goes,
And in his diligence his duty shows.
But Venus, anxious for her son's affairs,
New counsels tries, and new designs prepares:
That Cupid should assume the shape and face
Of sweet Ascanius, and the sprightly grace;
Should bring the presents, in her nephew's stead,
And in Eliza's veins the gentle poison shed:
For much she fear'd the Tyrians, double-tongued,

And knew the town to Juno's care belong'd.
These thoughts by night her golden slumbers broke,
And thus alarm'd, to winged Love she spoke:
"My son, my strength, whose mighty pow'r alone
Controls the Thund'rer on his awful throne,
To thee thy much-afflicted mother flies,
And on thy succor and thy faith relies.
Thou know'st, my son, how Jove's revengeful wife,
By force and fraud, attempts thy brother's life;
And often hast thou mourn'd with me his pains.
Him Dido now with blandishment detains;
But I suspect the town where Juno reigns.
For this 't is needful to prevent her art,
And fire with love the proud Phoenician's heart:
A love so violent, so strong, so sure,
As neither age can change, nor art can cure.
How this may be perform'd, now take my mind:
Ascanius by his father is design'd
To come, with presents laden, from the port,
To gratify the queen, and gain the court.
I mean to plunge the boy in pleasing sleep,
And, ravish'd, in Idalian bow'rs to keep,
Or high Cythera, that the sweet deceit
May pass unseen, and none prevent the cheat.
Take thou his form and shape. I beg the grace
But only for a night's revolving space:
Thyself a boy, assume a boy's dissembled face;
That when, amidst the fervor of the feast,
The Tyrian hugs and fonds thee on her breast,
And with sweet kisses in her arms constrains,
Thou may'st infuse thy venom in her veins."
The God of Love obeys, and sets aside
His bow and quiver, and his plumy pride;
He walks Iulus in his mother's sight,
And in the sweet resemblance takes delight.
The goddess then to young Ascanius flies,
And in a pleasing slumber seals his eyes:
Lull'd in her lap, amidst a train of Loves,
She gently bears him to her blissful groves,
Then with a wreath of myrtle crowns his head,
And softly lays him on a flow'ry bed.
Cupid meantime assum'd his form and face,
Foll'wing Achates with a shorter pace,
And brought the gifts. The queen already sate
Amidst the Trojan lords, in shining state,
High on a golden bed: her princely guest
Was next her side; in order sate the rest.
Then canisters with bread are heap'd on high;
Th' attendants water for their hands supply,
And, having wash'd, with silken towels dry.
Next fifty handmaids in long order bore
The censers, and with fumes the gods adore:
Then youths, and virgins twice as many, join
To place the dishes, and to serve the wine.
The Tyrian train, admitted to the feast,

Approach, and on the painted couches rest.
All on the Trojan gifts with wonder gaze,
But view the beauteous boy with more amaze,
His rosy-color'd cheeks, his radiant eyes,
His motions, voice, and shape, and all the god's disguise;
Nor pass unprais'd the vest and veil divine,
Which wand'ring foliage and rich flow'rs entwine.
But, far above the rest, the royal dame,
(Already doom'd to love's disastrous flame,)
With eyes insatiate, and tumultuous joy,
Beholds the presents, and admires the boy.
The guileful god about the hero long,
With children's play, and false embraces, hung;
Then sought the queen: she took him to her arms
With greedy pleasure, and devour'd his charms.
Unhappy Dido little thought what guest,
How dire a god, she drew so near her breast;
But he, not mindless of his mother's pray'r,
Works in the pliant bosom of the fair,
And molds her heart anew, and blots her former care.
The dead is to the living love resign'd;
And all Aeneas enters in her mind.
Now, when the rage of hunger was appeas'd,
The meat remov'd, and ev'ry guest was pleas'd,
The golden bowls with sparkling wine are crown'd,
And thro' the palace cheerful cries resound.
From gilded roofs depending lamps display
Nocturnal beams, that emulate the day.
A golden bowl, that shone with gems divine,
The queen commanded to be crown'd with wine:
The bowl that Belus us'd, and all the Tyrian line.
Then, silence thro' the hall proclaim'd, she spoke:
"O hospitable Jove! we thus invoke,
With solemn rites, thy sacred name and pow'r;
Bless to both nations this auspicious hour!
So may the Trojan and the Tyrian line
In lasting concord from this day combine.
Thou, Bacchus, god of joys and friendly cheer,
And gracious Juno, both be present here!
And you, my lords of Tyre, your vows address
To Heav'n with mine, to ratify the peace."
The goblet then she took, with nectar crown'd
(Sprinkling the first libations on the ground,)
And rais'd it to her mouth with sober grace;
Then, sipping, offer'd to the next in place.
'T was Bitias whom she call'd, a thirsty soul;
He took challenge, and embrac'd the bowl,
With pleasure swill'd the gold, nor ceas'd to draw,
Till he the bottom of the brimmer saw.
The goblet goes around: Iopas brought
His golden lyre, and sung what ancient Atlas taught:
The various labors of the wand'ring moon,
And whence proceed th' eclipses of the sun;
Th' original of men and beasts; and whence
The rains arise, and fires their warmth dispense,

And fix'd and erring stars dispose their influence;
What shakes the solid earth; what cause delays
The summer nights and shortens winter days.
With peals of shouts the Tyrians praise the song:
Those peals are echo'd by the Trojan throng.
Th' unhappy queen with talk prolong'd the night,
And drank large draughts of love with vast delight;
Of Priam much enquir'd, of Hector more;
Then ask'd what arms the swarthy Memnon wore,
What troops he landed on the Trojan shore;
The steeds of Diomede varied the discourse,
And fierce Achilles, with his matchless force;
At length, as fate and her ill stars requir'd,
To hear the series of the war desir'd.
"Relate at large, my godlike guest," she said,
"The Grecian stratagems, the town betray'd:
The fatal issue of so long a war,
Your flight, your wand'rings, and your woes, declare;
For, since on ev'ry sea, on ev'ry coast,
Your men have been distress'd, your navy toss'd,
Sev'n times the sun has either tropic view'd,
The winter banish'd, and the spring renew'd."

Book II

All were attentive to the godlike man,
When from his lofty couch he thus began:
"Great queen, what you command me to relate
Renews the sad remembrance of our fate:
An empire from its old foundations rent,
And ev'ry woe the Trojans underwent;
A peopled city made a desart place;
All that I saw, and part of which I was:
Not ev'n the hardest of our foes could hear,
Nor stern Ulysses tell without a tear.
And now the latter watch of wasting night,
And setting stars, to kindly rest invite;
But, since you take such int'rest in our woe,
And Troy's disastrous end desire to know,
I will restrain my tears, and briefly tell
What in our last and fatal night befell.
"By destiny compell'd, and in despair,
The Greeks grew weary of the tedious war,
And by Minerva's aid a fabric rear'd,
Which like a steed of monstrous height appear'd:
The sides were plank'd with pine; they feign'd it made
For their return, and this the vow they paid.
Thus they pretend, but in the hollow side
Selected numbers of their soldiers hide:
With inward arms the dire machine they load,
And iron bowels stuff the dark abode.
In sight of Troy lies Tenedos, an isle
(While Fortune did on Priam's empire smile)
Renown'd for wealth; but, since, a faithless bay,

Where ships expos'd to wind and weather lay.
There was their fleet conceal'd. We thought, for Greece
Their sails were hoisted, and our fears release.
The Trojans, coop'd within their walls so long,
Unbar their gates, and issue in a throng,
Like swarming bees, and with delight survey
The camp deserted, where the Grecians lay:
The quarters of the sev'ral chiefs they show'd;
Here Phoenix, here Achilles, made abode;
Here join'd the battles; there the navy rode.
Part on the pile their wond'ring eyes employ:
The pile by Pallas rais'd to ruin Troy.
Thymoetes first ('t is doubtful whether hir'd,
Or so the Trojan destiny requir'd)
Mov'd that the ramparts might be broken down,
To lodge the monster fabric in the town.
But Capys, and the rest of sounder mind,
The fatal present to the flames designed,
Or to the wat'ry deep; at least to bore
The hollow sides, and hidden frauds explore.
The giddy vulgar, as their fancies guide,
With noise say nothing, and in parts divide.
Laocoon, follow'd by a num'rous crowd,
Ran from the fort, and cried, from far, aloud:
'O wretched countrymen! what fury reigns?
What more than madness has possess'd your brains?
Think you the Grecians from your coasts are gone?
And are Ulysses' arts no better known?
This hollow fabric either must inclose,
Within its blind recess, our secret foes;
Or 't is an engine rais'd above the town,
T' o'erlook the walls, and then to batter down.
Somewhat is sure design'd, by fraud or force:
Trust not their presents, nor admit the horse.'
Thus having said, against the steed he threw
His forceful spear, which, hissing as flew,
Pierc'd thro' the yielding planks of jointed wood,
And trembling in the hollow belly stood.
The sides, transpierc'd, return a rattling sound,
And groans of Greeks inclos'd come issuing thro' the wound
And, had not Heav'n the fall of Troy design'd,
Or had not men been fated to be blind,
Enough was said and done t'inspire a better mind.
Then had our lances pierc'd the treach'rous wood,
And Ilian tow'rs and Priam's empire stood.
Meantime, with shouts, the Trojan shepherds bring
A captive Greek, in bands, before the king;
Taken to take; who made himself their prey,
T' impose on their belief, and Troy betray;
Fix'd on his aim, and obstinately bent
To die undaunted, or to circumvent.
About the captive, tides of Trojans flow;
All press to see, and some insult the foe.
Now hear how well the Greeks their wiles disguis'd;
Behold a nation in a man compris'd.

Trembling the miscreant stood, unarm'd and bound;
He star'd, and roll'd his haggard eyes around,
Then said: 'Alas! what earth remains, what sea
Is open to receive unhappy me?
What fate a wretched fugitive attends,
Scorn'd by my foes, abandon'd by my friends?'
He said, and sigh'd, and cast a rueful eye:
Our pity kindles, and our passions die.
We cheer youth to make his own defense,
And freely tell us what he was, and whence:
What news he could impart, we long to know,
And what to credit from a captive foe.
"His fear at length dismiss'd, he said: 'Whate'er
My fate ordains, my words shall be sincere:
I neither can nor dare my birth disclaim;
Greece is my country, Sinon is my name.
Tho' plung'd by Fortune's pow'r in misery,
'T is not in Fortune's pow'r to make me lie.
If any chance has hither brought the name
Of Palamedes, not unknown to fame,
Who suffer'd from the malice of the times,
Accus'd and sentenc'd for pretended crimes,
Because these fatal wars he would prevent;
Whose death the wretched Greeks too late lament-
Me, then a boy, my father, poor and bare
Of other means, committed to his care,
His kinsman and companion in the war.
While Fortune favor'd, while his arms support
The cause, and rul'd the counsels, of the court,
I made some figure there; nor was my name
Obscure, nor I without my share of fame.
But when Ulysses, with fallacious arts,
Had made impression in the people's hearts,
And forg'd a treason in my patron's name
(I speak of things too far divulg'd by fame),
My kinsman fell. Then I, without support,
In private mourn'd his loss, and left the court.
Mad as I was, I could not bear his fate
With silent grief, but loudly blam'd the state,
And curs'd the direful author of my woes.
'T was told again; and hence my ruin rose.
I threaten'd, if indulgent Heav'n once more
Would land me safely on my native shore,
His death with double vengeance to restore.
This mov'd the murderer's hate; and soon ensued
Th' effects of malice from a man so proud.
Ambiguous rumors thro' the camp he spread,
And sought, by treason, my devoted head;
New crimes invented; left unturn'd no stone,
To make my guilt appear, and hide his own;
Till Calchas was by force and threat'ning wrought-
But why- why dwell I on that anxious thought?
If on my nation just revenge you seek,
And 't is t' appear a foe, t' appear a Greek;
Already you my name and country know;

Assuage your thirst of blood, and strike the blow:
My death will both the kingly brothers please,
And set insatiate Ithacus at ease.'
This fair unfinish'd tale, these broken starts,
Rais'd expectations in our longing hearts:
Unknowing as we were in Grecian arts.
His former trembling once again renew'd,
With acted fear, the villain thus pursued:
"'Long had the Grecians (tir'd with fruitless care,
And wearied with an unsuccessful war)
Resolv'd to raise the siege, and leave the town;
And, had the gods permitted, they had gone;
But oft the wintry seas and southern winds
Withstood their passage home, and chang'd their minds.
Portents and prodigies their souls amaz'd;
But most, when this stupendous pile was rais'd:
Then flaming meteors, hung in air, were seen,
And thunders rattled thro' a sky serene.
Dismay'd, and fearful of some dire event,
Eurypylus t' enquire their fate was sent.
He from the gods this dreadful answer brought:
"O Grecians, when the Trojan shores you sought,
Your passage with a virgin's blood was bought:
So must your safe return be bought again,
And Grecian blood once more atone the main."
The spreading rumor round the people ran;
All fear'd, and each believ'd himself the man.
Ulysses took th' advantage of their fright;
Call'd Calchas, and produc'd in open sight:
Then bade him name the wretch, ordain'd by fate
The public victim, to redeem the state.
Already some presag'd the dire event,
And saw what sacrifice Ulysses meant.
For twice five days the good old seer withstood
Th' intended treason, and was dumb to blood,
Till, tir'd, with endless clamors and pursuit
Of Ithacus, he stood no longer mute;
But, as it was agreed, pronounc'd that I
Was destin'd by the wrathful gods to die.
All prais'd the sentence, pleas'd the storm should fall
On one alone, whose fury threaten'd all.
The dismal day was come; the priests prepare
Their leaven'd cakes, and fillets for my hair.
I follow'd nature's laws, and must avow
I broke my bonds and fled the fatal blow.
Hid in a weedy lake all night I lay,
Secure of safety when they sail'd away.
But now what further hopes for me remain,
To see my friends, or native soil, again;
My tender infants, or my careful sire,
Whom they returning will to death require;
Will perpetrate on them their first design,
And take the forfeit of their heads for mine?
Which, O! if pity mortal minds can move,
If there be faith below, or gods above,

If innocence and truth can claim desert,
Ye Trojans, from an injur'd wretch avert.'
"False tears true pity move; the king commands
To loose his fetters, and unbind his hands:
Then adds these friendly words: 'Dismiss thy fears;
Forget the Greeks; be mine as thou wert theirs.
But truly tell, was it for force or guile,
Or some religious end, you rais'd the pile?'
Thus said the king. He, full of fraudful arts,
This well-invented tale for truth imparts:
'Ye lamps of heav'n!' he said, and lifted high
His hands now free, 'thou venerable sky!
Inviolable pow'rs, ador'd with dread!
Ye fatal fillets, that once bound this head!
Ye sacred altars, from whose flames I fled!
Be all of you adjur'd; and grant I may,
Without a crime, th' ungrateful Greeks betray,
Reveal the secrets of the guilty state,
And justly punish whom I justly hate!
But you, O king, preserve the faith you gave,
If I, to save myself, your empire save.
The Grecian hopes, and all th' attempts they made,
Were only founded on Minerva's aid.
But from the time when impious Diomede,
And false Ulysses, that inventive head,
Her fatal image from the temple drew,
The sleeping guardians of the castle slew,
Her virgin statue with their bloody hands
Polluted, and profan'd her holy bands;
From thence the tide of fortune left their shore,
And ebb'd much faster than it flow'd before:
Their courage languish'd, as their hopes decay'd;
And Pallas, now averse, refus'd her aid.
Nor did the goddess doubtfully declare
Her alter'd mind and alienated care.
When first her fatal image touch'd the ground,
She sternly cast her glaring eyes around,
That sparkled as they roll'd, and seem'd to threat:
Her heav'nly limbs distill'd a briny sweat.
Thrice from the ground she leap'd, was seen to wield
Her brandish'd lance, and shake her horrid shield.
Then Calchas bade our host for flight
And hope no conquest from the tedious war,
Till first they sail'd for Greece; with pray'rs besought
Her injur'd pow'r, and better omens brought.
And now their navy plows the wat'ry main,
Yet soon expect it on your shores again,
With Pallas pleas'd; as Calchas did ordain.
But first, to reconcile the blue-ey'd maid
For her stol'n statue and her tow'r betray'd,
Warn'd by the seer, to her offended name
We rais'd and dedicate this wondrous frame,
So lofty, lest thro' your forbidden gates
It pass, and intercept our better fates:
For, once admitted there, our hopes are lost;

And Troy may then a new Palladium boast;
For so religion and the gods ordain,
That, if you violate with hands profane
Minerva's gift, your town in flames shall burn,
(Which omen, O ye gods, on Graecia turn!)
But if it climb, with your assisting hands,
The Trojan walls, and in the city stands;
Then Troy shall Argos and Mycenae burn,
And the reverse of fate on us return.'
"With such deceits he gain'd their easy hearts,
Too prone to credit his perfidious arts.
What Diomede, nor Thetis' greater son,
A thousand ships, nor ten years' siege, had done-
False tears and fawning words the city won.
"A greater omen, and of worse portent,
Did our unwary minds with fear torment,
Concurring to produce the dire event.
Laocoon, Neptune's priest by lot that year,
With solemn pomp then sacrific'd a steer;
When, dreadful to behold, from sea we spied
Two serpents, rank'd abreast, the seas divide,
And smoothly sweep along the swelling tide.
Their flaming crests above the waves they show;
Their bellies seem to burn the seas below;
Their speckled tails advance to steer their course,
And on the sounding shore the flying billows force.
And now the strand, and now the plain they held;
Their ardent eyes with bloody streaks were fill'd;
Their nimble tongues they brandish'd as they came,
And lick'd their hissing jaws, that sputter'd flame.
We fled amaz'd; their destin'd way they take,
And to Laocoon and his children make;
And first around the tender boys they wind,
Then with their sharpen'd fangs their limbs and bodies grind.
The wretched father, running to their aid
With pious haste, but vain, they next invade;
Twice round his waist their winding volumes roll'd;
And twice about his gasping throat they fold.
The priest thus doubly chok'd, their crests divide,
And tow'ring o'er his head in triumph ride.
With both his hands he labors at the knots;
His holy fillets the blue venom blots;
His roaring fills the flitting air around.
Thus, when an ox receives a glancing wound,
He breaks his bands, the fatal altar flies,
And with loud bellowings breaks the yielding skies.
Their tasks perform'd, the serpents quit their prey,
And to the tow'r of Pallas make their way:
Couch'd at her feet, they lie protected there
By her large buckler and protended spear.
Amazement seizes all; the gen'ral cry
Proclaims Laocoon justly doom'd to die,
Whose hand the will of Pallas had withstood,
And dared to violate the sacred wood.
All vote t' admit the steed, that vows be paid

And incense offer'd to th' offended maid.
A spacious breach is made; the town lies bare;
Some hoisting-levers, some the wheels prepare
And fasten to the horse's feet; the rest
With cables haul along th' unwieldly beast.
Each on his fellow for assistance calls;
At length the fatal fabric mounts the walls,
Big with destruction. Boys with chaplets crown'd,
And choirs of virgins, sing and dance around.
Thus rais'd aloft, and then descending down,
It enters o'er our heads, and threats the town.
O sacred city, built by hands divine!
O valiant heroes of the Trojan line!
Four times he struck: as oft the clashing sound
Of arms was heard, and inward groans rebound.
Yet, mad with zeal, and blinded with our fate,
We haul along the horse in solemn state;
Then place the dire portent within the tow'r.
Cassandra cried, and curs'd th' unhappy hour;
Foretold our fate; but, by the god's decree,
All heard, and none believ'd the prophecy.
With branches we the fanes adorn, and waste,
In jollity, the day ordain'd to be the last.
Meantime the rapid heav'ns roll'd down the light,
And on the shaded ocean rush'd the night;
Our men, secure, nor guards nor sentries held,
But easy sleep their weary limbs compell'd.
The Grecians had embark'd their naval pow'rs
From Tenedos, and sought our well-known shores,
Safe under covert of the silent night,
And guided by th' imperial galley's light;
When Sinon, favor'd by the partial gods,
Unlock'd the horse, and op'd his dark abodes;
Restor'd to vital air our hidden foes,
Who joyful from their long confinement rose.
Tysander bold, and Sthenelus their guide,
And dire Ulysses down the cable slide:
Then Thoas, Athamas, and Pyrrhus haste;
Nor was the Podalirian hero last,
Nor injur'd Menelaus, nor the fam'd
Epeus, who the fatal engine fram'd.
A nameless crowd succeed; their forces join
T' invade the town, oppress'd with sleep and wine.
Those few they find awake first meet their fate;
Then to their fellows they unbar the gate.
"'T was in the dead of night, when sleep repairs
Our bodies worn with toils, our minds with cares,
When Hector's ghost before my sight appears:
A bloody shroud he seem'd, and bath'd in tears;
Such as he was, when, by Pelides slain,
Thessalian coursers dragg'd him o'er the plain.
Swoln were his feet, as when the thongs were thrust
Thro' the bor'd holes; his body black with dust;
Unlike that Hector who return'd from toils
Of war, triumphant, in Aeacian spoils,

Or him who made the fainting Greeks retire,
And launch'd against their navy Phrygian fire.
His hair and beard stood stiffen'd with his gore;
And all the wounds he for his country bore
Now stream'd afresh, and with new purple ran.
I wept to see the visionary man,
And, while my trance continued, thus began:
'O light of Trojans, and support of Troy,
Thy father's champion, and thy country's joy!
O, long expected by thy friends! from whence
Art thou so late return'd for our defense?
Do we behold thee, wearied as we are
With length of labors, and with toils of war?
After so many fun'rals of thy own
Art thou restor'd to thy declining town?
But say, what wounds are these? What new disgrace
Deforms the manly features of thy face?'
"To this the specter no reply did frame,
But answer'd to the cause for which he came,
And, groaning from the bottom of his breast,
This warning in these mournful words express'd:
'O goddess-born! escape, by timely flight,
The flames and horrors of this fatal night.
The foes already have possess'd the wall;
Troy nods from high, and totters to her fall.
Enough is paid to Priam's royal name,
More than enough to duty and to fame.
If by a mortal hand my father's throne
Could be defended, 't was by mine alone.
Now Troy to thee commends her future state,
And gives her gods companions of thy fate:
From their assistance walls expect,
Which, wand'ring long, at last thou shalt erect.'
He said, and brought me, from their blest abodes,
The venerable statues of the gods,
With ancient Vesta from the sacred choir,
The wreaths and relics of th' immortal fire.
"Now peals of shouts come thund'ring from afar,
Cries, threats, and loud laments, and mingled war:
The noise approaches, tho' our palace stood
Aloof from streets, encompass'd with a wood.
Louder, and yet more loud, I hear th' alarms
Of human cries distinct, and clashing arms.
Fear broke my slumbers; I no longer stay,
But mount the terrace, thence the town survey,
And hearken what the frightful sounds convey.
Thus, when a flood of fire by wind is borne,
Crackling it rolls, and mows the standing corn;
Or deluges, descending on the plains,
Sweep o'er the yellow year, destroy the pains
Of lab'ring oxen and the peasant's gains;
Unroot the forest oaks, and bear away
Flocks, folds, and trees, and undistinguish'd prey:
The shepherd climbs the cliff, and sees from far
The wasteful ravage of the wat'ry war.

Then Hector's faith was manifestly clear'd,
And Grecian frauds in open light appear'd.
The palace of Deiphobus ascends
In smoky flames, and catches on his friends.
Ucalegon burns next: the seas are bright
With splendor not their own, and shine with Trojan light.
New clamors and new clangors now arise,
The sound of trumpets mix'd with fighting cries.
With frenzy seiz'd, I run to meet th' alarms,
Resolv'd on death, resolv'd to die in arms,
But first to gather friends, with them t' oppose
(If fortune favor'd) and repel the foes;
Spurr'd by my courage, by my country fir'd,
With sense of honor and revenge inspir'd.
"Pantheus, Apollo's priest, a sacred name,
Had scap'd the Grecian swords, and pass'd the flame:
With relics loaden. to my doors he fled,
And by the hand his tender grandson led.
'What hope, O Pantheus? whither can we run?
Where make a stand? and what may yet be done?'
Scarce had I said, when Pantheus, with a groan:
'Troy is no more, and Ilium was a town!
The fatal day, th' appointed hour, is come,
When wrathful Jove's irrevocable doom
Transfers the Trojan state to Grecian hands.
The fire consumes the town, the foe commands;
And armed hosts, an unexpected force,
Break from the bowels of the fatal horse.
Within the gates, proud Sinon throws about
The flames; and foes for entrance press without,
With thousand others, whom I fear to name,
More than from Argos or Mycenae came.
To sev'ral posts their parties they divide;
Some block the narrow streets, some scour the wide:
The bold they kill, th' unwary they surprise;
Who fights finds death, and death finds him who flies.
The warders of the gate but scarce maintain
Th' unequal combat, and resist in vain.'
"I heard; and Heav'n, that well-born souls inspires,
Prompts me thro' lifted swords and rising fires
To run where clashing arms and clamor calls,
And rush undaunted to defend the walls.
Ripheus and Iph'itus by my side engage,
For valor one renown'd, and one for age.
Dymas and Hypanis by moonlight knew
My motions and my mien, and to my party drew;
With young Coroebus, who by love was led
To win renown and fair Cassandra's bed,
And lately brought his troops to Priam's aid,
Forewarn'd in vain by the prophetic maid.
Whom when I saw resolv'd in arms to fall,
And that one spirit animated all:
'Brave souls!' said I,- 'but brave, alas! in vain-
Come, finish what our cruel fates ordain.
You see the desp'rate state of our affairs,

And heav'n's protecting pow'rs are deaf to pray'rs.
The passive gods behold the Greeks defile
Their temples, and abandon to the spoil
Their own abodes: we, feeble few, conspire
To save a sinking town, involv'd in fire.
Then let us fall, but fall amidst our foes:
Despair of life the means of living shows.'
So bold a speech incourag'd their desire
Of death, and added fuel to their fire.
"As hungry wolves, with raging appetite,
Scour thro' the fields, nor fear the stormy night-
Their whelps at home expect the promis'd food,
And long to temper their dry chaps in blood-
So rush'd we forth at once; resolv'd to die,
Resolv'd, in death, the last extremes to try.
We leave the narrow lanes behind, and dare
Th' unequal combat in the public square:
Night was our friend; our leader was despair.
What tongue can tell the slaughter of that night?
What eyes can weep the sorrows and affright?
An ancient and imperial city falls:
The streets are fill'd with frequent funerals;
Houses and holy temples float in blood,
And hostile nations make a common flood.
Not only Trojans fall; but, in their turn,
The vanquish'd triumph, and the victors mourn.
Ours take new courage from despair and night:
Confus'd the fortune is, confus'd the fight.
All parts resound with tumults, plaints, and fears;
And grisly Death in sundry shapes appears.
Androgeos fell among us, with his band,
Who thought us Grecians newly come to land.
'From whence,' said he, 'my friends, this long delay?
You loiter, while the spoils are borne away:
Our ships are laden with the Trojan store;
And you, like truants, come too late ashore.'
He said, but soon corrected his mistake,
Found, by the doubtful answers which we make:
Amaz'd, he would have shunn'd th' unequal fight;
But we, more num'rous, intercept his flight.
As when some peasant, in a bushy brake,
Has with unwary footing press'd a snake;
He starts aside, astonish'd, when he spies
His rising crest, blue neck, and rolling eyes;
So from our arms surpris'd Androgeos flies.
In vain; for him and his we compass'd round,
Possess'd with fear, unknowing of the ground,
And of their lives an easy conquest found.
Thus Fortune on our first endeavor smil'd.
Coroebus then, with youthful hopes beguil'd,
Swoln with success, and a daring mind,
This new invention fatally design'd.
'My friends,' said he, 'since Fortune shows the way,
'T is fit we should th' auspicious guide obey.
For what has she these Grecian arms bestow'd,

But their destruction, and the Trojans' good?
Then change we shields, and their devices bear:
Let fraud supply the want of force in war.
They find us arms.' This said, himself he dress'd
In dead Androgeos' spoils, his upper vest,
His painted buckler, and his plumy crest.
Thus Ripheus, Dymas, all the Trojan train,
Lay down their own attire, and strip the slain.
Mix'd with the Greeks, we go with ill presage,
Flatter'd with hopes to glut our greedy rage;
Unknown, assaulting whom we blindly meet,
And strew with Grecian carcasses the street.
Thus while their straggling parties we defeat,
Some to the shore and safer ships retreat;
And some, oppress'd with more ignoble fear,
Remount the hollow horse, and pant in secret there.
"But, ah! what use of valor can be made,
When heav'n's propitious pow'rs refuse their aid!
Behold the royal prophetess, the fair
Cassandra, dragg'd by her dishevel'd hair,
Whom not Minerva's shrine, nor sacred bands,
In safety could protect from sacrilegious hands:
On heav'n she cast her eyes, she sigh'd, she cried-
'T was all she could- her tender arms were tied.
So sad a sight Coroebus could not bear;
But, fir'd with rage, distracted with despair,
Amid the barb'rous ravishers he flew:
Our leader's rash example we pursue.
But storms of stones, from the proud temple's height,
Pour down, and on our batter'd helms alight:
We from our friends receiv'd this fatal blow,
Who thought us Grecians, as we seem'd in show.
They aim at the mistaken crests, from high;
And ours beneath the pond'rous ruin lie.
Then, mov'd with anger and disdain, to see
Their troops dispers'd, the royal virgin free,
The Grecians rally, and their pow'rs unite,
With fury charge us, and renew the fight.
The brother kings with Ajax join their force,
And the whole squadron of Thessalian horse.
"Thus, when the rival winds their quarrel try,
Contending for the kingdom of the sky,
South, east, and west, on airy coursers borne;
The whirlwind gathers, and the woods are torn:
Then Nereus strikes the deep; the billows rise,
And, mix'd with ooze and sand, pollute the skies.
The troops we squander'd first again appear
From several quarters, and enclose the rear.
They first observe, and to the rest betray,
Our diff'rent speech; our borrow'd arms survey.
Oppress'd with odds, we fall; Coroebus first,
At Pallas' altar, by Peneleus pierc'd.
Then Ripheus follow'd, in th' unequal fight;
Just of his word, observant of the right:
Heav'n thought not so. Dymas their fate attends,

With Hypanis, mistaken by their friends.
Nor, Pantheus, thee, thy miter, nor the bands
Of awful Phoebus, sav'd from impious hands.
Ye Trojan flames, your testimony bear,
What I perform'd, and what I suffer'd there;
No sword avoiding in the fatal strife,
Expos'd to death, and prodigal of life;
Witness, ye heavens! I live not by my fault:
I strove to have deserv'd the death I sought.
But, when I could not fight, and would have died,
Borne off to distance by the growing tide,
Old Iphitus and I were hurried thence,
With Pelias wounded, and without defense.
New clamors from th' invested palace ring:
We run to die, or disengage the king.
So hot th' assault, so high the tumult rose,
While ours defend, and while the Greeks oppose
As all the Dardan and Argolic race
Had been contracted in that narrow space;
Or as all Ilium else were void of fear,
And tumult, war, and slaughter, only there.
Their targets in a tortoise cast, the foes,
Secure advancing, to the turrets rose:
Some mount the scaling ladders; some, more bold,
Swerve upwards, and by posts and pillars hold;
Their left hand gripes their bucklers in th' ascent,
While with their right they seize the battlement.
From their demolish'd tow'rs the Trojans throw
Huge heaps of stones, that, falling, crush the foe;
And heavy beams and rafters from the sides
(Such arms their last necessity provides)
And gilded roofs, come tumbling from on high,
The marks of state and ancient royalty.
The guards below, fix'd in the pass, attend
The charge undaunted, and the gate defend.
Renew'd in courage with recover'd breath,
A second time we ran to tempt our death,
To clear the palace from the foe, succeed
The weary living, and revenge the dead.
"A postern door, yet unobserv'd and free,
Join'd by the length of a blind gallery,
To the king's closet led: a way well known
To Hector's wife, while Priam held the throne,
Thro' which she brought Astyanax, unseen,
To cheer his grandsire and his grandsire's queen.
Thro' this we pass, and mount the tow'r, from whence
With unavailing arms the Trojans make defense.
From this the trembling king had oft descried
The Grecian camp, and saw their navy ride.
Beams from its lofty height with swords we hew,
Then, wrenching with our hands, th' assault renew;
And, where the rafters on the columns meet,
We push them headlong with our arms and feet.
The lightning flies not swifter than the fall,
Nor thunder louder than the ruin'd wall:

Down goes the top at once; the Greeks beneath
Are piecemeal torn, or pounded into death.
Yet more succeed, and more to death are sent;
We cease not from above, nor they below relent.
Before the gate stood Pyrrhus, threat'ning loud,
With glitt'ring arms conspicuous in the crowd.
So shines, renew'd in youth, the crested snake,
Who slept the winter in a thorny brake,
And, casting off his slough when spring returns,
Now looks aloft, and with new glory burns;
Restor'd with poisonous herbs, his ardent sides
Reflect the sun; and rais'd on spires he rides;
High o'er the grass, hissing he rolls along,
And brandishes by fits his forky tongue.
Proud Periphas, and fierce Automedon,
His father's charioteer, together run
To force the gate; the Scyrian infantry
Rush on in crowds, and the barr'd passage free.
Ent'ring the court, with shouts the skies they rend;
And flaming firebrands to the roofs ascend.
Himself, among the foremost, deals his blows,
And with his ax repeated strokes bestows
On the strong doors; then all their shoulders ply,
Till from the posts the brazen hinges fly.
He hews apace; the double bars at length
Yield to his ax and unresisted strength.
A mighty breach is made: the rooms conceal'd
Appear, and all the palace is reveal'd;
The halls of audience, and of public state,
And where the lonely queen in secret sate.
Arm'd soldiers now by trembling maids are seen,
With not a door, and scarce a space, between.
The house is fill'd with loud laments and cries,
And shrieks of women rend the vaulted skies;
The fearful matrons run from place to place,
And kiss the thresholds, and the posts embrace.
The fatal work inhuman Pyrrhus plies,
And all his father sparkles in his eyes;
Nor bars, nor fighting guards, his force sustain:
The bars are broken, and the guards are slain.
In rush the Greeks, and all the apartments fill;
Those few defendants whom they find, they kill.
Not with so fierce a rage the foaming flood
Roars, when he finds his rapid course withstood;
Bears down the dams with unresisted sway,
And sweeps the cattle and the cots away.
These eyes beheld him when he march'd between
The brother kings: I saw th' unhappy queen,
The hundred wives, and where old Priam stood,
To stain his hallow'd altar with his brood.
The fifty nuptial beds (such hopes had he,
So large a promise, of a progeny),
The posts, of plated gold, and hung with spoils,
Fell the reward of the proud victor's toils.
Where'er the raging fire had left a space,

The Grecians enter and possess the place.
"Perhaps you may of Priam's fate enquire.
He, when he saw his regal town on fire,
His ruin'd palace, and his ent'ring foes,
On ev'ry side inevitable woes,
In arms, disus'd, invests his limbs, decay'd,
Like them, with age; a late and useless aid.
His feeble shoulders scarce the weight sustain;
Loaded, not arm'd, he creeps along with pain,
Despairing of success, ambitious to be slain!
Uncover'd but by heav'n, there stood in view
An altar; near the hearth a laurel grew,
Dodder'd with age, whose boughs encompass round
The household gods, and shade the holy ground.
Here Hecuba, with all her helpless train
Of dames, for shelter sought, but sought in vain.
Driv'n like a flock of doves along the sky,
Their images they hug, and to their altars fly.
The Queen, when she beheld her trembling lord,
And hanging by his side a heavy sword,
'What rage,' she cried, 'has seiz'd my husband's mind?
What arms are these, and to what use design'd?
These times want other aids! Were Hector here,
Ev'n Hector now in vain, like Priam, would appear.
With us, one common shelter thou shalt find,
Or in one common fate with us be join'd.'
She said, and with a last salute embrac'd
The poor old man, and by the laurel plac'd.
Behold! Polites, one of Priam's sons,
Pursued by Pyrrhus, there for safety runs.
Thro' swords and foes, amaz'd and hurt, he flies
Thro' empty courts and open galleries.
Him Pyrrhus, urging with his lance, pursues,
And often reaches, and his thrusts renews.
The youth, transfix'd, with lamentable cries,
Expires before his wretched parent's eyes:
Whom gasping at his feet when Priam saw,
The fear of death gave place to nature's law;
And, shaking more with anger than with age,
'The gods,' said he, 'requite thy brutal rage!
As sure they will, barbarian, sure they must,
If there be gods in heav'n, and gods be just-
Who tak'st in wrongs an insolent delight;
With a son's death t' infect a father's sight.
Not he, whom thou and lying fame conspire
To call thee his- not he, thy vaunted sire,
Thus us'd my wretched age: the gods he fear'd,
The laws of nature and of nations heard.
He cheer'd my sorrows, and, for sums of gold,
The bloodless carcass of my Hector sold;
Pitied the woes a parent underwent,
And sent me back in safety from his tent.'
"This said, his feeble hand a javelin threw,
Which, flutt'ring, seem'd to loiter as it flew:
Just, and but barely, to the mark it held,

And faintly tinkled on the brazen shield.
"Then Pyrrhus thus: 'Go thou from me to fate,
And to my father my foul deeds relate.
Now die!' With that he dragg'd the trembling sire,
Slidd'ring thro' clotter'd blood and holy mire,
(The mingled paste his murder'd son had made,)
Haul'd from beneath the violated shade,
And on the sacred pile the royal victim laid.
His right hand held his bloody falchion bare,
His left he twisted in his hoary hair;
Then, with a speeding thrust, his heart he found:
The lukewarm blood came rushing thro' the wound,
And sanguine streams distain'd the sacred ground.
Thus Priam fell, and shar'd one common fate
With Troy in ashes, and his ruin'd state:
He, who the scepter of all Asia sway'd,
Whom monarchs like domestic slaves obey'd.
On the bleak shore now lies th' abandon'd king,
A headless carcass, and a nameless thing.
"Then, not before, I felt my cruddled blood
Congeal with fear, my hair with horror stood:
My father's image fill'd my pious mind,
Lest equal years might equal fortune find.
Again I thought on my forsaken wife,
And trembled for my son's abandon'd life.
I look'd about, but found myself alone,
Deserted at my need! My friends were gone.
Some spent with toil, some with despair oppress'd,
Leap'd headlong from the heights; the flames consum'd the rest.
Thus, wand'ring in my way, without a guide,
The graceless Helen in the porch I spied
Of Vesta's temple; there she lurk'd alone;
Muffled she sate, and, what she could, unknown:
But, by the flames that cast their blaze around,
That common bane of Greece and Troy I found.
For Ilium burnt, she dreads the Trojan sword;
More dreads the vengeance of her injur'd lord;
Ev'n by those gods who refug'd her abhorr'd.
Trembling with rage, the strumpet I regard,
Resolv'd to give her guilt the due reward:
'Shall she triumphant sail before the wind,
And leave in flames unhappy Troy behind?
Shall she her kingdom and her friends review,
In state attended with a captive crew,
While unreveng'd the good old Priam falls,
And Grecian fires consume the Trojan walls?
For this the Phrygian fields and Xanthian flood
Were swell'd with bodies, and were drunk with blood?
'T is true, a soldier can small honor gain,
And boast no conquest, from a woman slain:
Yet shall the fact not pass without applause,
Of vengeance taken in so just a cause;
The punish'd crime shall set my soul at ease,
And murm'ring manes of my friends appease.'
Thus while I rave, a gleam of pleasing light

Spread o'er the place; and, shining heav'nly bright,
My mother stood reveal'd before my sight
Never so radiant did her eyes appear;
Not her own star confess'd a light so clear:
Great in her charms, as when on gods above
She looks, and breathes herself into their love.
She held my hand, the destin'd blow to break;
Then from her rosy lips began to speak:
'My son, from whence this madness, this neglect
Of my commands, and those whom I protect?
Why this unmanly rage? Recall to mind
Whom you forsake, what pledges leave behind.
Look if your helpless father yet survive,
Or if Ascanius or Creusa live.
Around your house the greedy Grecians err;
And these had perish'd in the nightly war,
But for my presence and protecting care.
Not Helen's face, nor Paris, was in fault;
But by the gods was this destruction brought.
Now cast your eyes around, while I dissolve
The mists and films that mortal eyes involve,
Purge from your sight the dross, and make you see
The shape of each avenging deity.
Enlighten'd thus, my just commands fulfil,
Nor fear obedience to your mother's will.
Where yon disorder'd heap of ruin lies,
Stones rent from stones; where clouds of dust arise-
Amid that smother Neptune holds his place,
Below the wall's foundation drives his mace,
And heaves the building from the solid base.
Look where, in arms, imperial Juno stands
Full in the Scaean gate, with loud commands,
Urging on shore the tardy Grecian bands.
See! Pallas, of her snaky buckler proud,
Bestrides the tow'r, refulgent thro' the cloud:
See! Jove new courage to the foe supplies,
And arms against the town the partial deities.
Haste hence, my son; this fruitless labor end:
Haste, where your trembling spouse and sire attend:
Haste; and a mother's care your passage shall befriend.'
She said, and swiftly vanish'd from my sight,
Obscure in clouds and gloomy shades of night.
I look'd, I listen'd; dreadful sounds I hear;
And the dire forms of hostile gods appear.
Troy sunk in flames I saw (nor could prevent),
And Ilium from its old foundations rent;
Rent like a mountain ash, which dar'd the winds,
And stood the sturdy strokes of lab'ring hinds.
About the roots the cruel ax resounds;
The stumps are pierc'd with oft-repeated wounds:
The war is felt on high; the nodding crown
Now threats a fall, and throws the leafy honors down.
To their united force it yields, tho' late,
And mourns with mortal groans th' approaching fate:
The roots no more their upper load sustain;

But down she falls, and spreads a ruin thro' the plain.
"Descending thence, I scape thro' foes and fire:
Before the goddess, foes and flames retire.
Arriv'd at home, he, for whose only sake,
Or most for his, such toils I undertake,
The good Anchises, whom, by timely flight,
I purpos'd to secure on Ida's height,
Refus'd the journey, resolute to die
And add his fun'rals to the fate of Troy,
Rather than exile and old age sustain.
'Go you, whose blood runs warm in ev'ry vein.
Had Heav'n decreed that I should life enjoy,
Heav'n had decreed to save unhappy Troy.
'T is, sure, enough, if not too much, for one,
Twice to have seen our Ilium overthrown.
Make haste to save the poor remaining crew,
And give this useless corpse a long adieu.
These weak old hands suffice to stop my breath;
At least the pitying foes will aid my death,
To take my spoils, and leave my body bare:
As for my sepulcher, let Heav'n take care.
'T is long since I, for my celestial wife
Loath'd by the gods, have dragg'd a ling'ring life;
Since ev'ry hour and moment I expire,
Blasted from heav'n by Jove's avenging fire.'
This oft repeated, he stood fix'd to die:
Myself, my wife, my son, my family,
Intreat, pray, beg, and raise a doleful cry-
'What, will he still persist, on death resolve,
And in his ruin all his house involve!'
He still persists his reasons to maintain;
Our pray'rs, our tears, our loud laments, are vain.
"Urg'd by despair, again I go to try
The fate of arms, resolv'd in fight to die:
'What hope remains, but what my death must give?
Can I, without so dear a father, live?
You term it prudence, what I baseness call:
Could such a word from such a parent fall?
If Fortune please, and so the gods ordain,
That nothing should of ruin'd Troy remain,
And you conspire with Fortune to be slain,
The way to death is wide, th' approaches near:
For soon relentless Pyrrhus will appear,
Reeking with Priam's blood- the wretch who slew
The son (inhuman) in the father's view,
And then the sire himself to the dire altar drew.
O goddess mother, give me back to Fate;
Your gift was undesir'd, and came too late!
Did you, for this, unhappy me convey
Thro' foes and fires, to see my house a prey?
Shall I my father, wife, and son behold,
Welt'ring in blood, each other's arms infold?
Haste! gird my sword, tho' spent and overcome:
'T is the last summons to receive our doom.
I hear thee, Fate; and I obey thy call!

Not unreveng'd the foe shall see my fall.
Restore me to the yet unfinish'd fight:
My death is wanting to conclude the night.'
Arm'd once again, my glitt'ring sword I wield,
While th' other hand sustains my weighty shield,
And forth I rush to seek th' abandon'd field.
I went; but sad Creusa stopp'd my way,
And cross the threshold in my passage lay,
Embrac'd my knees, and, when I would have gone,
Shew'd me my feeble sire and tender son:
'If death be your design, at least,' said she,
'Take us along to share your destiny.
If any farther hopes in arms remain,
This place, these pledges of your love, maintain.
To whom do you expose your father's life,
Your son's, and mine, your now forgotten wife!'
While thus she fills the house with clam'rous cries,
Our hearing is diverted by our eyes:
For, while I held my son, in the short space
Betwixt our kisses and our last embrace;
Strange to relate, from young Iulus' head
A lambent flame arose, which gently spread
Around his brows, and on his temples fed.
Amaz'd, with running water we prepare
To quench the sacred fire, and slake his hair;
But old Anchises, vers'd in omens, rear'd
His hands to heav'n, and this request preferr'd:
'If any vows, almighty Jove, can bend
Thy will; if piety can pray'rs commend,
Confirm the glad presage which thou art pleas'd to send.'
Scarce had he said, when, on our left, we hear
A peal of rattling thunder roll in air:
There shot a streaming lamp along the sky,
Which on the winged lightning seem'd to fly;
From o'er the roof the blaze began to move,
And, trailing, vanish'd in th' Idaean grove.
It swept a path in heav'n, and shone a guide,
Then in a steaming stench of sulphur died.
"The good old man with suppliant hands implor'd
The gods' protection, and their star ador'd.
'Now, now,' said he, 'my son, no more delay!
I yield, I follow where Heav'n shews the way.
Keep, O my country gods, our dwelling place,
And guard this relic of the Trojan race,
This tender child! These omens are your own,
And you can yet restore the ruin'd town.
At least accomplish what your signs foreshow:
I stand resign'd, and am prepar'd to go.'
"He said. The crackling flames appear on high.
And driving sparkles dance along the sky.
With Vulcan's rage the rising winds conspire,
And near our palace roll the flood of fire.
'Haste, my dear father, ('t is no time to wait,)
And load my shoulders with a willing freight.
Whate'er befalls, your life shall be my care;

One death, or one deliv'rance, we will share.
My hand shall lead our little son; and you,
My faithful consort, shall our steps pursue.
Next, you, my servants, heed my strict commands:
Without the walls a ruin'd temple stands,
To Ceres hallow'd once; a cypress nigh
Shoots up her venerable head on high,
By long religion kept; there bend your feet,
And in divided parties let us meet.
Our country gods, the relics, and the bands,
Hold you, my father, in your guiltless hands:
In me 't is impious holy things to bear,
Red as I am with slaughter, new from war,
Till in some living stream I cleanse the guilt
Of dire debate, and blood in battle spilt.'
Thus, ord'ring all that prudence could provide,
I clothe my shoulders with a lion's hide
And yellow spoils; then, on my bending back,
The welcome load of my dear father take;
While on my better hand Ascanius hung,
And with unequal paces tripp'd along.
Creusa kept behind; by choice we stray
Thro' ev'ry dark and ev'ry devious way.
I, who so bold and dauntless, just before,
The Grecian darts and shock of lances bore,
At ev'ry shadow now am seiz'd with fear,
Not for myself, but for the charge I bear;
Till, near the ruin'd gate arriv'd at last,
Secure, and deeming all the danger past,
A frightful noise of trampling feet we hear.
My father, looking thro' the shades, with fear,
Cried out: 'Haste, haste, my son, the foes are nigh;
Their swords and shining armor I descry.'
Some hostile god, for some unknown offense,
Had sure bereft my mind of better sense;
For, while thro' winding ways I took my flight,
And sought the shelter of the gloomy night,
Alas! I lost Creusa: hard to tell
If by her fatal destiny she fell,
Or weary sate, or wander'd with affright;
But she was lost for ever to my sight.
I knew not, or reflected, till I meet
My friends, at Ceres' now deserted seat.
We met: not one was wanting; only she
Deceiv'd her friends, her son, and wretched me.
"What mad expressions did my tongue refuse!
Whom did I not, of gods or men, accuse!
This was the fatal blow, that pain'd me more
Than all I felt from ruin'd Troy before.
Stung with my loss, and raving with despair,
Abandoning my now forgotten care,
Of counsel, comfort, and of hope bereft,
My sire, my son, my country gods I left.
In shining armor once again I sheathe
My limbs, not feeling wounds, nor fearing death.

Then headlong to the burning walls I run,
And seek the danger I was forc'd to shun.
I tread my former tracks; thro' night explore
Each passage, ev'ry street I cross'd before.
All things were full of horror and affright,
And dreadful ev'n the silence of the night.
Then to my father's house I make repair,
With some small glimpse of hope to find her there.
Instead of her, the cruel Greeks I met;
The house was fill'd with foes, with flames beset.
Driv'n on the wings of winds, whole sheets of fire,
Thro' air transported, to the roofs aspire.
From thence to Priam's palace I resort,
And search the citadel and desart court.
Then, unobserv'd, I pass by Juno's church:
A guard of Grecians had possess'd the porch;
There Phoenix and Ulysses watch prey,
And thither all the wealth of Troy convey:
The spoils which they from ransack'd houses brought,
And golden bowls from burning altars caught,
The tables of the gods, the purple vests,
The people's treasure, and the pomp of priests.
A rank of wretched youths, with pinion'd hands,
And captive matrons, in long order stands.
Then, with ungovern'd madness, I proclaim,
Thro' all the silent street, Creusa's name:
Creusa still I call; at length she hears,
And sudden thro' the shades of night appears-
Appears, no more Creusa, nor my wife,
But a pale specter, larger than the life.
Aghast, astonish'd, and struck dumb with fear,
I stood; like bristles rose my stiffen'd hair.
Then thus the ghost began to soothe my grief
'Nor tears, nor cries, can give the dead relief.
Desist, my much-lov'd lord,'t indulge your pain;
You bear no more than what the gods ordain.
My fates permit me not from hence to fly;
Nor he, the great controller of the sky.
Long wand'ring ways for you the pow'rs decree;
On land hard labors, and a length of sea.
Then, after many painful years are past,
On Latium's happy shore you shall be cast,
Where gentle Tiber from his bed beholds
The flow'ry meadows, and the feeding folds.
There end your toils; and there your fates provide
A quiet kingdom, and a royal bride:
There fortune shall the Trojan line restore,
And you for lost Creusa weep no more.
Fear not that I shall watch, with servile shame,
Th' imperious looks of some proud Grecian dame;
Or, stooping to the victor's lust, disgrace
My goddess mother, or my royal race.
And now, farewell! The parent of the gods
Restrains my fleeting soul in her abodes:
I trust our common issue to your care.'

She said, and gliding pass'd unseen in air.
I strove to speak: but horror tied my tongue;
And thrice about her neck my arms I flung,
And, thrice deceiv'd, on vain embraces hung.
Light as an empty dream at break of day,
Or as a blast of wind, she rush'd away.
"Thus having pass'd the night in fruitless pain,
I to my longing friends return again,
Amaz'd th' augmented number to behold,
Of men and matrons mix'd, of young and old;
A wretched exil'd crew together brought,
With arms appointed, and with treasure fraught,
Resolv'd, and willing, under my command,
To run all hazards both of sea and land.
The Morn began, from Ida, to display
Her rosy cheeks; and Phosphor led the day:
Before the gates the Grecians took their post,
And all pretense of late relief was lost.
I yield to Fate, unwillingly retire,
And, loaded, up the hill convey my sire."

Book IV

But anxious cares already seiz'd the queen:
She fed within her veins a flame unseen;
The hero's valor, acts, and birth inspire
Her soul with love, and fan the secret fire.
His words, his looks, imprinted in her heart,
Improve the passion, and increase the smart.
Now, when the purple morn had chas'd away
The dewy shadows, and restor'd the day,
Her sister first with early care she sought,
And thus in mournful accents eas'd her thought:
"My dearest Anna, what new dreams affright
My lab'ring soul! what visions of the night
Disturb my quiet, and distract my breast
With strange ideas of our Trojan guest!
His worth, his actions, and majestic air,
A man descended from the gods declare.
Fear ever argues a degenerate kind;
His birth is well asserted by his mind.
Then, what he suffer'd, when by Fate betray'd!
What brave attempts for falling Troy he made!
Such were his looks, so gracefully he spoke,
That, were I not resolv'd against the yoke
Of hapless marriage, never to be curst
With second love, so fatal was my first,
To this one error I might yield again;
For, since Sichaeus was untimely slain,
This only man is able to subvert
The fix'd foundations of my stubborn heart.
And, to confess my frailty, to my shame,
Somewhat I find within, if not the same,
Too like the sparkles of my former flame.
But first let yawning earth a passage rend,

And let me thro' the dark abyss descend;
First let avenging Jove, with flames from high,
Drive down this body to the nether sky,
Condemn'd with ghosts in endless night to lie,
Before I break the plighted faith I gave!
No! he who had my vows shall ever have;
For, whom I lov'd on earth, I worship in the grave."
She said: the tears ran gushing from her eyes,
And stopp'd her speech. Her sister thus replies:
"O dearer than the vital air I breathe,
Will you to grief your blooming years bequeath,
Condemn'd to waste in woes your lonely life,
Without the joys of mother or of wife?
Think you these tears, this pompous train of woe,
Are known or valued by the ghosts below?
I grant that, while your sorrows yet were green,
It well became a woman, and a queen,
The vows of Tyrian princes to neglect,
To scorn Hyarbas, and his love reject,
With all the Libyan lords of mighty name;
But will you fight against a pleasing flame!
This little spot of land, which Heav'n bestows,
On ev'ry side is hemm'd with warlike foes;
Gaetulian cities here are spread around,
And fierce Numidians there your frontiers bound;
Here lies a barren waste of thirsty land,
And there the Syrtes raise the moving sand;
Barcaean troops besiege the narrow shore,
And from the sea Pygmalion threatens more.
Propitious Heav'n, and gracious Juno, lead
This wand'ring navy to your needful aid:
How will your empire spread, your city rise,
From such a union, and with such allies?
Implore the favor of the pow'rs above,
And leave the conduct of the rest to love.
Continue still your hospitable way,
And still invent occasions of their stay,
Till storms and winter winds shall cease to threat,
And planks and oars repair their shatter'd fleet."
These words, which from a friend and sister came,
With ease resolv'd the scruples of her fame,
And added fury to the kindled flame.
Inspir'd with hope, the project they pursue;
On ev'ry altar sacrifice renew:
A chosen ewe of two years old they pay
To Ceres, Bacchus, and the God of Day;
Preferring Juno's pow'r, for Juno ties
The nuptial knot and makes the marriage joys.
The beauteous queen before her altar stands,
And holds the golden goblet in her hands.
A milk-white heifer she with flow'rs adorns,
And pours the ruddy wine betwixt her horns;
And, while the priests with pray'r the gods invoke,
She feeds their altars with Sabaean smoke,
With hourly care the sacrifice renews,

And anxiously the panting entrails views.
What priestly rites, alas! what pious art,
What vows avail to cure a bleeding heart!
A gentle fire she feeds within her veins,
Where the soft god secure in silence reigns.
Sick with desire, and seeking him she loves,
From street to street the raving Dido roves.
So when the watchful shepherd, from the blind,
Wounds with a random shaft the careless hind,
Distracted with her pain she flies the woods,
Bounds o'er the lawn, and seeks the silent floods,
With fruitless care; for still the fatal dart
Sticks in her side, and rankles in her heart.
And now she leads the Trojan chief along
The lofty walls, amidst the busy throng;
Displays her Tyrian wealth, and rising town,
Which love, without his labor, makes his own.
This pomp she shows, to tempt her wand'ring guest;
Her falt'ring tongue forbids to speak the rest.
When day declines, and feasts renew the night,
Still on his face she feeds her famish'd sight;
She longs again to hear the prince relate
His own adventures and the Trojan fate.
He tells it o'er and o'er; but still in vain,
For still she begs to hear it once again.
The hearer on the speaker's mouth depends,
And thus the tragic story never ends.
Then, when they part, when Phoebe's paler light
Withdraws, and falling stars to sleep invite,
She last remains, when ev'ry guest is gone,
Sits on the bed he press'd, and sighs alone;
Absent, her absent hero sees and hears;
Or in her bosom young Ascanius bears,
And seeks the father's image in the child,
If love by likeness might be so beguil'd.
Meantime the rising tow'rs are at a stand;
No labors exercise the youthful band,
Nor use of arts, nor toils of arms they know;
The mole is left unfinish'd to the foe;
The mounds, the works, the walls, neglected lie,
Short of their promis'd heighth, that seem'd to threat the sky,
But when imperial Juno, from above,
Saw Dido fetter'd in the chains of love,
Hot with the venom which her veins inflam'd,
And by no sense of shame to be reclaim'd,
With soothing words to Venus she begun:
"High praises, endless honors, you have won,
And mighty trophies, with your worthy son!
Two gods a silly woman have undone!
Nor am I ignorant, you both suspect
This rising city, which my hands erect:
But shall celestial discord never cease?
'T is better ended in a lasting peace.
You stand possess'd of all your soul desir'd:
Poor Dido with consuming love is fir'd.

Your Trojan with my Tyrian let us join;
So Dido shall be yours, Aeneas mine:
One common kingdom, one united line.
Eliza shall a Dardan lord obey,
And lofty Carthage for a dow'r convey."
Then Venus, who her hidden fraud descried,
Which would the scepter of the world misguide
To Libyan shores, thus artfully replied:
"Who, but a fool, would wars with Juno choose,
And such alliance and such gifts refuse,
If Fortune with our joint desires comply?
The doubt is all from Jove and destiny;
Lest he forbid, with absolute command,
To mix the people in one common land-
Or will the Trojan and the Tyrian line
In lasting leagues and sure succession join?
But you, the partner of his bed and throne,
May move his mind; my wishes are your own."
"Mine," said imperial Juno, "be the care;
Time urges, now, to perfect this affair:
Attend my counsel, and the secret share.
When next the Sun his rising light displays,
And gilds the world below with purple rays,
The queen, Aeneas, and the Tyrian court
Shall to the shady woods, for sylvan game, resort.
There, while the huntsmen pitch their toils around,
And cheerful horns from side to side resound,
A pitchy cloud shall cover all the plain
With hail, and thunder, and tempestuous rain;
The fearful train shall take their speedy flight,
Dispers'd, and all involv'd in gloomy night;
One cave a grateful shelter shall afford
To the fair princess and the Trojan lord.
I will myself the bridal bed prepare,
If you, to bless the nuptials, will be there:
So shall their loves be crown'd with due delights,
And Hymen shall be present at the rites."
The Queen of Love consents, and closely smiles
At her vain project, and discover'd wiles.
The rosy morn was risen from the main,
And horns and hounds awake the princely train:
They issue early thro' the city gate,
Where the more wakeful huntsmen ready wait,
With nets, and toils, and darts, beside the force
Of Spartan dogs, and swift Massylian horse.
The Tyrian peers and officers of state
For the slow queen in antechambers wait;
Her lofty courser, in the court below,
Who his majestic rider seems to know,
Proud of his purple trappings, paws the ground,
And champs the golden bit, and spreads the foam around.
The queen at length appears; on either hand
The brawny guards in martial order stand.
A flow'r'd simar with golden fringe she wore,
And at her back a golden quiver bore;

Her flowing hair a golden caul restrains,
A golden clasp the Tyrian robe sustains.
Then young Ascanius, with a sprightly grace,
Leads on the Trojan youth to view the chase.
But far above the rest in beauty shines
The great Aeneas, the troop he joins;
Like fair Apollo, when he leaves the frost
Of wint'ry Xanthus, and the Lycian coast,
When to his native Delos he resorts,
Ordains the dances, and renews the sports;
Where painted Scythians, mix'd with Cretan bands,
Before the joyful altars join their hands:
Himself, on Cynthus walking, sees below
The merry madness of the sacred show.
Green wreaths of bays his length of hair inclose;
A golden fillet binds his awful brows;
His quiver sounds: not less the prince is seen
In manly presence, or in lofty mien.
Now had they reach'd the hills, and storm'd the seat
Of salvage beasts, in dens, their last retreat.
The cry pursues the mountain goats: they bound
From rock to rock, and keep the craggy ground;
Quite otherwise the stags, a trembling train,
In herds unsingled, scour the dusty plain,
And a long chase in open view maintain.
The glad Ascanius, as his courser guides,
Spurs thro' the vale, and these and those outrides.
His horse's flanks and sides are forc'd to feel
The clanking lash, and goring of the steel.
Impatiently he views the feeble prey,
Wishing some nobler beast to cross his way,
And rather would the tusky boar attend,
Or see the tawny lion downward bend.
Meantime, the gath'ring clouds obscure the skies:
From pole to pole the forky lightning flies;
The rattling thunders roll; and Juno pours
A wintry deluge down, and sounding show'rs.
The company, dispers'd, to converts ride,
And seek the homely cots, or mountain's hollow side.
The rapid rains, descending from the hills,
To rolling torrents raise the creeping rills.
The queen and prince, as love or fortune guides,
One common cavern in her bosom hides.
Then first the trembling earth the signal gave,
And flashing fires enlighten all the cave;
Hell from below, and Juno from above,
And howling nymphs, were conscious of their love.
From this ill-omen'd hour in time arose
Debate and death, and all succeeding woes.
The queen, whom sense of honor could not move,
No longer made a secret of her love,
But call'd it marriage, by that specious name
To veil the crime and sanctify the shame.
The loud report thro' Libyan cities goes.
Fame, the great ill, from small beginnings grows:

Swift from the first; and ev'ry moment brings
New vigor to her flights, new pinions to her wings.
Soon grows the pigmy to gigantic size;
Her feet on earth, her forehead in the skies.
Inrag'd against the gods, revengeful Earth
Produc'd her last of the Titanian birth.
Swift is her walk, more swift her winged haste:
A monstrous phantom, horrible and vast.
As many plumes as raise her lofty flight,
So many piercing eyes inlarge her sight;
Millions of opening mouths to Fame belong,
And ev'ry mouth is furnish'd with a tongue,
And round with list'ning ears the flying plague is hung.
She fills the peaceful universe with cries;
No slumbers ever close her wakeful eyes;
By day, from lofty tow'rs her head she shews,
And spreads thro' trembling crowds disastrous news;
With court informers haunts, and royal spies;
Things done relates, not done she feigns, and mingles truth with lies.
Talk is her business, and her chief delight
To tell of prodigies and cause affright.
She fills the people's ears with Dido's name,
Who, lost to honor and the sense of shame,
Admits into her throne and nuptial bed
A wand'ring guest, who from his country fled:
Whole days with him she passes in delights,
And wastes in luxury long winter nights,
Forgetful of her fame and royal trust,
Dissolv'd in ease, abandon'd to her lust.
The goddess widely spreads the loud report,
And flies at length to King Hyarba's court.
When first possess'd with this unwelcome news
Whom did he not of men and gods accuse?
This prince, from ravish'd Garamantis born,
A hundred temples did with spoils adorn,
In Ammon's honor, his celestial sire;
A hundred altars fed with wakeful fire;
And, thro' his vast dominions, priests ordain'd,
Whose watchful care these holy rites maintain'd.
The gates and columns were with garlands crown'd,
And blood of victim beasts enrich'd the ground.
He, when he heard a fugitive could move
The Tyrian princess, who disdain'd his love,
His breast with fury burn'd, his eyes with fire,
Mad with despair, impatient with desire;
Then on the sacred altars pouring wine,
He thus with pray'rs implor'd his sire divine:
"Great Jove! propitious to the Moorish race,
Who feast on painted beds, with off'rings grace
Thy temples, and adore thy pow'r divine
With blood of victims, and with sparkling wine,
Seest thou not this? or do we fear in vain
Thy boasted thunder, and thy thoughtless reign?
Do thy broad hands the forky lightnings lance?

Thine are the bolts, or the blind work of chance?
A wand'ring woman builds, within our state,
A little town, bought at an easy rate;
She pays me homage, and my grants allow
A narrow space of Libyan lands to plow;
Yet, scorning me, by passion blindly led,
Admits a banish'd Trojan to her bed!
And now this other Paris, with his train
Of conquer'd cowards, must in Afric reign!
(Whom, what they are, their looks and garb confess,
Their locks with oil perfum'd, their Lydian dress.)
He takes the spoil, enjoys the princely dame;
And I, rejected I, adore an empty name."
His vows, in haughty terms, he thus preferr'd,
And held his altar's horns. The mighty Thund'rer heard;
Then cast his eyes on Carthage, where he found
The lustful pair in lawless pleasure drown'd,
Lost in their loves, insensible of shame,
And both forgetful of their better fame.
He calls Cyllenius, and the god attends,
By whom his menacing command he sends:
"Go, mount the western winds, and cleave the sky;
Then, with a swift descent, to Carthage fly:
There find the Trojan chief, who wastes his days
In slothful not and inglorious ease,
Nor minds the future city, giv'n by fate.
To him this message from my mouth relate:
'Not so fair Venus hop'd, when twice she won
Thy life with pray'rs, nor promis'd such a son.
Hers was a hero, destin'd to command
A martial race, and rule the Latian land,
Who should his ancient line from Teucer draw,
And on the conquer'd world impose the law.'
If glory cannot move a mind so mean,
Nor future praise from fading pleasure wean,
Yet why should he defraud his son of fame,
And grudge the Romans their immortal name!
What are his vain designs! what hopes he more
From his long ling'ring on a hostile shore,
Regardless to redeem his honor lost,
And for his race to gain th' Ausonian coast!
Bid him with speed the Tyrian court forsake;
With this command the slumb'ring warrior wake."
Hermes obeys; with golden pinions binds
His flying feet, and mounts the western winds:
And, whether o'er the seas or earth he flies,
With rapid force they bear him down the skies.
But first he grasps within his awful hand
The mark of sov'reign pow'r, his magic wand;
With this he draws the ghosts from hollow graves;
With this he drives them down the Stygian waves;
With this he seals in sleep the wakeful sight,
And eyes, tho' clos'd in death, restores to light.
Thus arm'd, the god begins his airy race,
And drives the racking clouds along the liquid space;

Now sees the tops of Atlas, as he flies,
Whose brawny back supports the starry skies;
Atlas, whose head, with piny forests crown'd,
Is beaten by the winds, with foggy vapors bound.
Snows hide his shoulders; from beneath his chin
The founts of rolling streams their race begin;
A beard of ice on his large breast depends.
Here, pois'd upon his wings, the god descends:
Then, rested thus, he from the tow'ring height
Plung'd downward, with precipitated flight,
Lights on the seas, and skims along the flood.
As waterfowl, who seek their fishy food,
Less, and yet less, to distant prospect show;
By turns they dance aloft, and dive below:
Like these, the steerage of his wings he plies,
And near the surface of the water flies,
Till, having pass'd the seas, and cross'd the sands,
He clos'd his wings, and stoop'd on Libyan lands:
Where shepherds once were hous'd in homely sheds,
Now tow'rs within the clouds advance their heads.
Arriving there, he found the Trojan prince
New ramparts raising for the town's defense.
A purple scarf, with gold embroider'd o'er,
(Queen Dido's gift,) about his waist he wore;
A sword, with glitt'ring gems diversified,
For ornament, not use, hung idly by his side.
Then thus, with winged words, the god began,
Resuming his own shape: "Degenerate man,
Thou woman's property, what mak'st thou here,
These foreign walls and Tyrian tow'rs to rear,
Forgetful of thy own? All-pow'rful Jove,
Who sways the world below and heav'n above,
Has sent me down with this severe command:
What means thy ling'ring in the Libyan land?
If glory cannot move a mind so mean,
Nor future praise from flitting pleasure wean,
Regard the fortunes of thy rising heir:
The promis'd crown let young Ascanius wear,
To whom th' Ausonian scepter, and the state
Of Rome's imperial name is ow'd by fate."
So spoke the god; and, speaking, took his flight,
Involv'd in clouds, and vanish'd out of sight.
The pious prince was seiz'd with sudden fear;
Mute was his tongue, and upright stood his hair.
Revolving in his mind the stern command,
He longs to fly, and loathes the charming land.
What should he say? or how should he begin?
What course, alas! remains to steer between
Th' offended lover and the pow'rful queen?
This way and that he turns his anxious mind,
And all expedients tries, and none can find.
Fix'd on the deed, but doubtful of the means,
After long thought, to this advice he leans:
Three chiefs he calls, commands them to repair
The fleet, and ship their men with silent care;

Some plausible pretense he bids them find,
To color what in secret he design'd.
Himself, meantime, the softest hours would choose,
Before the love-sick lady heard the news;
And move her tender mind, by slow degrees,
To suffer what the sov'reign pow'r decrees:
Jove will inspire him, when, and what to say.
They hear with pleasure, and with haste obey.
But soon the queen perceives the thin disguise:
(What arts can blind a jealous woman's eyes!)
She was the first to find the secret fraud,
Before the fatal news was blaz'd abroad.
Love the first motions of the lover hears,
Quick to presage, and ev'n in safety fears.
Nor impious Fame was wanting to report
The ships repair'd, the Trojans' thick resort,
And purpose to forsake the Tyrian court.
Frantic with fear, impatient of the wound,
And impotent of mind, she roves the city round.
Less wild the Bacchanalian dames appear,
When, from afar, their nightly god they hear,
And howl about the hills, and shake the wreathy spear.
At length she finds the dear perfidious man;
Prevents his form'd excuse, and thus began:
"Base and ungrateful! could you hope to fly,
And undiscover'd scape a lover's eye?
Nor could my kindness your compassion move.
Nor plighted vows, nor dearer bands of love?
Or is the death of a despairing queen
Not worth preventing, tho' too well foreseen?
Ev'n when the wintry winds command your stay,
You dare the tempests, and defy the sea.
False as you are, suppose you were not bound
To lands unknown, and foreign coasts to sound;
Were Troy restor'd, and Priam's happy reign,
Now durst you tempt, for Troy, the raging main?
See whom you fly! am I the foe you shun?
Now, by those holy vows, so late begun,
By this right hand, (since I have nothing more
To challenge, but the faith you gave before;)
I beg you by these tears too truly shed,
By the new pleasures of our nuptial bed;
If ever Dido, when you most were kind,
Were pleasing in your eyes, or touch'd your mind;
By these my pray'rs, if pray'rs may yet have place,
Pity the fortunes of a falling race.
For you I have provok'd a tyrant's hate,
Incens'd the Libyan and the Tyrian state;
For you alone I suffer in my fame,
Bereft of honor, and expos'd to shame.
Whom have I now to trust, ungrateful guest?
(That only name remains of all the rest!)
What have I left? or whither can I fly?
Must I attend Pygmalion's cruelty,
Or till Hyarba shall in triumph lead

A queen that proudly scorn'd his proffer'd bed?
Had you deferr'd, at least, your hasty flight,
And left behind some pledge of our delight,
Some babe to bless the mother's mournful sight,
Some young Aeneas, to supply your place,
Whose features might express his father's face;
I should not then complain to live bereft
Of all my husband, or be wholly left."
Here paus'd the queen. Unmov'd he holds his eyes,
By Jove's command; nor suffer'd love to rise,
Tho' heaving in his heart; and thus at length replies:
"Fair queen, you never can enough repeat
Your boundless favors, or I own my debt;
Nor can my mind forget Eliza's name,
While vital breath inspires this mortal frame.
This only let me speak in my defense:
I never hop'd a secret flight from hence,
Much less pretended to the lawful claim
Of sacred nuptials, or a husband's name.
For, if indulgent Heav'n would leave me free,
And not submit my life to fate's decree,
My choice would lead me to the Trojan shore,
Those relics to review, their dust adore,
And Priam's ruin'd palace to restore.
But now the Delphian oracle commands,
And fate invites me to the Latian lands.
That is the promis'd place to which I steer,
And all my vows are terminated there.
If you, a Tyrian, and a stranger born,
With walls and tow'rs a Libyan town adorn,
Why may not we- like you, a foreign race-
Like you, seek shelter in a foreign place?
As often as the night obscures the skies
With humid shades, or twinkling stars arise,
Anchises' angry ghost in dreams appears,
Chides my delay, and fills my soul with fears;
And young Ascanius justly may complain
Of his defrauded and destin'd reign.
Ev'n now the herald of the gods appear'd:
Waking I saw him, and his message heard.
From Jove he came commission'd, heav'nly bright
With radiant beams, and manifest to sight
(The sender and the sent I both attest)
These walls he enter'd, and those words express'd.
Fair queen, oppose not what the gods command;
Forc'd by my fate, I leave your happy land."
Thus while he spoke, already she began,
With sparkling eyes, to view the guilty man;
From head to foot survey'd his person o'er,
Nor longer these outrageous threats forebore:
"False as thou art, and, more than false, forsworn!
Not sprung from noble blood, nor goddess-born,
But hewn from harden'd entrails of a rock!
And rough Hyrcanian tigers gave thee suck!
Why should I fawn? what have I worse to fear?

Did he once look, or lent a list'ning ear,
Sigh'd when I sobb'd, or shed one kindly tear?-
All symptoms of a base ungrateful mind,
So foul, that, which is worse, 'tis hard to find.
Of man's injustice why should I complain?
The gods, and Jove himself, behold in vain
Triumphant treason; yet no thunder flies,
Nor Juno views my wrongs with equal eyes;
Faithless is earth, and faithless are the skies!
Justice is fled, and Truth is now no more!
I sav'd the shipwrack'd exile on my shore;
With needful food his hungry Trojans fed;
I took the traitor to my throne and bed:
Fool that I was- 't is little to repeat
The rest- I stor'd and rigg'd his ruin'd fleet.
I rave, I rave! A god's command he pleads,
And makes Heav'n accessary to his deeds.
Now Lycian lots, and now the Delian god,
Now Hermes is employ'd from Jove's abode,
To warn him hence; as if the peaceful state
Of heav'nly pow'rs were touch'd with human fate!
But go! thy flight no longer I detain-
Go seek thy promis'd kingdom thro' the main!
Yet, if the heav'ns will hear my pious vow,
The faithless waves, not half so false as thou,
Or secret sands, shall sepulchers afford
To thy proud vessels, and their perjur'd lord.
Then shalt thou call on injur'd Dido's name:
Dido shall come in a black sulph'ry flame,
When death has once dissolv'd her mortal frame;
Shall smile to see the traitor vainly weep:
Her angry ghost, arising from the deep,
Shall haunt thee waking, and disturb thy sleep.
At least my shade thy punishment shall know,
And Fame shall spread the pleasing news below."
Abruptly here she stops; then turns away
Her loathing eyes, and shuns the sight of day.
Amaz'd he stood, revolving in his mind
What speech to frame, and what excuse to find.
Her fearful maids their fainting mistress led,
And softly laid her on her ivory bed.
But good Aeneas, tho' he much desir'd
To give that pity which her grief requir'd;
Tho' much he mourn'd, and labor'd with his love,
Resolv'd at length, obeys the will of Jove;
Reviews his forces: they with early care
Unmoor their vessels, and for sea prepare.
The fleet is soon afloat, in all its pride,
And well-calk'd galleys in the harbor ride.
Then oaks for oars they fell'd; or, as they stood,
Of its green arms despoil'd the growing wood,
Studious of flight. The beach is cover'd o'er
With Trojan bands, that blacken all the shore:
On ev'ry side are seen, descending down,
Thick swarms of soldiers, loaden from the town.

Thus, in battalia, march embodied ants,
Fearful of winter, and of future wants,
T' invade the corn, and to their cells convey
The plunder'd forage of their yellow prey.
The sable troops, along the narrow tracks,
Scarce bear the weighty burthen on their backs:
Some set their shoulders to the pond'rous grain;
Some guard the spoil; some lash the lagging train;
All ply their sev'ral tasks, and equal toil sustain.
What pangs the tender breast of Dido tore,
When, from the tow'r, she saw the cover'd shore,
And heard the shouts of sailors from afar,
Mix'd with the murmurs of the wat'ry war!
All-pow'rful Love! what changes canst thou cause
In human hearts, subjected to thy laws!
Once more her haughty soul the tyrant bends:
To pray'rs and mean submissions she descends.
No female arts or aids she left untried,
Nor counsels unexplor'd, before she died.
"Look, Anna! look! the Trojans crowd to sea;
They spread their canvas, and their anchors weigh.
The shouting crew their ships with garlands bind,
Invoke the sea gods, and invite the wind.
Could I have thought this threat'ning blow so near,
My tender soul had been forewarn'd to bear.
But do not you my last request deny;
With yon perfidious man your int'rest try,
And bring me news, if I must live or die.
You are his fav'rite; you alone can find
The dark recesses of his inmost mind:
In all his trusted secrets you have part,
And know the soft approaches to his heart.
Haste then, and humbly seek my haughty foe;
Tell him, I did not with the Grecians go,
Nor did my fleet against his friends employ,
Nor swore the ruin of unhappy Troy,
Nor mov'd with hands profane his father's dust:
Why should he then reject a just!
Whom does he shun, and whither would he fly!
Can he this last, this only pray'r deny!
Let him at least his dang'rous flight delay,
Wait better winds, and hope a calmer sea.
The nuptials he disclaims I urge no more:
Let him pursue the promis'd Latian shore.
A short delay is all I ask him now;
A pause of grief, an interval from woe,
Till my soft soul be temper'd to sustain
Accustom'd sorrows, and inur'd to pain.
If you in pity grant this one request,
My death shall glut the hatred of his breast."
This mournful message pious Anna bears,
And seconds with her own her sister's tears:
But all her arts are still employ'd in vain;
Again she comes, and is refus'd again.
His harden'd heart nor pray'rs nor threat'nings move;

Fate, and the god, had stopp'd his ears to love.
As, when the winds their airy quarrel try,
Justling from ev'ry quarter of the sky,
This way and that the mountain oak they bend,
His boughs they shatter, and his branches rend;
With leaves and falling mast they spread the ground;
The hollow valleys echo to the sound:
Unmov'd, the royal plant their fury mocks,
Or, shaken, clings more closely to the rocks;
Far as he shoots his tow'ring head on high,
So deep in earth his fix'd foundations lie.
No less a storm the Trojan hero bears;
Thick messages and loud complaints he hears,
And bandied words, still beating on his ears.
Sighs, groans, and tears proclaim his inward pains;
But the firm purpose of his heart remains.
The wretched queen, pursued by cruel fate,
Begins at length the light of heav'n to hate,
And loathes to live. Then dire portents she sees,
To hasten on the death her soul decrees:
Strange to relate! for when, before the shrine,
She pours in sacrifice the purple wine,
The purple wine is turn'd to putrid blood,
And the white offer'd milk converts to mud.
This dire presage, to her alone reveal'd,
From all, and ev'n her sister, she conceal'd.
A marble temple stood within the grove,
Sacred to death, and to her murther'd love;
That honor'd chapel she had hung around
With snowy fleeces, and with garlands crown'd:
Oft, when she visited this lonely dome,
Strange voices issued from her husband's tomb;
She thought she heard him summon her away,
Invite her to his grave, and chide her stay.
Hourly 't is heard, when with a boding note
The solitary screech owl strains her throat,
And, on a chimney's top, or turret's height,
With songs obscene disturbs the silence of the night.
Besides, old prophecies augment her fears;
And stern Aeneas in her dreams appears,
Disdainful as by day: she seems, alone,
To wander in her sleep, thro' ways unknown,
Guideless and dark; or, in a desart plain,
To seek her subjects, and to seek in vain:
Like Pentheus, when, distracted with his fear,
He saw two suns, and double Thebes, appear;
Or mad Orestes, when his mother's ghost
Full in his face infernal torches toss'd,
And shook her snaky locks: he shuns the sight,
Flies o'er the stage, surpris'd with mortal fright;
The Furies guard the door and intercept his flight.
Now, sinking underneath a load of grief,
From death alone she seeks her last relief;
The time and means resolv'd within her breast,
She to her mournful sister thus address'd

(Dissembling hope, her cloudy front she clears,
And a false vigor in her eyes appears):
"Rejoice!" she said. "Instructed from above,
My lover I shall gain, or lose my love.
Nigh rising Atlas, next the falling sun,
Long tracts of Ethiopian climates run:
There a Massylian priestess I have found,
Honor'd for age, for magic arts renown'd:
Th' Hesperian temple was her trusted care;
'T was she supplied the wakeful dragon's fare.
She poppy seeds in honey taught to steep,
Reclaim'd his rage, and sooth'd him into sleep.
She watch'd the golden fruit; her charms unbind
The chains of love, or fix them on the mind:
She stops the torrents, leaves the channel dry,
Repels the stars, and backward bears the sky.
The yawning earth rebellows to her call,
Pale ghosts ascend, and mountain ashes fall.
Witness, ye gods, and thou my better part,
How loth I am to try this impious art!
Within the secret court, with silent care,
Erect a lofty pile, expos'd in air:
Hang on the topmost part the Trojan vest,
Spoils, arms, and presents, of my faithless guest.
Next, under these, the bridal bed be plac'd,
Where I my ruin in his arms embrac'd:
All relics of the wretch are doom'd to fire;
For so the priestess and her charms require."
Thus far she said, and farther speech forbears;
A mortal paleness in her face appears:
Yet the mistrustless Anna could not find
The secret fun'ral in these rites design'd;
Nor thought so dire a rage possess'd her mind.
Unknowing of a train conceal'd so well,
She fear'd no worse than when Sichaeus fell;
Therefore obeys. The fatal pile they rear,
Within the secret court, expos'd in air.
The cloven holms and pines are heap'd on high,
And garlands on the hollow spaces lie.
Sad cypress, vervain, yew, compose the wreath,
And ev'ry baleful green denoting death.
The queen, determin'd to the fatal deed,
The spoils and sword he left, in order spread,
And the man's image on the nuptial bed.
And now (the sacred altars plac'd around)
The priestess enters, with her hair unbound,
And thrice invokes the pow'rs below the ground.
Night, Erebus, and Chaos she proclaims,
And threefold Hecate, with her hundred names,
And three Dianas: next, she sprinkles round
With feign'd Avernian drops the hallow'd ground;
Culls hoary simples, found by Phoebe's light,
With brazen sickles reap'd at noon of night;
Then mixes baleful juices in the bowl,
And cuts the forehead of a newborn foal,

Robbing the mother's love. The destin'd queen
Observes, assisting at the rites obscene;
A leaven'd cake in her devoted hands
She holds, and next the highest altar stands:
One tender foot was shod, her other bare;
Girt was her gather'd gown, and loose her hair.
Thus dress'd, she summon'd, with her dying breath,
The heav'ns and planets conscious of her death,
And ev'ry pow'r, if any rules above,
Who minds, or who revenges, injur'd love.
"'T was dead of night, when weary bodies close
Their eyes in balmy sleep and soft repose:
The winds no longer whisper thro' the woods,
Nor murm'ring tides disturb the gentle floods.
The stars in silent order mov'd around;
And Peace, with downy wings, was brooding on the ground
The flocks and herds, and party-color'd fowl,
Which haunt the woods, or swim the weedy pool,
Stretch'd on the quiet earth, securely lay,
Forgetting the past labors of the day.
All else of nature's common gift partake:
Unhappy Dido was alone awake.
Nor sleep nor ease the furious queen can find;
Sleep fled her eyes, as quiet fled her mind.
Despair, and rage, and love divide her heart;
Despair and rage had some, but love the greater part.
Then thus she said within her secret mind:
"What shall I do? what succor can I find?
Become a suppliant to Hyarba's pride,
And take my turn, to court and be denied?
Shall I with this ungrateful Trojan go,
Forsake an empire, and attend a foe?
Himself I refug'd, and his train reliev'd-
'T is true- but am I sure to be receiv'd?
Can gratitude in Trojan souls have place!
Laomedon still lives in all his race!
Then, shall I seek alone the churlish crew,
Or with my fleet their flying sails pursue?
What force have I but those whom scarce before
I drew reluctant from their native shore?
Will they again embark at my desire,
Once more sustain the seas, and quit their second Tyre?
Rather with steel thy guilty breast invade,
And take the fortune thou thyself hast made.
Your pity, sister, first seduc'd my mind,
Or seconded too well what I design'd.
These dear-bought pleasures had I never known,
Had I continued free, and still my own;
Avoiding love, I had not found despair,
But shar'd with salvage beasts the common air.
Like them, a lonely life I might have led,
Not mourn'd the living, nor disturb'd the dead."
These thoughts she brooded in her anxious breast.
On board, the Trojan found more easy rest.
Resolv'd to sail, in sleep he pass'd the night;

And order'd all things for his early flight.
To whom once more the winged god appears;
His former youthful mien and shape he wears,
And with this new alarm invades his ears:
"Sleep'st thou, O goddess-born! and canst thou drown
Thy needful cares, so near a hostile town,
Beset with foes; nor hear'st the western gales
Invite thy passage, and inspire thy sails?
She harbors in her heart a furious hate,
And thou shalt find the dire effects too late;
Fix'd on revenge, and obstinate to die.
Haste swiftly hence, while thou hast pow'r to fly.
The sea with ships will soon be cover'd o'er,
And blazing firebrands kindle all the shore.
Prevent her rage, while night obscures the skies,
And sail before the purple morn arise.
Who knows what hazards thy delay may bring?
Woman's a various and a changeful thing."
Thus Hermes in the dream; then took his flight
Aloft in air unseen, and mix'd with night.
Twice warn'd by the celestial messenger,
The pious prince arose with hasty fear;
Then rous'd his drowsy train without delay:
"Haste to your banks; your crooked anchors weigh,
And spread your flying sails, and stand to sea.
A god commands: he stood before my sight,
And urg'd us once again to speedy flight.
O sacred pow'r, what pow'r soe'er thou art,
To thy blest orders I resign my heart.
Lead thou the way; protect thy Trojan bands,
And prosper the design thy will commands."
He said: and, drawing forth his flaming sword,
His thund'ring arm divides the many-twisted cord.
An emulating zeal inspires his train:
They run; they snatch; they rush into the main.
With headlong haste they leave the desert shores,
And brush the liquid seas with lab'ring oars.
Aurora now had left her saffron bed,
And beams of early light the heav'ns o'erspread,
When, from a tow'r, the queen, with wakeful eyes,
Saw day point upward from the rosy skies.
She look'd to seaward; but the sea was void,
And scarce in ken the sailing ships descried.
Stung with despite, and furious with despair,
She struck her trembling breast, and tore her hair.
"And shall th' ungrateful traitor go," she said,
"My land forsaken, and my love betray'd?
Shall we not arm? not rush from ev'ry street,
To follow, sink, and burn his perjur'd fleet?
Haste, haul my galleys out! pursue the foe!
Bring flaming brands! set sail, and swiftly row!
What have I said? where am I? Fury turns
My brain; and my distemper'd bosom burns.
Then, when I gave my person and my throne,
This hate, this rage, had been more timely shown.

See now the promis'd faith, the vaunted name,
The pious man, who, rushing thro' the flame,
Preserv'd his gods, and to the Phrygian shore
The burthen of his feeble father bore!
I should have torn him piecemeal; strow'd in floods
His scatter'd limbs, or left expos'd in woods;
Destroy'd his friends and son; and, from the fire,
Have set the reeking boy before the sire.
Events are doubtful, which on battles wait:
Yet where's the doubt, to souls secure of fate?
My Tyrians, at their injur'd queen's command,
Had toss'd their fires amid the Trojan band;
At once extinguish'd all the faithless name;
And I myself, in vengeance of my shame,
Had fall'n upon the pile, to mend the fun'ral flame.
Thou Sun, who view'st at once the world below;
Thou Juno, guardian of the nuptial vow;
Thou Hecate hearken from thy dark abodes!
Ye Furies, fiends, and violated gods,
All pow'rs invok'd with Dido's dying breath,
Attend her curses and avenge her death!
If so the Fates ordain, Jove commands,
Th' ungrateful wretch should find the Latian lands,
Yet let a race untam'd, and haughty foes,
His peaceful entrance with dire arms oppose:
Oppress'd with numbers in th' unequal field,
His men discourag'd, and himself expell'd,
Let him for succor sue from place to place,
Torn from his subjects, and his son's embrace.
First, let him see his friends in battle slain,
And their untimely fate lament in vain;
And when, at length, the cruel war shall cease,
On hard conditions may he buy his peace:
Nor let him then enjoy supreme command;
But fall, untimely, by some hostile hand,
And lie unburied on the barren sand!
These are my pray'rs, and this my dying will;
And you, my Tyrians, ev'ry curse fulfil.
Perpetual hate and mortal wars proclaim,
Against the prince, the people, and the name.
These grateful off'rings on my grave bestow;
Nor league, nor love, the hostile nations know!
Now, and from hence, in ev'ry future age,
When rage excites your arms, and strength supplies the rage
Rise some avenger of our Libyan blood,
With fire and sword pursue the perjur'd brood;
Our arms, our seas, our shores, oppos'd to theirs;
And the same hate descend on all our heirs!"
This said, within her anxious mind she weighs
The means of cutting short her odious days.
Then to Sichaeus' nurse she briefly said
(For, when she left her country, hers was dead):
"Go, Barce, call my sister. Let her care
The solemn rites of sacrifice prepare;
The sheep, and all th' atoning off'rings bring,

Sprinkling her body from the crystal spring
With living drops; then let her come, and thou
With sacred fillets bind thy hoary brow.
Thus will I pay my vows to Stygian Jove,
And end the cares of my disastrous love;
Then cast the Trojan image on the fire,
And, as that burns, my passions shall expire."
The nurse moves onward, with officious care,
And all the speed her aged limbs can bear.
But furious Dido, with dark thoughts involv'd,
Shook at the mighty mischief she resolv'd.
With livid spots distinguish'd was her face;
Red were her rolling eyes, and discompos'd her pace;
Ghastly she gaz'd, with pain she drew her breath,
And nature shiver'd at approaching death.
Then swiftly to the fatal place she pass'd,
And mounts the fun'ral pile with furious haste;
Unsheathes the sword the Trojan left behind
(Not for so dire an enterprise design'd).
But when she view'd the garments loosely spread,
Which once he wore, and saw the conscious bed,
She paus'd, and with a sigh the robes embrac'd;
Then on the couch her trembling body cast,
Repress'd the ready tears, and spoke her last:
"Dear pledges of my love, while Heav'n so pleas'd,
Receive a soul, of mortal anguish eas'd:
My fatal course is finish'd; and I go,
A glorious name, among the ghosts below.
A lofty city by my hands is rais'd,
Pygmalion punish'd, and my lord appeas'd.
What could my fortune have afforded more,
Had the false Trojan never touch'd my shore!"
Then kiss'd the couch; and, "Must I die," she said,
"And unreveng'd? 'T is doubly to be dead!
Yet ev'n this death with pleasure I receive:
On any terms, 't is better than to live.
These flames, from far, may the false Trojan view;
These boding omens his base flight pursue!"
She said, and struck; deep enter'd in her side
The piercing steel, with reeking purple dyed:
Clogg'd in the wound the cruel weapon stands;
The spouting blood came streaming on her hands.
Her sad attendants saw the deadly stroke,
And with loud cries the sounding palace shook.
Distracted, from the fatal sight they fled,
And thro' the town the dismal rumor spread.
First from the frighted court the yell began;
Redoubled, thence from house to house it ran:
The groans of men, with shrieks, laments, and cries
Of mixing women, mount the vaulted skies.
Not less the clamor, than if- ancient Tyre,
Or the new Carthage, set by foes on fire-
The rolling ruin, with their lov'd abodes,
Involv'd the blazing temples of their gods.
Her sister hears; and, furious with despair,

She beats her breast, and rends her yellow hair,
And, calling on Eliza's name aloud,
Runs breathless to the place, and breaks the crowd.
"Was all that pomp of woe for this prepar'd;
These fires, this fun'ral pile, these altars rear'd?
Was all this train of plots contriv'd," said she,
"All only to deceive unhappy me?
Which is the worst? Didst thou in death pretend
To scorn thy sister, or delude thy friend?
Thy summon'd sister, and thy friend, had come;
One sword had serv'd us both, one common tomb:
Was I to raise the pile, the pow'rs invoke,
Not to be present at the fatal stroke?
At once thou hast destroy'd thyself and me,
Thy town, thy senate, and thy colony!
Bring water; bathe the wound; while I in death
Lay close my lips to hers, and catch the flying breath."
This said, she mounts the pile with eager haste,
And in her arms the gasping queen embrac'd;
Her temples chaf'd; and her own garments tore,
To stanch the streaming blood, and cleanse the gore.
Thrice Dido tried to raise her drooping head,
And, fainting thrice, fell grov'ling on the bed;
Thrice op'd her heavy eyes, and sought the light,
But, having found it, sicken'd at the sight,
And clos'd her lids at last in endless night.
Then Juno, grieving that she should sustain
A death so ling'ring, and so full of pain,
Sent Iris down, to free her from the strife
Of lab'ring nature, and dissolve her life.
For since she died, not doom'd by Heav'n's decree,
Or her own crime, but human casualty,
And rage of love, that plung'd her in despair,
The Sisters had not cut the topmost hair,
Which Proserpine and they can only know;
Nor made her sacred to the shades below.
Downward the various goddess took her flight,
And drew a thousand colors from the light;
Then stood above the dying lover's head,
And said: "I thus devote thee to the dead.
This off'ring to th' infernal gods I bear."
Thus while she spoke, she cut the fatal hair:
The struggling soul was loos'd, and life dissolv'd in air.

Book VIII

When Turnus had assembled all his pow'rs,
His standard planted on Laurentum's tow'rs;
When now the sprightly trumpet, from afar,
Had giv'n the signal of approaching war,
Had rous'd the neighing steeds to scour the fields,
While the fierce riders clatter'd on their shields;
Trembling with rage, the Latian youth prepare
To join th' allies, and headlong rush to war.
Fierce Ufens, and Messapus, led the crowd,

With bold Mezentius, who blasphem'd aloud.
These thro' the country took their wasteful course,
The fields to forage, and to gather force.
Then Venulus to Diomede they send,
To beg his aid Ausonia to defend,
Declare the common danger, and inform
The Grecian leader of the growing storm:
Aeneas, landed on the Latian coast,
With banish'd gods, and with a baffled host,
Yet now aspir'd to conquest of the state,
And claim'd a title from the gods and fate;
What num'rous nations in his quarrel came,
And how they spread his formidable name.
What he design'd, what mischief might arise,
If fortune favor'd his first enterprise,
Was left for him to weigh, whose equal fears,
And common interest, was involv'd in theirs.
While Turnus and th' allies thus urge the war,
The Trojan, floating in a flood of care,
Beholds the tempest which his foes prepare.
This way and that he turns his anxious mind;
Thinks, and rejects the counsels he design'd;
Explores himself in vain, in ev'ry part,
And gives no rest to his distracted heart.
So, when the sun by day, or moon by night,
Strike on the polish'd brass their trembling light,
The glitt'ring species here and there divide,
And cast their dubious beams from side to side;
Now on the walls, now on the pavement play,
And to the ceiling flash the glaring day.
'T was night; and weary nature lull'd asleep
The birds of air, and fishes of the deep,
And beasts, and mortal men. The Trojan chief
Was laid on Tiber's banks, oppress'd with grief,
And found in silent slumber late relief.
Then, thro' the shadows of the poplar wood,
Arose the father of the Roman flood;
An azure robe was o'er his body spread,
A wreath of shady reeds adorn'd his head:
Thus, manifest to sight, the god appear'd,
And with these pleasing words his sorrow cheer'd:
"Undoubted offspring of ethereal race,
O long expected in this promis'd place!
Who thro' the foes hast borne thy banish'd gods,
Restor'd them to their hearths, and old abodes;
This is thy happy home, the clime where fate
Ordains thee to restore the Trojan state.
Fear not! The war shall end in lasting peace,
And all the rage of haughty Juno cease.
And that this nightly vision may not seem
Th' effect of fancy, or an idle dream,
A sow beneath an oak shall lie along,
All white herself, and white her thirty young.
When thirty rolling years have run their race,
Thy son Ascanius, on this empty space,

Shall build a royal town, of lasting fame,
Which from this omen shall receive the name.
Time shall approve the truth. For what remains,
And how with sure success to crown thy pains,
With patience next attend. A banish'd band,
Driv'n with Evander from th' Arcadian land,
Have planted here, and plac'd on high their walls;
Their town the founder Pallanteum calls,
Deriv'd from Pallas, his great-grandsire's name:
But the fierce Latians old possession claim,
With war infesting the new colony.
These make thy friends, and on their aid rely.
To thy free passage I submit my streams.
Wake, son of Venus, from thy pleasing dreams;
And, when the setting stars are lost in day,
To Juno's pow'r thy just devotion pay;
With sacrifice the wrathful queen appease:
Her pride at length shall fall, her fury cease.
When thou return'st victorious from the war,
Perform thy vows to me with grateful care.
The god am I, whose yellow water flows
Around these fields, and fattens as it goes:
Tiber my name; among the rolling floods
Renown'd on earth, esteem'd among the gods.
This is my certain seat. In times to come,
My waves shall wash the walls of mighty Rome."
He said, and plung'd below. While yet he spoke,
His dream Aeneas and his sleep forsook.
He rose, and looking up, beheld the skies
With purple blushing, and the day arise.
Then water in his hollow palm he took
From Tiber's flood, and thus the pow'rs bespoke:
"Laurentian nymphs, by whom the streams are fed,
And Father Tiber, in thy sacred bed
Receive Aeneas, and from danger keep.
Whatever fount, whatever holy deep,
Conceals thy wat'ry stores; where'er they rise,
And, bubbling from below, salute the skies;
Thou, king of horned floods, whose plenteous urn
Suffices fatness to the fruitful corn,
For this thy kind compassion of our woes,
Shalt share my morning song and ev'ning vows.
But, O be present to thy people's aid,
And firm the gracious promise thou hast made!"
Thus having said, two galleys from his stores,
With care he chooses, mans, and fits with oars.
Now on the shore the fatal swine is found.
Wondrous to tell!- She lay along the ground:
Her well-fed offspring at her udders hung;
She white herself, and white her thirty young.
Aeneas takes the mother and her brood,
And all on Juno's altar are bestow'd.
The foll'wing night, and the succeeding day,
Propitious Tiber smooth'd his wat'ry way:
He roll'd his river back, and pois'd he stood,

A gentle swelling, and a peaceful flood.
The Trojans mount their ships; they put from shore,
Borne on the waves, and scarcely dip an oar.
Shouts from the land give omen to their course,
And the pitch'd vessels glide with easy force.
The woods and waters wonder at the gleam
Of shields, and painted ships that stem the stream.
One summer's night and one whole day they pass
Betwixt the greenwood shades, and cut the liquid glass.
The fiery sun had finish'd half his race,
Look'd back, and doubted in the middle space,
When they from far beheld the rising tow'rs,
The tops of sheds, and shepherds' lowly bow'rs,
Thin as they stood, which, then of homely clay,
Now rise in marble, from the Roman sway.
These cots (Evander's kingdom, mean and poor)
The Trojan saw, and turn'd his ships to shore.
'T was on a solemn day: th' Arcadian states,
The king and prince, without the city gates,
Then paid their off'rings in a sacred grove
To Hercules, the warrior son of Jove.
Thick clouds of rolling smoke involve the skies,
And fat of entrails on his altar fries.
But, when they saw the ships that stemm'd the flood,
And glitter'd thro' the covert of the wood,
They rose with fear, and left th' unfinish'd feast,
Till dauntless Pallas reassur'd the rest
To pay the rites. Himself without delay
A jav'lin seiz'd, and singly took his way;
Then gain'd a rising ground, and call'd from far:
"Resolve me, strangers, whence, and what you are;
Your bus'ness here; and bring you peace or war?"
High on the stern Aeneas his stand,
And held a branch of olive in his hand,
While thus he spoke: "The Phrygians' arms you see,
Expell'd from Troy, provok'd in Italy
By Latian foes, with war unjustly made;
At first affianc'd, and at last betray'd.
This message bear: 'The Trojans and their chief
Bring holy peace, and beg the king's relief.'
Struck with so great a name, and all on fire,
The youth replies: "Whatever you require,
Your fame exacts. Upon our shores descend.
A welcome guest, and, what you wish, a friend."
He said, and, downward hasting to the strand,
Embrac'd the stranger prince, and join'd his hand.
Conducted to the grove, Aeneas broke
The silence first, and thus the king bespoke:
"Best of the Greeks, to whom, by fate's command,
I bear these peaceful branches in my hand,
Undaunted I approach you, tho' I know
Your birth is Grecian, and your land my foe;
From Atreus tho' your ancient lineage came,
And both the brother kings your kindred claim;
Yet, my self-conscious worth, your high renown,

Your virtue, thro' the neighb'ring nations blown,
Our fathers' mingled blood, Apollo's voice,
Have led me hither, less by need than choice.
Our founder Dardanus, as fame has sung,
And Greeks acknowledge, from Electra sprung:
Electra from the loins of Atlas came;
Atlas, whose head sustains the starry frame.
Your sire is Mercury, whom long before
On cold Cyllene's top fair Maia bore.
Maia the fair, on fame if we rely,
Was Atlas' daughter, who sustains the sky.
Thus from one common source our streams divide;
Ours is the Trojan, yours th' Areadian side.
Rais'd by these hopes, I sent no news before,
Nor ask'd your leave, nor did your faith implore;
But come, without a pledge, my own ambassador.
The same Rutulians, who with arms pursue
The Trojan race, are equal foes to you.
Our host expell'd, what farther force can stay
The victor troops from universal sway?
Then will they stretch their pow'r athwart the land,
And either sea from side to side command.
Receive our offer'd faith, and give us thine;
Ours is a gen'rous and experienc'd line:
We want not hearts nor bodies for the war;
In council cautious, and in fields we dare."
He said; and while spoke, with piercing eyes
Evander view'd the man with vast surprise,
Pleas'd with his action, ravish'd with his face:
Then answer'd briefly, with a royal grace:
"O valiant leader of the Trojan line,
In whom the features of thy father shine,
How I recall Anchises! how I see
His motions, mien, and all my friend, in thee!
Long tho' it be, 't is fresh within my mind,
When Priam to his sister's court design'd
A welcome visit, with a friendly stay,
And thro' th' Arcadian kingdom took his way.
Then, past a boy, the callow down began
To shade my chin, and call me first a man.
I saw the shining train with vast delight,
And Priam's goodly person pleas'd my sight:
But great Anchises, far above the rest,
With awful wonder fir'd my youthful breast.
I long'd to join in friendship's holy bands
Our mutual hearts, and plight our mutual hands.
I first accosted him: I sued, I sought,
And, with a loving force, to Pheneus brought.
He gave me, when at length constrain'd to go,
A Lycian quiver and a Gnossian bow,
A vest embroider'd, glorious to behold,
And two rich bridles, with their bits of gold,
Which my son's coursers in obedience hold.
The league you ask, I offer, as your right;
And, when to-morrow's sun reveals the light,

With swift supplies you shall be sent away.
Now celebrate with us this solemn day,
Whose holy rites admit no long delay.
Honor our annual feast; and take your seat,
With friendly welcome, at a homely treat."
Thus having said, the bowls (remov'd for fear)
The youths replac'd, and soon restor'd the cheer.
On sods of turf he set the soldiers round:
A maple throne, rais'd higher from the ground,
Receiv'd the Trojan chief; and, o'er the bed,
A lion's shaggy hide for ornament they spread.
The loaves were serv'd in canisters; the wine
In bowls; the priest renew'd the rites divine:
Broil'd entrails are their food, and beef's continued chine.
But when the rage of hunger was repress'd,
Thus spoke Evander to his royal guest:
"These rites, these altars, and this feast, O king,
From no vain fears or superstition spring,
Or blind devotion, or from blinder chance,
Or heady zeal, or brutal ignorance;
But, sav'd from danger, with a grateful sense,
The labors of a god we recompense.
See, from afar, yon rock that mates the sky,
About whose feet such heaps of rubbish lie;
Such indigested ruin; bleak and bare,
How desart now it stands, expos'd in air!
'T was once a robber's den, inclos'd around
With living stone, and deep beneath the ground.
The monster Cacus, more than half a beast,
This hold, impervious to the sun, possess'd.
The pavement ever foul with human gore;
Heads, and their mangled members, hung the door.
Vulcan this plague begot; and, like his sire,
Black clouds he belch'd, and flakes of livid fire.
Time, long expected, eas'd us of our load,
And brought the needful presence of a god.
Th' avenging force of Hercules, from Spain,
Arriv'd in triumph, from Geryon slain:
Thrice liv'd the giant, and thrice liv'd in vain.
His prize, the lowing herds, Alcides drove
Near Tiber's bank, to graze the shady grove.
Allur'd with hope of plunder, and intent
By force to rob, by fraud to circumvent,
The brutal Cacus, as by chance they stray'd,
Four oxen thence, and four fair kine convey'd;
And, lest the printed footsteps might be seen,
He dragg'd 'em backwards to his rocky den.
The tracks averse a lying notice gave,
And led the searcher backward from the cave.
"Meantime the herdsman hero shifts his place,
To find fresh pasture and untrodden grass.
The beasts, who miss'd their mates, fill'd all around
With bellowings, and the rocks restor'd the sound.
One heifer, who had heard her love complain,
Roar'd from the cave, and made the project vain.

Alcides found the fraud; with rage he shook,
And toss'd about his head his knotted oak.
Swift as the winds, or Scythian arrows' flight,
He clomb, with eager haste, th' aerial height.
Then first we saw the monster mend his pace;
Fear his eyes, and paleness in his face,
Confess'd the god's approach. Trembling he springs,
As terror had increas'd his feet with wings;
Nor stay'd for stairs; but down the depth he threw
His body, on his back the door he drew
(The door, a rib of living rock; with pains
His father hew'd it out, and bound with iron chains):
He broke the heavy links, the mountain clos'd,
And bars and levers to his foe oppos'd.
The wretch had hardly made his dungeon fast;
The fierce avenger came with bounding haste;
Survey'd the mouth of the forbidden hold,
And here and there his raging eyes he roll'd.
He gnash'd his teeth; and thrice he compass'd round
With winged speed the circuit of the ground.
Thrice at the cavern's mouth he pull'd in vain,
And, panting, thrice desisted from his pain.
A pointed flinty rock, all bare and black,
Grew gibbous from behind the mountain's back;
Owls, ravens, all ill omens of the night,
Here built their nests, and hither wing'd their flight.
The leaning head hung threat'ning o'er the flood,
And nodded to the left. The hero stood
Adverse, with planted feet, and, from the right,
Tugg'd at the solid stone with all his might.
Thus heav'd, the fix'd foundations of the rock
Gave way; heav'n echo'd at the rattling shock.
Tumbling, it chok'd the flood: on either side
The banks leap backward, and the streams divide;
The sky shrunk upward with unusual dread,
And trembling Tiber div'd beneath his bed.
The court of Cacus stands reveal'd to sight;
The cavern glares with new-admitted light.
So the pent vapors, with a rumbling sound,
Heave from below, and rend the hollow ground;
A sounding flaw succeeds; and, from on high,
The gods with hate beheld the nether sky:
The ghosts repine at violated night,
And curse th' invading sun, and sicken at the sight.
The graceless monster, caught in open day,
Inclos'd, and in despair to fly away,
Howls horrible from underneath, and fills
His hollow palace with unmanly yells.
The hero stands above, and from afar
Plies him with darts, and stones, and distant war.
He, from his nostrils huge mouth, expires
Black clouds of smoke, amidst his father's fires,
Gath'ring, with each repeated blast, the night,
To make uncertain aim, and erring sight.
The wrathful god then plunges from above,

And, where in thickest waves the sparkles drove,
There lights; and wades thro' fumes, and gropes his way,
Half sing'd, half stifled, till he grasps his prey.
The monster, spewing fruitless flames, he found;
He squeez'd his throat; he writh'd his neck around,
And in a knot his crippled members bound;
Then from their sockets tore his burning eyes:
Roll'd on a heap, the breathless robber lies.
The doors, unbarr'd, receive the rushing day,
And thoro' lights disclose the ravish'd prey.
The bulls, redeem'd, breathe open air again.
Next, by the feet, they drag him from his den.
The wond'ring neighborhood, with glad surprise,
Behold his shagged breast, his giant size,
His mouth that flames no more, and his extinguish'd eyes.
From that auspicious day, with rites divine,
We worship at the hero's holy shrine.
Potitius first ordain'd these annual vows:
As priests, were added the Pinarian house,
Who rais'd this altar in the sacred shade,
Where honors, ever due, for ever shall be paid.
For these deserts, and this high virtue shown,
Ye warlike youths, your heads with garlands crown:
Fill high the goblets with a sparkling flood,
And with deep draughts invoke our common god."
This said, a double wreath Evander twin'd,
And poplars black and white his temples bind.
Then brims his ample bowl. With like design
The rest invoke the gods, with sprinkled wine.
Meantime the sun descended from the skies,
And the bright evening star began to rise.
And now the priests, Potitius at their head,
In skins of beasts involv'd, the long procession led;
Held high the flaming tapers in their hands,
As custom had prescrib'd their holy bands;
Then with a second course the tables load,
And with full chargers offer to the god.
The Salii sing, and cense his altars round
With Saban smoke, their heads with poplar bound-
One choir of old, another of the young,
To dance, and bear the burthen of the song.
The lay records the labors, and the praise,
And all th' immortal acts of Hercules:
First, how the mighty babe, when swath'd in bands,
The serpents strangled with his infant hands;
Then, as in years and matchless force he grew,
Th' Oechalian walls, and Trojan, overthrew.
Besides, a thousand hazards they relate,
Procur'd by Juno's and Eurystheus' hate:
"Thy hands, unconquer'd hero, could subdue
The cloud-born Centaurs, and the monster crew:
Nor thy resistless arm the bull withstood,
Nor he, the roaring terror of the wood.
The triple porter of the Stygian seat,
With lolling tongue, lay fawning at thy feet,

And, seiz'd with fear, forgot his mangled meat.
Th' infernal waters trembled at thy sight;
Thee, god, no face of danger could affright;
Not huge Typhoeus, nor th' unnumber'd snake,
Increas'd with hissing heads, in Lerna's lake.
Hail, Jove's undoubted son! an added grace
To heav'n and the great author of thy race!
Receive the grateful off'rings which we pay,
And smile propitious on thy solemn day!"
In numbers thus they sung; above the rest,
The den and death of Cacus crown the feast.
The woods to hollow vales convey the sound,
The vales to hills, and hills the notes rebound.
The rites perform'd, the cheerful train retire.
Betwixt young Pallas and his aged sire,
The Trojan pass'd, the city to survey,
And pleasing talk beguil'd the tedious way.
The stranger cast around his curious eyes,
New objects viewing still, with new surprise;
With greedy joy enquires of various things,
And acts and monuments of ancient kings.
Then thus the founder of the Roman tow'rs:
"These woods were first the seat of sylvan pow'rs,
Of Nymphs and Fauns, and salvage men, who took
Their birth from trunks of trees and stubborn oak.
Nor laws they knew, nor manners, nor the care
Of lab'ring oxen, or the shining share,
Nor arts of gain, nor what they gain'd to spare.
Their exercise the chase; the running flood
Supplied their thirst, the trees supplied their food.
Then Saturn came, who fled the pow'r of Jove,
Robb'd of his realms, and banish'd from above.
The men, dispers'd on hills, to towns he brought,
And laws ordain'd, and civil customs taught,
And Latium call'd the land where safe he lay
From his unduteous son, and his usurping sway.
With his mild empire, peace and plenty came;
And hence the golden times deriv'd their name.
A more degenerate and discolor'd age
Succeeded this, with avarice and rage.
Th' Ausonians then, and bold Sicanians came;
And Saturn's empire often chang'd the name.
Then kings, gigantic Tybris, and the rest,
With arbitrary sway the land oppress'd:
For Tiber's flood was Albula before,
Till, from the tyrant's fate, his name it bore.
I last arriv'd, driv'n from my native home
By fortune's pow'r, and fate's resistless doom.
Long toss'd on seas, I sought this happy land,
Warn'd by my mother nymph, and call'd by Heav'n's command."
Thus, walking on, he spoke, and shew'd the gate,
Since call'd Carmental by the Roman state;
Where stood an altar, sacred to the name
Of old Carmenta, the prophetic dame,
Who to her son foretold th' Aenean race,

Sublime in fame, and Rome's imperial place:
Then shews the forest, which, in after times,
Fierce Romulus for perpetrated crimes
A sacred refuge made; with this, the shrine
Where Pan below the rock had rites divine:
Then tells of Argus' death, his murder'd guest,
Whose grave and tomb his innocence attest.
Thence, to the steep Tarpeian rock he leads;
Now roof'd with gold, then thatch'd with homely reeds.
A reverent fear (such superstition reigns
Among the rude) ev'n then possess'd the swains.
Some god, they knew- what god, they could not tell-
Did there amidst the sacred horror dwell.
Th' Arcadians thought him Jove; and said they saw
The mighty Thund'rer with majestic awe,
Who took his shield, and dealt his bolts around,
And scatter'd tempests on the teeming ground.
Then saw two heaps of ruins, (once they stood
Two stately towns, on either side the flood,)
Saturnia's and Janicula's remains;
And either place the founder's name retains.
Discoursing thus together, they resort
Where poor Evander kept his country court.
They view'd the ground of Rome's litigious hall;
(Once oxen low'd, where now the lawyers bawl;)
Then, stooping, thro' the narrow gate they press'd,
When thus the king bespoke his Trojan guest:
"Mean as it is, this palace, and this door,
Receiv'd Alcides, then a conqueror.
Dare to be poor; accept our homely food,
Which feasted him, and emulate a god."
Then underneath a lowly roof he led
The weary prince, and laid him on a bed;
The stuffing leaves, with hides of bears o'erspread.
Now Night had shed her silver dews around,
And with her sable wings embrac'd the ground,
When love's fair goddess, anxious for her son,
(New tumults rising, and new wars begun,)
Couch'd with her husband in his golden bed,
With these alluring words invokes his aid;
And, that her pleasing speech his mind may move,
Inspires each accent with the charms of love:
"While cruel fate conspir'd with Grecian pow'rs,
To level with the ground the Trojan tow'rs,
I ask'd not aid th' unhappy to restore,
Nor did the succor of thy skill implore;
Nor urg'd the labors of my lord in vain,
A sinking empire longer to sustain,
Tho'much I ow'd to Priam's house, and more
The dangers of Aeneas did deplore.
But now, by Jove's command, and fate's decree,
His race is doom'd to reign in Italy:
With humble suit I beg thy needful art,
O still propitious pow'r, that rules my heart!
A mother kneels a suppliant for her son.

By Thetis and Aurora thou wert won
To forge impenetrable shields, and grace
With fated arms a less illustrious race.
Behold, what haughty nations are combin'd
Against the relics of the Phrygian kind,
With fire and sword my people to destroy,
And conquer Venus twice, in conqu'ring Troy."
She said; and straight her arms, of snowy hue,
About her unresolving husband threw.
Her soft embraces soon infuse desire;
His bones and marrow sudden warmth inspire;
And all the godhead feels the wonted fire.
Not half so swift the rattling thunder flies,
Or forky lightnings flash along the skies.
The goddess, proud of her successful wiles,
And conscious of her form, in secret smiles.
Then thus the pow'r, obnoxious to her charms,
Panting, and half dissolving in her arms:
"Why seek you reasons for a cause so just,
Or your own beauties or my love distrust?
Long since, had you requir'd my helpful hand,
Th' artificer and art you might command,
To labor arms for Troy: nor Jove, nor fate,
Confin'd their empire to so short a date.
And, if you now desire new wars to wage,
My skill I promise, and my pains engage.
Whatever melting metals can conspire,
Or breathing bellows, or the forming fire,
Is freely yours: your anxious fears remove,
And think no task is difficult to love."
Trembling he spoke; and, eager of her charms,
He snatch'd the willing goddess to his arms;
Till in her lap infus'd, he lay possess'd
Of full desire, and sunk to pleasing rest.
Now when the Night her middle race had rode,
And his first slumber had refresh'd the god-
The time when early housewives leave the bed;
When living embers on the hearth they spread,
Supply the lamp, and call the maids to rise-
With yawning mouths, and with half-open'd eyes,
They ply the distaff by the winking light,
And to their daily labor add the night:
Thus frugally they earn their children's bread,
And uncorrupted keep the nuptial bed-
Not less concern'd, nor at a later hour,
Rose from his downy couch the forging pow'r.
Sacred to Vulcan's name, an isle there lay,
Betwixt Sicilia's coasts and Lipare,
Rais'd high on smoking rocks; and, deep below,
In hollow caves the fires of Aetna glow.
The Cyclops here their heavy hammers deal;
Loud strokes, and hissings of tormented steel,
Are heard around; the boiling waters roar,
And smoky flames thro' fuming tunnels soar.
Hether the Father of the Fire, by night,

Thro' the brown air precipitates his flight.
On their eternal anvils here he found
The brethren beating, and the blows go round.
A load of pointless thunder now there lies
Before their hands, to ripen for the skies:
These darts, for angry Jove, they daily cast;
Consum'd on mortals with prodigious waste.
Three rays of writhen rain, of fire three more,
Of winged southern winds and cloudy store
As many parts, the dreadful mixture frame;
And fears are added, and avenging flame.
Inferior ministers, for Mars, repair
His broken axletrees and blunted war,
And send him forth again with furbish'd arms,
To wake the lazy war with trumpets' loud alarms.
The rest refresh the scaly snakes that fold
The shield of Pallas, and renew their gold.
Full on the crest the Gorgon's head they place,
With eyes that roll in death, and with distorted face.
"My sons," said Vulcan, "set your tasks aside;
Your strength and master-skill must now be tried.
Arms for a hero forge; arms that require
Your force, your speed, and all your forming fire."
He said. They set their former work aside,
And their new toils with eager haste divide.
A flood of molten silver, brass, and gold,
And deadly steel, in the large furnace roll'd;
Of this, their artful hands a shield prepare,
Alone sufficient to sustain the war.
Sev'n orbs within a spacious round they close:
One stirs the fire, and one the bellows blows.
The hissing steel is in the smithy drown'd;
The grot with beaten anvils groans around.
By turns their arms advance, in equal time;
By turns their hands descend, and hammers chime.
They turn the glowing mass with crooked tongs;
The fiery work proceeds, with rustic songs.
While, at the Lemnian god's command, they urge
Their labors thus, and ply th' Aeolian forge,
The cheerful morn salutes Evander's eyes,
And songs of chirping birds invite to rise.
He leaves his lowly bed: his buskins meet
Above his ankles; sandals sheathe his feet:
He sets his trusty sword upon his side,
And o'er his shoulder throws a panther's hide.
Two menial dogs before their master press'd.
Thus clad, and guarded thus, he seeks his kingly guest.
Mindful of promis'd aid, he mends his pace,
But meets Aeneas in the middle space.
Young Pallas did his father's steps attend,
And true Achates waited on his friend.
They join their hands; a secret seat they choose;
Th' Arcadian first their former talk renews:
"Undaunted prince, I never can believe
The Trojan empire lost, while you survive.

Command th' assistance of a faithful friend;
But feeble are the succors I can send.
Our narrow kingdom here the Tiber bounds;
That other side the Latian state surrounds,
Insults our walls, and wastes our fruitful grounds.
But mighty nations I prepare, to join
Their arms with yours, and aid your just design.
You come, as by your better genius sent,
And fortune seems to favor your intent.
Not far from hence there stands a hilly town,
Of ancient building, and of high renown,
Torn from the Tuscans by the Lydian race,
Who gave the name of Caere to the place,
Once Agyllina call'd. It flourish'd long,
In pride of wealth and warlike people strong,
Till curs'd Mezentius, in a fatal hour,
Assum'd the crown, with arbitrary pow'r.
What words can paint those execrable times,
The subjects' suff'rings, and the tyrant's crimes!
That blood, those murthers, O ye gods, replace
On his own head, and on his impious race!
The living and the dead at his command
Were coupled, face to face, and hand to hand,
Till, chok'd with stench, in loath'd embraces tied,
The ling'ring wretches pin'd away and died.
Thus plung'd in ills, and meditating more-
The people's patience, tir'd, no longer bore
The raging monster; but with arms beset
His house, and vengeance and destruction threat.
They fire his palace: while the flame ascends,
They force his guards, and execute his friends.
He cleaves the crowd, and, favor'd by the night,
To Turnus' friendly court directs his flight.
By just revenge the Tuscans set on fire,
With arms, their king to punishment require:
Their num'rous troops, now muster'd on the strand,
My counsel shall submit to your command.
Their navy swarms upon the coasts; they cry
To hoist their anchors, but the gods deny.
An ancient augur, skill'd in future fate,
With these foreboding words restrains their hate:
'Ye brave in arms, ye Lydian blood, the flow'r
Of Tuscan youth, and choice of all their pow'r,
Whom just revenge against Mezentius arms,
To seek your tyrant's death by lawful arms;
Know this: no native of our land may lead
This pow'rful people; seek a foreign head.'
Aw'd with these words, in camps they still abide,
And wait with longing looks their promis'd guide.
Tarchon, the Tuscan chief, to me has sent
Their crown, and ev'ry regal ornament:
The people join their own with his desire;
And all my conduct, as their king, require.
But the chill blood that creeps within my veins,
And age, and listless limbs unfit for pains,

And a soul conscious of its own decay,
Have forc'd me to refuse imperial sway.
My Pallas were more fit to mount the throne,
And should, but he's a Sabine mother's son,
And half a native; but, in you, combine
A manly vigor, and a foreign line.
Where Fate and smiling Fortune shew the way,
Pursue the ready path to sov'reign sway.
The staff of my declining days, my son,
Shall make your good or ill success his own;
In fighting fields from you shall learn to dare,
And serve the hard apprenticeship of war;
Your matchless courage and your conduct view,
And early shall begin t' admire and copy you.
Besides, two hundred horse he shall command;
Tho' few, a warlike and well-chosen band.
These in my name are listed; and my son
As many more has added in his own."
Scarce had he said; Achates and his guest,
With downcast eyes, their silent grief express'd;
Who, short of succors, and in deep despair,
Shook at the dismal prospect of the war.
But his bright mother, from a breaking cloud,
To cheer her issue, thunder'd thrice aloud;
Thrice forky lightning flash'd along the sky,
And Tyrrhene trumpets thrice were heard on high.
Then, gazing up, repeated peals they hear;
And, in a heav'n serene, refulgent arms appear:
Redd'ning the skies, and glitt'ring all around,
The temper'd metals clash, and yield a silver sound.
The rest stood trembling, struck with awe divine;
Aeneas only, conscious to the sign,
Presag'd th' event, and joyful view'd, above,
Th' accomplish'd promise of the Queen of Love.
Then, to th' Arcadian king: "This prodigy
(Dismiss your fear) belongs alone to me.
Heav'n calls me to the war: th' expected sign
Is giv'n of promis'd aid, and arms divine.
My goddess mother, whose indulgent care
Foresaw the dangers of the growing war,
This omen gave, when bright Vulcanian arms,
Fated from force of steel by Stygian charms,
Suspended, shone on high: she then foreshow'd
Approaching fights, and fields to float in blood.
Turnus shall dearly pay for faith forsworn;
And corps, and swords, and shields, on Tiber borne,
Shall choke his flood: now sound the loud alarms;
And, Latian troops, prepare your perjur'd arms."
He said, and, rising from his homely throne,
The solemn rites of Hercules begun,
And on his altars wak'd the sleeping fires;
Then cheerful to his household gods retires;
There offers chosen sheep. Th' Arcadian king
And Trojan youth the same oblations bring.
Next, of his men and ships he makes review;

Draws out the best and ablest of the crew.
Down with the falling stream the refuse run,
To raise with joyful news his drooping son.
Steeds are prepar'd to mount the Trojan band,
Who wait their leader to the Tyrrhene land.
A sprightly courser, fairer than the rest,
The king himself presents his royal guest:
A lion's hide his back and limbs infold,
Precious with studded work, and paws of gold.
Fame thro' the little city spreads aloud
Th' intended march, amid the fearful crowd:
The matrons beat their breasts, dissolve in tears,
And double their devotion in their fears.
The war at hand appears with more affright,
And rises ev'ry moment to the sight.
Then old Evander, with a close embrace,
Strain'd his departing friend; and tears o'erflow his face.
"Would Heav'n," said he, "my strength and youth recall,
Such as I was beneath Praeneste's wall;
Then when I made the foremost foes retire,
And set whole heaps of conquer'd shields on fire;
When Herilus in single fight I slew,
Whom with three lives Feronia did endue;
And thrice I sent him to the Stygian shore,
Till the last ebbing soul return'd no more-
Such if I stood renew'd, not these alarms,
Nor death, should rend me from my Pallas' arms;
Nor proud Mezentius, thus unpunish'd, boast
His rapes and murthers on the Tuscan coast.
Ye gods, and mighty Jove, in pity bring
Relief, and hear a father and a king!
If fate and you reserve these eyes, to see
My son return with peace and victory;
If the lov'd boy shall bless his father's sight;
If we shall meet again with more delight;
Then draw my life in length; let me sustain,
In hopes of his embrace, the worst of pain.
But if your hard decrees- which, O! I dread-
Have doom'd to death his undeserving head;
This, O this very moment, let me die!
While hopes and fears in equal balance lie;
While, yet possess'd of all his youthful charms,
I strain him close within these aged arms;
Before that fatal news my soul shall wound!"
He said, and, swooning, sunk upon the ground.
His servants bore him off, and softly laid
His languish'd limbs upon his homely bed.
The horsemen march; the gates are open'd wide;
Aeneas at their head, Achates by his side.
Next these, the Trojan leaders rode along;
Last follows in the rear th' Arcadian throng.
Young Pallas shone conspicuous o'er the rest;
Gilded his arms, embroider'd was his vest.
So, from the seas, exerts his radiant head
The star by whom the lights of heav'n are led;

Shakes from his rosy locks the pearly dews,
Dispels the darkness, and the day renews.
The trembling wives the walls and turrets crowd,
And follow, with their eyes, the dusty cloud,
Which winds disperse by fits, and shew from far
The blaze of arms, and shields, and shining war.
The troops, drawn up in beautiful array,
O'er heathy plains pursue the ready way.
Repeated peals of shouts are heard around;
The neighing coursers answer to the sound,
And shake with horny hoofs the solid ground.
A greenwood shade, for long religion known,
Stands by the streams that wash the Tuscan town,
Incompass'd round with gloomy hills above,
Which add a holy horror to the grove.
The first inhabitants of Grecian blood,
That sacred forest to Silvanus vow'd,
The guardian of their flocks and fields; and pay
Their due devotions on his annual day.
Not far from hence, along the river's side,
In tents secure, the Tuscan troops abide,
By Tarchon led. Now, from a rising ground,
Aeneas cast his wond'ring eyes around,
And all the Tyrrhene army had in sight,
Stretch'd on the spacious plain from left to right.
Thether his warlike train the Trojan led,
Refresh'd his men, and wearied horses fed.
Meantime the mother goddess, crown'd with charms,
Breaks thro' the clouds, and brings the fated arms.
Within a winding vale she finds her son,
On the cool river's banks, retir'd alone.
She shews her heav'nly form without disguise,
And gives herself to his desiring eyes.
"Behold," she said, "perform'd in ev'ry part,
My promise made, and Vulcan's labor'd art.
Now seek, secure, the Latian enemy,
And haughty Turnus to the field defy."
She said; and, having first her son embrac'd,
The radiant arms beneath an oak she plac'd,
Proud of the gift, he roll'd his greedy sight
Around the work, and gaz'd with vast delight.
He lifts, he turns, he poises, and admires
The crested helm, that vomits radiant fires:
His hands the fatal sword and corslet hold,
One keen with temper'd steel, one stiff with gold:
Both ample, flaming both, and beamy bright;
So shines a cloud, when edg'd with adverse light.
He shakes the pointed spear, and longs to try
The plated cuishes on his manly thigh;
But most admires the shield's mysterious mold,
And Roman triumphs rising on the gold:
For these, emboss'd, the heav'nly smith had wrought
(Not in the rolls of future fate untaught)
The wars in order, and the race divine
Of warriors issuing from the Julian line.

The cave of Mars was dress'd with mossy greens:
There, by the wolf, were laid the martial twins.
Intrepid on her swelling dugs they hung;
The foster dam loll'd out her fawning tongue:
They suck'd secure, while, bending back her head,
She lick'd their tender limbs, and form'd them as they fed.
Not far from thence new Rome appears, with games
Projected for the rape of Sabine dames.
The pit resounds with shrieks; a war succeeds,
For breach of public faith, and unexampled deeds.
Here for revenge the Sabine troops contend;
The Romans there with arms the prey defend.
Wearied with tedious war, at length they cease;
And both the kings and kingdoms plight the peace.
The friendly chiefs before Jove's altar stand,
Both arm'd, with each a charger in his hand:
A fatted sow for sacrifice is led,
With imprecations on the perjur'd head.
Near this, the traitor Metius, stretch'd between
Four fiery steeds, is dragg'd along the green,
By Tullus' doom: the brambles drink his blood,
And his torn limbs are left the vulture's food.
There, Porsena to Rome proud Tarquin brings,
And would by force restore the banish'd kings.
One tyrant for his fellow-tyrant fights;
The Roman youth assert their native rights.
Before the town the Tuscan army lies,
To win by famine, or by fraud surprise.
Their king, half-threat'ning, half-disdaining stood,
While Cocles broke the bridge, and stemm'd the flood.
The captive maids there tempt the raging tide,
Scap'd from their chains, with Cloelia for their guide.
High on a rock heroic Manlius stood,
To guard the temple, and the temple's god.
Then Rome was poor; and there you might behold
The palace thatch'd with straw, now roof'd with gold.
The silver goose before the shining gate
There flew, and, by her cackle, sav'd the state.
She told the Gauls' approach; th' approaching Gauls,
Obscure in night, ascend, and seize the walls.
The gold dissembled well their yellow hair,
And golden chains on their white necks they wear.
Gold are their vests; long Alpine spears they wield,
And their left arm sustains a length of shield.
Hard by, the leaping Salian priests advance;
And naked thro' the streets the mad Luperci dance,
In caps of wool; the targets dropp'd from heav'n.
Here modest matrons, in soft litters driv'n,
To pay their vows in solemn pomp appear,
And odorous gums in their chaste hands they bear.
Far hence remov'd, the Stygian seats are seen;
Pains of the damn'd, and punish'd Catiline
Hung on a rock- the traitor; and, around,
The Furies hissing from the nether ground.
Apart from these, the happy souls he draws,

And Cato's holy ghost dispensing laws.
Betwixt the quarters flows a golden sea;
But foaming surges there in silver play.
The dancing dolphins with their tails divide
The glitt'ring waves, and cut the precious tide.
Amid the main, two mighty fleets engage
Their brazen beaks, oppos'd with equal rage.
Actium surveys the well-disputed prize;
Leucate's wat'ry plain with foamy billows fries.
Young Caesar, on the stern, in armor bright,
Here leads the Romans and their gods to fight:
His beamy temples shoot their flames afar,
And o'er his head is hung the Julian star.
Agrippa seconds him, with prosp'rous gales,
And, with propitious gods, his foes assails:
A naval crown, that binds his manly brows,
The happy fortune of the fight foreshows.
Rang'd on the line oppos'd, Antonius brings
Barbarian aids, and troops of Eastern kings;
Th' Arabians near, and Bactrians from afar,
Of tongues discordant, and a mingled war:
And, rich in gaudy robes, amidst the strife,
His ill fate follows him- th' Egyptian wife.
Moving they fight; with oars and forky prows
The froth is gather'd, and the water glows.
It seems, as if the Cyclades again
Were rooted up, and justled in the main;
Or floating mountains floating mountains meet;
Such is the fierce encounter of the fleet.
Fireballs are thrown, and pointed jav'lins fly;
The fields of Neptune take a purple dye.
The queen herself, amidst the loud alarms,
With cymbals toss'd her fainting soldiers warms-
Fool as she was! who had not yet divin'd
Her cruel fate, nor saw the snakes behind.
Her country gods, the monsters of the sky,
Great Neptune, Pallas, and Love's Queen defy:
The dog Anubis barks, but barks in vain,
Nor longer dares oppose th' ethereal train.
Mars in the middle of the shining shield
Is grav'd, and strides along the liquid field.
The Dirae souse from heav'n with swift descent;
And Discord, dyed in blood, with garments rent,
Divides the prease: her steps Bellona treads,
And shakes her iron rod above their heads.
This seen, Apollo, from his Actian height,
Pours down his arrows; at whose winged flight
The trembling Indians and Egyptians yield,
And soft Sabaeans quit the wat'ry field.
The fatal mistress hoists her silken sails,
And, shrinking from the fight, invokes the gales.
Aghast she looks, and heaves her breast for breath,
Panting, and pale with fear of future death.
The god had figur'd her as driv'n along
By winds and waves, and scudding thro' the throng.

Just opposite, sad Nilus opens wide
His arms and ample bosom to the tide,
And spreads his mantle o'er the winding coast,
In which he wraps his queen, and hides the flying host.
The victor to the gods his thanks express'd,
And Rome, triumphant, with his presence bless'd.
Three hundred temples in the town he plac'd;
With spoils and altars ev'ry temple grac'd.
Three shining nights, and three succeeding days,
The fields resound with shouts, the streets with praise,
The domes with songs, the theaters with plays.
All altars flame: before each altar lies,
Drench'd in his gore, the destin'd sacrifice.
Great Caesar sits sublime upon his throne,
Before Apollo's porch of Parian stone;
Accepts the presents vow'd for victory,
And hangs the monumental crowns on high.
Vast crowds of vanquish'd nations march along,
Various in arms, in habit, and in tongue.
Here, Mulciber assigns the proper place
For Carians, and th' ungirt Numidian race;
Then ranks the Thracians in the second row,
With Scythians, expert in the dart and bow.
And here the tam'd Euphrates humbly glides,
And there the Rhine submits her swelling tides,
And proud Araxes, whom no bridge could bind;
The Danes' unconquer'd offspring march behind,
And Morini, the last of humankind.
These figures, on the shield divinely wrought,
By Vulcan labor'd, and by Venus brought,
With joy and wonder fill the hero's thought.
Unknown the names, he yet admires the grace,
And bears aloft the fame and fortune of his race.

Book XII

When Turnus saw the Latins leave the field,
Their armies broken, and their courage quell'd,
Himself become the mark of public spite,
His honor question'd for the promis'd fight;
The more he was with vulgar hate oppress'd,
The more his fury boil'd within his breast:
He rous'd his vigor for the last debate,
And rais'd his haughty soul to meet his fate.
As, when the swains the Libyan lion chase,
He makes a sour retreat, nor mends his pace;
But, if the pointed jav'lin pierce his side,
The lordly beast returns with double pride:
He wrenches out the steel, he roars for pain;
His sides he lashes, and erects his mane:
So Turnus fares; his eyeballs flash with fire,
Thro' his wide nostrils clouds of smoke expire.
Trembling with rage, around the court he ran,
At length approach'd the king, and thus began:
"No more excuses or delays: I stand

In arms prepar'd to combat, hand to hand,
This base deserter of his native land.
The Trojan, by his word, is bound to take
The same conditions which himself did make.
Renew the truce; the solemn rites prepare,
And to my single virtue trust the war.
The Latians unconcern'd shall see the fight;
This arm unaided shall assert your right:
Then, if my prostrate body press the plain,
To him the crown and beauteous bride remain."
To whom the king sedately thus replied:
"Brave youth, the more your valor has been tried,
The more becomes it us, with due respect,
To weigh the chance of war, which you neglect.
You want not wealth, or a successive throne,
Or cities which your arms have made your own:
My towns and treasures are at your command,
And stor'd with blooming beauties is my land;
Laurentum more than one Lavinia sees,
Unmarried, fair, of noble families.
Now let me speak, and you with patience hear,
Things which perhaps may grate a lover's ear,
But sound advice, proceeding from a heart
Sincerely yours, and free from fraudful art.
The gods, by signs, have manifestly shown,
No prince Italian born should heir my throne:
Oft have our augurs, in prediction skill'd,
And oft our priests, foreign son reveal'd.
Yet, won by worth that cannot be withstood,
Brib'd by my kindness to my kindred blood,
Urg'd by my wife, who would not be denied,
I promis'd my Lavinia for your bride:
Her from her plighted lord by force I took;
All ties of treaties, and of honor, broke:
On your account I wag'd an impious war-
With what success, 't is needless to declare;
I and my subjects feel, and you have had your share.
Twice vanquish'd while in bloody fields we strive,
Scarce in our walls we keep our hopes alive:
The rolling flood runs warm with human gore;
The bones of Latians blanch the neighb'ring shore.
Why put I not an end to this debate,
Still unresolv'd, and still a slave to fate?
If Turnus' death a lasting peace can give,
Why should I not procure it whilst you live?
Should I to doubtful arms your youth betray,
What would my kinsmen the Rutulians say?
And, should you fall in fight, (which Heav'n defend!)
How curse the cause which hasten'd to his end
The daughter's lover and the father's friend?
Weigh in your mind the various chance of war;
Pity your parent's age, and ease his care."
Such balmy words he pour'd, but all in vain:
The proffer'd med'cine but provok'd the pain.
The wrathful youth, disdaining the relief,

With intermitting sobs thus vents his grief:
"The care, O best of fathers, which you take
For my concerns, at my desire forsake.
Permit me not to languish out my days,
But make the best exchange of life for praise.
This arm, this lance, can well dispute the prize;
And the blood follows, where the weapon flies.
His goddess mother is not near, to shroud
The flying coward with an empty cloud."
But now the queen, who fear'd for Turnus' life,
And loath'd the hard conditions of the strife,
Held him by force; and, dying in his death,
In these sad accents gave her sorrow breath:
"O Turnus, I adjure thee by these tears,
And whate'er price Amata's honor bears
Within thy breast, since thou art all my hope,
My sickly mind's repose, my sinking age's prop;
Since on the safety of thy life alone
Depends Latinus, and the Latian throne:
Refuse me not this one, this only pray'r,
To waive the combat, and pursue the war.
Whatever chance attends this fatal strife,
Think it includes, in thine, Amata's life.
I cannot live a slave, or see my throne
Usurp'd by strangers or a Trojan son."
At this, a flood of tears Lavinia shed;
A crimson blush her beauteous face o'erspread,
Varying her cheeks by turns with white and red.
The driving colors, never at a stay,
Run here and there, and flush, and fade away.
Delightful change! Thus Indian iv'ry shows,
Which with the bord'ring paint of purple glows;
Or lilies damask'd by the neighb'ring rose.
The lover gaz'd, and, burning with desire,
The more he look'd, the more he fed the fire:
Revenge, and jealous rage, and secret spite,
Roll in his breast, and rouse him to the fight.
Then fixing on the queen his ardent eyes,
Firm to his first intent, he thus replies:
"O mother, do not by your tears prepare
Such boding omens, and prejudge the war.
Resolv'd on fight, I am no longer free
To shun my death, if Heav'n my death decree."
Then turning to the herald, thus pursues:
"Go, greet the Trojan with ungrateful news;
Denounce from me, that, when to-morrow's light
Shall gild the heav'ns, he need not urge the fight;
The Trojan and Rutulian troops no more
Shall dye, with mutual blood, the Latian shore:
Our single swords the quarrel shall decide,
And to the victor be the beauteous bride."
He said, and striding on, with speedy pace,
He sought his coursers of the Thracian race.
At his approach they toss their heads on high,
And, proudly neighing, promise victory.

The sires of these Orythia sent from far,
To grace Pilumnus, when he went to war.
The drifts of Thracian snows were scarce so white,
Nor northern winds in fleetness match'd their flight.
Officious grooms stand ready by his side;
And some with combs their flowing manes divide,
And others stroke their chests and gently soothe their pride
He sheath'd his limbs in arms; a temper'd mass
Of golden metal those, and mountain brass.
Then to his head his glitt'ring helm he tied,
And girt his faithful fauchion to his side.
In his Aetnaean forge, the God of Fire
That fauchion labor'd for the hero's sire;
Immortal keenness on the blade bestow'd,
And plung'd it hissing in the Stygian flood.
Propp'd on a pillar, which the ceiling bore,
Was plac'd the lance Auruncan Actor wore;
Which with such force he brandish'd in his hand,
The tough ash trembled like an osier wand:
Then cried: "O pond'rous spoil of Actor slain,
And never yet by Turnus toss'd in vain,
Fail not this day thy wonted force; but go,
Sent by this hand, to pierce the Trojan foe!
Give me to tear his corslet from his breast,
And from that eunuch head to rend the crest;
Dragg'd in the dust, his frizzled hair to soil,
Hot from the vexing ir'n, and smear'd with fragrant oil!"
Thus while he raves, from his wide nostrils flies
A fiery steam, and sparkles from his eyes.
So fares the bull in his lov'd female's sight:
Proudly he bellows, and preludes the fight;
He tries his goring horns against a tree,
And meditates his absent enemy;
He pushes at the winds; he digs the strand
With his black hoofs, and spurns the yellow sand.
Nor less the Trojan, in his Lemnian arms,
To future fight his manly courage warms:
He whets his fury, and with joy prepares
To terminate at once the ling'ring wars;
To cheer his chiefs and tender son, relates
What Heav'n had promis'd, and expounds the fates.
Then to the Latian king he sends, to cease
The rage of arms, and ratify the peace.
The morn ensuing, from the mountain's height,
Had scarcely spread the skies with rosy light;
Th' ethereal coursers, bounding from the sea,
From out their flaming nostrils breath'd the day;
When now the Trojan and Rutulian guard,
In friendly labor join'd, the list prepar'd.
Beneath the walls they measure out the space;
Then sacred altars rear, on sods of grass,
Where, with religious their common gods they place.
In purest white the priests their heads attire;
And living waters bear, and holy fire;
And, o'er their linen hoods and shaded hair,

Long twisted wreaths of sacred veryain wear,
In order issuing from the town appears
The Latin legion, arm'd with pointed spears;
And from the fields, advancing on a line,
The Trojan and the Tuscan forces join:
Their various arms afford a pleasing sight;
A peaceful train they seem, in peace prepar'd for fight.
Betwixt the ranks the proud commanders ride,
Glitt'ring with gold, and vests in purple dyed;
Here Mnestheus, author of the Memmian line,
And there Messapus, born of seed divine.
The sign is giv'n; and, round the listed space,
Each man in order fills his proper place.
Reclining on their ample shields, they stand,
And fix their pointed lances in the sand.
Now, studious of the sight, a num'rous throng
Of either sex promiscuous, old and young,
Swarm the town: by those who rest behind,
The gates and walls and houses' tops are lin'd.
Meantime the Queen of Heav'n beheld the sight,
With eyes unpleas'd, from Mount Albano's height
(Since call'd Albano by succeeding fame,
But then an empty hill, without a name).
She thence survey'd the field, the Trojan pow'rs,
The Latian squadrons, and Laurentine tow'rs.
Then thus the goddess of the skies bespoke,
With sighs and tears, the goddess of the lake,
King Turnus' sister, once a lovely maid,
Ere to the lust of lawless Jove betray'd:
Compress'd by force, but, by the grateful god,
Now made the Nais of the neighb'ring flood.
"O nymph, the pride of living lakes," said she,
"O most renown'd, and most belov'd by me,
Long hast thou known, nor need I to record,
The wanton sallies of my wand'ring lord.
Of ev'ry Latian fair whom Jove misled
To mount by stealth my violated bed,
To thee alone I grudg'd not his embrace,
But gave a part of heav'n, and an unenvied place.
Now learn from me thy near approaching grief,
Nor think my wishes want to thy relief.
While fortune favor'd, nor Heav'n's King denied
To lend my succor to the Latian side,
I sav'd thy brother, and the sinking state:
But now he struggles with unequal fate,
And goes, with gods averse, o'ermatch'd in might,
To meet inevitable death in fight;
Nor must I break the truce, nor can sustain the sight.
Thou, if thou dar'st thy present aid supply;
It well becomes a sister's care to try."
At this the lovely nymph, with grief oppress'd,
Thrice tore her hair, and beat her comely breast.
To whom Saturnia thus: "Thy tears are late:
Haste, snatch him, if he can be snatch'd from fate:
New tumults kindle; violate the truce:

Who knows what changeful fortune may produce?
'T is not a crime t' attempt what I decree;
Or, if it were, discharge the crime on me."
She said, and, sailing on the winged wind,
Left the sad nymph suspended in her mind.
And now pomp the peaceful kings appear:
Four steeds the chariot of Latinus bear;
Twelve golden beams around his temples play,
To mark his lineage from the God of Day.
Two snowy coursers Turnus' chariot yoke,
And in his hand two massy spears he shook:
Then issued from the camp, in arms divine,
Aeneas, author of the Roman line;
And by his side Ascanius took his place,
The second hope of Rome's immortal race.
Adorn'd in white, a rev'rend priest appears,
And off'rings to the flaming altars bears;
A porket, and a lamb that never suffer'd shears.
Then to the rising sun he turns his eyes,
And strews the beasts, design'd for sacrifice,
With salt and meal: with like officious care
He marks their foreheads, and he clips their hair.
Betwixt their horns the purple wine he sheds;
With the same gen'rous juice the flame he feeds.
Aeneas then unsheath'd his shining sword,
And thus with pious pray'rs the gods ador'd:
"All-seeing sun, and thou, Ausonian soil,
For which I have sustain'd so long a toil,
Thou, King of Heav'n, and thou, the Queen of Air,
Propitious now, and reconcil'd by pray'r;
Thou, God of War, whose unresisted sway
The labors and events of arms obey;
Ye living fountains, and ye running floods,
All pow'rs of ocean, all ethereal gods,
Hear, and bear record: if I fall in field,
Or, recreant in the fight, to Turnus yield,
My Trojans shall encrease Evander's town;
Ascanius shall renounce th' Ausonian crown:
All claims, all questions of debate, shall cease;
Nor he, nor they, with force infringe the peace.
But, if my juster arms prevail in fight,
(As sure they shall, if I divine aright,)
My Trojans shall not o'er th' Italians reign:
Both equal, both unconquer'd shall remain,
Join'd in their laws, their lands, and their abodes;
I ask but altars for my weary gods.
The care of those religious rites be mine;
The crown to King Latinus I resign:
His be the sov'reign sway. Nor will I share
His pow'r in peace, or his command in war.
For me, my friends another town shall frame,
And bless the rising tow'rs with fair Lavinia's name."
Thus he. Then, with erected eyes and hands,
The Latian king before his altar stands.
"By the same heav'n," said he, "and earth, and main,

And all the pow'rs that all the three contain;
By hell below, and by that upper god
Whose thunder signs the peace, who seals it with his nod;
So let Latona's double offspring hear,
And double-fronted Janus, what I swear:
I touch the sacred altars, touch the flames,
And all those pow'rs attest, and all their names;
Whatever chance befall on either side,
No term of time this union shall divide:
No force, no fortune, shall my vows unbind,
Or shake the steadfast tenor of my mind;
Not tho' the circling seas should break their bound,
O'erflow the shores, or sap the solid ground;
Not tho' the lamps of heav'n their spheres forsake,
Hurl'd down, and hissing in the nether lake:
Ev'n as this royal scepter" (for he bore
A scepter in his hand) "shall never more
Shoot out in branches, or renew the birth:
An orphan now, cut from the mother earth
By the keen ax, dishonor'd of its hair,
And cas'd in brass, for Latian kings to bear."
When thus in public view the peace was tied
With solemn vows, and sworn on either side,
All dues perform'd which holy rites require;
The victim beasts are slain before the fire,
The trembling entrails from their bodies torn,
And to the fatten'd flames in chargers borne.
Already the Rutulians deem their man
O'ermatch'd in arms, before the fight began.
First rising fears are whisper'd thro' the crowd;
Then, gath'ring sound, they murmur more aloud.
Now, side to side, they measure with their eyes
The champions' bulk, their sinews, and their size:
The nearer they approach, the more is known
Th' apparent disadvantage of their own.
Turnus himself appears in public sight
Conscious of fate, desponding of the fight.
Slowly he moves, and at his altar stands
With eyes dejected, and with trembling hands;
And, while he mutters undistinguish'd pray'rs,
A livid deadness in his cheeks appears.
With anxious pleasure when Juturna view'd
Th' increasing fright of the mad multitude,
When their short sighs and thick'ning sobs she heard,
And found their ready minds for change prepar'd;
Dissembling her immortal form, she took
Camertus' mien, his habit, and his look;
A chief of ancient blood; in arms well known
Was his great sire, and he his greater son.
His shape assum'd, amid the ranks she ran,
And humoring their first motions, thus began:
"For shame, Rutulians, can you bear the sight
Of one expos'd for all, in single fight?
Can we, before the face of heav'n, confess
Our courage colder, or our numbers less?

View all the Trojan host, th' Arcadian band,
And Tuscan army; count 'em as they stand:
Undaunted to the battle if we go,
Scarce ev'ry second man will share a foe.
Turnus, 't is true, in this unequal strife,
Shall lose, with honor, his devoted life,
Or change it rather for immortal fame,
Succeeding to the gods, from whence he came:
But you, a servile and inglorious band,
For foreign lords shall sow your native land,
Those fruitful fields your fighting fathers gain'd,
Which have so long their lazy sons sustain'd."
With words like these, she carried her design:
A rising murmur runs along the line.
Then ev'n the city troops, and Latians, tir'd
With tedious war, seem with new souls inspir'd:
Their champion's fate with pity they lament,
And of the league, so lately sworn, repent.
Nor fails the goddess to foment the rage
With lying wonders, and a false presage;
But adds a sign, which, present to their eyes,
Inspires new courage, and a glad surprise.
For, sudden, in the fiery tracts above,
Appears in pomp th' imperial bird of Jove:
A plump of fowl he spies, that swim the lakes,
And o'er their heads his sounding pinions shakes;
Then, stooping on the fairest of the train,
In his strong talons truss'd a silver swan.
Th' Italians wonder at th' unusual sight;
But, while he lags, and labors in his flight,
Behold, the dastard fowl return anew,
And with united force the foe pursue:
Clam'rous around the royal hawk they fly,
And, thick'ning in a cloud, o'ershade the sky.
They cuff, they scratch, they cross his airy course;
Nor can th' incumber'd bird sustain their force;
But vex'd, not vanquish'd, drops the pond'rous prey,
And, lighten'd of his burthen, wings his way.
Th' Ausonian bands with shouts salute the sight,
Eager of action, and demand the fight.
Then King Tolumnius, vers'd in augurs' arts,
Cries out, and thus his boasted skill imparts:
"At length 't is granted, what I long desir'd!
This, this is what my frequent vows requir'd.
Ye gods, I take your omen, and obey.
Advance, my friends, and charge! I lead the way.
These are the foreign foes, whose impious band,
Like that rapacious bird, infest our land:
But soon, like him, they shall be forc'd to sea
By strength united, and forego the prey.
Your timely succor to your country bring,
Haste to the rescue, and redeem your king."
He said; and, pressing onward thro' the crew,
Pois'd in his lifted arm, his lance he threw.
The winged weapon, whistling in the wind,

Came driving on, nor miss'd the mark design'd.
At once the cornel rattled in the skies;
At once tumultuous shouts and clamors rise.
Nine brothers in a goodly band there stood,
Born of Arcadian mix'd with Tuscan blood,
Gylippus' sons: the fatal jav'lin flew,
Aim'd at the midmost of the friendly crew.
A passage thro' the jointed arms it found,
Just where the belt was to the body bound,
And struck the gentle youth extended on the ground.
Then, fir'd with pious rage, the gen'rous train
Run madly forward to revenge the slain.
And some with eager haste their jav'lins throw;
And some with sword in hand assault the foe.
The wish'd insult the Latine troops embrace,
And meet their ardor in the middle space.
The Trojans, Tuscans, and Arcadian line,
With equal courage obviate their design.
Peace leaves the violated fields, and hate
Both armies urges to their mutual fate.
With impious haste their altars are o'erturn'd,
The sacrifice half-broil'd, and half-unburn'd.
Thick storms of steel from either army fly,
And clouds of clashing darts obscure the sky;
Brands from the fire are missive weapons made,
With chargers, bowls, and all the priestly trade.
Latinus, frighted, hastens from the fray,
And bears his unregarded gods away.
These on their horses vault; those yoke the car;
The rest, with swords on high, run headlong to the war.
Messapus, eager to confound the peace,
Spurr'd his hot courser thro' the fighting prease,
At King Aulestes, by his purple known
A Tuscan prince, and by his regal crown;
And, with a shock encount'ring, bore him down.
Backward he fell; and, as his fate design'd,
The ruins of an altar were behind:
There, pitching on his shoulders and his head,
Amid the scatt'ring fires he lay supinely spread.
The beamy spear, descending from above,
His cuirass pierc'd, and thro' his body drove.
Then, with a scornful smile, the victor cries:
"The gods have found a fitter sacrifice."
Greedy of spoils, th' Italians strip the dead
Of his rich armor, and uncrown his head.
Priest Corynaeus, arm'd his better hand,
From his own altar, with a blazing brand;
And, as Ebusus with a thund'ring pace
Advanc'd to battle, dash'd it on his face:
His bristly beard shines out with sudden fires;
The crackling crop a noisome scent expires.
Following the blow, he seiz'd his curling crown
With his left hand; his other cast him down.
The prostrate body with his knees he press'd,
And plung'd his holy poniard in his breast.

While Podalirius, with his sword, pursued
The shepherd Alsus thro' the flying crowd,
Swiftly he turns, and aims a deadly blow
Full on the front of his unwary foe.
The broad ax enters with a crashing sound,
And cleaves the chin with one continued wound;
Warm blood, and mingled brains, besmear his arms around
An iron sleep his stupid eyes oppress'd,
And seal'd their heavy lids in endless rest.
But good Aeneas rush'd amid the bands;
Bare was his head, and naked were his hands,
In sign of truce: then thus he cries aloud:
"What sudden rage, what new desire of blood,
Inflames your alter'd minds? O Trojans, cease
From impious arms, nor violate the peace!
By human sanctions, and by laws divine,
The terms are all agreed; the war is mine.
Dismiss your fears, and let the fight ensue;
This hand alone shall right the gods and you:
Our injur'd altars, and their broken vow,
To this avenging sword the faithless Turnus owe."
Thus while he spoke, unmindful of defense,
A winged arrow struck the pious prince.
But, whether from some human hand it came,
Or hostile god, is left unknown by fame:
No human hand or hostile god was found,
To boast the triumph of so base a wound.
When Turnus saw the Trojan quit the plain,
His chiefs dismay'd, his troops a fainting train,
Th' unhop'd event his heighten'd soul inspires:
At once his arms and coursers he requires;
Then, with a leap, his lofty chariot gains,
And with a ready hand assumes the reins.
He drives impetuous, and, where'er he goes,
He leaves behind a lane of slaughter'd foes.
These his lance reaches; over those he rolls
His rapid car, and crushes out their souls:
In vain the vanquish'd fly; the victor sends
The dead men's weapons at their living friends.
Thus, on the banks of Hebrus' freezing flood,
The God of Battles, in his angry mood,
Clashing his sword against his brazen shield,
Let loose the reins, and scours along the field:
Before the wind his fiery coursers fly;
Groans the sad earth, resounds the rattling sky.
Wrath, Terror, Treason, Tumult, and Despair
(Dire faces, and deform'd) surround the car;
Friends of the god, and followers of the war.
With fury not unlike, nor less disdain,
Exulting Turnus flies along the plain:
His smoking horses, at their utmost speed,
He lashes on, and urges o'er the dead.
Their fetlocks run with blood; and, when they bound,
The gore and gath'ring dust are dash'd around.
Thamyris and Pholus, masters of the war,

He kill'd at hand, but Sthenelus afar:
From far the sons of Imbracus he slew,
Glaucus and Lades, of the Lycian crew;
Both taught to fight on foot, in battle join'd,
Or mount the courser that outstrips the wind.
Meantime Eumedes, vaunting in the field,
New fir'd the Trojans, and their foes repell'd.
This son of Dolon bore his grandsire's name,
But emulated more his father's fame;
His guileful father, sent a nightly spy,
The Grecian camp and order to descry:
Hard enterprise! and well he might require
Achilles' car and horses, for his hire:
But, met upon the scout, th' Aetolian prince
In death bestow'd a juster recompense.
Fierce Turnus view'd the Trojan from afar,
And launch'd his jav'lin from his lofty car;
Then lightly leaping down, pursued the blow,
And, pressing with his foot his prostrate foe,
Wrench'd from his feeble hold the shining sword,
And plung'd it in the bosom of its lord.
"Possess," said he, "the fruit of all thy pains,
And measure, at thy length, our Latian plains.
Thus are my foes rewarded by my hand;
Thus may they build their town, and thus enjoy the land!"
Then Dares, Butes, Sybaris he slew,
Whom o'er his neck his flound'ring courser threw.
As when loud Boreas, with his blust'ring train,
Stoops from above, incumbent on the main;
Where'er he flies, he drives the rack before,
And rolls the billows on th' Aegaean shore:
So, where resistless Turnus takes his course,
The scatter'd squadrons bend before his force;
His crest of horses' hair is blown behind
By adverse air, and rustles in the wind.
This haughty Phegeus saw with high disdain,
And, as the chariot roll'd along the plain,
Light from the ground he leapt, and seiz'd the rein.
Thus hung in air, he still retain'd his hold,
The coursers frighted, and their course controll'd.
The lance of Turnus reach'd him as he hung,
And pierc'd his plated arms, but pass'd along,
And only raz'd the skin. He turn'd, and held
Against his threat'ning foe his ample shield;
Then call'd for aid: but, while he cried in vain,
The chariot bore him backward on the plain.
He lies revers'd; the victor king descends,
And strikes so justly where his helmet ends,
He lops the head. The Latian fields are drunk
With streams that issue from the bleeding trunk.
While he triumphs, and while the Trojans yield,
The wounded prince is forc'd to leave the field:
Strong Mnestheus, and Achates often tried,
And young Ascanius, weeping by his side,
Conduct him to his tent. Scarce can he rear

His limbs from earth, supported on his spear.
Resolv'd in mind, regardless of the smart,
He tugs with both his hands, and breaks the dart.
The steel remains. No readier way he found
To draw the weapon, than t' inlarge the wound.
Eager of fight, impatient of delay,
He begs; and his unwilling friends obey.
Iapis was at hand to prove his art,
Whose blooming youth so fir'd Apollo's heart,
That, for his love, he proffer'd to bestow
His tuneful harp and his unerring bow.
The pious youth, more studious how to save
His aged sire, now sinking to the grave,
Preferr'd the pow'r of plants, and silent praise
Of healing arts, before Phoebean bays.
Propp'd on his lance the pensive hero stood,
And heard and saw, unmov'd, the mourning crowd.
The fam'd physician tucks his robes around
With ready hands, and hastens to the wound.
With gentle touches he performs his part,
This way and that, soliciting the dart,
And exercises all his heav'nly art.
All soft'ning simples, known of sov'reign use,
He presses out, and pours their noble juice.
These first infus'd, to lenify the pain,
He tugs with pincers, but he tugs in vain.
Then to the patron of his art he pray'd:
The patron of his art refus'd his aid.
Meantime the war approaches to the tents;
Th' alarm grows hotter, and the noise augments:
The driving dust proclaims the danger near;
And first their friends, and then their foes appear:
Their friends retreat; their foes pursue the rear.
The camp is fill'd with terror and affright:
The hissing shafts within the trench alight;
An undistinguish'd noise ascends the sky,
The shouts those who kill, and groans of those who die.
But now the goddess mother, mov'd with grief,
And pierc'd with pity, hastens her relief.
A branch of healing dittany she brought,
Which in the Cretan fields with care she sought:
Rough is the stern, which woolly leafs surround;
The leafs with flow'rs, the flow'rs with purple crown'd,
Well known to wounded goats; a sure relief
To draw the pointed steel, and ease the grief.
This Venus brings, in clouds involv'd, and brews
Th' extracted liquor with ambrosian dews,
And odorous panacee. Unseen she stands,
Temp'ring the mixture with her heav'nly hands,
And pours it in a bowl, already crown'd
With juice of med'c'nal herbs prepar'd to bathe the wound.
The leech, unknowing of superior art
Which aids the cure, with this foments the part;
And in a moment ceas'd the raging smart.
Stanch'd is the blood, and in the bottom stands:

The steel, but scarcely touch'd with tender hands,
Moves up, and follows of its own accord,
And health and vigor are at once restor'd.
Iapis first perceiv'd the closing wound,
And first the footsteps of a god he found.
"Arms! arms!" he cries; "the sword and shield prepare,
And send the willing chief, renew'd, to war.
This is no mortal work, no cure of mine,
Nor art's effect, but done by hands divine.
Some god our general to the battle sends;
Some god preserves his life for greater ends."
The hero arms in haste; his hands infold
His thighs with cuishes of refulgent gold:
Inflam'd to fight, and rushing to the field,
That hand sustaining the celestial shield,
This gripes the lance, and with such vigor shakes,
That to the rest the beamy weapon quakes.
Then with a close embrace he strain'd his son,
And, kissing thro' his helmet, thus begun:
"My son, from my example learn the war,
In camps to suffer, and in fields to dare;
But happier chance than mine attend thy care!
This day my hand thy tender age shall shield,
And crown with honors of the conquer'd field:
Thou, when thy riper years shall send thee forth
To toils of war, be mindful of my worth;
Assert thy birthright, and in arms be known,
For Hector's nephew, and Aeneas' son."
He said; and, striding, issued on the plain.
Anteus and Mnestheus, and a num'rous train,
Attend his steps; the rest their weapons take,
And, crowding to the field, the camp forsake.
A cloud of blinding dust is rais'd around,
Labors beneath their feet the trembling ground.
Now Turnus, posted on a hill, from far
Beheld the progress of the moving war:
With him the Latins view'd the cover'd plains,
And the chill blood ran backward in their veins.
Juturna saw th' advancing troops appear,
And heard the hostile sound, and fled for fear.
Aeneas leads; and draws a sweeping train,
Clos'd in their ranks, and pouring on the plain.
As when a whirlwind, rushing to the shore
From the mid ocean, drives the waves before;
The painful hind with heavy heart foresees
The flatted fields, and slaughter of the trees;
With like impetuous rage the prince appears
Before his doubled front, nor less destruction bears.
And now both armies shock in open field;
Osiris is by strong Thymbraeus kill'd.
Archetius, Ufens, Epulon, are slain
(All fam'd in arms, and of the Latian train)
By Gyas', Mnestheus', and Achates' hand.
The fatal augur falls, by whose command
The truce was broken, and whose lance, embrued

With Trojan blood, th' unhappy fight renew'd.
Loud shouts and clamors rend the liquid sky,
And o'er the field the frighted Latins fly.
The prince disdains the dastards to pursue,
Nor moves to meet in arms the fighting few;
Turnus alone, amid the dusky plain,
He seeks, and to the combat calls in vain.
Juturna heard, and, seiz'd with mortal fear,
Forc'd from the beam her brother's charioteer;
Assumes his shape, his armor, and his mien,
And, like Metiscus, in his seat is seen.
As the black swallow near the palace plies;
O'er empty courts, and under arches, flies;
Now hawks aloft, now skims along the flood,
To furnish her loquacious nest with food:
So drives the rapid goddess o'er the plains;
The smoking horses run with loosen'd reins.
She steers a various course among the foes;
Now here, now there, her conqu'ring brother shows;
Now with a straight, now with a wheeling flight,
She turns, and bends, but shuns the single fight.
Aeneas, fir'd with fury, breaks the crowd,
And seeks his foe, and calls by name aloud:
He runs within a narrower ring, and tries
To stop the chariot; but the chariot flies.
If he but gain a glimpse, Juturna fears,
And far away the Daunian hero bears.
What should he do! Nor arts nor arms avail;
And various cares in vain his mind assail.
The great Messapus, thund'ring thro' the field,
In his left hand two pointed jav'lins held:
Encount'ring on the prince, one dart he drew,
And with unerring aim and utmost vigor threw.
Aeneas saw it come, and, stooping low
Beneath his buckler, shunn'd the threat'ning blow.
The weapon hiss'd above his head, and tore
The waving plume which on his helm he wore.
Forced by this hostile act, and fir'd with spite,
That flying Turnus still declin'd the fight,
The Prince, whose piety had long repell'd
His inborn ardor, now invades the field;
Invokes the pow'rs of violated peace,
Their rites and injur'd altars to redress;
Then, to his rage abandoning the rein,
With blood and slaughter'd bodies fills the plain.
What god can tell, what numbers can display,
The various labors of that fatal day;
What chiefs and champions fell on either side,
In combat slain, or by what deaths they died;
Whom Turnus, whom the Trojan hero kill'd;
Who shar'd the fame and fortune of the field!
Jove, could'st thou view, and not avert thy sight,
Two jarring nations join'd in cruel fight,
Whom leagues of lasting love so shortly shall unite!
Aeneas first Rutulian Sucro found,

Whose valor made the Trojans quit their ground;
Betwixt his ribs the jav'lin drove so just,
It reach'd his heart, nor needs a second thrust.
Now Turnus, at two blows, two brethren slew;
First from his horse fierce Amycus he threw:
Then, leaping on the ground, on foot assail'd
Diores, and in equal fight prevail'd.
Their lifeless trunks he leaves upon the place;
Their heads, distilling gore, his chariot grace.
Three cold on earth the Trojan hero threw,
Whom without respite at one charge he slew:
Cethegus, Tanais, Tagus, fell oppress'd,
And sad Onythes, added to the rest,
Of Theban blood, whom Peridia bore.
Turnus two brothers from the Lycian shore,
And from Apollo's fane to battle sent,
O'erthrew; nor Phoebus could their fate prevent.
Peaceful Menoetes after these he kill'd,
Who long had shunn'd the dangers of the field:
On Lerna's lake a silent life he led,
And with his nets and angle earn'd his bread;
Nor pompous cares, nor palaces, he knew,
But wisely from th' infectious world withdrew:
Poor was his house; his father's painful hand
Discharg'd his rent, and plow'd another's land.
As flames among the lofty woods are thrown
On diff'rent sides, and both by winds are blown;
The laurels crackle in the sputt'ring fire;
The frighted sylvans from their shades retire:
Or as two neighb'ring torrents fall from high;
Rapid they run; the foamy waters fry;
They roll to sea with unresisted force,
And down the rocks precipitate their course:
Not with less rage the rival heroes take
Their diff'rent ways, nor less destruction make.
With spears afar, with swords at hand, they strike;
And zeal of slaughter fires their souls alike.
Like them, their dauntless men maintain the field;
And hearts are pierc'd, unknowing how to yield:
They blow for blow return, and wound for wound;
And heaps of bodies raise the level ground.
Murranus, boasting of his blood, that springs
From a long royal race of Latian kings,
Is by the Trojan from his chariot thrown,
Crush'd with the weight of an unwieldy stone:
Betwixt the wheels he fell; the wheels, that bore
His living load, his dying body tore.
His starting steeds, to shun the glitt'ring sword,
Paw down his trampled limbs, forgetful of their lord.
Fierce Hyllus threaten'd high, and, face to face,
Affronted Turnus in the middle space:
The prince encounter'd him in full career,
And at his temples aim'd the deadly spear;
So fatally the flying weapon sped,
That thro' his helm it pierc'd his head.

Nor, Cisseus, couldst thou scape from Turnus' hand,
In vain the strongest of th' Arcadian band:
Nor to Cupentus could his gods afford
Availing aid against th' Aenean sword,
Which to his naked heart pursued the course;
Nor could his plated shield sustain the force.
Iolas fell, whom not the Grecian pow'rs,
Nor great subverter of the Trojan tow'rs,
Were doom'd to kill, while Heav'n prolong'd his date;
But who can pass the bounds, prefix'd by fate?
In high Lyrnessus, and in Troy, he held
Two palaces, and was from each expell'd:
Of all the mighty man, the last remains
A little spot of foreign earth contains.
And now both hosts their broken troops unite
In equal ranks, and mix in mortal fight.
Serestthus and undaunted Mnestheus join
The Trojan, Tuscan, and Arcadian line:
Sea-born Messapus, with Atinas, heads
The Latin squadrons, and to battle leads.
They strike, they push, they throng the scanty space,
Resolv'd on death, impatient of disgrace;
And, where one falls, another fills his place.
The Cyprian goddess now inspires her son
To leave th' unfinish'd fight, and storm the town:
For, while he rolls his eyes around the plain
In quest of Turnus, whom he seeks in vain,
He views th' unguarded city from afar,
In careless quiet, and secure of war.
Occasion offers, and excites his mind
To dare beyond the task he first design'd.
Resolv'd, he calls his chiefs; they leave the fight:
Attended thus, he takes a neighb'ring height;
The crowding troops about their gen'ral stand,
All under arms, and wait his high command.
Then thus the lofty prince: "Hear and obey,
Ye Trojan bands, without the least delay
Jove is with us; and what I have decreed
Requires our utmost vigor, and our speed.
Your instant arms against the town prepare,
The source of mischief, and the seat of war.
This day the Latian tow'rs, that mate the sky,
Shall level with the plain in ashes lie:
The people shall be slaves, unless in time
They kneel for pardon, and repent their crime.
Twice have our foes been vanquish'd on the plain:
Then shall I wait till Turnus will be slain?
Your force against the perjur'd city bend.
There it began, and there the war shall end.
The peace profan'd our rightful arms requires;
Cleanse the polluted place with purging fires."
He finish'd; and, one soul inspiring all,
Form'd in a wedge, the foot approach the wall.
Without the town, an unprovided train
Of gaping, gazing citizens are slain.

Some firebrands, others scaling ladders bear,
And those they toss aloft, and these they rear:
The flames now launch'd, the feather'd arrows fly,
And clouds of missive arms obscure the sky.
Advancing to the front, the hero stands,
And, stretching out to heav'n his pious hands,
Attests the gods, asserts his innocence,
Upbraids with breach of faith th' Ausonian prince;
Declares the royal honor doubly stain'd,
And twice the rites of holy peace profan'd.
Dissenting clamors in the town arise;
Each will be heard, and all at once advise.
One part for peace, and one for war contends;
Some would exclude their foes, and some admit their friends.
The helpless king is hurried in the throng,
And, whate'er tide prevails, is borne along.
Thus, when the swain, within a hollow rock,
Invades the bees with suffocating smoke,
They run around, or labor on their wings,
Disus'd to flight, and shoot their sleepy stings;
To shun the bitter fumes in vain they try;
Black vapors, issuing from the vent, involve the sky.
But fate and envious fortune now prepare
To plunge the Latins in the last despair.
The queen, who saw the foes invade the town,
And brands on tops of burning houses thrown,
Cast round her eyes, distracted with her fear-
No troops of Turnus in the field appear.
Once more she stares abroad, but still in vain,
And then concludes the royal youth is slain.
Mad with her anguish, impotent to bear
The mighty grief, she loathes the vital air.
She calls herself the cause of all this ill,
And owns the dire effects of her ungovern'd will;
She raves against the gods; she beats her breast;
She tears with both her hands her purple vest:
Then round a beam a running noose she tied,
And, fasten'd by the neck, obscenely died.
Soon as the fatal news by Fame was blown,
And to her dames and to her daughter known,
The sad Lavinia rends her yellow hair
And rosy cheeks; the rest her sorrow share:
With shrieks the palace rings, and madness of despair.
The spreading rumor fills the public place:
Confusion, fear, distraction, and disgrace,
And silent shame, are seen in ev'ry face.
Latinus tears his garments as he goes,
Both for his public and his private woes;
With filth his venerable beard besmears,
And sordid dust deforms his silver hairs.
And much he blames the softness of his mind,
Obnoxious to the charms of womankind,
And soon seduc'd to change what he so well design'd;
To break the solemn league so long desir'd,
Nor finish what his fates, and those of Troy, requir'd.

Now Turnus rolls aloof o'er empty plains,
And here and there some straggling foes he gleans.
His flying coursers please him less and less,
Asham'd of easy fight and cheap success.
Thus half-contented, anxious in his mind,
The distant cries come driving in the wind,
Shouts from the walls, but shouts in murmurs drown'd;
A jarring mixture, and a boding sound.
"Alas!" said he, "what mean these dismal cries?
What doleful clamors from the town arise?"
Confus'd, he stops, and backward pulls the reins.
She who the driver's office now sustains,
Replies: "Neglect, my lord, these new alarms;
Here fight, and urge the fortune of your arms:
There want not others to defend the wall.
If by your rival's hand th' Italians fall,
So shall your fatal sword his friends oppress,
In honor equal, equal in success."
To this, the prince: "O sister- for I knew
The peace infring'd proceeded first from you;
I knew you, when you mingled first in fight;
And now in vain you would deceive my sight-
Why, goddess, this unprofitable care?
Who sent you down from heav'n, involv'd in air,
Your share of mortal sorrows to sustain,
And see your brother bleeding on the plain?
For to what pow'r can Turnus have recourse,
Or how resist his fate's prevailing force?
These eyes beheld Murranus bite the ground:
Mighty the man, and mighty was the wound.
I heard my dearest friend, with dying breath,
My name invoking to revenge his death.
Brave Ufens fell with honor on the place,
To shun the shameful sight of my disgrace.
On earth supine, a manly corpse he lies;
His vest and armor are the victor's prize.
Then, shall I see Laurentum in a flame,
Which only wanted, to complete my shame?
How will the Latins hoot their champion's flight!
How Drances will insult and point them to the sight!
Is death so hard to bear? Ye gods below,
(Since those above so small compassion show,)
Receive a soul unsullied yet with shame,
Which not belies my great forefather's name!"
He said; and while he spoke, with flying speed
Came Sages urging on his foamy steed:
Fix'd on his wounded face a shaft he bore,
And, seeking Turnus, sent his voice before:
"Turnus, on you, on you alone, depends
Our last relief: compassionate your friends!
Like lightning, fierce Aeneas, rolling on,
With arms invests, with flames invades the town:
The brands are toss'd on high; the winds conspire
To drive along the deluge of the fire.
All eyes are fix'd on you: your foes rejoice;

Ev'n the king staggers, and suspends his choice;
Doubts to deliver or defend the town,
Whom to reject, or whom to call his son.
The queen, on whom your utmost hopes were plac'd,
Herself suborning death, has breath'd her last.
'T is true, Messapus, fearless of his fate,
With fierce Atinas' aid, defends the gate:
On ev'ry side surrounded by the foe,
The more they kill, the greater numbers grow;
An iron harvest mounts, and still remains to mow.
You, far aloof from your forsaken bands,
Your rolling chariot drive o'er empty
Stupid he sate, his eyes on earth declin'd,
And various cares revolving in his mind:
Rage, boiling from the bottom of his breast,
And sorrow mix'd with shame, his soul oppress'd;
And conscious worth lay lab'ring in his thought,
And love by jealousy to madness wrought.
By slow degrees his reason drove away
The mists of passion, and resum'd her sway.
Then, rising on his car, he turn'd his look,
And saw the town involv'd in fire and smoke.
A wooden tow'r with flames already blaz'd,
Which his own hands on beams and rafters rais'd;
And bridges laid above to join the space,
And wheels below to roll from place to place.
"Sister, the Fates have vanquish'd: let us go
The way which Heav'n and my hard fortune show.
The fight is fix'd; nor shall the branded name
Of a base coward blot your brother's fame.
Death is my choice; but suffer me to try
My force, and vent my rage before I die."
He said; and, leaping down without delay,
Thro' crowds of scatter'd foes he freed his way.
Striding he pass'd, impetuous as the wind,
And left the grieving goddess far behind.
As when a fragment, from a mountain torn
By raging tempests, or by torrents borne,
Or sapp'd by time, or loosen'd from the roots- Prone thro' the void the rocky ruin shoots,
Rolling from crag to crag, from steep to steep;
Down sink, at once, the shepherds and their sheep:
Involv'd alike, they rush to nether ground;
Stunn'd with the shock they fall, and stunn'd from earth rebound:
So Turnus, hasting headlong to the town,
Should'ring and shoving, bore the squadrons down.
Still pressing onward, to the walls he drew,
Where shafts, and spears, and darts promiscuous flew,
And sanguine streams the slipp'ry ground embrue.
First stretching out his arm, in sign of peace,
He cries aloud, to make the combat cease:
"Rutulians, hold; and Latin troops, retire!
The fight is mine; and me the gods require.
'T is just that I should vindicate alone
The broken truce, or for the breach atone.

This day shall free from wars th' Ausonian state,
Or finish my misfortunes in my fate."
Both armies from their bloody work desist,
And, bearing backward, form a spacious list.
The Trojan hero, who receiv'd from fame
The welcome sound, and heard the champion's name,
Soon leaves the taken works and mounted walls,
Greedy of war where greater glory calls.
He springs to fight, exulting in his force
His jointed armor rattles in the course.
Like Eryx, or like Athos, great he shows,
Or Father Apennine, when, white with snows,
His head divine obscure in clouds he hides,
And shakes the sounding forest on his sides.
The nations, overaw'd, surcease the fight;
Immovable their bodies, fix'd their sight.
Ev'n death stands still; nor from above they throw
Their darts, nor drive their batt'ring-rams below.
In silent order either army stands,
And drop their swords, unknowing, from their hands.
Th' Ausonian king beholds, with wond'ring sight,
Two mighty champions match'd in single fight,
Born under climes remote, and brought by fate,
With swords to try their titles to the state.
Now, in clos'd field, each other from afar
They view; and, rushing on, begin the war.
They launch their spears; then hand to hand they meet;
The trembling soil resounds beneath their feet:
Their bucklers clash; thick blows descend from high,
And flakes of fire from their hard helmets fly.
Courage conspires with chance, and both ingage
With equal fortune yet, and mutual rage.
As when two bulls for their fair female fight
In Sila's shades, or on Taburnus' height;
With horns adverse they meet; the keeper flies;
Mute stands the herd; the heifers roll their eyes,
And wait th' event; which victor they shall bear,
And who shall be the lord, to rule the lusty year:
With rage of love the jealous rivals burn,
And push for push, and wound for wound return;
Their dewlaps gor'd, their sides are lav'd in blood;
Loud cries and roaring sounds rebellow thro' the wood:
Such was the combat in the listed ground;
So clash their swords, and so their shields resound.
Jove sets the beam; in either scale he lays
The champions' fate, and each exactly weighs.
On this side, life and lucky chance ascends;
Loaded with death, that other scale descends.
Rais'd on the stretch, young Turnus aims a blow
Full on the helm of his unguarded foe:
Shrill shouts and clamors ring on either side,
As hopes and fears their panting hearts divide.
But all in pieces flies the traitor sword,
And, in the middle stroke, deserts his lord.
Now is but death, or flight; disarm'd he flies,

When in his hand an unknown hilt he spies.
Fame says that Turnus, when his steeds he join'd,
Hurrying to war, disorder'd in his mind,
Snatch'd the first weapon which his haste could find.
'T was not the fated sword his father bore,
But that his charioteer Metiscus wore.
This, while the Trojans fled, the toughness held;
But, vain against the great Vulcanian shield,
The mortal-temper'd steel deceiv'd his hand:
The shiver'd fragments shone amid the sand.
Surpris'd with fear, he fled along the field,
And now forthright, and now in orbits wheel'd;
For here the Trojan troops the list surround,
And there the pass is clos'd with pools and marshy ground.
Aeneas hastens, tho' with heavier pace-
His wound, so newly knit, retards the chase,
And oft his trembling knees their aid refuse-
Yet, pressing foot by foot, his foe pursues.
Thus, when a fearful stag is clos'd around
With crimson toils, or in a river found,
High on the bank the deep-mouth'd hound appears,
Still opening, following still, where'er he steers;
The persecuted creature, to and fro,
Turns here and there, to scape his Umbrian foe:
Steep is th' ascent, and, if he gains the land,
The purple death is pitch'd along the strand.
His eager foe, determin'd to the chase,
Stretch'd at his length, gains ground at ev'ry pace;
Now to his beamy head he makes his way,
And now he holds, or thinks he holds, his prey:
Just at the pinch, the stag springs out with fear;
He bites the wind, and fills his sounding jaws with air:
The rocks, the lakes, the meadows ring with cries;
The mortal tumult mounts, and thunders in the skies.
Thus flies the Daunian prince, and, flying, blames
His tardy troops, and, calling by their names,
Demands his trusty sword. The Trojan threats
The realm with ruin, and their ancient seats
To lay in ashes, if they dare supply
With arms or aid his vanquish'd enemy:
Thus menacing, he still pursues the course,
With vigor, tho' diminish'd of his force.
Ten times already round the listed place
One chief had fled, and t' other giv'n the chase:
No trivial prize is play'd; for on the life
Or death of Turnus now depends the strife.
Within the space, an olive tree had stood,
A sacred shade, a venerable wood,
For vows to Faunus paid, the Latins' guardian god.
Here hung the vests, and tablets were ingrav'd,
Of sinking mariners from shipwrack sav'd.
With heedless hands the Trojans fell'd the tree,
To make the ground inclos'd for combat free.
Deep in the root, whether by fate, or chance,
Or erring haste, the Trojan drove his lance;

Then stoop'd, and tugg'd with force immense, to free
Th' incumber'd spear from the tenacious tree;
That, whom his fainting limbs pursued in vain,
His flying weapon might from far attain.
Confus'd with fear, bereft of human aid,
Then Turnus to the gods, and first to Faunus pray'd:
"O Faunus, pity! and thou Mother Earth,
Where I thy foster son receiv'd my birth,
Hold fast the steel! If my religious hand
Your plant has honor'd, which your foes profan'd,
Propitious hear my pious pray'r!" He said,
Nor with successless vows invok'd their aid.
Th' incumbent hero wrench'd, and pull'd, and strain'd;
But still the stubborn earth the steel detain'd.
Juturna took her time; and, while in vain
He strove, assum'd Meticus' form again,
And, in that imitated shape, restor'd
To the despairing prince his Daunian sword.
The Queen of Love, who, with disdain and grief,
Saw the bold nymph afford this prompt relief,
T' assert her offspring with a greater deed,
From the tough root the ling'ring weapon freed.
Once more erect, the rival chiefs advance:
One trusts the sword, and one the pointed lance;
And both resolv'd alike to try their fatal chance.
Meantime imperial Jove to Juno spoke,
Who from a shining cloud beheld the shock:
"What new arrest, O Queen of Heav'n, is sent
To stop the Fates now lab'ring in th' event?
What farther hopes are left thee to pursue?
Divine Aeneas, (and thou know'st it too,)
Foredoom'd, to these celestial seats are due.
What more attempts for Turnus can be made,
That thus thou ling'rest in this lonely shade?
Is it becoming of the due respect
And awful honor of a god elect,
A wound unworthy of our state to feel,
Patient of human hands and earthly steel?
Or seems it just, the sister should restore
A second sword, when one was lost before,
And arm a conquer'd wretch against his conqueror?
For what, without thy knowledge and avow,
Nay more, thy dictate, durst Juturna do?
At last, in deference to my love, forbear
To lodge within thy soul this anxious care;
Reclin'd upon my breast, thy grief unload:
Who should relieve the goddess, but the god?
Now all things to their utmost issue tend,
Push'd by the Fates to their appointed
While leave was giv'n thee, and a lawful hour
For vengeance, wrath, and unresisted pow'r,
Toss'd on the seas, thou couldst thy foes distress,
And, driv'n ashore, with hostile arms oppress;
Deform the royal house; and, from the side
Of the just bridegroom, tear the plighted bride:

Now cease at my command." The Thund'rer said;
And, with dejected eyes, this answer Juno made:
"Because your dread decree too well I knew,
From Turnus and from earth unwilling I withdrew.
Else should you not behold me here, alone,
Involv'd in empty clouds, my friends bemoan,
But, girt with vengeful flames, in open sight
Engag'd against my foes in mortal fight.
'T is true, Juturna mingled in the strife
By my command, to save her brother's life-
At least to try; but, by the Stygian lake,
(The most religious oath the gods can take,)
With this restriction, not to bend the bow,
Or toss the spear, or trembling dart to throw.
And now, resign'd to your superior might,
And tir'd with fruitless toils, I loathe the fight.
This let me beg (and this no fates withstand)
Both for myself and for your father's land,
That, when the nuptial bed shall bind the peace,
(Which I, since you ordain, consent to bless,)
The laws of either nation be the same;
But let the Latins still retain their name,
Speak the same language which they spoke before,
Wear the same habits which their grandsires wore.
Call them not Trojans: perish the renown
And name of Troy, with that detested town.
Latium be Latium still; let Alba reign
And Rome's immortal majesty remain."
Then thus the founder of mankind replies
(Unruffled was his front, serene his eyes)
"Can Saturn's issue, and heav'n's other heir,
Such endless anger in her bosom bear?
Be mistress, and your full desires obtain;
But quench the choler you foment in vain.
From ancient blood th' Ausonian people sprung,
Shall keep their name, their habit, and their tongue.
The Trojans to their customs shall be tied:
I will, myself, their common rites provide;
The natives shall command, the foreigners subside.
All shall be Latium; Troy without a name;
And her lost sons forget from whence they came.
From blood so mix'd, a pious race shall flow,
Equal to gods, excelling all below.
No nation more respect to you shall pay,
Or greater off'rings on your altars lay."
Juno consents, well pleas'd that her desires
Had found success, and from the cloud retires.
The peace thus made, the Thund'rer next prepares
To force the wat'ry goddess from the wars.
Deep in the dismal regions void of light,
Three daughters at a birth were born to Night:
These their brown mother, brooding on her care,
Indued with windy wings to flit in air,
With serpents girt alike, and crown'd with hissing hair.
In heav'n the Dirae call'd, and still at hand,

Before the throne of angry Jove they stand,
His ministers of wrath, and ready still
The minds of mortal men with fears to fill,
Whene'er the moody sire, to wreak his hate
On realms or towns deserving of their fate,
Hurls down diseases, death and deadly care,
And terrifies the guilty world with war.
One sister plague if these from heav'n he sent,
To fright Juturna with a dire portent.
The pest comes whirling down: by far more slow
Springs the swift arrow from the Parthian bow,
Or Cydon yew, when, traversing the skies,
And drench'd in pois'nous juice, the sure destruction flies.
With such a sudden and unseen a flight
Shot thro' the clouds the daughter of the night.
Soon as the field inclos'd she had in view,
And from afar her destin'd quarry knew,
Contracted, to the boding bird she turns,
Which haunts the ruin'd piles and hallow'd urns,
And beats about the tombs with nightly wings,
Where songs obscene on sepulchers she sings.
Thus lessen'd in her form, with frightful cries
The Fury round unhappy Turnus flies,
Flaps on his shield, and flutters o'er his eyes.
A lazy chillness crept along his blood;
Chok'd was his voice; his hair with horror stood.
Juturna from afar beheld her fly,
And knew th' ill omen, by her screaming cry
And stridor of her wings. Amaz'd with fear,
Her beauteous breast she beat, and rent her flowing hair.
"Ah me!" she cries, "in this unequal strife
What can thy sister more to save thy life?
Weak as I am, can I, alas! contend
In arms with that inexorable fiend?
Now, now, I quit the field! forbear to fright
My tender soul, ye baleful birds of night;
The lashing of your wings I know too well,
The sounding flight, and fun'ral screams of hell!
These are the gifts you bring from haughty Jove,
The worthy recompense of ravish'd love!
Did he for this exempt my life from fate?
O hard conditions of immortal state,
Tho' born to death, not privileg'd to die,
But forc'd to bear impos'd eternity!
Take back your envious bribes, and let me go
Companion to my brother's ghost below!
The joys are vanish'd: nothing now remains,
Of life immortal, but immortal pains.
What earth will open her devouring womb,
To rest a weary goddess in the tomb!"
She drew a length of sighs; nor more she said,
But in her azure mantle wrapp'd her head,
Then plung'd into her stream, with deep despair,
And her last sobs came bubbling up in air.
Now stern Aeneas his weighty spear

Against his foe, and thus upbraids his fear:
"What farther subterfuge can Turnus find?
What empty hopes are harbor'd in his mind?
'T is not thy swiftness can secure thy flight;
Not with their feet, but hands, the valiant fight.
Vary thy shape in thousand forms, and dare
What skill and courage can attempt in war;
Wish for the wings of winds, to mount the sky;
Or hid, within the hollow earth to lie!"
The champion shook his head, and made this short reply:
"No threats of thine my manly mind can move;
'T is hostile heav'n I dread, and partial Jove."
He said no more, but, with a sigh, repress'd
The mighty sorrow in his swelling breast.
Then, as he roll'd his troubled eyes around,
An antique stone he saw, the common bound
Of neighb'ring fields, and barrier of the ground;
So vast, that twelve strong men of modern days
Th' enormous weight from earth could hardly raise.
He heav'd it at a lift, and, pois'd on high,
Ran stagg'ring on against his enemy,
But so disorder'd, that he scarcely knew
His way, or what unwieldly weight he threw.
His knocking knees are bent beneath the load,
And shiv'ring cold congeals his vital blood.
The stone drops from his arms, and, falling short
For want of vigor, mocks his vain effort.
And as, when heavy sleep has clos'd the sight,
The sickly fancy labors in the night;
We seem to run; and, destitute of force,
Our sinking limbs forsake us in the course:
In vain we heave for breath; in vain we cry;
The nerves, unbrac'd, their usual strength deny;
And on the tongue the falt'ring accents die:
So Turnus far'd; whatever means he tried,
All force of arms and points of art employ'd,
The Fury flew athwart, and made th' endeavor void.
A thousand various thoughts his soul confound;
He star'd about, nor aid nor issue found;
His own men stop the pass, and his own walls surround.
Once more he pauses, and looks out again,
And seeks the goddess charioteer in vain.
Trembling he views the thund'ring chief advance,
And brandishing aloft the deadly lance:
Amaz'd he cow'rs beneath his conqu'ring foe,
Forgets to ward, and waits the coming blow.
Astonish'd while he stands, and fix'd with fear,
Aim'd at his shield he sees th' impending spear.
The hero measur'd first, with narrow view,
The destin'd mark; and, rising as he threw,
With its full swing the fatal weapon flew.
Not with less rage the rattling thunder falls,
Or stones from batt'ring-engines break the walls:
Swift as a whirlwind, from an arm so strong,
The lance drove on, and bore the death along.

Naught could his sev'nfold shield the prince avail,
Nor aught, beneath his arms, the coat of mail:
It pierc'd thro' all, and with a grisly wound
Transfix'd his thigh, and doubled him to ground.
With groans the Latins rend the vaulted sky:
Woods, hills, and valleys, to the voice reply.
Now low on earth the lofty chief is laid,
With eyes cast upward, and with arms display'd,
And, recreant, thus to the proud victor pray'd:
"I know my death deserv'd, nor hope to live:
Use what the gods and thy good fortune give.
Yet think, O think, if mercy may be shown-
Thou hadst a father once, and hast a son-
Pity my sire, now sinking to the grave;
And for Anchises' sake old Daunus save!
Or, if thy vow'd revenge pursue my death,
Give to my friends my body void of breath!
The Latian chiefs have seen me beg my life;
Thine is the conquest, thine the royal wife:
Against a yielded man, 't is mean ignoble strife."
In deep suspense the Trojan seem'd to stand,
And, just prepar'd to strike, repress'd his hand.
He roll'd his eyes, and ev'ry moment felt
His manly soul with more compassion melt;
When, casting down a casual glance, he spied
The golden belt that glitter'd on his side,
The fatal spoils which haughty Turnus tore
From dying Pallas, and in triumph wore.
Then, rous'd anew to wrath, he loudly cries
(Flames, while he spoke, came flashing from his eyes)
"Traitor, dost thou, dost thou to grace pretend,
Clad, as thou art, in trophies of my friend?
To his sad soul a grateful off'ring go!
'T is Pallas, Pallas gives this deadly blow."
He rais'd his arm aloft, and, at the word,
Deep in his bosom drove the shining sword.
The streaming blood distain'd his arms around,
And the disdainful soul came rushing thro' the wound.

Insights to the Aeneid

1. Virgil deliberately models his poem after Homer. What aspects of this piece are most obviously mimicking Homer's greatest works?
2. Discuss the character of Aeneas as compared to other heroes like Achilles, Odysseus, and Rama. Does Aeneas deserve the bad rap he's received over the years?
3. How are women portrayed in the Aeneid and how is that different than the Ramayana?

APUS ePress Colophon

For end matter, APUS ePress draws on a convention from the birth of writing on clay tablets to the days of the handwritten codex. Our colophon, the final stroke, identifies the source of the manuscript-but also a bit more. APUS ePress volumes are designed for Web output. Print is a secondary option. As befits a Web conceit, the colophon thus goes a step further to point the reader beyond the covers.

APUS ePress publications are designed to avoid such printed book trappings as indexes and bibliographies. Instead, the index function is subsumed by the ability for electronic searching across the full text. At the low level, this assumes the simple employ word/string matching with wildcards. At a higher plane and especially if employing our Online Library's copy, you may be able to use a relevance engine and even search across multiple volumes. Rather than a bibliography, we also typically proffer a related campus guide with its range of librarian-vetted Web resources. In this case: LITR 201, World Literature through the Renaissance-http://apus.campusguides.com/LITR201.

Frederick J. Stielow, Ph.D., M.L.S.
Chief Editor, APUS ePress
111 W. Congress Street
Charles Town, WV 25414

CPSIA information can be obtained at www.ICGtesting.com
Printed in the USA
LVOW07s1138050315

429154LV00039B/307/P

9 781937 381004